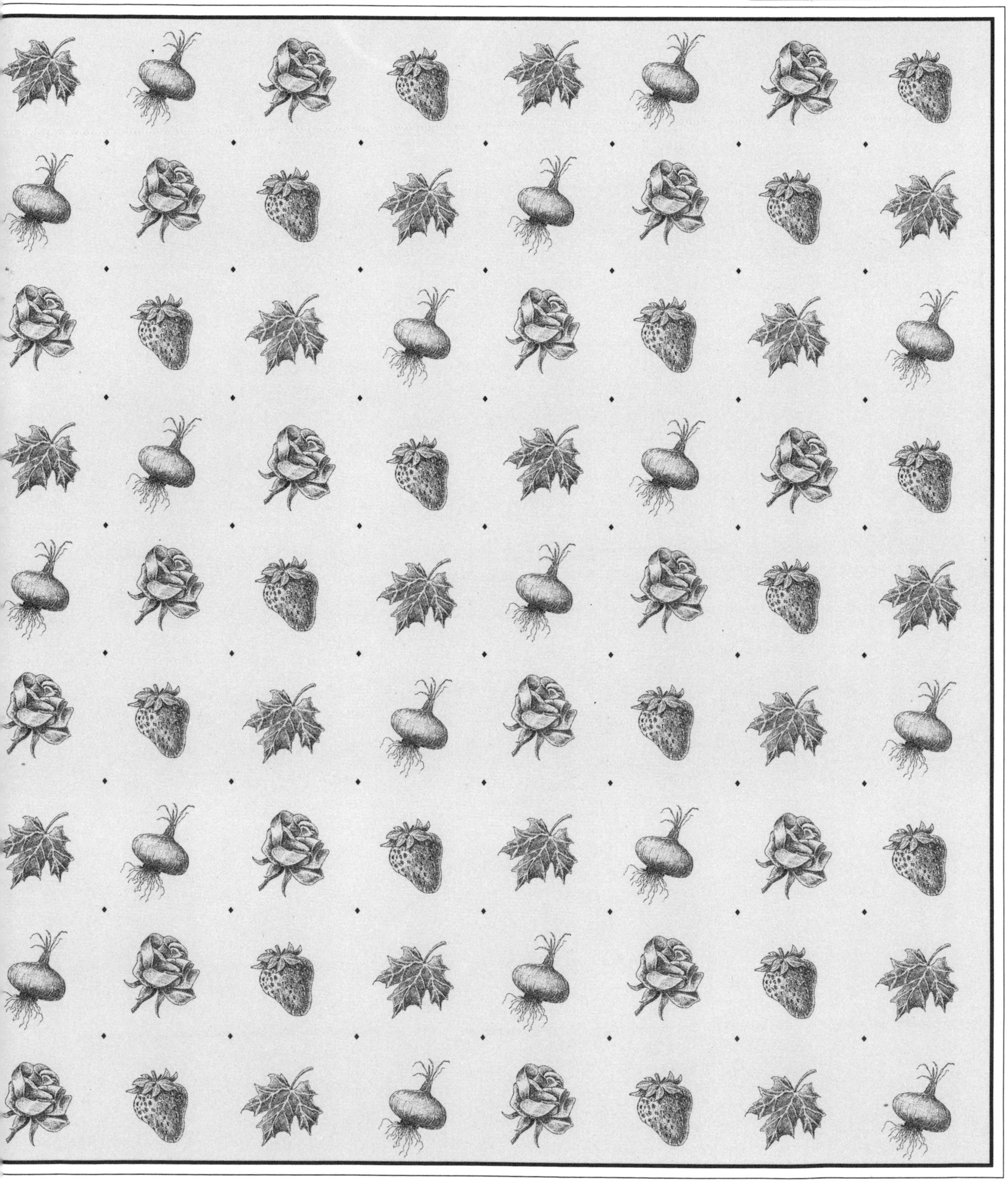

A GARDENER'S JOURNAL

The great value of a journal
is that it can keep a confusing
world in perspective.
Spring may come late in any
one year, but it always comes.
A journal serves to reinforce
such simple truths.
More important, it can be a
record for future generations,
not only of what happened
but of what we hoped would
happen — what would grow
from our gardens.
I think that most of us wish
our forebears had kept such
journals so that we could
know them better, if only
through their gardens.

Lee Valley

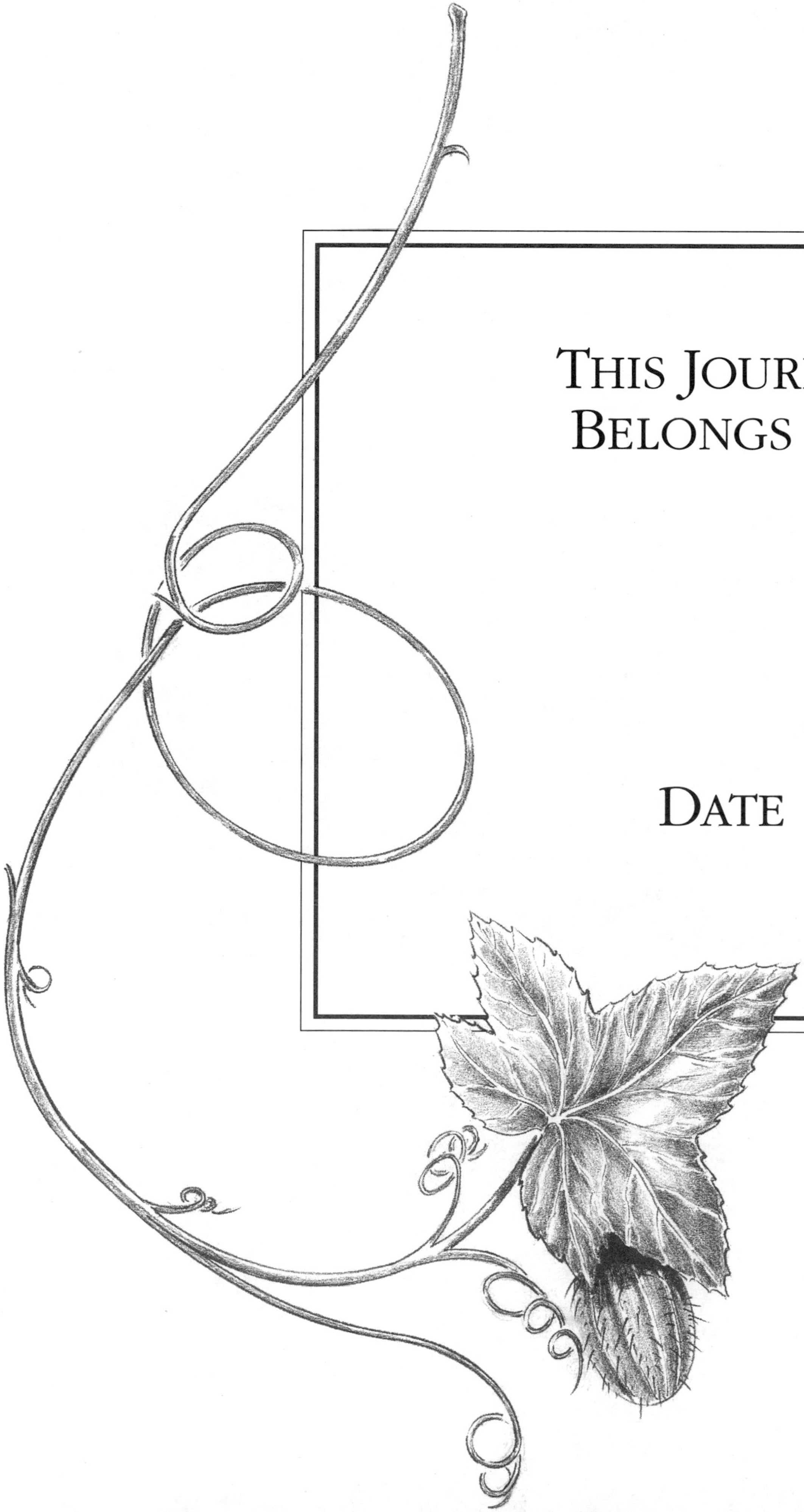

THIS JOURNAL BELONGS TO

DATE

Lee Valley Tools Ltd.
1080 Morrison Drive
Ottawa, Ontario K2H 8K7

Distributed in the United States by:
Veritas Tools Inc.
12 East River Street
Ogdensburg, New York 13669

Distributed in Canada by:
Lee Valley Tools Ltd.
1080 Morrison Drive
Ottawa, Ontario K2H 8K7

Canadian Cataloguing in Publication Data

Lunan, Robert R., 1960-
A gardener's journal: a ten year chronicle of your garden
Includes index.
ISBN 0-921335-34-2
1. Gardening. I. Lee Valley Tools. II. Title.
SB450.96.L86 1993 635 C93-090324-2

Printed in Canada

Table of Contents

♦ *Indicates record pages*

HOW TO USE THE GARDENER'S JOURNAL

A special note to the journal owner:

Although this book is designed to be a useful record of your gardening activities, the diary pages are the heart of the book. As the years pass, it becomes even more enjoyable reading past entries. Don't let the book restrict your imagination. There is nothing wrong with putting non-gardening entries in the diary. In fact, we hope that you use it to record the first date that the robins returned or what you did the day your first grandchild was born. The book has ample space for ten years of entries and can be started any time. There is a perpetual calendar at the back which will serve until 2099 A.D. Don't let yourself be restricted to the lines allocated for one year. On any specific date you will have much to say one year, the next, very little. You will find that the random entries have a way of balancing the space. It is far more important to make this book enjoyable than it is to make it a sterile record. The how-to-use guide should be treated as a guide only. Write in this book often and anywhere you see fit. It is your record.

THE GARDEN LAYOUT

A sketch of your garden helps your planning and your memory. A perennial bed may only need to be sketched once or twice in ten years with update notes between times. The organization of your vegetable garden, on the other hand, should be recorded every year to help maintain good crop rotation. The thirty pages give you lots of scope.

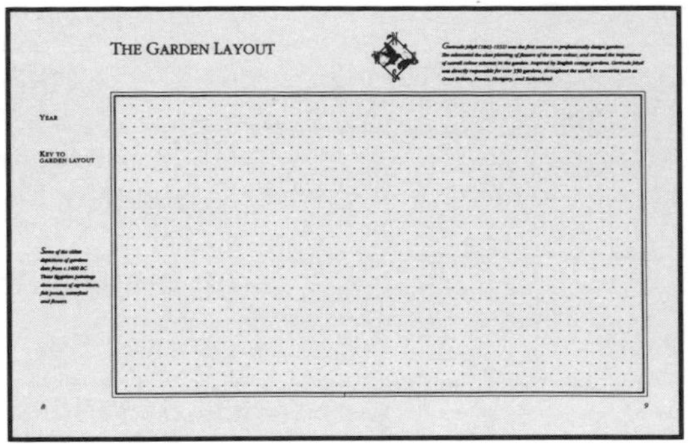

SOIL TEST RECORD

Soil tests can be referenced to points on your garden layout. Both the test results and any corrective action taken (addition of fertilizer, lime, etc.) establish a base on which you can build good soil history and results.

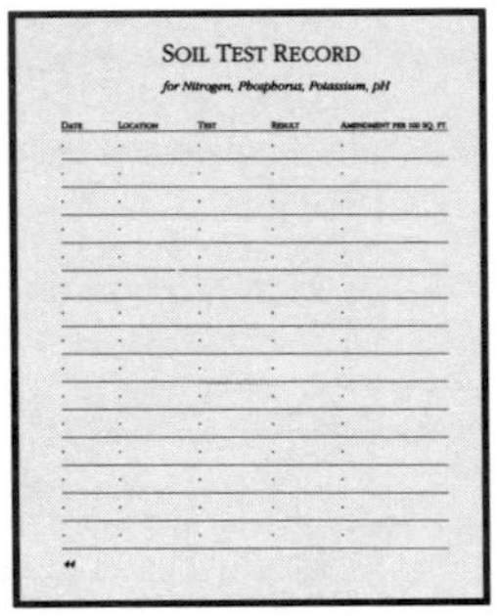

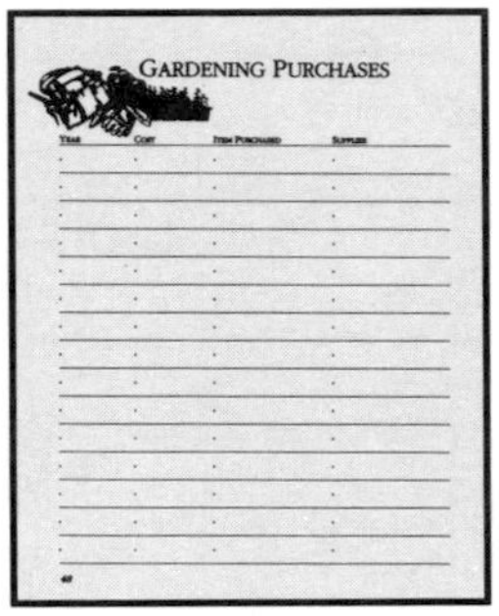

GARDENING PURCHASES

While a cost record for plants is useful, the record of sources is often more important since plant quality is known only after a growing season. It is nice to know just where your best and worst came from.

PLANTING/HARVESTING RECORD

Used to record the planting and harvesting of vegetables, herbs and other annuals. Having the key dates on facing pages makes it particularly easy to use. If you use succession plantings you may want to use a number beside the plant name (such as carrot nantes 1, carrot nantes 2, etc.) to keep them differentiated.

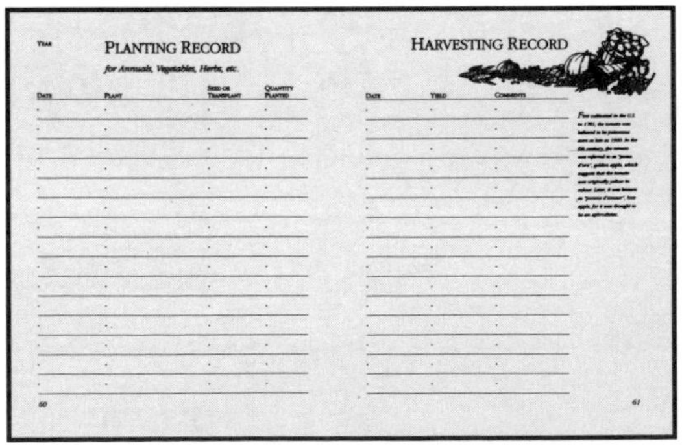

PERENNIAL INVENTORY

This inventory is used to record herbaceous perennials, bulbs, etc. The column for flowering date is useful for planning as well as indicating annual variability. The section "number of plants remaining in year..." is used to record the number of plants that have survived the rigors of winter. Ten columns are provided for the ten years. The last column entitled "See notes on..." is a useful cross reference to other parts of the book. Probably the most used cross reference will be to the 366 diary pages that are described later.

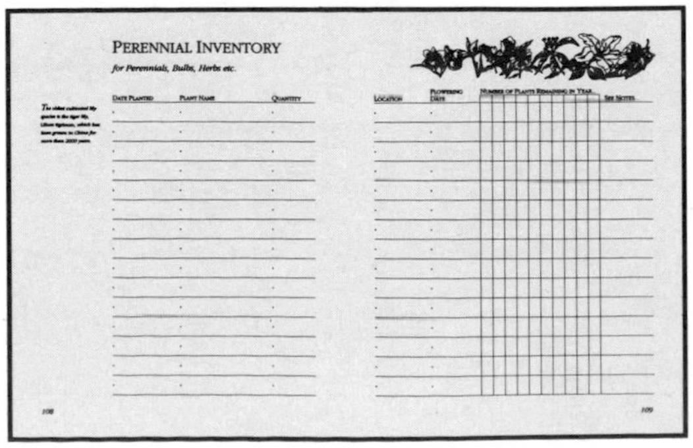

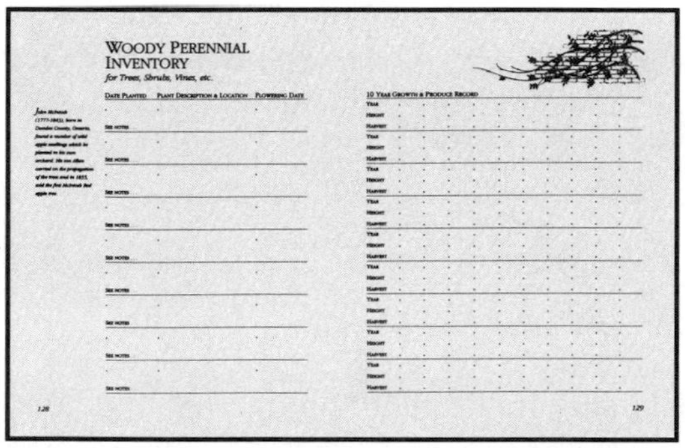

WOODY PERENNIAL INVENTORY

The "Woody Perennial Inventory", is used to record non-herbaceous perennials such as trees, shrubs, roses, etc. Use is similar to the perennials inventory except it also has a section to record heights and harvests (such as from apple trees, currant bushes, etc.).

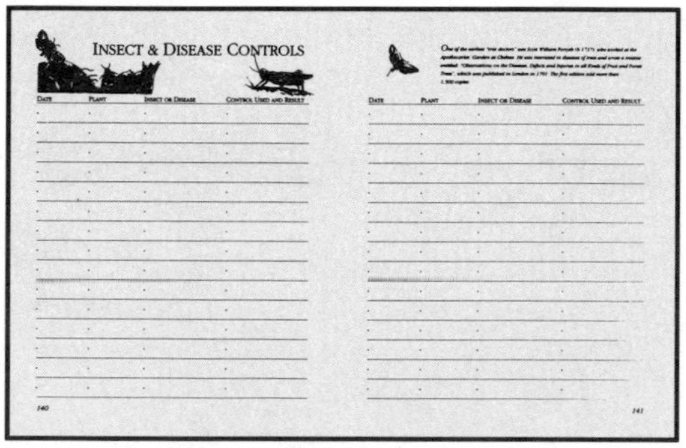

INSECT & DISEASE CONTROLS

A record of insect and disease controls is useful to track insect infestations over the years as well as which controls worked and which did not. Make sure to record the insect stage (larva, nymph, adult) as some controls only work in certain stages.

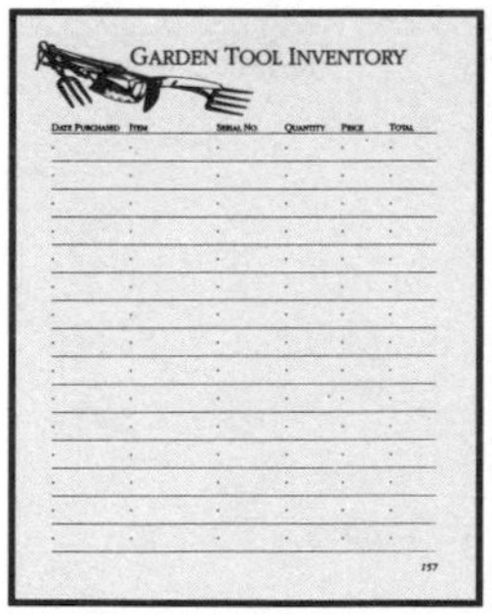

GARDEN TOOL INVENTORY

As well as tracking the original cost and source of tools, this is a useful record for insurance purposes, just in case disaster strikes.

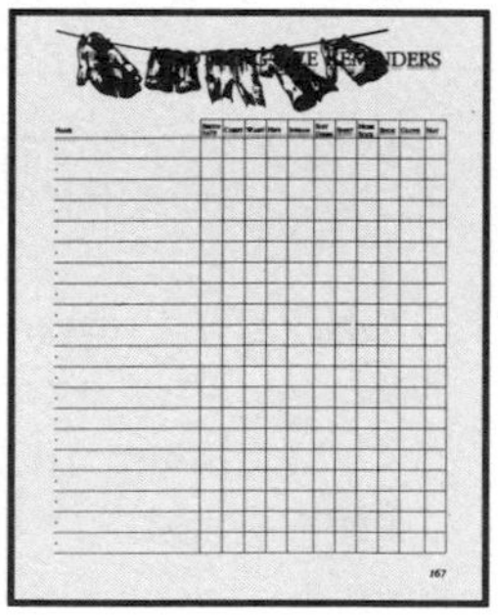

CLOTHING SIZE REMINDERS

Not really a necessity in a gardening journal, but where else can you be sure to track down the various clothing sizes of the special people in your life?

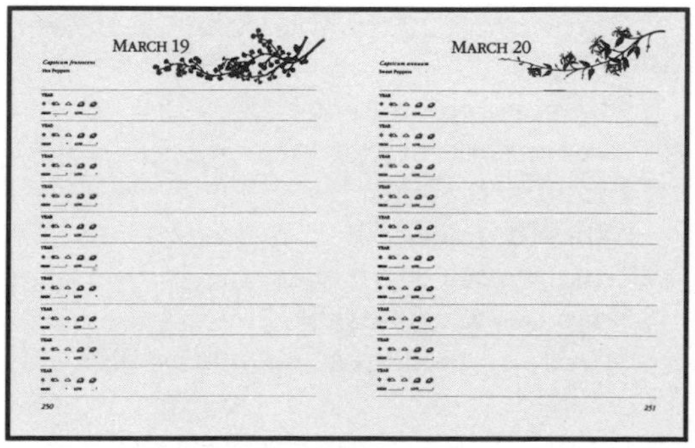

THE DIARY PAGES

The daily diary is the heart of this book. Arranged for easy recording of the date, the weather and the temperature, each page is divided into ten sections to record a decade of notes, observations, reminders, etc., for every day of the year. Don't be overly concerned about using only the five lines provided for each year; it all tends to balance out in the long run. Cross reference can be made to other sections for additional information. The diary pages also serve as a brief dictionary of the most common Latin names in gardening.

For your amusement and enlightenment, historical tidbits are sprinkled throughout the journal. Our hope is that this book will heighten your enjoyment of gardening, not only by organizing information, but by providing pleasant browsing now and in the years ahead.

Home Garden Schedule

for most areas in Northeast North America

(West Coast and Southern gardeners should adjust it accordingly)

In October, 1851, on Canada's west coast, James Douglas ordered seeds from England, with instructions that they be sent overland immediately, so that they would arrive, he hoped, in time for spring sowing in 1853.

January

All outdoor plants dormant

- Plan gardens
- Order seeds and propagation equipment
- Prune shade trees
- Start slow-germinating seeds indoors
- Inspect bulbs in storage

February

All outdoor plants dormant

- Sharpen garden tools in storage
- Prune shade trees
- Start seeds indoors

March

Some growth starts outdoors toward end of month

- Prune fruit trees and shrubs
- Apply dormant oil spray
- Examine garden tools
  Fix, sharpen and replace as necessary
- Check plants for mouse and rabbit damage
  Repair if possible, replace if necessary

April

- Dig over and prepare growing beds for planting
- Rake lawn. Seed bare patches
- Fertilize lawn with a slow release fertilizer
- Plant bareroot trees and shrubs
- Start lawn mowing toward end of month
- Remove protective cover from roses and prune them
- Plant perennials
- Plant peas, onions, leeks, sweet peas, lettuce, radish, chervil, swiss chard, spinach and chives outdoors
- Plant asparagus and rhubarb
- Start to build a compost pile
- Remove winter mulch from perennial beds to allow soil to warm up
- Apply a general purpose fertilizer to perennial beds and to shrubs
- Edge around growing areas
- Spray dormant oil and lime-sulphur on fruit and ornamental trees

May

Last light frosts toward middle of month

- Set out annuals when danger of frost is past
- Plant container-grown plants
- Mow lawn weekly; only remove the clippings if they smother the turf
- Apply manure or compost to growing areas
- Fertilize and mulch beds
- Dust roses
- Seed new lawns
- Plant perennials and summer flowering bulbs
- Plant evergreen hedges
- Set out brassica crops (broccoli, cabbage, cauliflower, etc.)
- When danger of frost is past, plant and sow frost tender vegetables including tomatoes, snap beans and corn
- Weed growing areas weekly or biweekly as needed

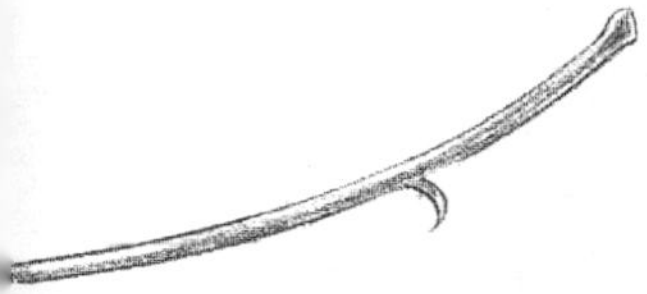

June

- Mow lawn weekly
- Fertilize and mulch beds
- Prune evergreens
- Spot kill or dig persistent lawn weeds
- Support tall perennials as needed
- Prune spring flowering shrubs to remove dead flower heads
- Thin vegetable garden
- Pinch chrysanthemums to force lower growth
- Plant successive crops (lettuce, carrots, beans, etc.)
- Weed growing areas as needed
- Dust roses

July

- Mow lawn weekly or as needed, cut no shorter than 2″
- Make sure growing beds receive enough water during dry periods
- Prune out old raspberry canes when done fruiting
- Water lawns as necessary
- Stake tall perennials such as delphinium and peony
- Continue to dust roses
- Weed as needed

August

- Water lawn as necessary
- Prune climbing roses
- Seed new lawns toward end of month
- Sow fall vegetables (radish, spinach, lettuce, etc.)
- Mow lawn as needed, no shorter than 2″ in hot weather
- Harvest vegetables
- Remove sucker growth from weeping grafted trees (e.g., weeping peashrub and weeping mulberry)

September

First light frosts

- Plant spring flowering bulbs and perennials
- Mow lawn weekly or as needed
- Harvest vegetables
- Divide perennials if needed
- Compost frost-killed annuals
- Apply fall fertilizer (high phosphate, low nitrogen) to lawn
- Aerate lawn
- Plant evergreens
- Seed lawns
- Bring tender plants indoors

October

First heavy frosts

- Dig and store frost tender summer flowering bulbs
- Plant trees and shrubs
- Dig over vegetable and annual beds
- Plant spring flowering bulbs
- Water evergreens liberally until freezeup to prevent winter sun scalding
- Rake leaves
- Aerate lawn
- Edge beds

November

All outdoor plants dormant

- Mound rose bushes with soil to protect from freeze-thaw cycles
- Wrap evergreens to protect from wind, sun and snow damage
- When the ground is slightly frozen, cut back perennials and cover with a 3″ layer of leaf or straw mulch
- Protect trees from animals with tree guards and rodent repellent
- Clean and oil hand tools before storage. Rub wooden handles with tung oil
- Drain hoses and sprinklers. Store in shed or basement

December

All outdoor plants dormant

- Rest

The first almanac in the United States was published in Cambridge, Massachusetts, in 1639. Over the subsequent years, many other almanacs were published, containing calendars and astronomical information in addition to month-by-month gardening tips. The most enduring is Robert B. Thomas's "The Farmer's Almanac", which began publication in 1793 and was used by both farmers and gardeners.

THE GARDEN LAYOUT

YEAR

KEY TO
GARDEN LAYOUT

Some of the oldest depictions of gardens date from c.1400 BC. These Egyptian paintings show scenes of agriculture, fish ponds, waterfowl and flowers.

Gertrude Jekyll (1843-1932) was the first woman to professionally design gardens. She advocated the close planting of flowers of the same colour, and stressed the importance of overall colour schemes in the garden. Inspired by English cottage gardens, Gertrude Jekyll was directly responsible for over 350 gardens, throughout the world, in countries such as Great Britain, France, Hungary, and Switzerland.

THE GARDEN LAYOUT

YEAR

KEY TO GARDEN LAYOUT

The ruins of the temple of Sibyl at Tivoli, located overlooking the banks of the Anio River, was a source of fascination for painters and gardeners alike. In the 18th century, such a temple, with its round plan, fluted columns, and crumbling stonework, was the most frequently imitated garden building – either complete or in mock ruin.

The French Impressionist painter Claude Monet (1840-1926) moved to Giverny, between Paris and Rouen, where he painted the local scenery as well as his own garden. His paintings, which show his attention to the overall colour and shape of his garden, have inspired other gardeners since then.

THE GARDEN LAYOUT

YEAR

KEY TO
GARDEN LAYOUT

The notion of water fountains in gardens goes back to the 1st century AD and the work of Hero of Alexandria, who wrote a text called the "Pneumatica". He included in it all kinds of odd machines which worked with steam, air pressure or water. The water works he described provided inspiration for the elaborate fountains of Europe from the Renaissance period on.

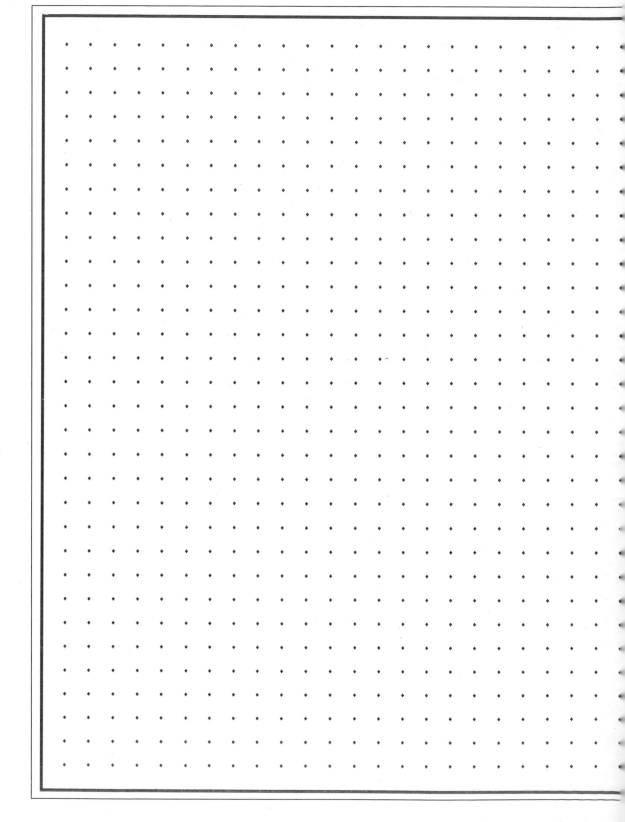

"Turf seats" were a part of the medieval garden. Placed around a tree or against a wall, these raised areas provided a natural setting for sitting and enjoying the garden. A 13th-century gardening manual reveals that amid the flowers, one could "refresh the senses" and allow one's self to "rest with pleasure".

The Garden Layout

Year

Key to
garden layout

In the late 3rd century BC, Hiero II, ruler of Syracuse, was so extravagant that he had a pleasure boat made, the upper deck of which had all sorts of garden beds made of barrels of earth with luxuriant plants, with hidden lead tiles to provide irrigation. This idea appeared again many centuries later when the Duchess of Kingston, on a visit to Russia in the 18th century, included a garden on her yacht.

Probably the oldest botanical garden still in existence, that in Padua, Italy, was founded in 1545. It also had one of the first greenhouses, a heated building used for protecting tender plants in winter.

THE GARDEN LAYOUT

YEAR

KEY TO
GARDEN LAYOUT

At the end of the 19th century, allotment gardening first appeared in North America in Philadelphia. By 1910, this movement in Canada included vacant lot gardening, which was designed for the "moral and financial improvement" of city dwellers, and over the next decade had resulted in large crops being harvested from otherwise unused land.

The influence of the garden design at Versailles was far-reaching. In 1680, Nicodemus Tessin the Younger visited Versailles and, upon returning to his native Sweden, designed a huge garden in the French style for the Swedish king at Drottningholm, near Stockholm.

THE GARDEN LAYOUT

YEAR

KEY TO
GARDEN LAYOUT

John Parkinson (1567-1650), an apothecary, was herbalist to James I. His writings on gardening were addressed primarily to women. His most famous work, "Paradisi in Sole Paradisus Terrestris", published in 1629, was a treasury of flowers of the period. Parkinson suggested, in selecting the location of the garden, that the house be located on the north side to offer protection to the plants.

The real age of imported garden plants occurred between the years of 1500 and 1700. Plants arriving in England from abroad included mulberry, crown imperial, sunflower, lobelia and nasturtium. Such plants were grown more as curiosities than for their decorative value.

The Garden Layout

Year

Key to
garden layout

Medieval gardens had grass within their enclosed spaces, which was meant to replicate a natural spot in the country, for as a writer of the period suggested, "Nothing refreshes the sight so much as fine short grass". Instructions from 1260, on how to achieve such a spot include pouring boiling water over the surface of the ground before the turf is laid to ensure that all roots and seeds are dead.

The most famous botanist of the 19th century was Joseph D. Hooker (1817-1911), who introduced the rhododendron from the Himalayas to Britain. The plant became so popular that the amount spent on the plant over a 20-year period ending in 1871 was roughly equal to the national debt.

THE GARDEN LAYOUT

YEAR

KEY TO
GARDEN LAYOUT

The modern method of plant classification was devised by Swedish botanist Carolus Linnaeus (1707-1778). Each plant name was composed of two parts: the plant genus which came first, and the second for the individual species, which distinguishes the plant among the others in the same class.

The Arts and Crafts Movement aided in the topiary's popularity. Members of the movement, such as William Morris, liked the more architectural approach to garden design, and in particular the use of trees and shrubs clipped and trained into formal shapes.

The Garden Layout

Year

Key to
Garden Layout

In China's Sui dynasty (589-618), the emperor, Yangdi, built what were the world's largest and most extensive gardens, and sought to collect a number of rare and unusual flowers.

In the 18th century, the view of the land surrounding the garden was often hampered by the fences needed to keep cows out. The solution to the problem was to use a sunken, not raised, barrier which the cows could not cross. These were called "ha-has", for as Walpole (1717-1797) wrote concerning these astonishing ditches that "the common people called them Ha! Ha! to express their surprise at finding such a sudden and unperceived check to their walk."

The Garden Layout

Year

Key to
Garden Layout

Mrs. Loudon's "Gardening for Ladies" and "Ladies' Companion to the Flower Garden", published in England, appeared together as one volume in the United States in 1843. The American editor stated that this book was intended for "the benefit of lady gardeners" especially to increase the number of women who would delight in these "occupations in the open air, which are so conducive to their own health, and to the beauty and interest of our homes."

The camellia came to Europe from the Far East in the early 18th century. By the 19th century, it became such a popular plant that in keeping with the Victorian craze for garden structures, special "camellia houses" were constructed. When it was discovered that the camellia could survive out of doors, the need for camellia houses declined.

THE GARDEN LAYOUT

YEAR

KEY TO
GARDEN LAYOUT

When Vesuvius erupted in AD 79, the towns of Pompeii and Herculaneum were destroyed along with approximately 480 gardens of every conceivable variety, including those for villas, public spaces, temples, baths, theatres, restaurants, hotels and tombs. Most of the gardens were attached to homes where the house enclosed the garden, thereby offering a measure of privacy from the street.

The Arabs had a strong influence on European Gardens. As early as the 16th century, large shipments of plants were transported from the Ottoman Empire, consisting of such cultivated and therefore improved-upon species as narcissus, lily, iris, carnation, hollyhock, jasmine and primrose.

The Garden Layout

Year

Key to
Garden Layout

Medieval gardens were square or rectangular, a shape which imitated the plan of the cloisters from which they developed.

Dioscorides, the Greek physician of the 1st century AD and author of "De Materia Medica", was the first to suggest that in order to truly learn from plants, one must study them "in situ", not as dead specimens. This had tremendous effect on botanists, and from that time on, living plants were examined over a period of time, in contrast to learning from gathered and dried collections.

THE GARDEN LAYOUT

YEAR

KEY TO
GARDEN LAYOUT

Cincinnati was America's original grape and wine centre. Nicholas Longworth (1783-1863), a lawyer and a banker, introduced the Catawba grape to the Ohio River area around 1825, giving the area the nickname, "The Rhine of America". It is estimated that by 1850, there were more than 1,500 acres of grapes grown there.

One of the seven wonders of the world, the Hanging Gardens of Babylon were thought to have been created by Nebuchadnezzar II (604-562 BC). These gardens were terraced on a hillside, with arches as high as 170 feet and walls 22 feet thick. An elaborate system of irrigation brought water from the Euphrates to the gardens via conduits.

THE GARDEN LAYOUT

YEAR

KEY TO
GARDEN LAYOUT

While the topiary has existed since Roman times, it was not always admired. The English poet Alexander Pope (1688-1744) expressed his displeasure in 1712: "Our trees rise in cones, globes and pyramids. I would rather look upon a tree when in all its luxuriancy and diffusion and branches, than when it is thus cut and trimmed into a mathematical figure."

Early English writings on gardening are in manuscript form, as they predate the printed book. A very early example, dating from around 1440, by Mayster Ion Gardener, lists 78 plants that can be cultivated. Most of the plants are herbs for cooking or for medicine, but garden vegetables, such as the radish, leek, spinach, cabbage and lettuce are also mentioned.

The Garden Layout

Year

Key to
Garden Layout

The word "paradise" comes from the old Persian term, "pairidaeza", meaning an enclosure, and pertained to the enclosed grounds in which the king went hunting. In the Old Testament, this word was adopted as the Hebrew "pardes", an enclosed garden or park, which in turn became the Greek "paradeisos", a kingly or sumptuous park.

The use of greenhouse structures for entertainment as well as for growing plants began in the 17th century. Queen Anne served summer suppers in the orangery at her palace in Kensington, London.

How Plants Grow

By Anstace and Larry Esmonde-White

The heavily polluted air of 19th-century London made growing plants in the city nearly impossible. In an effort to keep his ferns alive, Nathaniel Bagshaw Ward (1791-1868) devised a method of growing plants under glass in structures called Wardian cases. These terrariums found widespread use in transporting plants around the world. The modified cases with wire netting protecting the glass were lashed to the decks of the ships and served to greatly increase the survival rate of plants including banana, tea and rubber.

A plant is a carefully balanced mechanism, which requires specific physical and chemical conditions to keep it healthy and functioning correctly. Each part of a plant plays an individual role and contributes to its overall development, which we call growth. The process of growth is controlled by *photosynthesis,* which in the presence of light is the manufacture of carbon-containing compounds, which may be used by the plant. This process requires light, carbon dioxide and water, and occurs in all green-pigmented tissue.

By a process which we call *osmosis,* roots absorb water and nutrients which are transported to the stems and leaves by conducting vessels called *xylem* (see diagram). Manufactured compounds are then moved within the plants by the *phloem,* which are also conducting tissues.

The leaf is the work centre of the plant with its continuous manufacture of compounds and their subsequent distribution within the plant for storage or use in the many biochemical processes which occur. It is designed to absorb light, exchange gases of oxygen and carbon dioxide, release excess moisture, and control excessive moisture loss during periods of stress such as drought. These processes take place in the leaf through structures called *stomata,* or "pores". The opening and closing of the pores is controlled by the guard cells and is dependent upon environmental conditions. As their name implies, they are protective mechanisms that prevent excessive stress on the plant during unfavourable weather conditions.

The green pigment within the leaves and some stems is *chlorophyll,* an essential requirement of photosynthesis. Chlorophyll contains carbon, hydrogen and oxygen, as well as nitrogen and magnesium. Deficiencies of various mineral elements inhibit chlorophyll synthesis and cause the development of *chlorosis* (yellowing). In the absence of normal amounts of chlorophyll, the upper leaves quickly become yellow and photosynthesis is reduced.

The utilization of the manufactured carbon-containing compounds (sugars) is called *respiration,* which takes place at all times within the plant, but the rate varies with temperature. The higher the temperature, the more rapid the rate. Oxygen is essential for respiration, which yields carbon dioxide, water and energy. The energy may be released as heat or as chemical energy, which is important in causing cell division, absorption of minerals, movement of nutrients and the synthesis of amino acids and proteins. Photosynthesis and respiration are controlled by favourable environmental conditions. Good soil drainage and aeration, sufficient nutrients of the correct kinds, optimum soil moisture and an abundance of sunlight result in growth.

The plant roots absorb nutrients, primarily in a soluble form. Commercial fertilizers are usually water soluble, at least in part, and are therefore immediately utilized. Organic fertilizers are not soluble and must first be broken down by soil micro-organisms. The chemical minerals will then be released and become soluble in water. By the time the minerals reach the roots, both the manufactured (synthetic) and the organic fertilizers are identical.

The acidity or pH of soil plays an important role in the availability of nutrients as it affects the activity of micro-organisms. Most minerals, if present in the soil, are available to the plants when the pH is in the 6 to 6.8 range. When a soil analysis has been made for a home vegetable garden, the recommendations are based on bringing the pH to an optimum level.

A plant grows as a result of an increase in size or number of cells. Cell elongation takes place in many parts of the plant; cell division, or *mitosis,* occurs in certain areas called *meristems,* the most important being the shoot, root tips, lateral buds and cambium layer. These meristematic tissues are very delicate and sensitive to physical damage, pests and diseases. Stress conditions, which may result in an imbalance or disruption of cell growth, can cause increased vulnerability to disease.

Thickening of stems is the result of the continuously accumulating xylem tissue. The cambium layer surrounding the xylem is increasing by cell division as the stems develop. This can be seen on woody perennials such as the stump of a tree as annual growth rings. Certain cells eventually die, but they are continually replaced. In vegetable plants that are growing for only one season, this process is not apparent, whereas in woody plants such as trees and shrubs these cells become support tissue.♦

The preceding was reproduced with permission from the book "Vegetables from a Country Garden", written by Anstace and Larry Esmonde-White, and published by Lee Valley Tools. The Esmonde-Whites are hosts of a popular TV series seen on most PBS stations. For more information or to order this book please write:
Lee Valley Tools Ltd.
1080 Morrison Dr.
Ottawa, Ontario, Canada
K2H 8K7

William Bartram was the first person in America to hybridize plants. In 1739, he wrote on what he termed "the male and female parts in vegetables". He experimented in joining species of the same genus, producing new colours in the flowers.

Diagram showing simplified plant process

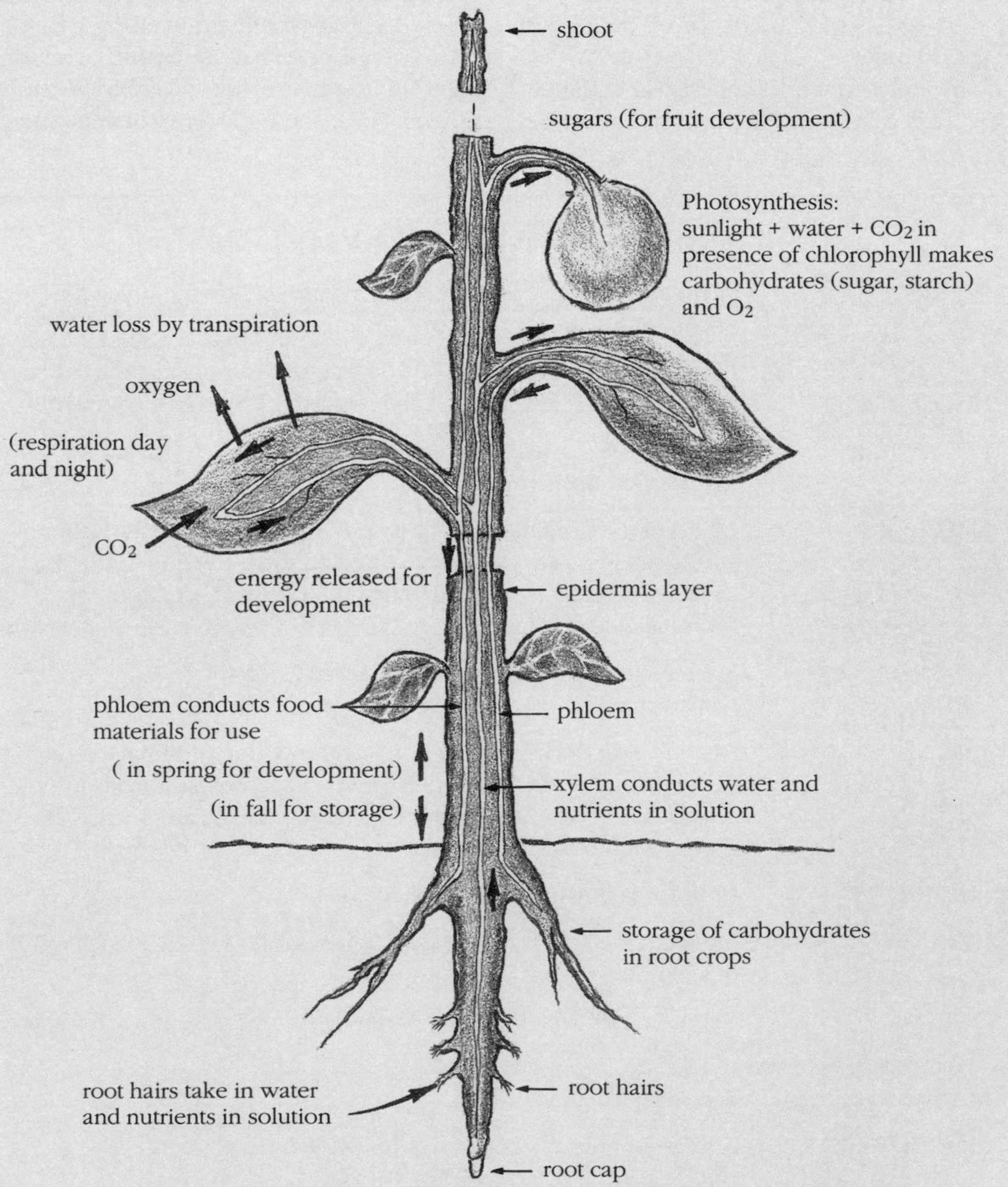

The Importance of Soil

In the 19th century, the French agricultural chemist Jean-Baptiste Boussaingault raised the first hydroponic plants in pots of sand and charcoal watered with nutrient solutions. Not until 1930 in the United States was the technique recommended for commercial growing, either outdoors or in greenhouses.

Soil has only two purposes from a plant's point of view, first, to provide a medium of support and second, to provide nourishment to the plant's roots. (This is quite apparent when plants are grown hydroponically, without soil. In this case plastic frames, gravel or rock wool provide the support, and nutrients are supplied in the water. In soil culture the nutrients are held by the soil particles and released for use by the plant as they are dissolved by rain or irrigation water.)

If any soil is to work properly for a plant it must meet three conditions. First, it must be chemically correct. This includes the pH and the nutrients available. Second, it must be structurally correct. This is determined by the ratio of different particles that make up the soil, such as sand, silt, clay and organic matter. And third, there must be a sufficient volume of chemically correct and structurally correct soil. The top six inches of soil in your vegetable garden may be correct, but if there is a hard packed layer of clay below that, your vegetables won't do well.

The pH of your soil is important because some nutrients are not available in certain ranges. For instance, iron availability drops

Nutrient Deficiency Symptoms

Nitrogen	Small leaves; short, thin growth. Uniform yellowing of leaves, becoming red in severe cases. Leaf abscission (removal) occurs, beginning with older leaves.
Phosphorus	Bronze to red coloration of dull-green leaves. Shoots short and thin.
Potassium	On older leaves, marginal chlorosis (yellowing) followed by marginal necrosis (death or dead areas).
Calcium	Death of the terminal bud, often preceded by chlorosis of the young foliage. Leaves may be distorted, with the tips hooked back. Root system is damaged first, usually with death of the root tips.
Magnesium	Interveinal (between leaf veins) chlorosis on the foliage, followed by interveinal necrosis.
Boron	Distortion or thickening, or both, of the young terminal foliage. Some yellow spots may appear on the foliage. Terminal bud ceases development and lateral growth begins. Lateral growth soon goes through same cycle.
Sulfur	Uniform yellowing of new foliage.
Iron	Interveinal chlorosis of the new foliage, followed by bleaching of leaf color.
Copper	Necrosis and white mottling of newer foliage. This may result in small, linear, distorted leaves. Shoots die back.
Manganese	Yellowing of foliage.
Molybdenum	Leaves do not fully expand; color often bluish-green; chlorosis and necrosis also present.
Zinc	Small, narrow leaves in a rosette-like whorl.

off rapidly at a pH in excess of 6.5 and nitrogen availability drops off rapidly at a pH of less than 5.0. Test your soil for pH. Inexpensive home test kits can be purchased from major garden centres and specialty mail order sources. These kits often test for pH and the major nutrients. If your garden is found to have an unbalanced pH (generally 6.5 is good for most plants) then it can be changed by adding limestone to raise it or peat moss to lower it. If the soil has been given liberal amounts of compost and organic matter, it will usually be in the correct pH range.

In addition to pH, the level of nutrients in your soil is very important to good plant growth. Nitrogen, phosphorus and potassium are the nutrients supplied in most commercial fertilizer mixes. Good mixes from organic sources often contain other nutrients as well. The nutrients that plants use in major quantities are: nitrogen, phosphorus, potassium, calcium, magnesium and sulphur. Plants also need small quantities of chlorine, boron, iron, manganese, zinc, copper and molybdenum. This is why a garden that is given a good top dressing of compost every year performs so well, in comparison to a garden that gets only a feeding of N-P-K (nitrogen, phosphorus and potassium).

Soil must also have the right structure to encourage root growth. Roots need air to grow, so a soil with many air spaces in it will encourage root growth. Generally, the healthier the roots are, the healthier the plant as a whole will be and the more it will produce. If your soil has a high content of clay, most plants will grow slowly in it compared to a loose, airy soil high in organic matter. In fact, soil structure is so important that the differences in performance and health between plants growing in a poor and a good soil structure are often spectacular. Adding copious amounts of organic matter (such as composted manure) to your soil and mixing it in deeply will usually provide the structure required for optimum plant growth.

As a related point, a good structure is useless if the growing area is poorly drained. If the soil stays soggy long after a rain, try growing in raised beds. They will capitalize on the good soil structure and drain rapidly, while the organic content will hold the moisture at an optimum level.

All the previous points rely on you providing sufficient quantities of this good soil. If you are growing in containers, they must be large enough to hold enough moisture and provide enough nutrients for the plants being grown. They must also be large enough to allow the roots to spread sufficiently. If you are growing right in the ground, then the growing area must have been loosened to a sufficient depth. Many gardeners don't realize that the roots of a vegetable such as carrot or tomato grow four feet down. The fine roots of a beet can grow ten feet down! Obviously if these plants run into hardpan at six inches, growth will be less than optimum. The answer is to deeply cultivate your soil. Another article in this book covers double digging and that is a good place to start. ♦

The first chemical fertilizers used were probably limestone dusts, and later, gypsum on the mostly acidic soil of eastern United States. One writer noted in 1748 of limestone, "The people pretend that this stone is a very good manure, if it is scattered upon the cornfields..."

PH EFFECT ON NUTRIENT AVAILABILITY

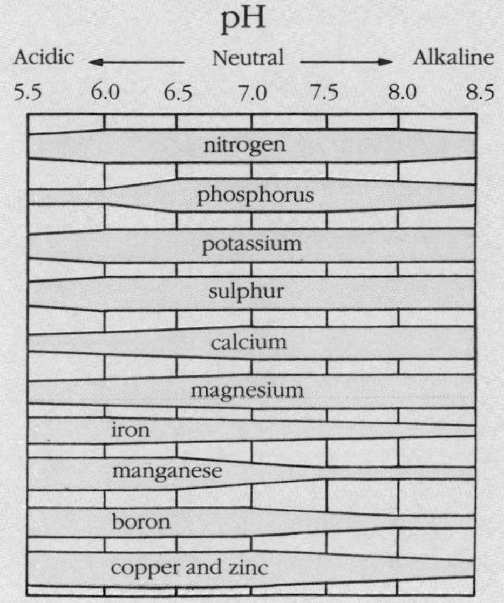

NITROGEN (N), PHOSPHORUS (P), & POTASSIUM (K)

Pounds of Fertilizer to add per 100 square feet

Test Rating	Nitrogen (N)	Phosphorus (P)	Potassium (K)
HIGH	1.5 lbs. blood meal or 2 lbs. fish meal	1.5 lbs. bone or 3 lbs. phosphate rock	1.5 lbs. wood ashes* and 2.5 lbs. crushed granite
MEDIUM	2.25 lbs. blood meal or 3 lbs. fish meal	2 lbs. bone or 4 lbs. phosphate rock	1.5 lbs. wood ashes and 4.5 lbs. crushed granite
LOW	3 lbs. blood meal or 4 lbs. fish meal	2.5 lbs. bone or 5 lbs. phosphate rock	1.5 lbs. wood ashes and 6.5 lbs. crushed granite
VERY LOW	4 lbs. blood meal or 5 lbs. fish meal	3 lbs. bone or 6 lbs. phosphate rock	1.5 lbs. wood ashes and 8.5 lbs. crushed granite

* *Wood ash application is not recommended for soils with a pH above 6.5.*

COMPOSTING

In 1834, British gardener and author John Loudon listed the types of manure that had been found valuable: animal urine, dead animals (if available for any reason), animal blood, fish, blubber, bones, horn, hair, woolen rags, feathers, leather manufacturers' refuse, human night soil, soot, malt dust, linseed cake, seaweed and "all green succulent plants", best dug into the soil as green manure.

One of the most rewarding things about gardening surely must be the way we can manipulate the powers of nature with seemingly little effort. It is interesting how many people find using and understanding personal computers to be highly complex but at the same time find a hobby such as gardening to be simple, or at least simpler. The fact, of course, is just the opposite. With just a few years of study the average person can fully understand the inner workings of any computer or program. However, even with a lifetime of study a person can only understand a small part of the life processes in plants, animals or the environment. The deception lies in the interface. The interface with computers is still crude, and demands that you conform to its strict and rigid rules for any hope of success, making it seem complex. The interface with a plant on the other hand is more forgiving. Producing fruits and vegetables can be as easy as scratching a bare spot in the soil, planting a seed, and then abandoning it until harvest time. The sun, the rain and the soil take care of the rest.

Even so, most gardeners know it is not quite as easy as that in practice. A plant left to fend for itself suffers from the ravages of insects, animals, weed competition, and marginally fertile soil. Composting is one thing we can do to improve the soil and increase a plant's chances of success.

Compost is the decomposed remains of plant material. It is similar to the material that is found on the natural forest floor, and it is the best fertilizer and soil conditioner available (not the most potent but the best for the plant). In the home garden we can "make" compost by throwing excess organic matter in a pile, keeping it moist and letting it rot until black and crumbly. Typically this may take up to two years to happen. The methods that follow will permit you to create finished compost in as little as fourteen days.

All organic matter will decompose; however, compost is usually made from kitchen scraps, garden waste and animal manures. Meat, fat and human excrement are undesirable because they often attract vermin and carry disease. For rapid decomposition the compost pile needs four conditions: heat,

FIG. 1
CARBON CYCLE

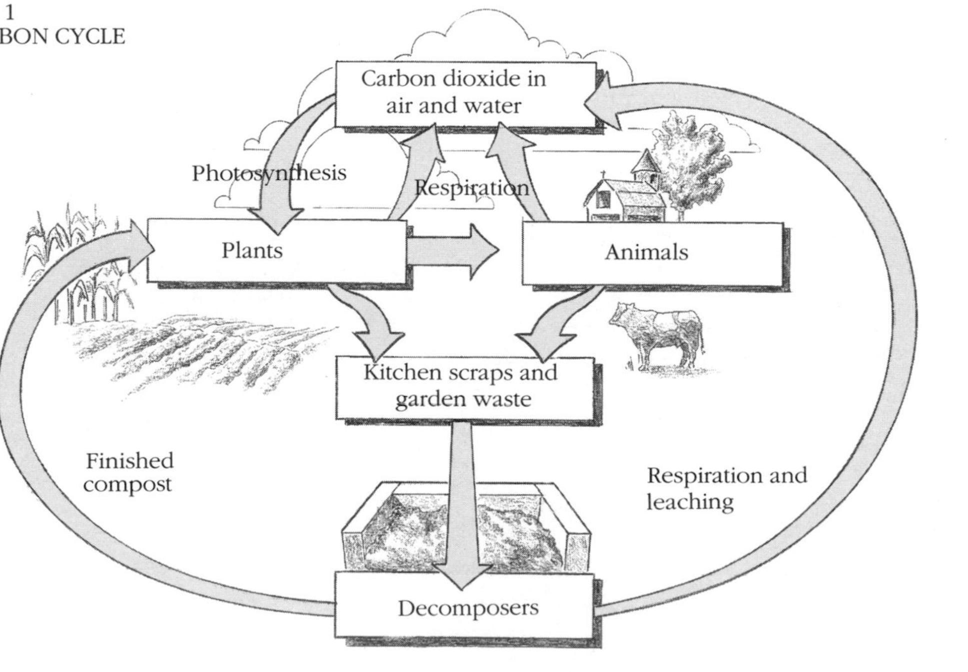

FIG. 1
Green plants use carbon dioxide gas, water, and sunlight in making sugars and other carbon-containing compounds that animals use as food. These compounds in plant and animal wastes provide food for decomposers in the compost pile. Having passed through the decomposers' bodies and the microbial bodies, they themselves contain nutrients used by plants to continue the cycle.

moisture, aeration and a proper carbon to nitrogen ratio (C/N ratio).

Early in the history of mankind (or so it is thought) someone probably noticed how easily plants grew on garbage heaps and manure piles when compared to the adjacent unfertilized ground. That would have led this person to start seeding those piles or adding the compost to the surrounding fields. Obviously it was so successful that it became the predominant method of fertilization of agricultural lands up until the early part of this century, and in fact still is in most non-industrialized nations.

In 1840 the German scientist Justus von Liebig was the first to demonstrate that plants obtained nutrients from chemicals in solution. In the decades that followed, the mind set became increasingly chemical and ignored the other benefits of manures and composts, which include improving soil structure, resistance to erosion and the improved and necessary symbiotic relationships with soil fungi and other micro-organisms.

After several decades of using mostly chemical fertilizers, compost was rediscovered by a whole new generation of gardeners – the baby boomers – who were astonished by the results of using rich compost on their garden plants. It also calmed their concerns about the growing mountains of waste in municipal landfill sites.

The usual way to build a compost pile (called the modified Indore or California method) is to start with a layer of small sticks or brush and on to that alternate layers of dry and fresh materials, with the odd layer of soil to provide micronutrients and add soil-borne organisms. The minimum pile size should be 3′x3′x3′. Smaller piles can be made to work if they have insulated sides to hold in the heat. Fresh green materials and manures are high in nitrogen while dry materials are high in carbon. The proper ratio of carbon to nitrogen is about 25:1. However, it is almost impossible for the average home owner to measure this ratio. The thing to watch is whether the pile is heating up inside or not.

A properly built pile will heat enough to kill weed seeds and pathogens harmful to plant growth. If the pile is kept moist, and turned on the third, seventh and tenth days after starting, the interior temperature should reach 130 degrees F. The compost will be ready to use on the fourteenth day, thanks mainly to rapid bacterial and fungal action.

Turning the pile adds air to it and increases the bacterial action within. Only about half of the decomposition is done anaerobically (without air); the remainder needs air. The air can be added to the pile in various ways: turning it with a fork, spearing holes in it with a compost aerating tool, raising on a platform and inserting air tubes, using a compost tumbling drum, etc.

Experimentation will provide gardeners with the method of composting most suited to their needs.♦

In 1840, guano was imported into England as fertilizer from Peru and Chile. From the Quechua word for dung, "huano", guano could be found in deposits 100 feet deep along the coastlines. The Incas knew of its properties: it is strong in nitrogen and phosphates, with one ton of guano being roughly equal to 33 tons of farmyard fertilizer. More than 5 million tons were exported from Chile over the next 6 decades.

FIG. 2

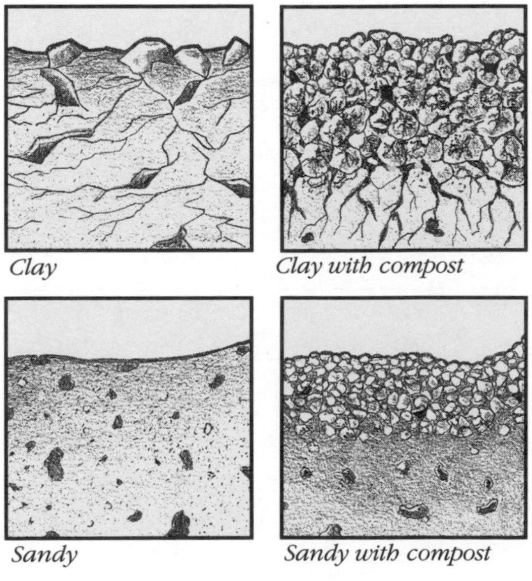

FIG. 3

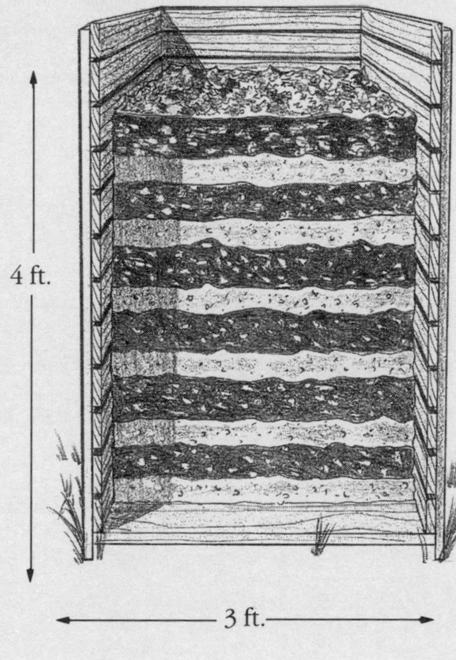

FIG. 2
Compost helps to loosen heavy soils by opening pore spaces, allowing air and water to penetrate into the soil. In addition, sand particles are united into larger ones that can hold greater amounts of water in films on their surfaces.

FIG. 3
The minimum dimensions of a bin for the California method should be 3 feet by 3 feet, with a height of 3 to 6 feet.

Soil Test Record

for Nitrogen, Phosphorus, Potassium, pH

Date	Location	Test	Result	Amendment per 100 sq. ft.
•	•	•	•	•
•	•	•	•	•
•	•	•	•	•
•	•	•	•	•
•	•	•	•	•
•	•	•	•	•
•	•	•	•	•
•	•	•	•	•
•	•	•	•	•
•	•	•	•	•
•	•	•	•	•
•	•	•	•	•
•	•	•	•	•
•	•	•	•	•
•	•	•	•	•

George Washington Carver (1864-1943) is known for encouraging the cultivation of the peanut and the sweet potato as alternatives to cotton, which depleted the soil of its nutrients. He found that peanuts could be used in the making of over 300 products, including cheese, milk, dyes and soaps.

DATE	LOCATION	TEST	RESULT	AMENDMENT PER 100 SQ. FT.
•	•	•	•	•
•	•	•	•	•
•	•	•	•	•
•	•	•	•	•
•	•	•	•	•
•	•	•	•	•
•	•	•	•	•
•	•	•	•	•
•	•	•	•	•
•	•	•	•	•
•	•	•	•	•
•	•	•	•	•
•	•	•	•	•
•	•	•	•	•
•	•	•	•	•

GARDENING PURCHASES

YEAR	COST	ITEM PURCHASED	SUPPLIER
•	•	•	•
•	•	•	•
•	•	•	•
•	•	•	•
•	•	•	•
•	•	•	•
•	•	•	•
•	•	•	•
•	•	•	•
•	•	•	•
•	•	•	•
•	•	•	•
•	•	•	•
•	•	•	•
•	•	•	•

Garden trellises probably date to Roman times. By the 14th and 15th centuries, they became a regular feature in European gardens. The usefulness of such devices was explained in a mid-16th century treatise on trellises which stated that "the branches of Vine, Melon, or Cucumber, running and spreading all over, might so shadow and keep both the heat and sun from the walkers and sitters thereunder."

YEAR	COST	ITEM PURCHASED	SUPPLIER
•	•	•	•
•	•	•	•
•	•	•	•
•	•	•	•
•	•	•	•
•	•	•	•
•	•	•	•
•	•	•	•
•	•	•	•
•	•	•	•
•	•	•	•
•	•	•	•
•	•	•	•
•	•	•	•
•	•	•	•

Gardening Purchases

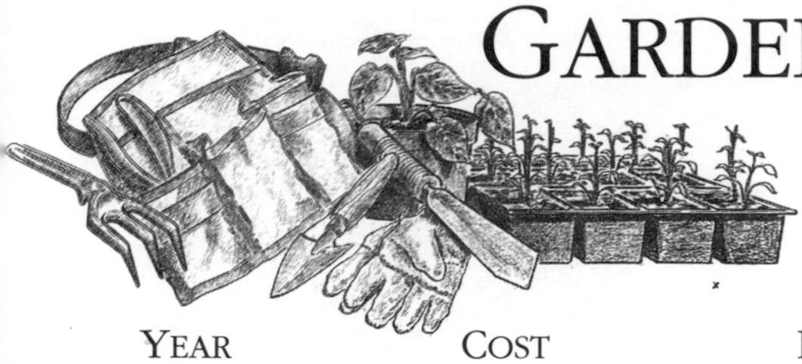

Year	Cost	Item Purchased	Supplier
•	•	•	•
•	•	•	•
•	•	•	•
•	•	•	•
•	•	•	•
•	•	•	•
•	•	•	•
•	•	•	•
•	•	•	•
•	•	•	•
•	•	•	•
•	•	•	•
•	•	•	•
•	•	•	•
•	•	•	•

"Carpet bedding" – using masses of plants – only became possible with the invention of the greenhouse, which could provide the abundance of annual plants that were needed.

YEAR	COST	ITEM PURCHASED	SUPPLIER
•	•	•	•
•	•	•	•
•	•	•	•
•	•	•	•
•	•	•	•
•	•	•	•
•	•	•	•
•	•	•	•
•	•	•	•
•	•	•	•
•	•	•	•
•	•	•	•
•	•	•	•
•	•	•	•
•	•	•	•

GARDENING PURCHASES

YEAR	COST	ITEM PURCHASED	SUPPLIER
•	•	•	•
•	•	•	•
•	•	•	•
•	•	•	•
•	•	•	•
•	•	•	•
•	•	•	•
•	•	•	•
•	•	•	•
•	•	•	•
•	•	•	•
•	•	•	•
•	•	•	•
•	•	•	•
•	•	•	•

The cylinder or reel mower was invented in England in 1830. Before then, lawns had been cut with scythes. The lawn mower was adapted to the gasoline-driven power motor around 1900.

YEAR	COST	ITEM PURCHASED	SUPPLIER
•	•	•	•
•	•	•	•
•	•	•	•
•	•	•	•
•	•	•	•
•	•	•	•
•	•	•	•
•	•	•	•
•	•	•	•
•	•	•	•
•	•	•	•
•	•	•	•
•	•	•	•
•	•	•	•
•	•	•	•

GARDENING PURCHASES

YEAR	COST	ITEM PURCHASED	SUPPLIER
•	•	•	•
•	•	•	•
•	•	•	•
•	•	•	•
•	•	•	•
•	•	•	•
•	•	•	•
•	•	•	•
•	•	•	•
•	•	•	•
•	•	•	•
•	•	•	•
•	•	•	•
•	•	•	•
•	•	•	•

In colonial New England, the pumpkin was very popular, so much so that Thanksgiving Day was derisively referred to as St. Pumpkin's Day. The pumpkin pie of this period was made in a manner much different than it is today: the top was cut off the pumpkin, the seeds and surrounding flesh were removed, and the shell was filled with spices, apples, milk, sugar, and then baked.

YEAR	COST	ITEM PURCHASED	SUPPLIER
•	•	•	•
•	•	•	•
•	•	•	•
•	•	•	•
•	•	•	•
•	•	•	•
•	•	•	•
•	•	•	•
•	•	•	•
•	•	•	•
•	•	•	•
•	•	•	•
•	•	•	•
•	•	•	•
•	•	•	•

GARDENING PURCHASES

YEAR	COST	ITEM PURCHASED	SUPPLIER
•	•	•	•
•	•	•	•
•	•	•	•
•	•	•	•
•	•	•	•
•	•	•	•
•	•	•	•
•	•	•	•
•	•	•	•
•	•	•	•
•	•	•	•
•	•	•	•
•	•	•	•
•	•	•	•
•	•	•	•

The tulip was introduced to Europe by the Viennese ambassador to Turkey, Ogier de Besbeque, in the 16th century. By 1610, the demand for the bulbs was so great that prices rose dramatically. One brewery in France was said to have been purchased with a single bulb. In the Netherlands, tulipomania raged from 1633-1637, a time when homes were mortgaged in order to acquire tulip bulbs.

YEAR	COST	ITEM PURCHASED	SUPPLIER
•	•	•	•
•	•	•	•
•	•	•	•
•	•	•	•
•	•	•	•
•	•	•	•
•	•	•	•
•	•	•	•
•	•	•	•
•	•	•	•
•	•	•	•
•	•	•	•
•	•	•	•
•	•	•	•
•	•	•	•

Deeply Dug Planting Beds

In his "Opus Agriculturae", the Roman writer Palladius advised raising or lowering beds in the vegetable garden according to the drainage, to prevent the soil from being washed away. Later, in the mid-9th century, another author suggested using planks around raised beds for this purpose.

Planting in beds instead of rows is a wise plan. When you plant in rows the space between the rows gets constantly walked on and the soil compacts, leading to all sorts of problems, including lessened root growth. In addition, the spaces between the rows must be constantly hoed or tilled and it ends up as wasted space. When you plant in a deeply dug bed the plants can be equidistantly spaced for optimum usage of the area and, because the bed is never walked on, the soil will be of such a structure to encourage maximum root growth.

The first step in preparing these beds is to double dig them. This is a process where the soil is loosened to a depth equal to two spade blades. If it is now an area covered with sod you will need to remove the sod and soak the ground, and leave it for a day or two until it is ready for digging. Mark out the areas of the beds (3′ wide by 10′ long is a size favoured by many gardeners) and for each bed perform the following:

- Dig a trench along one end of the bed, one spade length (10″) deep. Place the soil in a wheelbarrow. Bring the wheelbarrow around to the other end of the bed where the soil will be used again (figure 1).
- Loosen the soil in the bottom of the trench with a spading fork to a depth of 10″ (figure 2).
- Dig another trench beside the first one by moving the soil over and filling in the first trench. Don't walk on the prepared portion of the bed or it will compact the soil (figure 3).
- Loosen the soil in the bottom of the second trench and continue digging trenches and loosening soil until you reach the other end of the bed.

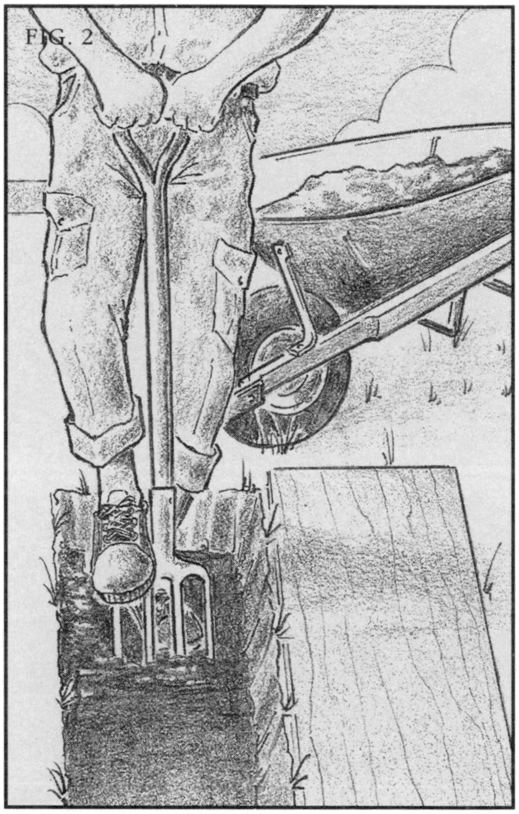

FIG. 1
Dig a trench a spade blade deep and put the soil into a wheel barrow or onto a sheet of plastic.

FIG. 2
Loosen subsoil with a spading fork.

- When you reach the other end of the bed you will notice that you don't have any soil to fill in the last trench that was dug. Figure 4 shows where the soil in the wheelbarrow is used. Fill in the last trench and rake the bed smooth. This loosened soil should now stand two or three inches above the surrounding pathways. You can also shovel the topsoil out of the pathways, where it will only be compacted anyway, and on to the top of nearby beds. Raising the beds like this will improve drainage and aeration.
- You can now add soil amendments and fertilizers to the soil before planting. Rake them into the top several inches of soil.

Most plants will do best when planted equidistantly, that is, with equal spacing on all sides. The following chart (titled "Guide for Planting Intensive Beds") gives the recommended spacing for most common vegetables. A good way to mark the bed for equidistant planting is by making up a series of plywood or cardboard templates (figure 5). These templates allow you to quickly mark out the planting points.

The yield mentioned is the maximum possible in optimum conditions. However, even in the worst of conditions an intensely planted, deeply dug bed will produce a yield three times that of conventional row gardening.♦

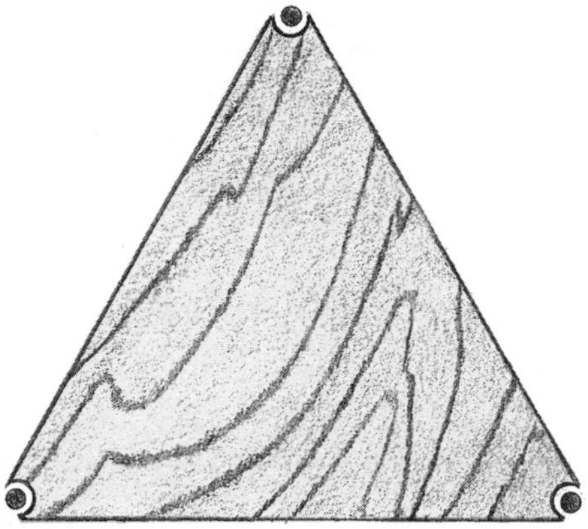

FIG. 5
A plywood template helps in placing seeds and plants at equidistant spacing.

The oldest surviving seed catalogue is that of William Lucas (d.1679), a milliner by profession. His catalogue of 1677 mentions a wide variety of seeds for purchase, as well as some trees and plants.

FIG. 3
Dig the next trench, filling in the previous one.

FIG. 4
Fill in the last trench with the soil in the wheelbarrow.

GUIDE FOR PLANTING INTENSIVE BEDS

PLANT	MAXIMUM YIELD PER 100 SQ. FT. IN LBS.	IN BED SPACING IN INCHES	WEEKS IN FLATS	WEEKS TO MATURITY	HEAVY OR LIGHT FEEDER
Asparagus	30	12	0	perennial	H
Beans, Snap or Pole	90	6	0	9	L
Beets	50	4	0	9	L
Broccoli	55	15	6	9	H
Brussels Sprouts	125	18	6	10	H
Cabbage	300	15	6	10	H
Carrots	300	3	0	10	L
Cauliflower	200	15	7	10	H
Celery	500	6	9	12	H
Cucumbers	400	12	4	6	H
Eggplant	120	18	7	4	H
Garlic	180	4	0	16-25	L
Jerusalem Artichoke	300	15	0	17-25	H
Kohlrabi	190	4	0	9	L
Leeks	600	6	8	12	L
Lettuce, Head	200	12	5	7	H
Lettuce, Leaf	350	8	4	5	H
Melons	95	15	4	10	H
Okra	105	12	0	9	H
Onion	350	4	0	14	L
Onion, Bunching	350	3	0	9	L
Parsley	90	5	0	12	H
Parsnips	330	4	5	10	L
Peas, Bush	85	3	0	9	L
Peas, Pole	85	4	0	10	L
Peppers, Green	130	12	7	10	M
Peppers, Hot	30	12	7	10	M
Potatoes, Irish	450	9	0	15	L
Potatoes, Sweet	320	9	0	17	L
Pumpkin	120	20	4	12	H
Radishes	350	2	0	4	L
Rhubarb	200	24	0	perennial	H
Rutabagas	600	6	4	8	L
Spinach	150	6	0	7	H
Sunflowers	7	15	0	12	H
Sweet Corn	50	18	0	12	H
Swiss Chard	600	8	0	8	H
Tomatoes	320	18	8	10	H
Turnips	250	4	0	9	L
Watermelon	200	18	4	12	H
Winter Squash	220	18	4	10	H
Zucchini	350	18	4	6	H

PLANTING A KNOT GARDEN

Knot gardens (or parterres) were popular in England and France from as early as the 15th century up to the end of the last century. However, they make an especially eye-catching addition to a modern landscape. They can be as simple or as complex a design as you choose. The main idea here is to lay out an edge or border of low-growing hedging plants, between which are planted contrasting herbs, vegetables or flowers. When properly constructed and looked at from a distance, the knot looks like a colourful geometric design laid on the ground. Larger knots often have gravel or stone walkways running through them, and may have a fountain in the middle.

The traditional material used for the low hedge is boxwood. Unfortunately, unless you propagate your own, boxwood is expensive. Other materials can be readily substituted, such as various types of deciduous hedging or even some herbs. Whatever material you choose, make sure it is suitable for your particular region, and that it will hold its shape when clipped.

Start your knot by removing all sod and weeds from the planting area. Measure and mark out the lines where the border plants are to be planted. These can be clearly marked on the soil with a thin line of dry sand. Dry sand is light in colour and provides a good contrast when placed on dark soil. Use string lines to guide you when making straight lines. Plant small hedging along these lines 6-9 inches apart. When all these plants are in position, dig over the planting areas and lay gravel or flagstone in the pathways. Finally, plant the areas inside the edging with herbs, flowers or vegetables. For larger knots, also use flowering shrubs, evergreens and small trees for contrast. ♦

Mazes were a part of gardens from the late 15th century. They were low at first, usually made of scented herbs. Extant mazes in the gardens of Europe are of later date, when taller shrubs were used.

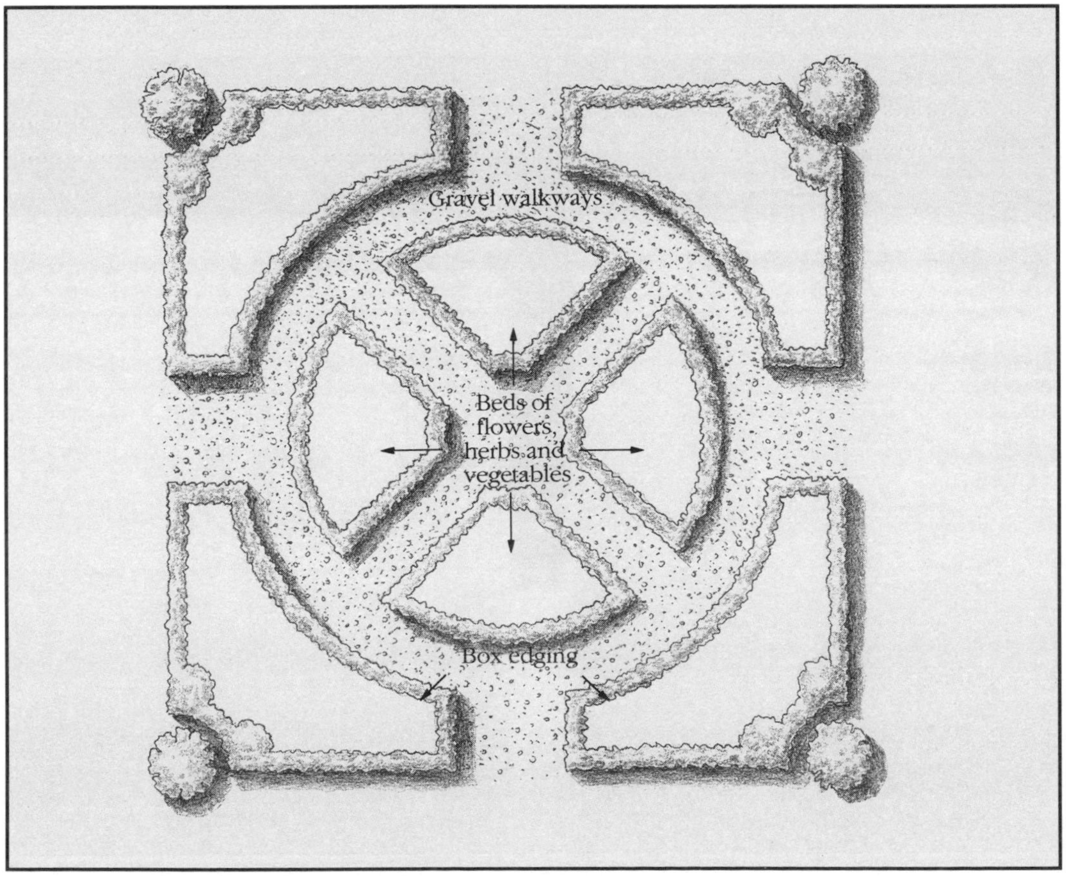

A simple knot garden design.

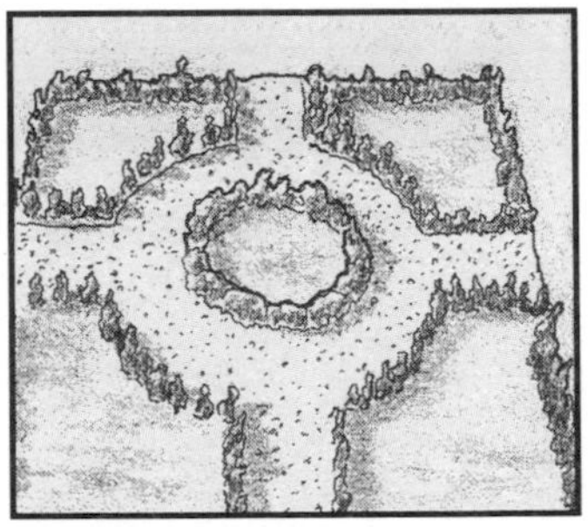

Low hedges outline the knot garden.

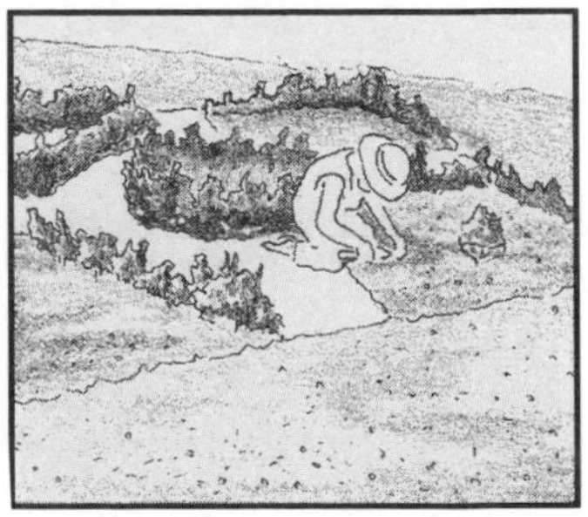

Plant hedging plants along lines marked with sand.

Year

Planting Record

for Annuals, Vegetables, Herbs, etc.

Date	Plant	Seed or Transplant	Quantity Planted
•	•	•	•
•	•	•	•
•	•	•	•
•	•	•	•
•	•	•	•
•	•	•	•
•	•	•	•
•	•	•	•
•	•	•	•
•	•	•	•
•	•	•	•
•	•	•	•
•	•	•	•
•	•	•	•
•	•	•	•

HARVESTING RECORD

DATE	YIELD	COMMENTS
•	•	•
•	•	•
•	•	•
•	•	•
•	•	•
•	•	•
•	•	•
•	•	•
•	•	•
•	•	•
•	•	•
•	•	•
•	•	•
•	•	•
•	•	•

First cultivated in the U.S. in 1781, the tomato was believed to be poisonous even as late as 1900. In the 6th century, the tomato was referred to as "pomo d'oro", golden apple, which suggests that the tomato was originally yellow in colour. Later, it was known as "pomme d'amour", love apple, for it was thought to be an aphrodisiac.

YEAR

PLANTING RECORD

for Annuals, Vegetables, Herbs, etc.

DATE	PLANT	SEED OR TRANSPLANT	QUANTITY PLANTED
•	•	•	•
•	•	•	•
•	•	•	•
•	•	•	•
•	•	•	•
•	•	•	•
•	•	•	•
•	•	•	•
•	•	•	•
•	•	•	•
•	•	•	•
•	•	•	•
•	•	•	•
•	•	•	•
•	•	•	•

HARVESTING RECORD

DATE	YIELD	COMMENTS
•	•	•
•	•	•
•	•	•
•	•	•
•	•	•
•	•	•
•	•	•
•	•	•
•	•	•
•	•	•
•	•	•
•	•	•
•	•	•
•	•	•
•	•	•

The bountiful yield of apple orchards in America in the late 18th and early 19th centuries did not always go into cider. One writer of the period tells of feeding the large surpluses to hogs, and also of drying the fruit. Apples were cored, peeled and quartered, and then set out in the garden on boards to dry, where they "were soon covered with all the bees and wasps and sucking flies of the neighbourhood which accelerates the operation of drying". In this way, he wrote, the farmers were able "to have apple pies and apple dumplings almost the year round".

Year

Planting Record

for Annuals, Vegetables, Herbs, etc.

Date	Plant	Seed or Transplant	Quantity Planted
•	•	•	•
•	•	•	•
•	•	•	•
•	•	•	•
•	•	•	•
•	•	•	•
•	•	•	•
•	•	•	•
•	•	•	•
•	•	•	•
•	•	•	•
•	•	•	•
•	•	•	•
•	•	•	•
•	•	•	•

HARVESTING RECORD

DATE	YIELD	COMMENTS
•	•	•
•	•	•
•	•	•
•	•	•
•	•	•
•	•	•
•	•	•
•	•	•
•	•	•
•	•	•
•	•	•
•	•	•
•	•	•
•	•	•
•	•	•

Carrots may be white or purple, but the orange offspring of a yellow mutation, found in western Europe around the 6th century, has become by far the favourite type. The orange colour indicates the presence of large amounts of beta-carotene, making carrots an excellent source of dietary vitamin A.

YEAR

PLANTING RECORD

for Annuals, Vegetables, Herbs, etc.

DATE	PLANT	SEED OR TRANSPLANT	QUANTITY PLANTED
•	•	•	•
•	•	•	•
•	•	•	•
•	•	•	•
•	•	•	•
•	•	•	•
•	•	•	•
•	•	•	•
•	•	•	•
•	•	•	•
•	•	•	•
•	•	•	•
•	•	•	•
•	•	•	•
•	•	•	•

HARVESTING RECORD

DATE	YIELD	COMMENTS
•	•	•
•	•	•
•	•	•
•	•	•
•	•	•
•	•	•
•	•	•
•	•	•
•	•	•
•	•	•
•	•	•
•	•	•
•	•	•
•	•	•
•	•	•

Nicholas Appert, a Frenchman, discovered in 1795 that fruits and vegetables could be preserved in their natural juices in hermetically-sealed containers. In 1810, Peter Durand patented the process and, in 1815, the discovery was brought to America by Ezra Dagget, who with his son-in-law Thomas Kennett, patented the art of canning foods.

YEAR

PLANTING RECORD

for Annuals, Vegetables, Herbs, etc.

DATE	PLANT	SEED OR TRANSPLANT	QUANTITY PLANTED
•	•	•	•
•	•	•	•
•	•	•	•
•	•	•	•
•	•	•	•
•	•	•	•
•	•	•	•
•	•	•	•
•	•	•	•
•	•	•	•
•	•	•	•
•	•	•	•
•	•	•	•
•	•	•	•
•	•	•	•

HARVESTING RECORD

DATE	YIELD	COMMENTS
•	•	•
•	•	•
•	•	•
•	•	•
•	•	•
•	•	•
•	•	•
•	•	•
•	•	•
•	•	•
•	•	•
•	•	•
•	•	•
•	•	•
•	•	•

Yellow-fleshed potatoes have recently become popular among gardeners, with Yukon Gold, developed in Ontario and licensed in 1980, taking the lead in both Canada and the United States.

Year

Planting Record

for Annuals, Vegetables, Herbs, etc.

Date	Plant	Seed or Transplant	Quantity Planted

HARVESTING RECORD

DATE	YIELD	COMMENTS
•	•	•
•	•	•
•	•	•
•	•	•
•	•	•
•	•	•
•	•	•
•	•	•
•	•	•
•	•	•
•	•	•
•	•	•
•	•	•
•	•	•
•	•	•

The Jerusalem artichoke, which is neither an artichoke nor from Jerusalem, is a sunflower relative and one of the few vegetables native to North America. Its edible roots were introduced to Europe in 1570 but, like the tomato and potato, it was not an immediate success there.

Year

Planting Record

for Annuals, Vegetables, Herbs, etc.

Date	Plant	Seed or Transplant	Quantity Planted
•	•	•	•
•	•	•	•
•	•	•	•
•	•	•	•
•	•	•	•
•	•	•	•
•	•	•	•
•	•	•	•
•	•	•	•
•	•	•	•
•	•	•	•
•	•	•	•
•	•	•	•
•	•	•	•
•	•	•	•

HARVESTING RECORD

DATE	YIELD	COMMENTS
•	•	•
•	•	•
•	•	•
•	•	•
•	•	•
•	•	•
•	•	•
•	•	•
•	•	•
•	•	•
•	•	•
•	•	•
•	•	•
•	•	•
•	•	•

Most garden weeds such as dandelion, lamb's-quarters, pigweed and burdock are Old World natives that immigrated along with the explorers and settlers, either brought by accident or carried intentionally, as medicinal or food plants.

Year

Planting Record

for Annuals, Vegetables, Herbs, etc.

Date	Plant	Seed or Transplant	Quantity Planted
•	•	•	•
•	•	•	•
•	•	•	•
•	•	•	•
•	•	•	•
•	•	•	•
•	•	•	•
•	•	•	•
•	•	•	•
•	•	•	•
•	•	•	•
•	•	•	•
•	•	•	•
•	•	•	•
•	•	•	•

Harvesting Record

Date	Yield	Comments
•	•	•
•	•	•
•	•	•
•	•	•
•	•	•
•	•	•
•	•	•
•	•	•
•	•	•
•	•	•
•	•	•
•	•	•
•	•	•
•	•	•
•	•	•

Corn is one of the plants that profited most from hybridization, which significantly increased both productivity and vigour. Although corn has been eaten for more than 6,000 years, most of the hybridizing work took place in this century. Only one percent of North American commercial corn was hybrid in 1935, but now virtually all of it is.

Year

Planting Record

for Annuals, Vegetables, Herbs, etc.

Date	Plant	Seed or Transplant	Quantity Planted
•	•	•	•
•	•	•	•
•	•	•	•
•	•	•	•
•	•	•	•
•	•	•	•
•	•	•	•
•	•	•	•
•	•	•	•
•	•	•	•
•	•	•	•
•	•	•	•
•	•	•	•
•	•	•	•
•	•	•	•

HARVESTING RECORD

DATE	YIELD	COMMENTS
•	•	•
•	•	•
•	•	•
•	•	•
•	•	•
•	•	•
•	•	•
•	•	•
•	•	•
•	•	•
•	•	•
•	•	•
•	•	•
•	•	•
•	•	•

Tillering, the sending off of side shoots from the stem just below the first set of leaves, actually increases the yield of cereal crops. For this reason, grazing on cereal plants by animals does not harm the plant but actually encourages tillering, which when mature will yield grain.

Year

Planting Record

for Annuals, Vegetables, Herbs, etc.

Date	Plant	Seed or Transplant	Quantity Planted
•	•	•	•
•	•	•	•
•	•	•	•
•	•	•	•
•	•	•	•
•	•	•	•
•	•	•	•
•	•	•	•
•	•	•	•
•	•	•	•
•	•	•	•
•	•	•	•
•	•	•	•
•	•	•	•
•	•	•	•

HARVESTING RECORD

DATE	YIELD	COMMENTS
•	•	•
•	•	•
•	•	•
•	•	•
•	•	•
•	•	•
•	•	•
•	•	•
•	•	•
•	•	•
•	•	•
•	•	•
•	•	•
•	•	•
•	•	•

Squashes were probably domesticated not for their flesh but for their seeds, which are sweet and nutritious. Mexican archaeological deposits dating back to 7000 BC include remains of squashes that had little or no flesh.

YEAR

PLANTING RECORD

for Annuals, Vegetables, Herbs, etc.

DATE	PLANT	SEED OR TRANSPLANT	QUANTITY PLANTED
•	•	•	•
•	•	•	•
•	•	•	•
•	•	•	•
•	•	•	•
•	•	•	•
•	•	•	•
•	•	•	•
•	•	•	•
•	•	•	•
•	•	•	•
•	•	•	•
•	•	•	•
•	•	•	•
•	•	•	•

HARVESTING RECORD

DATE	YIELD	COMMENTS
•	•	•
•	•	•
•	•	•
•	•	•
•	•	•
•	•	•
•	•	•
•	•	•
•	•	•
•	•	•
•	•	•
•	•	•
•	•	•
•	•	•
•	•	•

One of the most important moments in the development of the tomato was the introduction of the hybrid known as the Trophy in the mid-19th century. The small, smooth love-apple, a common ornamental of the period, was crossed with the large fluted garden tomato. The resulting Trophy was fleshy and juicy, with small seeds and smooth skin, and is the ancestor of many of the varieties grown today.

YEAR

PLANTING RECORD

for Annuals, Vegetables, Herbs, etc.

DATE	PLANT	SEED OR TRANSPLANT	QUANTITY PLANTED
•	•	•	•
•	•	•	•
•	•	•	•
•	•	•	•
•	•	•	•
•	•	•	•
•	•	•	•
•	•	•	•
•	•	•	•
•	•	•	•
•	•	•	•
•	•	•	•
•	•	•	•
•	•	•	•
•	•	•	•

HARVESTING RECORD

DATE	YIELD	COMMENTS
•	•	•
•	•	•
•	•	•
•	•	•
•	•	•
•	•	•
•	•	•
•	•	•
•	•	•
•	•	•
•	•	•
•	•	•
•	•	•
•	•	•
•	•	•

The green pea, a native of Eurasia and grown as a vegetable for thousands of years, was planted by Columbus on Isabella Island in 1493 and had arrived in New England by 1602. During Samuel de Champlain's fourth voyage to the Ottawa River in 1613, he wrote that the gardens of the Indians were filled with nothing but squash, beans and European peas.

Year

Planting Record

for Annuals, Vegetables, Herbs, etc.

Date	Plant	Seed or Transplant	Quantity Planted
•	•	•	•
•	•	•	•
•	•	•	•
•	•	•	•
•	•	•	•
•	•	•	•
•	•	•	•
•	•	•	•
•	•	•	•
•	•	•	•
•	•	•	•
•	•	•	•
•	•	•	•
•	•	•	•
•	•	•	•

HARVESTING RECORD

DATE	YIELD	COMMENTS
•	•	•
•	•	•
•	•	•
•	•	•
•	•	•
•	•	•
•	•	•
•	•	•
•	•	•
•	•	•
•	•	•
•	•	•
•	•	•
•	•	•
•	•	•

The Aztecs practiced plant cultivation and grew a number of crops, many of which are still used today, including maize, pumpkins, beans, vanilla, cotton, tobacco, tomatoes and cacao. Cacao was one of the most important products, and was used both as food and as currency. One of Montezuma's favourite drinks was made of cacao flavoured with vanilla and spices.

YEAR

PLANTING RECORD

for Annuals, Vegetables, Herbs, etc.

DATE	PLANT	SEED OR TRANSPLANT	QUANTITY PLANTED
•	•	•	•
•	•	•	•
•	•	•	•
•	•	•	•
•	•	•	•
•	•	•	•
•	•	•	•
•	•	•	•
•	•	•	•
•	•	•	•
•	•	•	•
•	•	•	•
•	•	•	•
•	•	•	•
•	•	•	•

HARVESTING RECORD

DATE	YIELD	COMMENTS
•	•	•
•	•	•
•	•	•
•	•	•
•	•	•
•	•	•
•	•	•
•	•	•
•	•	•
•	•	•
•	•	•
•	•	•
•	•	•
•	•	•
•	•	•

Jonathan Chapman (1774-1847) travelled for over 40 years, mostly on foot, between the Ohio River and northern Pennsylvania planting thousands of apple seeds. This eccentric, who walked barefoot until the ground was covered with snow, is best known by his nickname of Johnny Appleseed.

YEAR

PLANTING RECORD

for Annuals, Vegetables, Herbs, etc.

DATE	PLANT	SEED OR TRANSPLANT	QUANTITY PLANTED
•	•	•	•
•	•	•	•
•	•	•	•
•	•	•	•
•	•	•	•
•	•	•	•
•	•	•	•
•	•	•	•
•	•	•	•
•	•	•	•
•	•	•	•
•	•	•	•
•	•	•	•
•	•	•	•
•	•	•	•

HARVESTING RECORD

DATE	YIELD	COMMENTS
•	•	•
•	•	•
•	•	•
•	•	•
•	•	•
•	•	•
•	•	•
•	•	•
•	•	•
•	•	•
•	•	•
•	•	•
•	•	•
•	•	•
•	•	•

Radishes, which have been grown since the time of the Pharaohs, are used mostly as small salad ingredients in the west, but there are Japanese varieties that reach a weight of several pounds and are valued for their ability to last all winter in cold storage.

YEAR

PLANTING RECORD

for Annuals, Vegetables, Herbs, etc.

DATE	PLANT	SEED OR TRANSPLANT	QUANTITY PLANTED
•	•	•	•
•	•	•	•
•	•	•	•
•	•	•	•
•	•	•	•
•	•	•	•
•	•	•	•
•	•	•	•
•	•	•	•
•	•	•	•
•	•	•	•
•	•	•	•
•	•	•	•
•	•	•	•
•	•	•	•

HARVESTING RECORD

DATE	YIELD	COMMENTS
•	•	•
•	•	•
•	•	•
•	•	•
•	•	•
•	•	•
•	•	•
•	•	•
•	•	•
•	•	•
•	•	•
•	•	•
•	•	•
•	•	•
•	•	•

*The potato (*Solanum tuberosum*), was introduced to Ireland in the 16th century, and within half a century became the main food in the Irish diet. Unfortunately, the potato blight, caused by the fungus* Phytophthora infestans, *struck in 1845 and 1846, and a large portion of the population either starved to death or were forced to emigrate, the tragic result of relying too heavily on a single source of food.*

YEAR

PLANTING RECORD

for Annuals, Vegetables, Herbs, etc.

DATE	PLANT	SEED OR TRANSPLANT	QUANTITY PLANTED
•	•	•	•
•	•	•	•
•	•	•	•
•	•	•	•
•	•	•	•
•	•	•	•
•	•	•	•
•	•	•	•
•	•	•	•
•	•	•	•
•	•	•	•
•	•	•	•
•	•	•	•
•	•	•	•
•	•	•	•

HARVESTING RECORD

DATE	YIELD	COMMENTS
•	•	•
•	•	•
•	•	•
•	•	•
•	•	•
•	•	•
•	•	•
•	•	•
•	•	•
•	•	•
•	•	•
•	•	•
•	•	•
•	•	•
•	•	•

Garlic, one of the world's most common seasonings, was given to the Egyptian slaves every day as a strength-sustaining medicine when they constructed the pyramid of Cheops.

Year

Planting Record

for Annuals, Vegetables, Herbs, etc.

Date	Plant	Seed or Transplant	Quantity Planted
•	•	•	•
•	•	•	•
•	•	•	•
•	•	•	•
•	•	•	•
•	•	•	•
•	•	•	•
•	•	•	•
•	•	•	•
•	•	•	•
•	•	•	•
•	•	•	•
•	•	•	•
•	•	•	•
•	•	•	•

HARVESTING RECORD

DATE	YIELD	COMMENTS
•	•	•
•	•	•
•	•	•
•	•	•
•	•	•
•	•	•
•	•	•
•	•	•
•	•	•
•	•	•
•	•	•
•	•	•
•	•	•
•	•	•
•	•	•

An "apple" was an early term for many round fruits, so tomatoes were once called love apples or apples of Peru, eggplants were mad apples, and the French word for potatoes remains "pommes de terre", apples of the earth. The pineapple is named for its fancied resemblance to a pine cone.

YEAR

PLANTING RECORD

for Annuals, Vegetables, Herbs, etc.

DATE	PLANT	SEED OR TRANSPLANT	QUANTITY PLANTED
•	•	•	•
•	•	•	•
•	•	•	•
•	•	•	•
•	•	•	•
•	•	•	•
•	•	•	•
•	•	•	•
•	•	•	•
•	•	•	•
•	•	•	•
•	•	•	•
•	•	•	•
•	•	•	•
•	•	•	•

HARVESTING RECORD

DATE	YIELD	COMMENTS
•	•	•
•	•	•
•	•	•
•	•	•
•	•	•
•	•	•
•	•	•
•	•	•
•	•	•
•	•	•
•	•	•
•	•	•
•	•	•
•	•	•
•	•	•

The first European description of chili peppers, in 1494, was by Chauca, physician with Columbus on his second voyage to the West Indies. The substance that makes peppers taste hot, capsaicin, is sensed not by taste buds but by pain receptors in the mouth.

Year

Planting Record

for Annuals, Vegetables, Herbs, etc.

Date	Plant	Seed or Transplant	Quantity Planted
•	•	•	•
•	•	•	•
•	•	•	•
•	•	•	•
•	•	•	•
•	•	•	•
•	•	•	•
•	•	•	•
•	•	•	•
•	•	•	•
•	•	•	•
•	•	•	•
•	•	•	•
•	•	•	•
•	•	•	•

HARVESTING RECORD

DATE	YIELD	COMMENTS
•	•	•
•	•	•
•	•	•
•	•	•
•	•	•
•	•	•
•	•	•
•	•	•
•	•	•
•	•	•
•	•	•
•	•	•
•	•	•
•	•	•
•	•	•

The French perfected the art of growing lettuce year round. Their plants grow in a variety of shapes, colours and textures, from crunchy to buttery. Louis XIV preferred his lettuce in a salad of tarragon, pimpernel, basil, and violets.

20 Gardening Tips

Orchid enthusiasts of 13th century China believed that rain water, collected in earthenware pots and exposed to the sun until it turned green, would enable orchids to thrive.

1 Before you transplant a tree from the wild, prune the roots to encourage fibrous roots closer to the trunk. Do this by digging a trench halfway around the tree in the spring of year one and then refilling it again, and then around the other half in year two. By the fall of year two it will be ready to transplant with a much greater chance of survival.

2 Any pruning saw should only be used to cut material up to half its blade length; otherwise, some teeth will never be clear of the cut and able to free trapped sawdust. For example, a pruning saw with an 8″ blade will cut branches up to 4″ thick.

3 Before you perform a soil test, make sure the sample taken is representative of your garden. Do this by taking soil from several points in the garden and then mixing them together to get an averaged test sample.

4 For best results, build your compost pile in layers. Use 2″ of dry vegetation, 2″ of green vegetation and kitchen scraps and ½″ of soil. Repeat this process until the whole pile is built.

5 Many insects are repelled by the smell of dead bodies of their own species. To repel any specific insect, trap a handful, grind them up, then add water to make a sprayable liquid (try one part insects to two parts water). Spray every day for five days for best control.

6 Use red worms to process your food scraps into compost. They can be used outside in your compost pile or indoors in a large plastic bin. When ideally maintained, the worm population can double every three months.

7 A weeding hoe should be kept sharp at all times. A sharp hoe will cut weeds with minimal effort, but a dull hoe has to be used with a chopping motion that is hard on the arms and back. A good general purpose file for sharpening hoes and shovels is an eight or ten inch mill file. This file cuts well, removing metal rapidly.

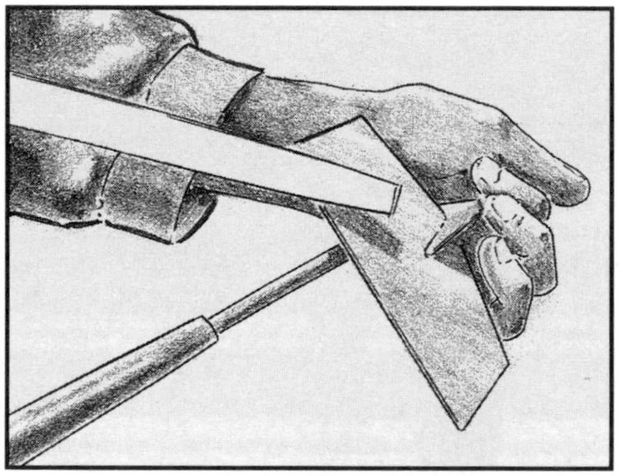

8 Seeds from the plant anise (*Pimpinella anisum*) are commonly used to flavour medicines and foods such as licorice. However, in the 16th century, it found its widest application as a mousetrap bait. Apparently mice find it irresistible.

9 When pruning branches with a saw, always make the starting cut on the bottom of the branch and then revert to the top. It avoids the problem of torn bark and a ragged scar.

10 To save time during watering, always use a large diameter hose. At 50 psi a ⅝″ diameter hose delivers 2⅔ gallons in 10 seconds, but a ½″ diameter hose delivers only 1⅓ gallons in 10 seconds.

11 If you get leaking at a hose coupling and a new washer doesn't solve the problem, add a second washer. This often fills the gap that is causing the leak.

12 If you have problems with whiteflies, try the following. Paint a one square foot board bright yellow and cover it with a sticky substance and hang it near the affected plants. The insects will be drawn to the yellow colour and stick to the surface. Each board will treat 150 sq. ft. of greenhouse area.

13 If you have trouble evenly sowing small seed such as turnip or carrot, mix 4 parts dry sand with 1 part seed and then sow. The result will be a more even distribution of seed with little thinning needed later.

14 To grow head lettuce all summer long, make sure it is given a partly shaded spot, or cover it with shade cloth during the hottest months of the summer.

15 Make your hedges do double duty by planting one that provides fruit as well as a screen. Highbush blueberry or bush cherry works well for this.

16 Avoid transplant shock by growing seedlings in peat pots, or soil blocks, hardening them off in a cold frame before transplanting and by providing a fertilizer high in phosphorus when setting out.

17 To protect seedlings against cutworms, surround the stems with 3″ pieces of cardboard buried halfway into the soil.

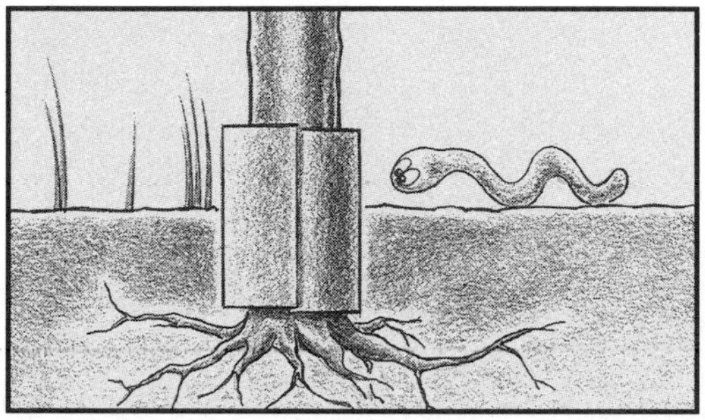

18 Sunflower seeds can quickly be removed from mature flower heads by scraping them across a homemade seed remover. Make the seed remover by clamping ½″ wire screen in a wooden frame. Place it over a pail and rub the seed heads over it face down. The seeds readily drop from the flower head into the pail below.

19 Make your own liquid organic fertilizer by filling a cotton bag with compost or well rotted manure, tying the top and soaking it in water in a pail or drum for several days. Remove the bag, wring it out and the resulting "tea" can be used as a very effective liquid fertilizer.

20 Gardeners who live close to the ocean have an additional source of free fertilizer. Many types of seaweed make effective fertilizers in either dry or liquid form. Not only are they high in potash, but they also contain natural growth stimulants. ♦

In North America the dandelion, (Taraxacum officinale), *is considered to be an annoying weed. Its name comes from the French dent-de-lion, lion's tooth, for its notched leaves. The leaves of the dandelion, though bitter, are edible and may be used as salad greens; the roots, when roasted and ground, are a coffee substitute.*

A Selection of Perennials

Perennial Name	Flower Colour	Plant Height 4-12″	12-24″	24-36″	36″+	Plant Conditions	Blooming Season	Uses
		10-30	31-60	61-90	90+cm			
Aster	Red, pink, blue	•	•			Sun	Fall	Mass planting, cut flowers, rockery
Astilbe	White, red, pink		•	•		Sun, partial shade	Early summer to fall	Mass planting, cut flowers
Baby's Breath *Gypsophila paniculata*	White, pink		•	•		Sun	Early summer to fall	Cut flowers, rockery
Bee Balm *Monarda*	White, red, pink, purple			•		Sun, partial shade	Early summer to fall	Mass planting, cut flowers
Bell Flower *Campanula carpatica*	White, blue	•	•			Sun, partial shade	Early summer to fall	Rockery, border
Bleeding Heart *Dicentra spectabilis*	White, pink		•			Sun, shade	Spring	Mass planting, cut flowers
Buttercup *Ranunculus*	White, yellow		•			Sun, partial shade	Spring & early summer	Border, rockery
Cardinal Flower *Lobelia*	Red				•	Partial shade, shade	Early summer & fall	Mass planting, cut flowers
Carnation *Dianthus caryophyllus*	White, red, pink, yellow, mixed		•			Sun	Summer	Border, cut flowers
Carpet Bugle *Ajuga reptans Rubra*	Coloured foliage, flowers purple-red	•				Sun, shade	Spring	Ground cover, rockery
Chinese Balloon Flower *Platycodon*	White, blue		•			Sun, partial shade	Summer	Mass planting, cut flowers
Chrysanthemum, Daisy *Chrysanthemum maximum*	White, red, yellow		•	•		Sun, partial shade	Early summer & summer	Mass planting, cut flowers
Columbine *Aquilegia*	White, red, yellow, blue, mixed		•			Sun, partial shade	Spring & early summer	Mass planting, cut flowers
Common Thrift *Armeria*	White, red, pink	•				Sun	Spring to summer	Border, rockery

The centaurea, or cornflower, derives its name from Chiron the Centaur, whose wounds, legend reveals, the plant healed.

PERENNIAL NAME	FLOWER COLOUR	PLANT HEIGHT				PLANT CONDITIONS	BLOOMING SEASON	USES
		4-12″	12-24″	24-36″	36″+			
		10-30	31-60	61-90	90+cm			
Cornflower *Centaurea cyanus*	White, blue, pink		•			Sun	Summer to fall	Cut flowers
Coral Bells *Heuchera sanguinea*	White, red, pink		•			Sun, partial shade	Early summer	Mass planting, cut flowers
Cup and Saucer *Campanula calycanthema*	White, pink, blue		•		•	Sun, partial shade	Early summer	Ground cover, mass planting
Day Lily *Hemerocallis*	Red, pink, yellow, orange			•		Sun, partial shade	Summer	Ground cover, mass planting
Delphinium	White, pink, blue, mixed, purple			•	•	Sun	Early summer to fall	Mass planting, cut flowers
Evening Primrose *Oenothera*	Yellow	•	•			Sun	Early summer to fall	Mass planting, cut flowers
Flax *Linum*	White, red, yellow, blue		•			Sun	Early summer & summer	Mass planting, cut flowers
Fleabane *Erigeron*	Red, orange, blue, purple		•			Sun	Early summer & summer	Mass planting, cut flowers
Gaillardia *G. aristata*	Red, yellow, mixed	•				Sun	Early summer to fall	Border, rockery
Geneva Bugle *Ajuga genevensis*	Purple	•				Sun, partial shade	Spring	Ground cover, rockery
Globe Thistle *Echinops*	Blue				•	Sun	Late summer & fall	Mass planting, cut flowers
Goutweed *Aegopodium variegatum*	White	•				Partial shade	Early summer	Border
Hens & Chickens *Sempervivum*	Pink	•				Sun	Summer	Border, rockery
Iris	White, red, pink, yellow, blue, purple	•				Sun	Spring	Border, cut flowers

A Selection of Perennials

Perennial Name	Flower Colour	Plant Height				Plant Conditions	Blooming Season	Uses
		4-12″	12-24″	24-36″	36″+			
		10-30	31-60	61-90	90+cm			
Italian Bugloss *Anchusa 'Blue Angel'*	Blue		•			Sun	Early summer	Mass planting, rockery
Lavender *Lavandula*	Blue, purple		•			Sun	Early summer	Mass planting, cut flowers
Lily of the Valley *Convallaria*	White, pink	•				Partial shade, shade	Spring	Mass planting, rockery
Loosestrife *Lythrum*	Pink, purple				•	Sun, partial shade	Summer to early fall	Mass planting, cut flowers
Moss Pink *Phlox*	White, red, pink, blue	•				Sun	Spring	Border, rockery, container
Mullein *Verbascum*	Mixed			•		Sun	Summer	Mass planting, cut flowers
Sunflower *Heliopsis*	Yellow				•	Sun	Summer & early fall	Mass planting, cut flowers
Oriental Poppy *Papaver orientale*	White, red, pink			•		Sun	Spring	Mass planting
Pachysandra terminalis	White	•				Sun, shade	Spring	Ground cover
Painted Daisy *Pyrethrum*	White, red, pink, mixed			•		Sun	Early summer	Mass planting, cut flowers
Plantain Lily *Hosta*	Coloured foliage		•			Sun, shade	Late summer	Border, mass planting
Primrose *Primula pacific*	White, red, pink, yellow, blue	•				Partial shade	Spring	Border, rockery
Red-hot Poker *Kniphofia*	Red, yellow, orange			•		Sun	Summer	Border, cut flowers
Rock Cress *Aubrieta*	Purple	•				Sun, partial shade	Spring & early summer	Border, rockery

Some plants, which today are regarded as ornamental, were of much more practical use in the 9th century. The iris, the lily and the rose were grown in the small garden for their medicinal or culinary value. The lily, for example, was thought to cure snake bite.

PERENNIAL NAME	FLOWER COLOUR	PLANT HEIGHT 4-12"	12-24"	24-36"	36"+	PLANT CONDITIONS	BLOOMING SEASON	USES
		10-30	31-60	61-90	90+cm			
Rock Cress *Arabis caucasica*	White, coloured foliage	•				Sun	Spring	Border, ground cover, container
Russell Lupine *Lupinus*	White, red, pink, yellow, orange, blue, purple			•		Sun	Summer	Border, cut flowers
Sage *Salvia*	Blue		•			Sun	Early summer to fall	Mass planting, cut flowers
Silver Mound *Artemisia*	Coloured foliage	•				Sun	Early summer to fall	Border, rockery
Snow-in-Summer *Cerastium*	White, coloured foliage	•				Sun	Spring	Ground cover, rockery
Speedwell *Veronica*	White, red, pink, blue		•			Sun, partial shade	Early summer to fall	Border, ground cover, cut flowers, rockery
Stone Crop *Sedum*	Red, pink		•			Sun	Summer & fall	Ground cover, rockery
Summer Phlox *P. paniculata*	Red, white, pink, blue, purple			•		Sun	Late summer	Mass planting, cut flowers
Thyme *Thymus*	Red, pink, purple	•				Sun	Early summer to fall	Ground cover, rockery
Tickseed *Coreopsis*	Yellow		•			Sun	Early summer to fall	Border, mass planting, cut flowers, rockery
Tradescantia	White, red, blue, purple		•			Sun, partial shade	Early summer to fall	Border, mass planting
Viola	White, red, yellow, orange, blue, purple	•				Sun, partial shade	Full season	Mass planting, cut flowers, rockery
Yarrow *Achilea*	White, red, yellow		•	•		Sun	Early summer to fall	Border, mass planting, container
Yellow Flowering Spurge *Euphorbia*	Yellow	•	•			Sun	Spring	Border, rockery

PERENNIAL INVENTORY

for Perennials, Bulbs, Herbs etc.

Hundreds of ornamental plants, such as the well-known Shasta daisy, were introduced by plant breeder and hybridizer Luther Burbank (1849-1926). Born in Lancaster, Massachusetts, Burbank moved to California in 1875 where he developed his so-called "new creations." His main interest was not in making new scientific discoveries but rather of developing better plants.

DATE PLANTED	PLANT NAME	QUANTITY
•	•	•
•	•	•
•	•	•
•	•	•
•	•	•
•	•	•
•	•	•
•	•	•
•	•	•
•	•	•
•	•	•
•	•	•
•	•	•
•	•	•
•	•	•

Location	Flowering Date	Number of Plants Remaining in Year...										See Notes...
•	•											
•	•											
•	•											
•	•											
•	•											
•	•											
•	•											
•	•											
•	•											
•	•											
•	•											
•	•											
•	•											
•	•											
•	•											

PERENNIAL INVENTORY

for Perennials, Bulbs, Herbs etc.

The oldest cultivated lily species is the tiger lily, Lilium tigrinum, *which has been grown in China for more than 2000 years.*

DATE PLANTED	PLANT NAME	QUANTITY
•	•	•
•	•	•
•	•	•
•	•	•
•	•	•
•	•	•
•	•	•
•	•	•
•	•	•
•	•	•
•	•	•
•	•	•
•	•	•
•	•	•
•	•	•

Location	Flowering Date	Number of Plants Remaining in Year...										See Notes...
•	•											
•	•											
•	•											
•	•											
•	•											
•	•											
•	•											
•	•											
•	•											
•	•											
•	•											
•	•											
•	•											
•	•											
•	•											

PERENNIAL INVENTORY

for Perennials, Bulbs, Herbs etc.

The cornflower, Centaurea cyanus, *and Jacob's Ladder,* Polemonium caeruleum, *are two plants which grew as early as 10,000 B.C. It is the fossils of pollen grains, not the plants themselves, which yield this information.*

DATE PLANTED	PLANT NAME	QUANTITY
•	•	•
•	•	•
•	•	•
•	•	•
•	•	•
•	•	•
•	•	•
•	•	•
•	•	•
•	•	•
•	•	•
•	•	•
•	•	•
•	•	•
•	•	•

Location	Flowering Date	Number of Plants Remaining in Year...										See Notes...
•	•											
•	•											
•	•											
•	•											
•	•											
•	•											
•	•											
•	•											
•	•											
•	•											
•	•											
•	•											
•	•											
•	•											
•	•											

Perennial Inventory

for Perennials, Bulbs, Herbs etc.

The garden hollyhock, Althaea rosea, *is a Chinese native first grown in Europe in the 16th century, when it was considered not only ornamental but also edible and medicinal.*

Date Planted	Plant Name	Quantity
•	•	•
•	•	•
•	•	•
•	•	•
•	•	•
•	•	•
•	•	•
•	•	•
•	•	•
•	•	•
•	•	•
•	•	•
•	•	•
•	•	•
•	•	•

Location	Flowering Date	Number of Plants Remaining in Year...										See Notes...
•	•											
•	•											
•	•											
•	•											
•	•											
•	•											
•	•											
•	•											
•	•											
•	•											
•	•											
•	•											
•	•											
•	•											
•	•											

PERENNIAL INVENTORY

for Perennials, Bulbs, Herbs etc.

The peony, Paeonia officinalis, *was named after Paeon, son of Apollo and physician to the Greek gods. The roots of the plant are believed to have toning qualities.*

DATE PLANTED	PLANT NAME	QUANTITY
•	•	•
•	•	•
•	•	•
•	•	•
•	•	•
•	•	•
•	•	•
•	•	•
•	•	•
•	•	•
•	•	•
•	•	•
•	•	•
•	•	•
•	•	•

Location	Flowering Date	Number of Plants Remaining in Year...										See Notes...
•	•											
•	•											
•	•											
•	•											
•	•											
•	•											
•	•											
•	•											
•	•											
•	•											
•	•											
•	•											
•	•											
•	•											
•	•											

PERENNIAL INVENTORY

for Perennials, Bulbs, Herbs etc.

In China's Han dynasty (206 BC-220 AD), chrysanthemum wine was drunk each year on the ninth day of the ninth month in order to give everlasting life and promote good health. To make the wine, the foliage and twigs were collected when the flower was in full bloom. It was then mixed with glutinous rice and allowed to ferment. It was ready to drink the next year.

DATE PLANTED	PLANT NAME	QUANTITY
•	•	•
•	•	•
•	•	•
•	•	•
•	•	•
•	•	•
•	•	•
•	•	•
•	•	•
•	•	•
•	•	•
•	•	•
•	•	•
•	•	•
•	•	•

Location	Flowering Date	Number of Plants Remaining in Year...										See Notes...
•	•											
•	•											
•	•											
•	•											
•	•											
•	•											
•	•											
•	•											
•	•											
•	•											
•	•											
•	•											
•	•											
•	•											
•	•											

Perennial Inventory

for Perennials, Bulbs, Herbs etc.

A number of plant names are linked to gods from Greek mythology. The iris is named for Juno's messenger, Iris, who walked between heaven and earth on a bridge made of a rainbow. The many hues of the iris flower are linked to the colours of Iris's rainbow.

Date Planted	Plant Name	Quantity
•	•	•
•	•	•
•	•	•
•	•	•
•	•	•
•	•	•
•	•	•
•	•	•
•	•	•
•	•	•
•	•	•
•	•	•
•	•	•
•	•	•
•	•	•

Location	Flowering Date	Number of Plants Remaining in Year...										See Notes...
•	•											
•	•											
•	•											
•	•											
•	•											
•	•											
•	•											
•	•											
•	•											
•	•											
•	•											
•	•											
•	•											
•	•											
•	•											

PERENNIAL INVENTORY

for Perennials, Bulbs, Herbs etc.

In the late 18th century, Dr. William Wuthering discovered that the dried leaves of the foxglove, Digitalis purpurea, *yielded the powerful cardiac stimulant that we now call digitalis. Both the common English name of the plant, foxglove, and the continental name, digitalis (from the Latin word* digitus, *meaning finger), come from the similarity of the flowers to the fingertips of gloves.*

DATE PLANTED	PLANT NAME	QUANTITY
•	•	•
•	•	•
•	•	•
•	•	•
•	•	•
•	•	•
•	•	•
•	•	•
•	•	•
•	•	•
•	•	•
•	•	•
•	•	•
•	•	•
•	•	•

Location	Flowering Date	Number of Plants Remaining in Year...										See Notes...
•	•											
•	•											
•	•											
•	•											
•	•											
•	•											
•	•											
•	•											
•	•											
•	•											
•	•											
•	•											
•	•											
•	•											
•	•											

PERENNIAL INVENTORY

for Perennials, Bulbs, Herbs etc.

The modern-day herb garden traces its roots back to the kitchen gardens of the Greeks and Romans, and the monastic gardens of medieval times. The plants were chosen for their uses in medicine, perfumes, as decoration, and as a flavouring in food. Eleanor Sinclair Rhode (1882-1950), whose writings encouraged the use of herbs, is responsible for interest in herb gardens today.

DATE PLANTED	PLANT NAME	QUANTITY
•	•	•
•	•	•
•	•	•
•	•	•
•	•	•
•	•	•
•	•	•
•	•	•
•	•	•
•	•	•
•	•	•
•	•	•
•	•	•
•	•	•
•	•	•

Location	Flowering Date	Number of Plants Remaining in Year...										See Notes...
•	•											
•	•											
•	•											
•	•											
•	•											
•	•											
•	•											
•	•											
•	•											
•	•											
•	•											
•	•											
•	•											
•	•											
•	•											

Repairing Tree Wounds

The tree-of-heaven (Ailanthus altissima), *now a popular tree for city streets because of its disease resistance, fast growth and durability, is a Chinese native introduced to England in 1751 and to the United States in 1800.*

There are three common types of tree injuries: damage caused by weather (where limbs are torn off by gusts of wind, lightning strikes or the weight of ice and snow), damage caused by automobiles or machinery (usually limited to bark or sapwood being ripped from the tree) and damage caused by animals, the most serious of which is girdling (where the bark is chewed off the trunk in a band completely around the tree). If girdling isn't repaired the tree will die. After a storm, assess the damage to your tree. If it has been hit by lightning, determine how much of the bark has been affected. A lightning strike often transmits enough energy to the tree to boil the liquids inside. The boiling creates steam, forcing the wood to split open and the bark to peel away. If a strip of bark has come off all around the circumference of the tree, unless you attach a bridge graft, life support to the roots will be severed and the tree will starve to death within a year. If six feet (1.8 m) or more of bark has split away all around the trunk, the tree can also be saved by bridge grafting; however, the resulting repair will be so disfiguring that it's usually better to cut down the tree.

FIG. 1
Correct method for limb removal.

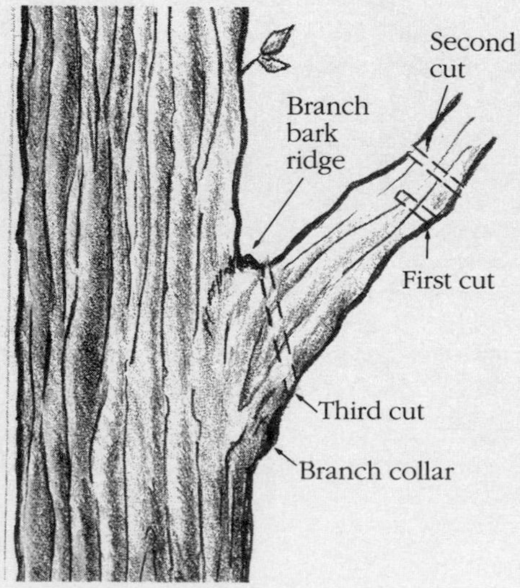

Torn Branches

Wind, ice or lightning can also rip off branches (as can undue contact with cars or machinery). If a fractured stub remains, it should be cut back to the branch collar (the bulge where the branch joins the trunk). Don't cut the collar off, as it protects the tree from insects and fungal infections (see figure 1). If the branch was torn off at the trunk, a more serious wound has occurred. The exposed sapwood should be smoothed (with a chisel, gouge or sharp adze) and the frayed bark trimmed back to where it is firmly attached to the tree. As you trim back the bark, smooth the opening into a shape that resembles an upside down flame; the downward flow of food will move more easily around this shape than any other (see figures 2 & 3). The controversy surrounding tree paints, which are used for sealing wounds, is never ending. Recent research tends to support the view that pruning paints don't benefit trees. Even so, a rubber-based compound or a sheet of polyethylene will often speed callus formation around the wound. If the wound is large, painting may be more valuable for aesthetic reasons. Stay away from compounds that form thick skins and tend to peel away from the wood surface, providing a nesting site for insects and micro-organisms.

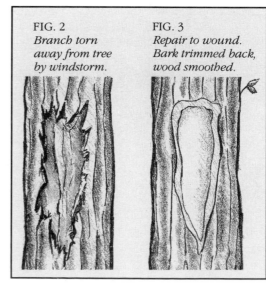

FIG. 2
Branch torn away from tree by windstorm.

FIG. 3
Repair to wound. Bark trimmed back, wood smoothed.

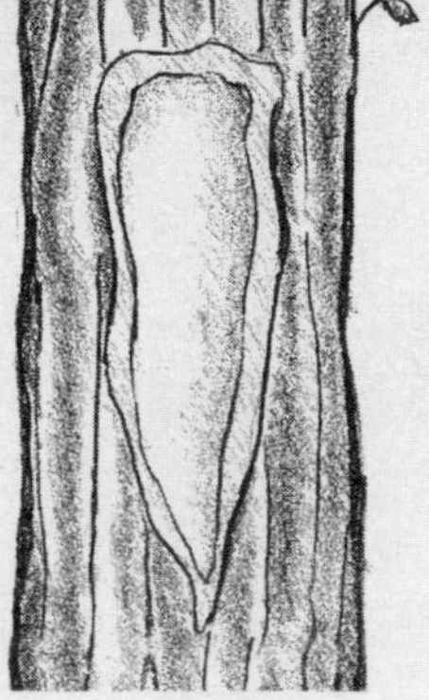

GIRDLING

A girdled trunk is one of the gardener's worst nightmares. It's usually caused by hungry mice, rabbits or deer looking for food while the ground is covered with snow. It can also be caused by the careless use of a string trimmer. This wound is serious not just because it will kill the tree if left alone, but because most gardeners don't know how to treat it. The procedure to repair a girdling wound, called bridge grafting, is quite simple and if done carefully is usually successful. By using a simple graft to join the two disconnected sections of bark, a new path is provided for foods travelling from the leaves to the roots. A small tree of one inch (2.5 cm) in diameter can be saved by one bridge. Larger trees should have a bridge for every inch (2.5 cm) of trunk diameter. In grafting terminology the bridges (thin, flexible branches) are called scions. Grafting must be carried out as soon as the scions are cut.

BRIDGE GRAFTING

By using these procedures you should be able to repair most common injuries to trees. For extensive damage or where you feel repairing the tree would be hazardous to yourself or others, a competent arborist should be consulted.

FIG.4 *Bridging by rind grafting.*

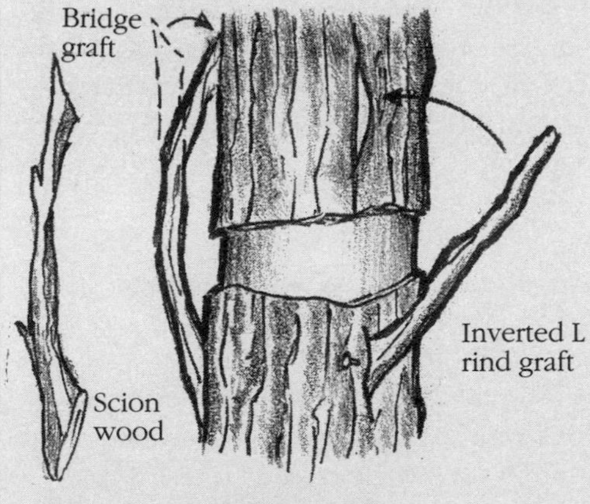

FIG.5 *Mature bridge graft.*

1 Trim back the rough sections of bark.

2 Using a sharp knife, collect scions from the branches of the affected tree or from another tree of exactly the same genus and species. Take last year's growth, either dormant or freshly defoliated.

3 The scions should be collected in such a way that you will remember which is the apical end (the end pointing toward the branch tip) and which is the basal end (the end pointing towards the main trunk). This can be accomplished by making a square cut on the basal end and a sloping cut on the apical end. This is important as the scion must be inserted with the apical end pointing up. Always make the end cuts on the scion wood near a bud, as it's here that most growth activity occurs.

4 One of the most successful graft types is the inverted L rind bridge graft. This must be done in late spring or early summer, when the bark lifts away from the cambium easily.

5 Make an inverted L cut into the bark a short distance below and above the girdle. The cut should be just wide enough to hold the scion. Make sure it passes through to the sapwood (if the bark won't lift off you haven't cut far enough).

6 Twist the knife and the bark should lift away from the sapwood right at the cambium layer (a thin layer of green tissue).

7 Turn the square cut on the basal end into a sloping cut to match the one on the apical end.

8 Insert the ends of the scion under the bark (see figure 4), taking note of which end is pointing up and making sure there is good firm contact between the scion and trunk's cambium.

9 Tack the scion in place with a small nail. Make sure it's bowed in the middle away from the trunk to exert pressure under the bark at both ends. Seal the grafts with grafting wax.♦

In the late 18th century, one recipe for treating diseased trees was to make a plaster of "one bushel of fresh cow dung, half a bushel of lime rubbish of old buildings (that from the ceilings of rooms is preferable), half a bushel of wood ashes, and a sixteenth of a bushel of pit or river sand", which were mixed together and applied to the areas of the tree where the decay had been cut away.

PRUNING TREES

The Roman word toparius *was applied to all gardeners before the 1st century AD, when topiaries as we know them began to be created, and when Pliny the Younger described "representations of divers animals in box" and "evergreens shaped into a variety of forms".*

When pruning a tree you should keep in mind that in order for the tree to survive, it must be able to defend the open wound. The more you do to help the tree heal itself, the more likely it is to survive. You can promote rapid and complete healing by not cutting through the tree's natural protective barriers. Looking carefully at a tree, you will see a bulge at the point where the branch joins the trunk. This bulge is known as the branch collar (see figure 1). Inside the branch collar are terpines (in conifers) and phenols (in hardwoods). These are the chemicals that protect the tree from invading pests and diseases. Cutting a branch off flush with the trunk destroys the branch collar and gives the tree little defense against marauding insects and fungal infection.

Use the following procedure for pruning a branch. Always use a good pruning saw for branches thicker than 1½″. Japanese saws are excellent, giving a smooth cut with little tearing of bark. You may use bypass hand pruners or bypass loppers for small branches. Bypass blades make a cleaner cut than the anvil type which tends to crush the stem as it cuts. Using hand pruners, cut as close to the branch collar as possible but not into it. Hold the pruners with the blade side toward the tree (for the smoothest cut) and grip the branch with your other hand. Gently push down on the branch as you squeeze the pruner. This makes cutting much easier. If you have trouble finding the branch collar – they are nearly flat on some conifers – first locate the branch bark ridge, the raised bark between the bark and trunk and then make a cut at an angle that mirrors the angle between the branch bark ridge and the trunk (see figure 2).

For branches larger than 1½″ in diameter, first stub cut the branch six inches out from the branch collar. Use a pruning saw and make the first cut up from the bottom halfway through the limb. Make the next cut down from the top and right through the limb. This procedure prevents the weight of the limb from pulling down and tearing out a long strip of bark and wood toward the trunk. Now that most of the weight of the branch has been removed, you can safely make the final cut. Make your saw cut as close to the branch collar as possible but don't damage it. Use the rule of equal values shown in figure 2 if you cannot clearly see the branch collar.

Paint or tar-based wound dressings are of little use and sometimes even harm the tree by trapping micro-organisms under the skin, providing a cozy breeding ground. The best wound dressing comes from inside the tree itself. However, recent research has shown dressings that form a plastic-like sheet speed callus formation.

As a general rule, the best time to prune broadleaf plants is late dormant season (March in most of Canada). The best time to prune evergreens is early summer (late June). For ornamental purposes, you may wish to delay pruning flowering shrubs until after they bloom. This is acceptable; however, don't prune when food reserves are low. Food reserves are lowest just after leaf formation.

In the years following branch removal you will see the branch collar growing over the wound. It should grow evenly all around the cut. If the cut was made too close to the trunk (i.e., damaging the branch collar) the wound-wood will be seen growing over only the sides of the wound.

When cutting back the ends of branches, always cut close to a bud or secondary branch. Make sure the bud or secondary branch is pointing in the direction that you wish the tree branch to grow (see figure 3). In this way, a plant can be trained for growth patterns (such as in espalier).

When a tree forks, sometimes called a double leader or co-dominant stem, there is no branch collar to prune back to. The best way to make a cut that the tree can defend and eventually close is as follows. Start the cut beside the top of the stem bark ridge and end directly across from the bottom of the ridge with the angle of the cut the same as the remaining branch (see figure 4).

By using these methods your trees and shrubs are assured long and healthy lives.♦

FIG. 1

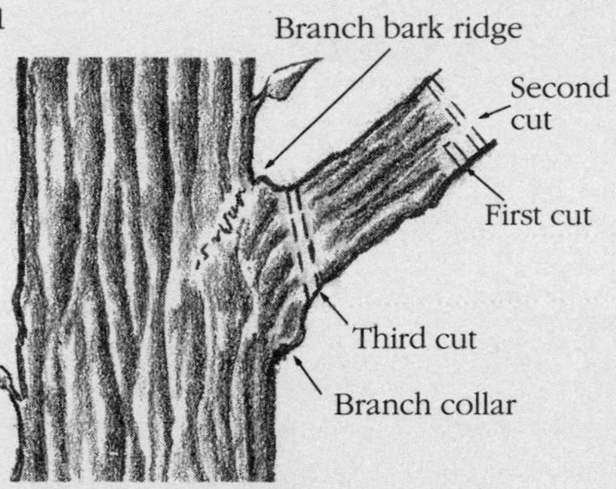

Branches are best pruned with bypass pruners or loppers. Large branches should be removed with a pruning saw: stub cut the branch 5" from the branch collar, then prune the branch. Make your pruning cut directly in front of the collar, being careful not to injure it.

FIG. 2

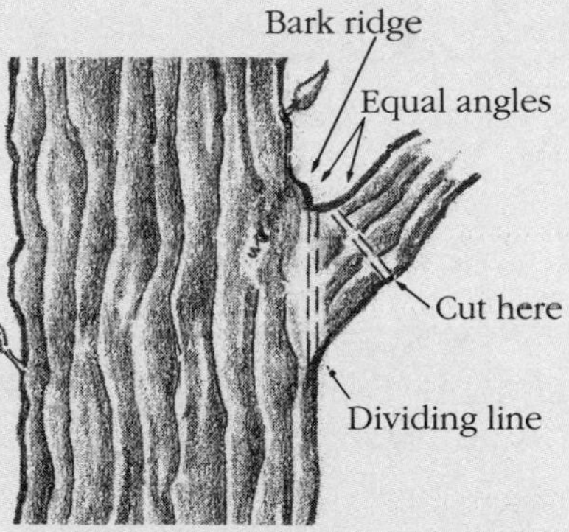

If it is difficult to see the bottom of the branch collar, locate the branch's bark ridge, then imagine a line drawn straight up from the point where the bottom of the branch meets the trunk. Make your cut on the opposite side of the line, at the same angle as the bark ridge.

FIG. 3

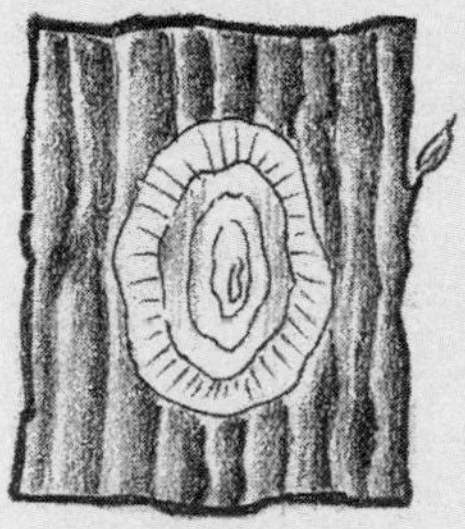

Proper wound-wood formations; correct pruning has left branch collar intact.

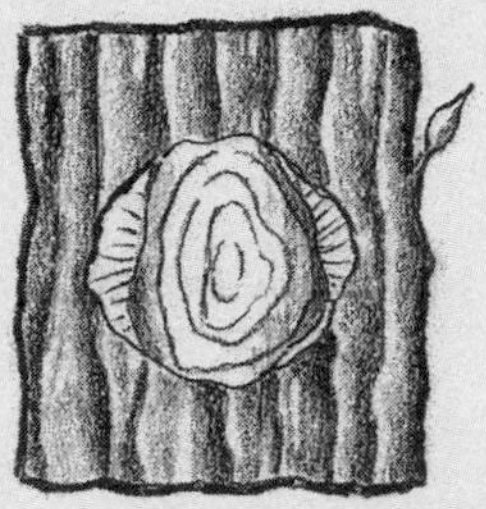

Incomplete wound-wood formation; branch collar has been injured.

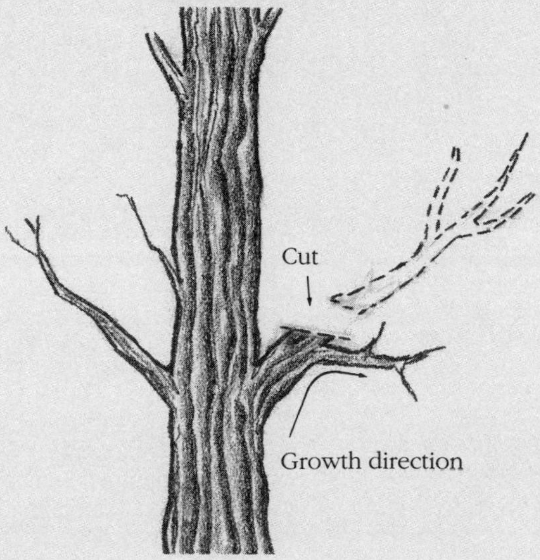

FIG. 4

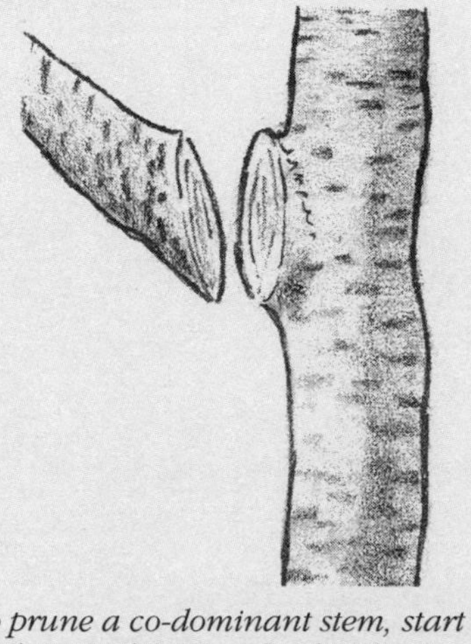

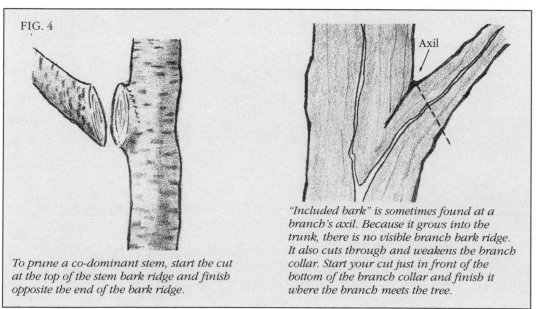

To prune a co-dominant stem, start the cut at the top of the stem bark ridge and finish opposite the end of the bark ridge.

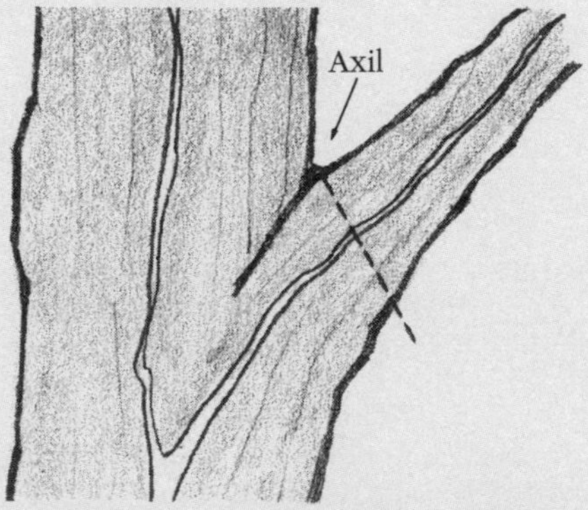

"Included bark" is sometimes found at a branch's axil. Because it grows into the trunk, there is no visible branch bark ridge. It also cuts through and weakens the branch collar. Start your cut just in front of the bottom of the branch collar and finish it where the branch meets the tree.

By the time of China's Sung dynasty (960-1279), grafting and cultivation were already well developed. For the highly-esteemed tree peony, buds were grafted onto the Chinese mohagany tree (Cedrela sinensis). *The resulting plants were ten feet in height, perfect for viewing flowers from an upper-storey window.*

Woody Perennial Inventory

for Trees, Shrubs, Vines, etc.

John McIntosh (1777-1843), born in Dundas County, Ontario, found a number of wild apple seedlings which he planted in his own orchard. His son Allan carried on the propagation of the trees and in 1835, sold the first McIntosh Red apple tree.

Date Planted	Plant Description & Location	Flowering Date
•	•	•
See notes . . .		
•	•	•
See notes . . .		
•	•	•
See notes . . .		
•	•	•
See notes . . .		
•	•	•
See notes . . .		
•	•	•
See notes . . .		
•	•	•
See notes . . .		
•	•	•
See notes . . .		
•	•	•
See notes . . .		

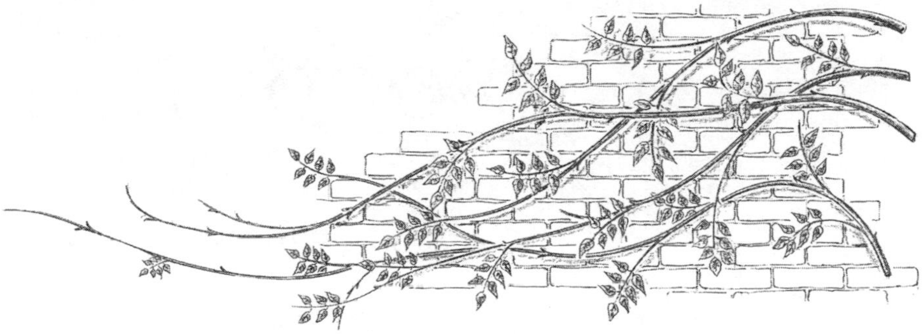

10 Year Growth & Produce Record

Year										
Height										
Harvest										
Year										
Height										
Harvest										
Year										
Height										
Harvest										
Year										
Height										
Harvest										
Year										
Height										
Harvest										
Year										
Height										
Harvest										
Year										
Height										
Harvest										
Year										
Height										
Harvest										
Year										
Height										
Harvest										

WOODY PERENNIAL INVENTORY

for Trees, Shrubs, Vines, etc.

In 16th-century England, the rose was a popular flower in the writings of Shakespeare and his contemporaries. The white and red roses, representing the house of York and Lancaster during the 15th century War of the Roses, *were united during the reign of the Tudors, whose symbol – the Tudor rose – is a five-lobed figure of a red rose encircling a white rose. Under the (relatively) peaceful reign of Elizabeth I, the rose became a symbol of peace, instead of war.*

DATE PLANTED	PLANT DESCRIPTION & LOCATION	FLOWERING DATE
•	•	•
SEE NOTES . . .		
•	•	•
SEE NOTES . . .		
•	•	•
SEE NOTES . . .		
•	•	•
SEE NOTES . . .		
•	•	•
SEE NOTES . . .		
•	•	•
SEE NOTES . . .		
•	•	•
SEE NOTES . . .		
•	•	•
SEE NOTES . . .		
•	•	•
SEE NOTES . . .		

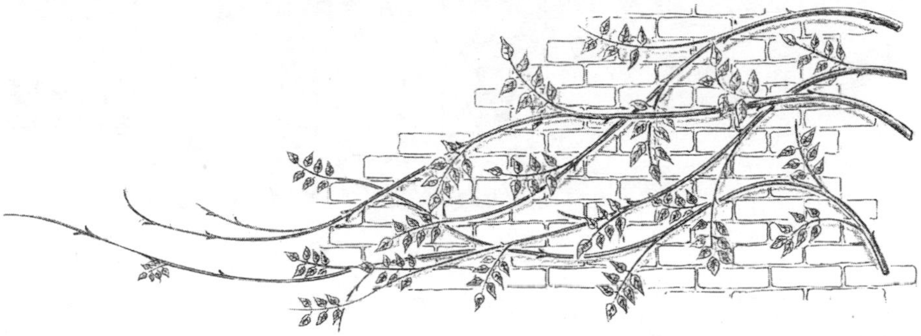

10 Year Growth & Produce Record

YEAR	•	•	•	•	•	•	•	•	•	•
HEIGHT	•	•	•	•	•	•	•	•	•	•
HARVEST	•	•	•	•	•	•	•	•	•	•
YEAR	•	•	•	•	•	•	•	•	•	•
HEIGHT	•	•	•	•	•	•	•	•	•	•
HARVEST	•	•	•	•	•	•	•	•	•	•
YEAR	•	•	•	•	•	•	•	•	•	•
HEIGHT	•	•	•	•	•	•	•	•	•	•
HARVEST	•	•	•	•	•	•	•	•	•	•
YEAR	•	•	•	•	•	•	•	•	•	•
HEIGHT	•	•	•	•	•	•	•	•	•	•
HARVEST	•	•	•	•	•	•	•	•	•	•
YEAR	•	•	•	•	•	•	•	•	•	•
HEIGHT	•	•	•	•	•	•	•	•	•	•
HARVEST	•	•	•	•	•	•	•	•	•	•
YEAR	•	•	•	•	•	•	•	•	•	•
HEIGHT	•	•	•	•	•	•	•	•	•	•
HARVEST	•	•	•	•	•	•	•	•	•	•
YEAR	•	•	•	•	•	•	•	•	•	•
HEIGHT	•	•	•	•	•	•	•	•	•	•
HARVEST	•	•	•	•	•	•	•	•	•	•
YEAR	•	•	•	•	•	•	•	•	•	•
HEIGHT	•	•	•	•	•	•	•	•	•	•
HARVEST	•	•	•	•	•	•	•	•	•	•
YEAR	•	•	•	•	•	•	•	•	•	•
HEIGHT	•	•	•	•	•	•	•	•	•	•
HARVEST	•	•	•	•	•	•	•	•	•	•

Woody Perennial Inventory

for Trees, Shrubs, Vines, etc.

Cranberries in North America were mentioned as early as 1780, where they were said to be like "cherries for colour and bigness". The first cultivated cranberry bogs were established on Cape Cod, and by 1845 had spread to other areas including Long Island, and parts of New Jersey. The recorded yields of these plants grew from 400 bushels in 1830 to more than one million a century later.

Date Planted	Plant Description & Location	Flowering Date
•	•	•
See notes . . .		
•	•	•
See notes . . .		
•	•	•
See notes . . .		
•	•	•
See notes . . .		
•	•	•
See notes . . .		
•	•	•
See notes . . .		
•	•	•
See notes . . .		
•	•	•
See notes . . .		
•	•	•
See notes . . .		

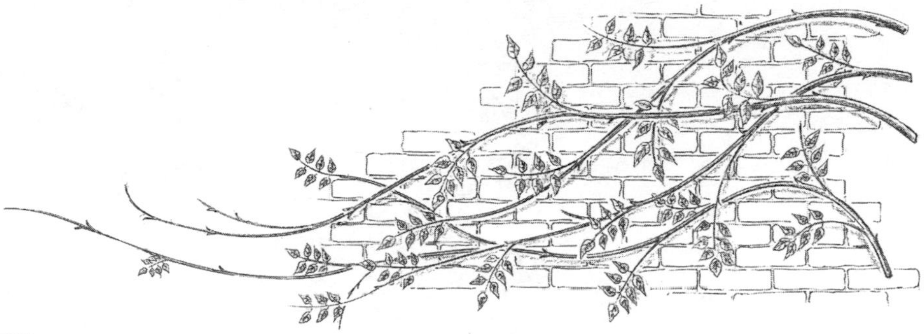

10 Year Growth & Produce Record

YEAR	•	•	•	•	•	•	•	•	•	•
HEIGHT	•	•	•	•	•	•	•	•	•	•
HARVEST	•	•	•	•	•	•	•	•	•	•
YEAR	•	•	•	•	•	•	•	•	•	•
HEIGHT	•	•	•	•	•	•	•	•	•	•
HARVEST	•	•	•	•	•	•	•	•	•	•
YEAR	•	•	•	•	•	•	•	•	•	•
HEIGHT	•	•	•	•	•	•	•	•	•	•
HARVEST	•	•	•	•	•	•	•	•	•	•
YEAR	•	•	•	•	•	•	•	•	•	•
HEIGHT	•	•	•	•	•	•	•	•	•	•
HARVEST	•	•	•	•	•	•	•	•	•	•
YEAR	•	•	•	•	•	•	•	•	•	•
HEIGHT	•	•	•	•	•	•	•	•	•	•
HARVEST	•	•	•	•	•	•	•	•	•	•
YEAR	•	•	•	•	•	•	•	•	•	•
HEIGHT	•	•	•	•	•	•	•	•	•	•
HARVEST	•	•	•	•	•	•	•	•	•	•
YEAR	•	•	•	•	•	•	•	•	•	•
HEIGHT	•	•	•	•	•	•	•	•	•	•
HARVEST	•	•	•	•	•	•	•	•	•	•
YEAR	•	•	•	•	•	•	•	•	•	•
HEIGHT	•	•	•	•	•	•	•	•	•	•
HARVEST	•	•	•	•	•	•	•	•	•	•

WOODY PERENNIAL INVENTORY

for Trees, Shrubs, Vines, etc.

Apples have been popular in England from early times, not only to eat, or to drink as cider, but also for cosmetics. John Gerard in his "Herball" of 1597, mentions the apple's use to soften the skin and remove freckles. "Pomatum" was a mixture of apple pulp, rose water and swine grease.

DATE PLANTED	PLANT DESCRIPTION & LOCATION	FLOWERING DATE
•	•	•
SEE NOTES . . .		
•	•	•
SEE NOTES . . .		
•	•	•
SEE NOTES . . .		
•	•	•
SEE NOTES . . .		
•	•	•
SEE NOTES . . .		
•	•	•
SEE NOTES . . .		
•	•	•
SEE NOTES . . .		
•	•	•
SEE NOTES . . .		
•	•	•
SEE NOTES . . .		

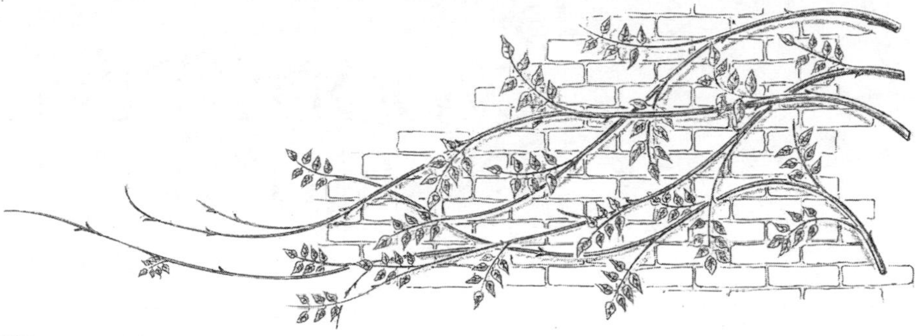

10 Year Growth & Produce Record

Year	•	•	•	•	•	•	•	•	•	•
Height	•	•	•	•	•	•	•	•	•	•
Harvest	•	•	•	•	•	•	•	•	•	•
Year	•	•	•	•	•	•	•	•	•	•
Height	•	•	•	•	•	•	•	•	•	•
Harvest	•	•	•	•	•	•	•	•	•	•
Year	•	•	•	•	•	•	•	•	•	•
Height	•	•	•	•	•	•	•	•	•	•
Harvest	•	•	•	•	•	•	•	•	•	•
Year	•	•	•	•	•	•	•	•	•	•
Height	•	•	•	•	•	•	•	•	•	•
Harvest	•	•	•	•	•	•	•	•	•	•
Year	•	•	•	•	•	•	•	•	•	•
Height	•	•	•	•	•	•	•	•	•	•
Harvest	•	•	•	•	•	•	•	•	•	•
Year	•	•	•	•	•	•	•	•	•	•
Height	•	•	•	•	•	•	•	•	•	•
Harvest	•	•	•	•	•	•	•	•	•	•
Year	•	•	•	•	•	•	•	•	•	•
Height	•	•	•	•	•	•	•	•	•	•
Harvest	•	•	•	•	•	•	•	•	•	•
Year	•	•	•	•	•	•	•	•	•	•
Height	•	•	•	•	•	•	•	•	•	•
Harvest	•	•	•	•	•	•	•	•	•	•

WOODY PERENNIAL INVENTORY

for Trees, Shrubs, Vines, etc.

The Pennsylvania Dutch were known for their bountiful orchards. From their produce, they made and sold cider, apple-butter and dried fruit. To dry peaches, for example, the pitted peaches were first mashed, then spread in a thin layer on a tray, and dried in an oven. This "peach leather" could be kept indefinitely, and became soft again after soaking it in water.

DATE PLANTED	PLANT DESCRIPTION & LOCATION	FLOWERING DATE
•	•	•
SEE NOTES . . .		
•	•	•
SEE NOTES . . .		
•	•	•
SEE NOTES . . .		
•	•	•
SEE NOTES . . .		
•	•	•
SEE NOTES . . .		
•	•	•
SEE NOTES . . .		
•	•	•
SEE NOTES . . .		
•	•	•
SEE NOTES . . .		
•	•	•
SEE NOTES . . .		

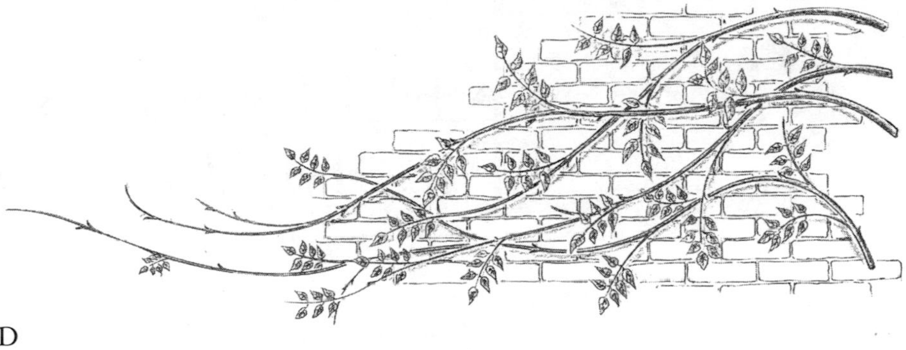

10 Year Growth & Produce Record

YEAR										
HEIGHT										
HARVEST										
YEAR										
HEIGHT										
HARVEST										
YEAR										
HEIGHT										
HARVEST										
YEAR										
HEIGHT										
HARVEST										
YEAR										
HEIGHT										
HARVEST										
YEAR										
HEIGHT										
HARVEST										
YEAR										
HEIGHT										
HARVEST										
YEAR										
HEIGHT										
HARVEST										
YEAR										
HEIGHT										
HARVEST										

KEEPING INSECT PROBLEMS TO A MINIMUM

The Colorado potato beetle, an innocuous native of the Colorado River basin when it was first described in 1823, took to settlers' potatoes and spread to Europe by 1876 and then around the world, dining also on potato relatives such as eggplant and tomato.

By following a few simple rules, you can keep your garden insect problems to a minimum. Keep in mind that it is natural for insects to be eating plants and that they interfere with the plant's ability to produce food. Preventative maintenance is the best path, rather than trying to annihilate a species after it has built up into a problem population.

1 KEEP THE GARDEN CLEAN

Insects hide in weeds and garden trash. Keep your garden weeded and use a clean mulch.

2 USE INTER-PLANTING

Insects feed on plants belonging to a certain family and usually reject others. By mixing your plantings and avoiding monocropping you can keep insect populations to a minimum.

3 CROP ROTATION

Many insects winter in, on or around their host plants. To avoid instant re-infestations every year do not plant the same crop in the same place each season.

4 HAND PICKING

Many insects can be controlled by hand picking and crushing or dropping into a can of kerosene. The Colorado potato beetle larva is easily controlled in this way.

5 INSECT BARRIERS

Insects can be discouraged from attacking plants by setting up physical barriers between them and the plants. A good example of this is a cardboard collar wrapped around a transplant to prevent cutworm damage.

6 PLANT VARIETIES

Some varieties of a plant may be more resistant to insects than others. Check the seed catalogues for insect-resistant varieties.

7 SPRAYS

Use natural, environment-friendly sprays as a last resort. A blast of plain water will wash off aphids, mites and many other small insects. Potassium based soaps (as contained in many Safer's products) don't make suds but do smother many soft-bodied insects such as aphids, whiteflies, mealybugs, and mites. For more serious infestations, stronger, organic (plant derived and non-residual) compounds can be used, such as pyrethrum (an extract from chrysanthemum flowers) rotenone, diatomaceous earth, or Bt (bacteria that affect only larvae). All of these are harmless to mammals. By following these rules you should have a relatively pest-free garden throughout the season.♦

1. *Squash Bug*
2. *Tomato Hornworm*
3. *Cabbage Looper*
4. *Striped Cucumber Beetle*
5. *Earwig*
6. *Squash Vine Borer*
7. *Grasshoppers*
8. *Slugs & Snails*
9. *Cutworm*
10. *Bean Aphid*
11. *Colorado Potato Beetle*
12. *Codling Moth*

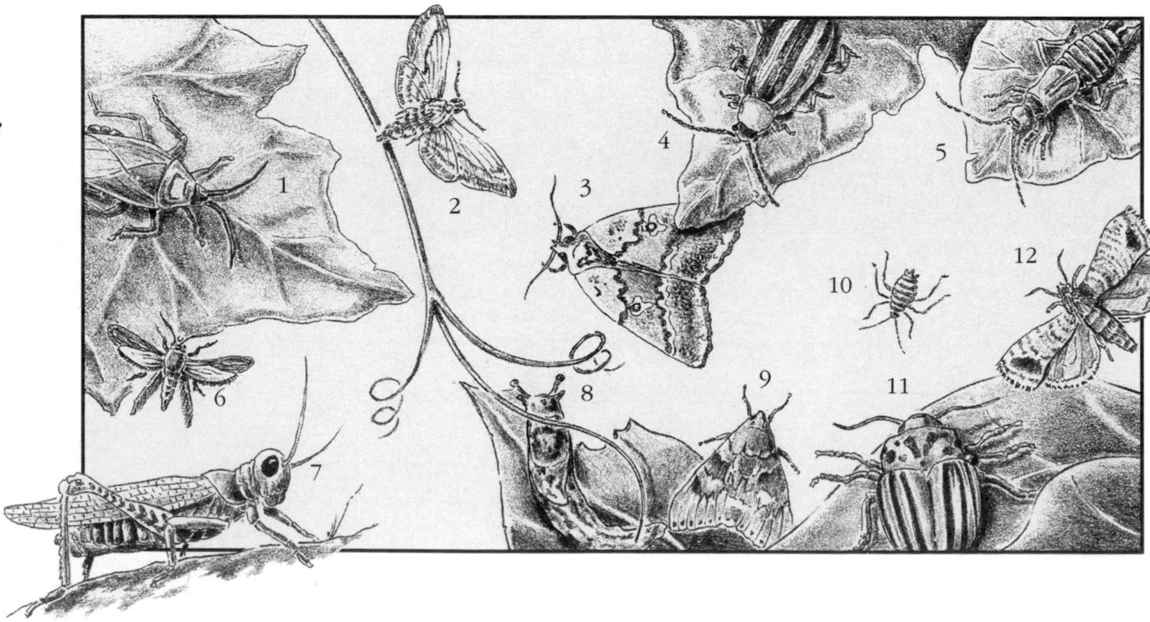

Insect & Disease Controls

Date	Plant	Insect or Disease	Control Used and Result
•	•	•	•
•	•	•	•
•	•	•	•
•	•	•	•
•	•	•	•
•	•	•	•
•	•	•	•
•	•	•	•
•	•	•	•
•	•	•	•
•	•	•	•
•	•	•	•
•	•	•	•
•	•	•	•
•	•	•	•

INSECT & DISEASE CONTROLS

DATE	PLANT	INSECT OR DISEASE	CONTROL USED AND RESULT
•	•	•	•
•	•	•	•
•	•	•	•
•	•	•	•
•	•	•	•
•	•	•	•
•	•	•	•
•	•	•	•
•	•	•	•
•	•	•	•
•	•	•	•
•	•	•	•
•	•	•	•
•	•	•	•
•	•	•	•

One of the earliest "tree doctors" was Scott William Forsyth (b.1737), who worked at the Apothecaries' Garden at Chelsea. He was interested in diseases of trees and wrote a treatise entitled: "Observations on the Diseases, Defects and Injuries in all Kinds of Fruit and Forest Trees", which was published in London in 1791. The first edition sold more than 1,500 copies.

DATE	PLANT	INSECT OR DISEASE	CONTROL USED AND RESULT
•	•	•	•
•	•	•	•
•	•	•	•
•	•	•	•
•	•	•	•
•	•	•	•
•	•	•	•
•	•	•	•
•	•	•	•
•	•	•	•
•	•	•	•
•	•	•	•
•	•	•	•
•	•	•	•
•	•	•	•

INSECT & DISEASE CONTROLS

DATE	PLANT	INSECT OR DISEASE	CONTROL USED AND RESULT
•	•	•	•
•	•	•	•
•	•	•	•
•	•	•	•
•	•	•	•
•	•	•	•
•	•	•	•
•	•	•	•
•	•	•	•
•	•	•	•
•	•	•	•
•	•	•	•
•	•	•	•
•	•	•	•
•	•	•	•

The gypsy moth was accidentally introduced to North America in 1869 by Leopold Trouvelt, who had brought gypsy moth eggs from his native France to Medford, Massachusetts, in the hope of producing a disease-resistant silkworm. By 1923, all of New England was infested. The gypsy moth now inhabits about 13 million acres throughout the Northeast and has made forays into the west.

Date	Plant	Insect or Disease	Control Used and Result
•	•	•	•
•	•	•	•
•	•	•	•
•	•	•	•
•	•	•	•
•	•	•	•
•	•	•	•
•	•	•	•
•	•	•	•
•	•	•	•
•	•	•	•
•	•	•	•
•	•	•	•
•	•	•	•
•	•	•	•

INSECT & DISEASE CONTROLS

DATE	PLANT	INSECT OR DISEASE	CONTROL USED AND RESULT
•	•	•	•
•	•	•	•
•	•	•	•
•	•	•	•
•	•	•	•
•	•	•	•
•	•	•	•
•	•	•	•
•	•	•	•
•	•	•	•
•	•	•	•
•	•	•	•
•	•	•	•
•	•	•	•
•	•	•	•

Dutch elm disease, characterized by the wilting of leaves, is spread by the bark beetle or may be transmitted between the roots of adjacent trees. There is no cure once a tree has contracted the fungus, Ceratocystis ulmi, *which was first noted in the Netherlands in 1920. It entered North America around 1930, and since that time, has killed millions of trees.*

DATE	PLANT	INSECT OR DISEASE	CONTROL USED AND RESULT
•	•	•	•
•	•	•	•
•	•	•	•
•	•	•	•
•	•	•	•
•	•	•	•
•	•	•	•
•	•	•	•
•	•	•	•
•	•	•	•
•	•	•	•
•	•	•	•
•	•	•	•
•	•	•	•
•	•	•	•

Insect & Disease Controls

Date	Plant	Insect or Disease	Control Used and Result
•	•	•	•
•	•	•	•
•	•	•	•
•	•	•	•
•	•	•	•
•	•	•	•
•	•	•	•
•	•	•	•
•	•	•	•
•	•	•	•
•	•	•	•
•	•	•	•
•	•	•	•
•	•	•	•
•	•	•	•

The name of the insect commonly known as the earwig, Forficula auricularia, *comes from an Anglo-Saxon word meaning "ear-structure." It was so named because of an ancient superstition, which held that the earwig was thought to penetrate the head by entering the ear of sleeping persons.*

DATE	PLANT	INSECT OR DISEASE	CONTROL USED AND RESULT
•	•	•	•
•	•	•	•
•	•	•	•
•	•	•	•
•	•	•	•
•	•	•	•
•	•	•	•
•	•	•	•
•	•	•	•
•	•	•	•
•	•	•	•
•	•	•	•
•	•	•	•
•	•	•	•
•	•	•	•

INSECT & DISEASE CONTROLS

DATE	PLANT	INSECT OR DISEASE	CONTROL USED AND RESULT
•	•	•	•
•	•	•	•
•	•	•	•
•	•	•	•
•	•	•	•
•	•	•	•
•	•	•	•
•	•	•	•
•	•	•	•
•	•	•	•
•	•	•	•
•	•	•	•
•	•	•	•
•	•	•	•
•	•	•	•

A mixture of tobacco, sulphur, unslaked lime, and elder-buds, placed in boiling water, left to stand until cold, and allowed to settle for two or three days, was one recipe for dealing with severe cases of mildew on trees in the 19th century.

Date	Plant	Insect or Disease	Control Used and Result
•	•	•	•
•	•	•	•
•	•	•	•
•	•	•	•
•	•	•	•
•	•	•	•
•	•	•	•
•	•	•	•
•	•	•	•
•	•	•	•
•	•	•	•
•	•	•	•
•	•	•	•
•	•	•	•
•	•	•	•

INSECT & DISEASE CONTROLS

DATE	PLANT	INSECT OR DISEASE	CONTROL USED AND RESULT
•	•	•	•
•	•	•	•
•	•	•	•
•	•	•	•
•	•	•	•
•	•	•	•
•	•	•	•
•	•	•	•
•	•	•	•
•	•	•	•
•	•	•	•
•	•	•	•
•	•	•	•
•	•	•	•
•	•	•	•

Fire blight, a bacterial disease that infects pears, mountain ashes, hawthorns and many other members of the rose family, originated in North America and reached northern Europe and the British Isles during this century. Fire blight is the most serious limitation, besides climate, to growing pears in Canada and in the United States.

Date	Plant	Insect or Disease	Control Used and Result
•	•	•	•
•	•	•	•
•	•	•	•
•	•	•	•
•	•	•	•
•	•	•	•
•	•	•	•
•	•	•	•
•	•	•	•
•	•	•	•
•	•	•	•
•	•	•	•
•	•	•	•
•	•	•	•
•	•	•	•

INSECT & DISEASE CONTROLS

DATE	PLANT	INSECT OR DISEASE	CONTROL USED AND RESULT
•	•	•	•
•	•	•	•
•	•	•	•
•	•	•	•
•	•	•	•
•	•	•	•
•	•	•	•
•	•	•	•
•	•	•	•
•	•	•	•
•	•	•	•
•	•	•	•
•	•	•	•
•	•	•	•
•	•	•	•

In 1943, the first DDT was imported into North America from the Swiss company that manufactured it. It was first recommended for the military against body lice, and was soon found an effective poison against more than 500 pests, and birds, mammals and humans, via the food chain. It has since been banned from use in most industrialized nations; however, it is still used in many third world nations.

DATE	PLANT	INSECT OR DISEASE	CONTROL USED AND RESULT
•	•	•	•
•	•	•	•
•	•	•	•
•	•	•	•
•	•	•	•
•	•	•	•
•	•	•	•
•	•	•	•
•	•	•	•
•	•	•	•
•	•	•	•
•	•	•	•
•	•	•	•
•	•	•	•
•	•	•	•

GARDEN TOOL CARE

What to do with your tools while your garden hibernates

When European settlers observed North American natives in Virginia in the 16th century, they wrote that the Indians made holes for seeds with "a crooked piece of wood, being scraped on both sides in fashion of a gardener's paring iron". A report from Florida described "a kind of hoe made from fishes' bones".

After the final harvests are brought in and the gardens prepared for the onslaught of winter, garden tools are often hastily tossed into a corner of the garage, basement or garden shed until they are needed again in the spring. Then, when spring arrives, we often groan over our rusted, chipped, splintered and dull tools.

This scene need not be played out again this year. A few hours of attention and planning before storage will keep your garden tools neatly placed, accessible and in good condition. It's never too late. All it takes is a little effort, elbow grease and patience.

Maintaining your tools means nothing more than protecting them from the weather, making sure the soil is removed, keeping the metal parts oiled and rust-free and the wooden parts oiled and splinter-free. It also means keeping sharp edges sharp and moving parts moving smoothly. Finally, tools should be stored in a dry place in such a way that you can get to them easily when the warm weather comes around again.

Most tools can be kept clean and rust free by hosing them off after each use. Stubborn dirt can be removed with a wire brush or with steel wool. Then the tools should be wiped down with an oily rag. This cleaning and oiling can be accomplished in one step by plunging the tool head into a five-gallon bucket filled with coarse sand and a quart of motor oil. If you find minor rust on your tools, use steel wool or a sandpaper-like material on the rusty spot, then cover with a rust-penetrating oil. Wipe clean. If your tools are seriously rusted, they may have to be discarded. If you have tools with wooden handles, keep them splinter-free by giving the handles a light sanding at least once a year, followed by a coat of tung oil or linseed oil. Let the handle dry, then wipe off any excess oil.

KEEPING YOUR BLADES SHARP

Garden tools invariably perform better and with less effort when they are sharp. This is true not only for cutting tools, such as pruners and shears, but also for spades, hoes, edgers and other tools that come into contact with the soil. Maintaining a sharp edge will greatly reduce the effort needed each time the blade is pushed into the soil.

Digging will be made easier if a 35 degree bevel is put across the edge. However, the exact angle is not as important as keeping

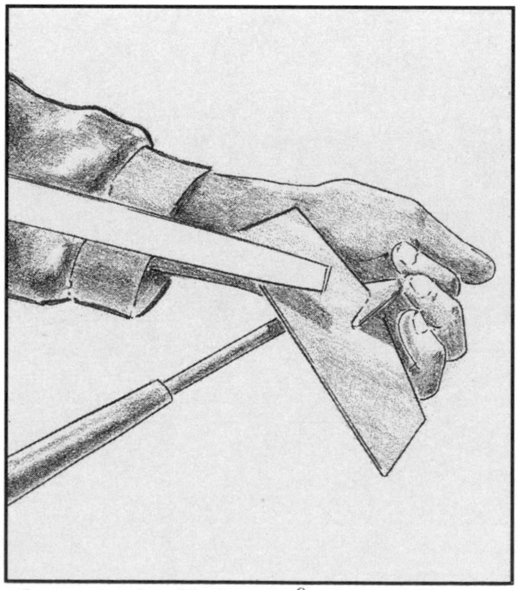

Sharpening hoe blade to 35° with mill file.

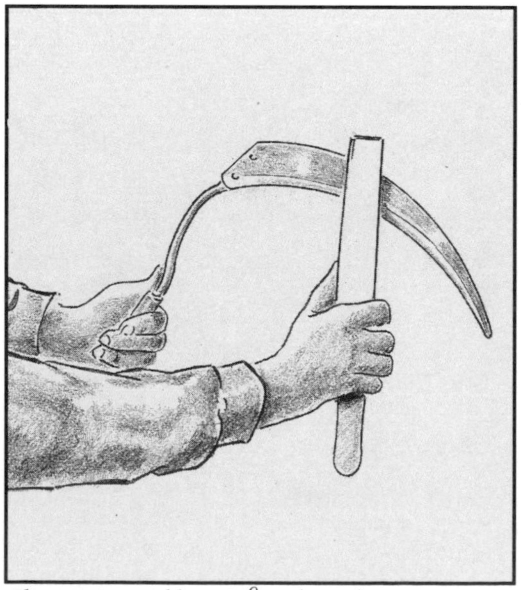

Sharpening sickle to 20° with scythe stone.

the angle constant across the entire edge, as the thinnest parts will wear down first. Using an eight- or ten-inch mill file with a bastard cut, put a bevel on one edge of the blade. Spades used for heavy chopping, where the edge is more likely to roll, should have a bevel of about 45 degrees. Use a 20 degree bevel for pruners, scythes and sickles. Knives can take a fine bevel of 22 degrees, 11 degrees on each side. Finer cutting tools should be sharpened with a stone.

Pruning saws edged with the Japanese tooth-pattern are increasingly popular. While they give a superior cut, they come with a unique problem – how to sharpen them. The only way to do this properly is to use a feather-edge file. Designed to fit into narrow, tightly-angled spots, this file is perfect for getting in between the long narrow teeth. Japanese saws are made with a harder steel than Western saws and do not dull as quickly. Even when used regularly, they will not need sharpening for several years. When they do become dull, re-file the teeth at the same angle as they were originally cut.

WHAT TO DO AND HOW TO DO IT

- SCYTHES AND SICKLES
Sand and oil wooden handles. Rub down rusty blades with sandpaper or steel wool. Sharpen with a good scythe stone by drawing the stone repeatedly across the blade, in one direction only. Lightly oil the blade, then hang in a dry place.

- SPADES, FORKS, HOES AND EDGE KNIVES
Remove soil and debris. Sand wooden handles until smooth and apply tung oil or boiled linseed oil. Sharpen blade. Lightly oil unpainted metal parts and hang in a dry place.

- TROWELS AND HAND FORKS
Remove dirt and debris. Lightly oil any exposed metal and store in a dry place.

- WATERING CANS
Empty and rinse out watering cans. Hang with the nozzle pointing down. Keep plastic cans out of sunlight as ultraviolet rays will eventually cause them to deteriorate.

- HOSES
Drain hoses by pulling them over a beam or the top of a door. Coil neatly and hang in a dry place. Keep away from sunlight, as ultraviolet rays eventually destroy plastic, vinyl or nylon products.

- SHEARS, PRUNERS, LOPPERS AND KNIVES
Wipe clean. Commercial solvents can be used to remove sap and chlorophyll residues. Sharpen using fine grit stone. Lightly oil moving parts and exposed metal. Hang in a dry spot.

- SPREADERS
Thoroughly wash inside and outside. Fertilizer residues are often corrosive. Clean with steel wool and lightly oil metal parts. Lubricate all moving parts. Store in a dry place. Keep plastic spreaders away from sunlight.

The greenhouse was developed in England in the mid-19th century when techniques for glass manufacture allowed large, thin, transparent sheets to be made. However, an earlier version existed in New York in 1764 and was of simple design: a shingle-roofed building with glass panels on the side and at the ends. Some greenhouses also had a second storey to provide accommodation for the gardener.

Sharpening spade to 35° with mill file.

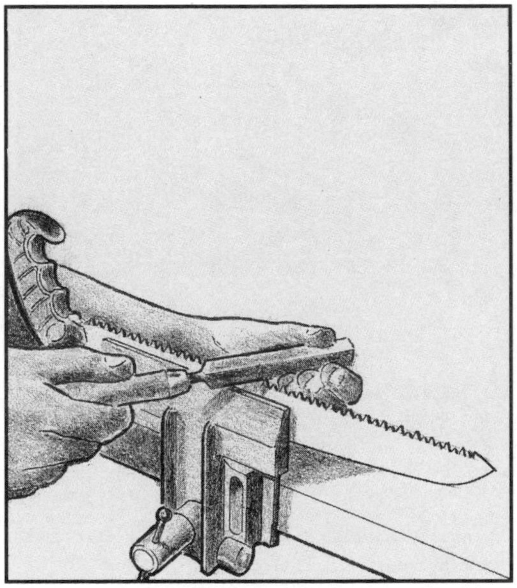

Sharpening Japanese saw with feather-edge file.

The lawn-mower was invented in 1830 by Edwin Beard Budding, who did not like the bare patches and the circular cuts caused by the scythes. The apparatus was pushed from the rear, but for difficult mowing it could also be helped along with someone pulling at the front. "The Ladies' Companion to the Flower Garden" of 1844 found the mower gave "excellent exercise to the arms and every part of the body".

- GARDEN CARTS AND WHEELBARROWS
  Remove dirt and debris. Paint or stain exposed surfaces. Tighten loose nuts and screws. Lubricate bearings. Store on end in a dry sheltered place.

- POWER MOWERS AND ROTOTILLERS
  Drain gas tank. Run engine until carburetor empties. Remove spark plug wire from spark plug to prevent ignition. Clean air filter. Change oil on four-cycle engines. Clean and sharpen blades and tines. Scrape grass and mud from housing. Remove rust and repaint exposed surfaces. Clean debris from cylinder cooling fins. Tighten loose nuts and screws. Store in a dry place.

- PUSH MOWERS
  Keep moving parts, reel axle shaft, wheels and cutting surfaces lubricated. Clean out any dry grass or dirt. Repaint exposed metal surfaces (other than cutting surfaces). Tighten any loose screws or nuts. A new push mower, if properly adjusted and lubricated, is self-sharpening. However, after several years of use the blade may need sharpening. This can be accomplished by either strapping a cylinder mower sharpening device to the cutter bar or by applying industrial grinding or valve lapping compound (180-240 grit) to the cutter bar and then operating the mower over a smooth surface for several minutes until the front edge of the cutter bar blade is polished. If the blades are chipped or bent, you may need to use a professional sharpening service.

STORAGE

All tools should be stored in a dry place away from the ravages of the weather. If the floor in your storage area is damp, use tool hooks to keep them off the floor and easy to get at. Hanging tools on a wall gives a neat, organized appearance. Use corners for lawnmowers and spreaders and store wheelbarrows and garden carts on end up against a bare wall.

Protecting wood and steel from moisture, and the moving parts from dirt, and storing tools in an organized manner will make the springtime reunion with your garden tools an enjoyable, not a dreaded, experience. Enjoyment, after all, is what gardening is all about. ♦

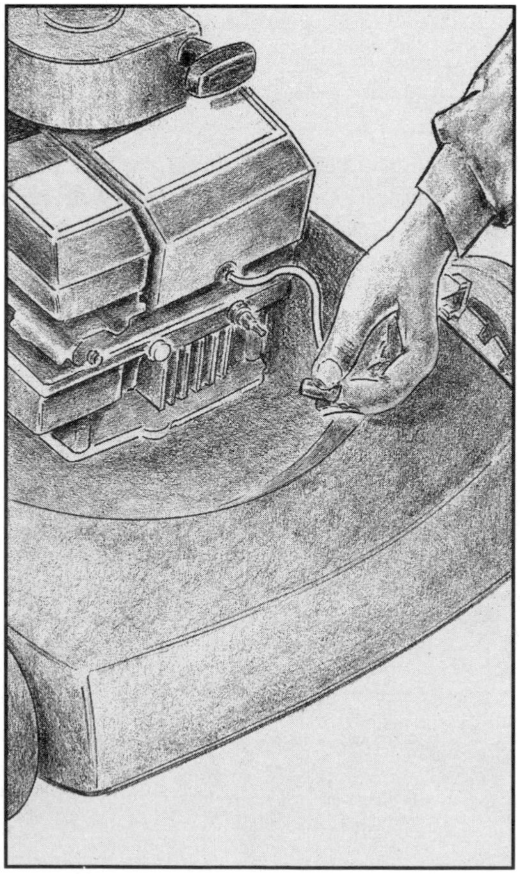

Removing spark plug wire before working on lawn-mower.

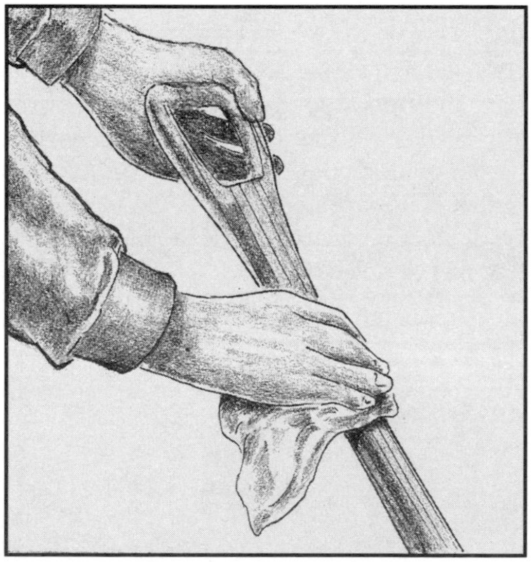

Wiping down handle of spade with linseed oil or tung oil.

GARDEN TOOL INVENTORY

DATE PURCHASED	ITEM	SERIAL NO.	QUANTITY	PRICE	TOTAL
•	•	•	•	•	•
•	•	•	•	•	•
•	•	•	•	•	•
•	•	•	•	•	•
•	•	•	•	•	•
•	•	•	•	•	•
•	•	•	•	•	•
•	•	•	•	•	•
•	•	•	•	•	•
•	•	•	•	•	•
•	•	•	•	•	•
•	•	•	•	•	•
•	•	•	•	•	•
•	•	•	•	•	•
•	•	•	•	•	•

Garden Tool Inventory

Date Purchased	Item	Serial No.	Quantity	Price	Total
•	•	•	•	•	•
•	•	•	•	•	•
•	•	•	•	•	•
•	•	•	•	•	•
•	•	•	•	•	•
•	•	•	•	•	•
•	•	•	•	•	•
•	•	•	•	•	•
•	•	•	•	•	•
•	•	•	•	•	•
•	•	•	•	•	•
•	•	•	•	•	•
•	•	•	•	•	•
•	•	•	•	•	•
•	•	•	•	•	•

In the early 17th century, women were encouraged to work in the garden. "The Countrie Housewife's Garden" of 1618, written by William Lawson, advised: "If you be not able or willing to hire a gardener, keep your profits to yourself, but then you must take all the pain."

Date Purchased	Item	Serial No.	Quantity	Price	Total
•	•	•	•	•	•
•	•	•	•	•	•
•	•	•	•	•	•
•	•	•	•	•	•
•	•	•	•	•	•
•	•	•	•	•	•
•	•	•	•	•	•
•	•	•	•	•	•
•	•	•	•	•	•
•	•	•	•	•	•
•	•	•	•	•	•
•	•	•	•	•	•
•	•	•	•	•	•
•	•	•	•	•	•
•	•	•	•	•	•

Constructing a Better Garden Pond

The Aztecs, who were enthusiastic gardeners, created floating gardens called chinampas. Made of willow branches and roots, and covered with mud, these rectangularly-shaped islands were set with great numbers of plants, including fruit trees. As much as 300 feet in length, they produced up to seven crops a year.

Most suppliers of garden pond equipment suggest the sequences illustrated in figure 1 for constructing a pond. This will create a troublesome edge as illustrated in figure 2. After a rain it will overflow, eventually eroding the soil and causing the edge rocks to shift and be unstable when walked on. During dry spells the water level will drop, leaving an unsightly ring on the liner and exposing it to the damaging rays of the sun.

There are two better ways to construct a garden pond. One has a stone edge and the other a natural-looking edge. Figure 3 illustrates the stone edge method to protect the liner. It holds the liner in place under water and behind the edge rocks. Now the water level can drop a full six inches before the liner is exposed.

Figure 4 illustrates a method of creating a natural look to the edge of your pond. Although it uses more pond liner, it creates an environment friendly to short-legged wading birds and certain plants. The choice of which edge to use depends on your personal preferences and intentions for garden usage.

Regardless of the type of edge you end up using, every pond should have a planned overflow point. The most logical point is toward the lowest ground surrounding the pond. Position the liner lower at this point, and out from it plant flood-tolerant plants An alternative is to make the spill point very narrow and have it run into a drain pipe, which then carries the water away to another part of the garden. ♦

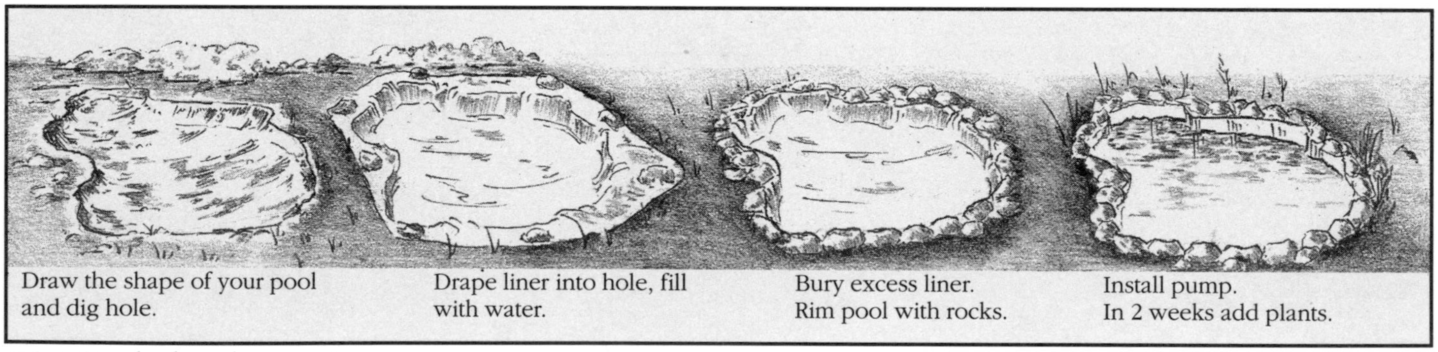

Draw the shape of your pool and dig hole.
Drape liner into hole, fill with water.
Bury excess liner.
Rim pool with rocks.
Install pump.
In 2 weeks add plants.

FIG. 1 *Standard pond construction.*

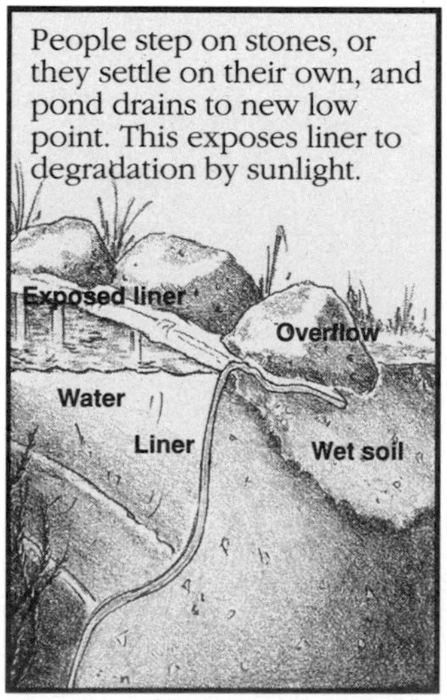

People step on stones, or they settle on their own, and pond drains to new low point. This exposes liner to degradation by sunlight.
Exposed liner

FIG. 2 *Problems with standard construction.*

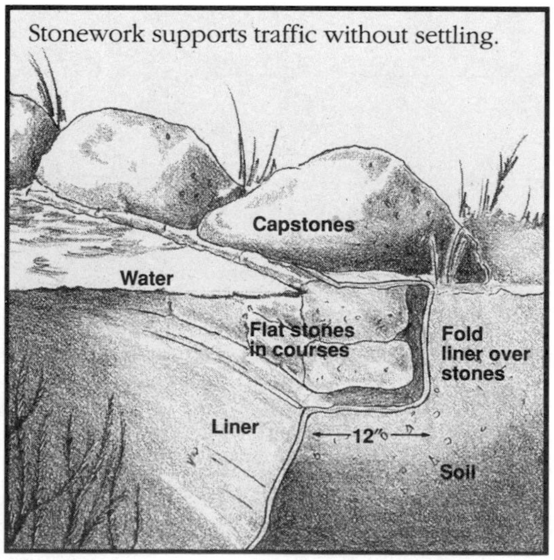

Stonework supports traffic without settling.
Capstones

Flat stones in courses
Fold liner over stones

FIG. 3 *A better stone edge for garden ponds.*

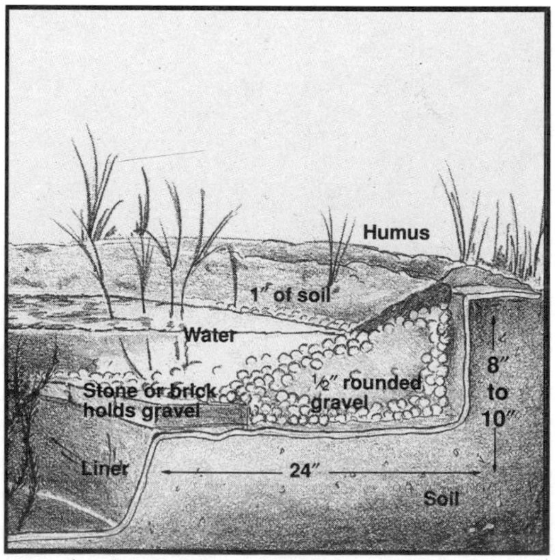

Stone or brick holds gravel
½" rounded gravel

FIG. 4 *A better natural bank for ponds.*

PREPARING FOR WINTER

There are many things that can be done to prepare your garden to come through the winter with as little damage as possible.

PERENNIALS

After the first light frosts, divide perennials if needed. Dig and store frost tender (summer flowering) bulbs. When the ground is partially frozen, cut back the remaining foliage on the perennials and cover the beds with a 3″ layer of straw or leaf mulch.

EVERGREENS AND SMALL TREES

All evergreens should be watered liberally before freeze-up. Smaller evergreens should be wrapped with burlap. This will help the tissues to stay green through the winter months, despite the drying effects of the sun and wind. Tall upright evergreens planted near the roof line of a building, but too large to wrap with burlap, should have their branches supported by a wrap of netting to prevent damage from falling ice and snow. Small trees should have their trunks protected from animals by using wrap-around guards and rodent repellents.

LAWNS

Areas covered with turf should be raked clean and the grass cut to no shorter than 2″. Leaves should be composted for use next year. A fertilizer with a low nitrogen and high phosphorus and potassium content can be applied to strengthen the root system. Lawns can also be aerated at this time with a coring tool to increase the air, water and nutrients getting to the roots of the turf.

VEGETABLE AND ANNUAL BEDS

Dig over the vegetable and annual beds, burying old plant residue to allow it to decompose over the winter. Rake smooth any areas you may want to sow very early in the spring, to save time preparing the soil later.

ROSES

Starting in the spring, in areas zone 5 or colder, hybrid tea roses should be planted with the graft union four inches below the soil surface. (This one little trick will give you a spectacular increase in survival rates.) In the fall, just before freeze-up, soil should be mounded up around them to a level of eight to twelve inches. ♦

Francis Peabody Sharp was the first breeder of hardy fruits in Canada. He introduced a number of hardy fruits, such as cold climate apples, from England and the United States to his New Brunswick nursery in 1844, having as many as 2000 seedlings at one time.

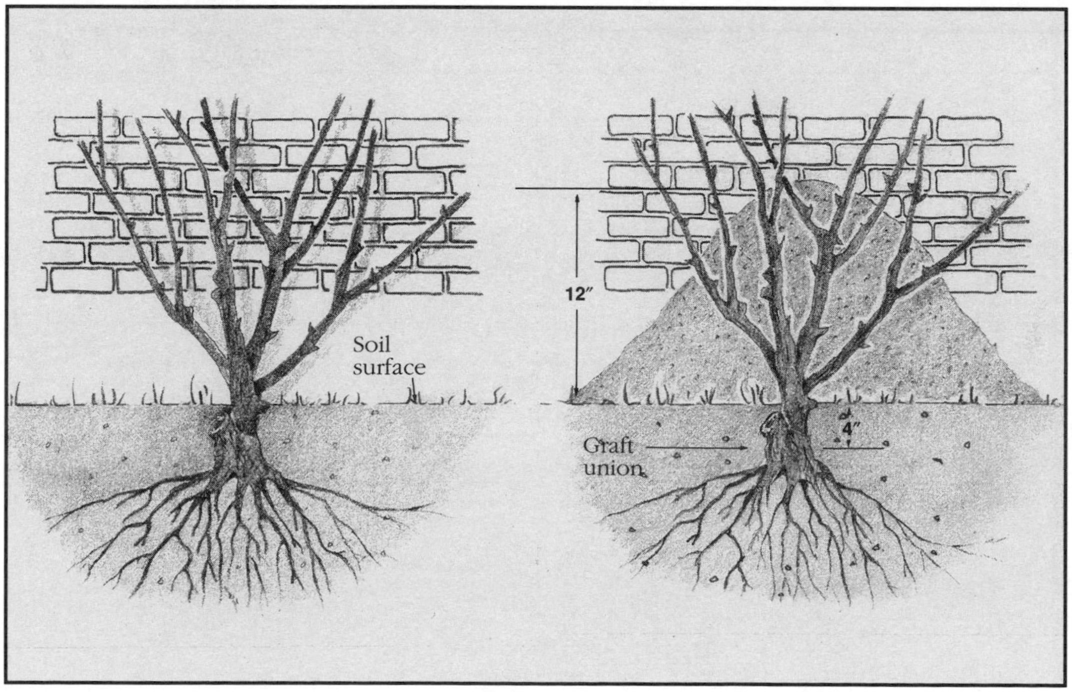

Proper planting and winter protection will spectacularly increase the survival rate of a hybrid tea rose.

BULB PLANTING GUIDE

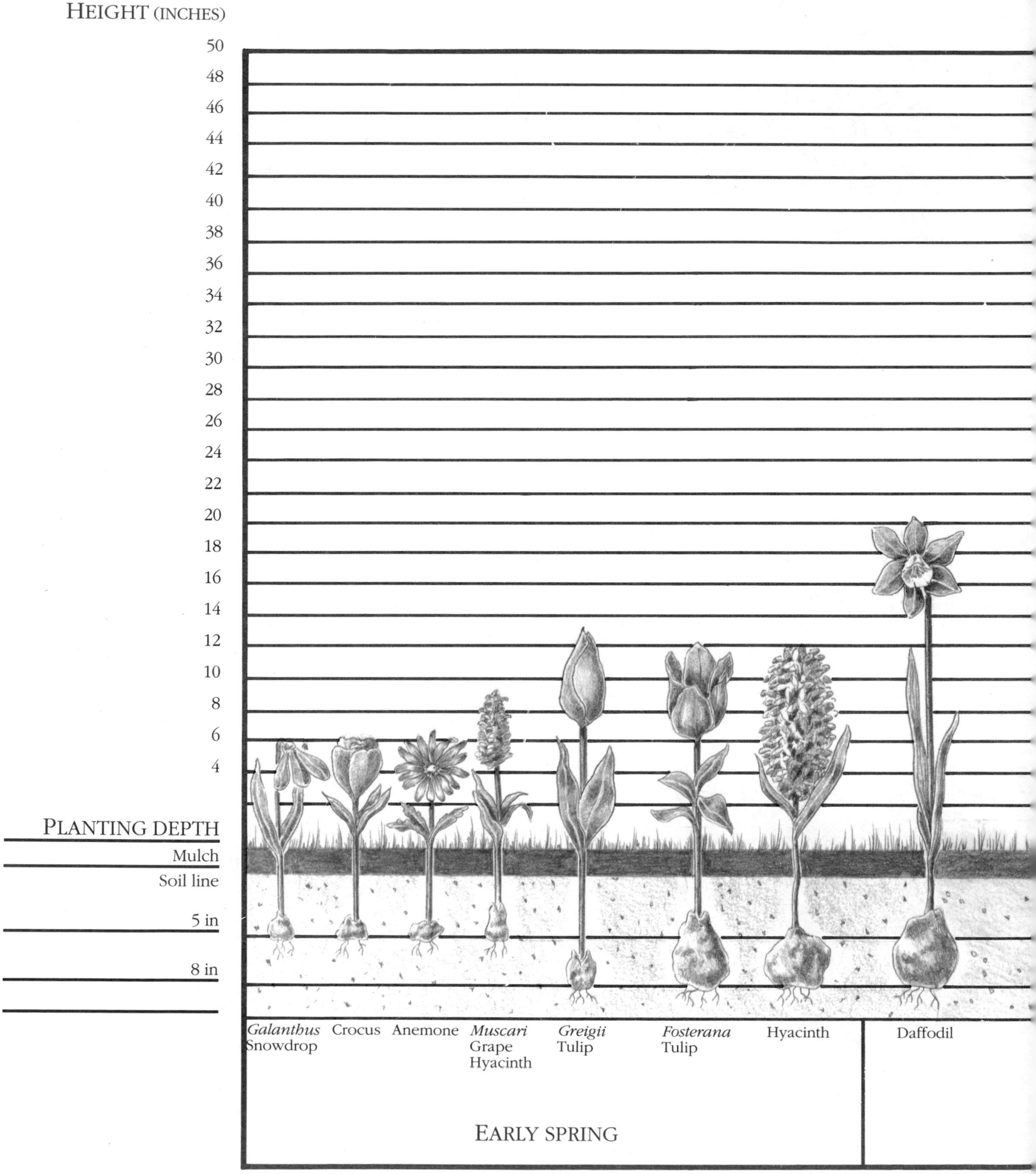

HEIGHT (INCHES)
50
48
46
44
42
40
38
36
34
32
30
28
26
24
22
20
18
16
14
12
10
8
6
4
PLANTING DEPTH
Mulch
Soil line
5 in
8 in
Galanthus Snowdrop
Crocus
Anemone
Muscari Grape Hyacinth
Greigii Tulip
Fosterana Tulip
Hyacinth
Daffodil
EARLY SPRING

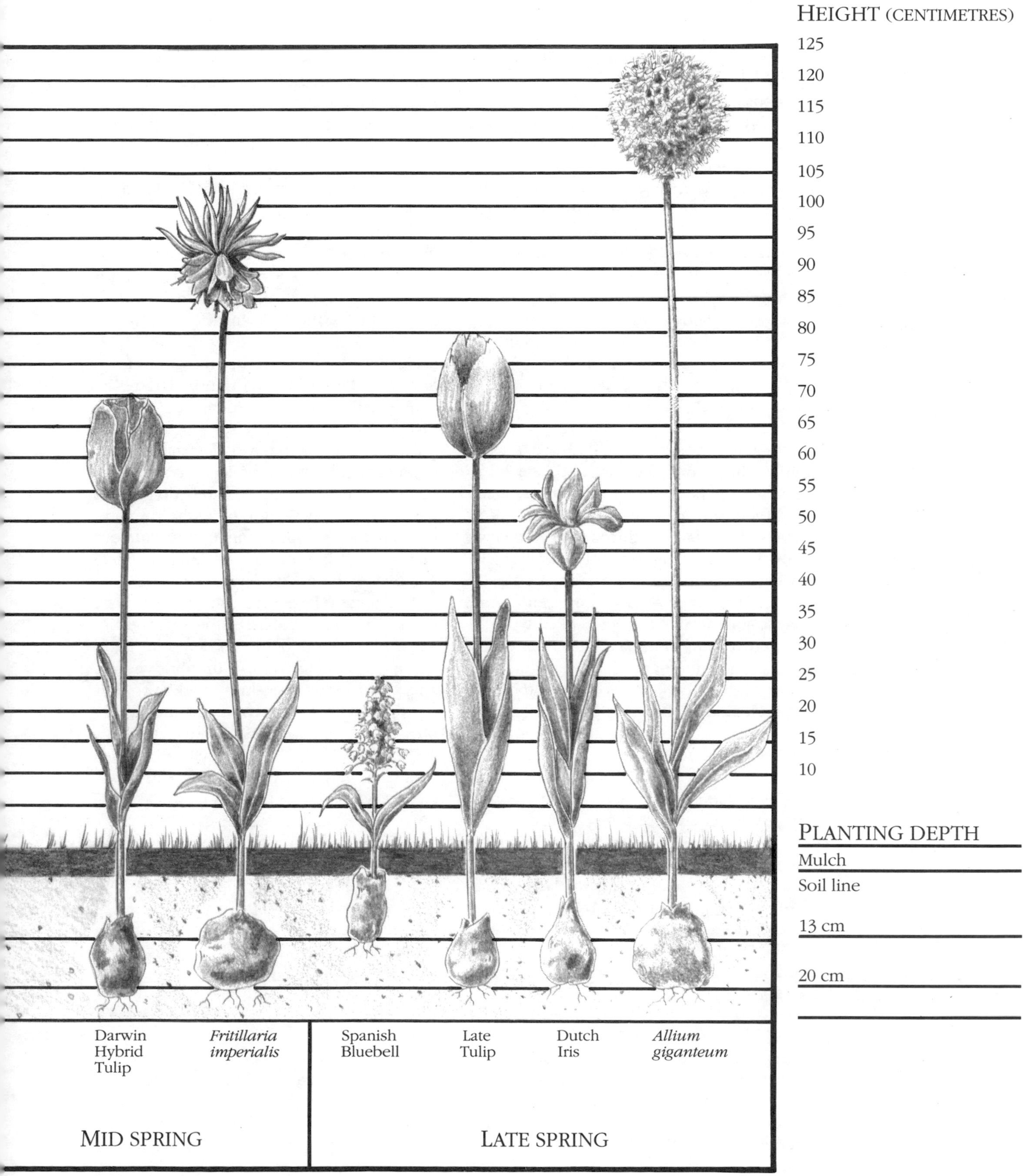
HEIGHT (CENTIMETRES)
125
120
115
110
105
100
95
90
85
80
75
70
65
60
55
50
45
40
35
30
25
20
15
10
PLANTING DEPTH
Mulch
Soil line
13 cm
20 cm
Darwin Hybrid Tulip
Fritillaria imperialis
Spanish Bluebell
Late Tulip
Dutch Iris
Allium giganteum
MID SPRING
LATE SPRING

WEIGHTS & MEASURES

*Barley (*Hordeum vulgare*) was the first cereal grain to be cultivated. Its use has been traced back to Neolithic times. Now more than 70 percent of farm land worldwide is planted in cereal grains, which provide humanity, directly or indirectly via livestock, with more than 50 percent of its calories.*

THE METRIC SYSTEM

An explanation of metric weights and measures may seem out of place in this book, since the system is hardly used in the United States and it has received less than whole-hearted welcome in Canada. However, the rest of the developed world operates in the metric system, and you will find yourself encountering it more and more often during the upcoming decade. Since this book is a ten year chronicle, we wanted to ease your transition from nostalgic tradition to ruthless efficiency.

The original metric system was developed by scientists on purely logical grounds; it rapidly spread throughout the scientific community. Pharmacists were among the early users, moving to metric to avoid the errors arising from the drachm and dram, the minim, the scruple, the grain and the gill.

There have been numerous metric systems developed to fit particular scientific disciplines. The modern metric system, known as SI or the International System, is the result of an international effort to develop a totally consistent system, suitable for science, and practical in meeting the needs of daily life. It has a small number of base units from which all the others are derived. The fact that the derived units are multiples of ten of the base units eliminates the need for an extensive series of tables for weights and measures.

SI has eliminated a great deal of calculation necessary when using the traditional system, just as introduction of decimals in the 16th century greatly reduced the calculation necessary when dealing with other than whole numbers, which were at that time expressed in fractions. Decimals meant that as many as three multiplications followed by tedious division were replaced by a single multiplication. Similarly today, measuring a rectangular piece of ground in metres, multiplying length by width and shifting the decimal place to get the area directly in hectares is an improvement over measuring the sides in feet, multiplying to get square feet, then dividing by 43,560 to get acres.

The primary problem with the traditional systems is the odd multiples that units of increasing size bear to one another; for example, the length units of inch, foot, yard, rod, furlong and mile increase according to the series 12, 3, 5.5, 40 and 8. This creates a formidable test for the school child's memory, compared to the millimetre, centimetre, metre, kilometre series, related by multiples of 10.

Volume presents a greater problem for the child to cope with. Any need to express volume in gallons as a result of measuring a tank's dimensions results in a complex calculation, relating the cubic inches or feet to the gallons required as an answer. How much easier it is to measure in metres or centimetres and get the result directly in litres or cubic metres, by a mere shifting of the decimal point.

The traditionalists often justify continued use of an unwieldy system by their preference to stay with what they know. Rarely do they, in fact, know the definition of all the common units. There are, for example, four different ounces used in Canada (two fluid volumes, two by weight) and three in the U.S.A.

SI's common base units are the metre (m), the kilogram (kg), the second (s), and the ampere (A). From these, and units for light, chemical substance, and thermodynamic temperature, all other units are derived. For example, the watt, a derived unit, may be expressed in the basic units as $kg.m^2/s^3$. This may look awkward, but is very handy in calculations that mix units of force, power, current, volume and time, as electrical engineers may be called upon to do.

It is necessary to know the meanings of the prefixes that form parts of the names of many units, in order to see their relative sizes. The table in figure 1 shows the major ones.

In general, names of units come from the name for the base unit and, if needed, a prefix to show how many of the base units make up the new unit. For example, a kilometre is 1000 metres, a centimetre is a hundredth of a metre.

Custom has entrenched exceptions to the rule of deriving names of units from the base unit and a prefix. The litre is well established as the common name for the cubic decimetre. The long ton has its rough equivalent in the metric ton (or tonne, which is really a megagram). Similarly, conventional names for time units have been retained outside of scientific calculation, even though the hour is an inconvenient 3600 seconds, and although surveyors now use SI exclusively, there has wisely been no attempt to convert old land survey records.

Written metric units are represented by standard symbols, which are not abbreviations, do not have a period after them, and are the same for the singular as for the plural. Square and cubic units are shown with a small superscript 2 and 3 respectively.

Note: Spelling of unit names in the table in fig. 2 is as authorized in Canada's Weights and Measures Act, and as used in most other countries, including Great Britain and Australia. In the United States, except by some technical organizations, the -er ending is used, for example, liter and meter.

FIG. 1

PREFIX	SYMBOL	MULTIPLYING FACTOR
nano	n	.000,000,001
micro	µ	.000,001
milli	m	.001
centi	c	.01
deci	d	.1
deka	da	10
hecto	h	100
kilo	k	1000
mega	M	1,000,000
giga	G	1,000,000,000

FIG. 2

UNIT	SYMBOL
kilogram	kg
gram	g
kilometre	km
metre	m
centimetre	cm
millimetre	mm
hectare	ha
kilopascal	kPa
watt	W
joule	J

METRIC AND TRADITIONAL UNITS CONVERSION TABLES

LINEAR MEASURE

1 km = 0.6214 mile
1 m = 39.37 inches
1 m = 3.2808 feet
1 m = 1.0936 yards
1 cm = 0.3937 inch

1 mile = 1.609 km
1 yard = 0.9144 m
1 foot = 0.3048 m
1 inch = 2.54 cm
1 inch = 25.4 mm

SQUARE MEASURE

1 km^2 = 0.3861 square mile
10,000 m^2 = 1 ha = 2.471 acres
1 m^2 = 10.764 square feet = 1.196 square yards
1 cm^2 = 0.1550 square inch

1 square mile = 2.5900 km^2
1 acre = 0.4047 ha
1 square yard = 0.8361 m^2
1 square foot = 0.09290 m^2
1 square inch = 6.452 cm^2

CUBIC (VOLUME) MEASURE

1 m^3 = 35.315 cubic feet = 1.308 cubic yards
1 m^3 = 264.2 U.S. gallons
1 m^3 = 220.0 Imperial gallons
1 litre = 0.2642 U.S. gallon
1 litre = 0.2200 Imperial gallon
1 litre = 1.057 U.S. quarts
1 litre = 0.8799 Imperial quart

1 cubic yard = 0.7646 m^3
1 cubic foot = 0.02832 m^3 = 28.32 litres
1 cubic inch = 16.387 cm^3
1 U.S. gallon = 3.785 litres
1 U.S. quart = 0.9464 litre
1 Imp. gallon = 4.546 litres
1 Imp. quart = 1.1365 litres

WEIGHT

1 metric ton (tonne) = 2204.6 pounds
1 kg = 2.2046 pounds = 35.274 ounces avoirdupois
1 g = 0.03215 ounce troy = 0.03527 ounce avoirdupois
1 g = 15.432 grains

1 long ton (2240 pounds) = 1.016 tonne = 1016 kg
1 pound = 0.4536 kg = 453.6 g
1 ounce avoirdupois = 28.35 g
1 ounce troy = 31.103 g
1 grain = 0.0648 g

PRESSURE

1 kPa = 0.1450 psi

1 std. atmosphere = 101.325 kPa
1" Hg = 3.377 kPa
1" water = 0.2488 kPa
1 psi = 6.895 kPa

OTHER

1 BTU = 1055 J
1 hp = 747.7 W
degrees Fahrenheit = 32 + (1.8 x degrees Celsius)
degrees Celsius = (degrees Fahrenheit - 32) / 1.8

MEASURES OF LENGTH

1 mile = 1760 yards = 5280 feet
1 yard = 3 feet = 36 inches   1 foot = 12 inches
1 mil = 0.001 inch   1 fathom = 2 yards = 6 feet
1 rod = 5.5 yards = 16.5 feet   1 hand = 4 inches
1 span = 9 inches
1 mile = 8 furlongs = 80 chains
1 furlong = 10 chains = 220 yards
1 chain = 4 rods = 22 yards = 66 feet = 100 links
1 link = 7.92 inches
1 league = 3 nautical miles
1 nautical mile = 6076 feet = 1.1508 statue miles
(The knot, which is a nautical unit of speed, is equivalent to a speed of 1 nautical mile per hour).

SQUARE MEASURE

1 square mile = 640 acres
1 acre = 10 square chains = 4840 square yards = 43,560 square feet
1 square yard = 9 square feet
1 square foot = 144 square inches
An acre is equivalent to the area of a square 208.7 feet on a side

CUBIC MEASURE

1 cubic yard = 27 cubic feet
1 cubic foot = 1728 cubic inches
The following measures are also used for wood and masonry:
1 cord of wood = 4 x 4 x 8 feet = 128 cubic feet
1 perch of masonry = 16 ½ x 1½ x 1 foot = 24¾ cubic feet
1 bushel (U.S. or Winchester struck bushel) = 1.2445 cubic foot = 2150.42 cubic inches
1 bushel = 4 peck = 32 quarts = 64 pints
1 peck = 8 quarts = 16 pints   1 quart = 2 pints
1 heaped bushel = 1¼ struck bushel
1 cubic foot = 0.8036 struck bushel
1 British Imperial bushel = 8 Imperial gallons = 1.2837 cubic foot = 2218.19 cubic inches

LIQUID MEASURE

1 U.S. gallon = 0.1337 cubic foot = 231 cubic inches = 4 quarts = 8 pints
1 quart = 2 pints = 8 gills
1 pint = 4 gills
1 British Imperial gallon = 1.2009 U.S. gallon = 277.42 cubic inches
1 cubic foot = 7.48 U.S. gallons

SHIPPING MEASURE

For measuring entire internal capacity of a vessel:
1 register ton = 100 cubic feet
For measurement of cargo:
Approximately 40 cubic feet of merchandise is considered a shipping ton, unless that bulk would weigh more than 2000 pounds, in which case the freight charge may be based upon weight.

AVOIRDUPOIS OR COMMERCIAL WEIGHT MEASURE

1 gross or long ton = 2240 pounds
1 net or short ton = 2000 pounds
1 pound = 16 ounces = 7000 grains
1 ounce = 16 drachms = 437.5 grains

TROY & APOTHECARIES' MEASURE

1 U.S. fluid ounce = 8 drachms = 1.805 cubic inch = 1/128 U.S. gallon
1 fluid drachm = 60 minims
1 British fluid ounce = 1.732 cubic inch
1 pound = 12 ounces = 5760 grains
1 ounce = 8 drachms = 480 grains
1 drachm = 3 scruples = 60 grains
1 scruple = 20 grains
1 pennyweight = 24 grains
1 carat (used in weighing diamonds) = 3.086 grains
1 grain Troy = 1 grain avoirdupois = 1 grain apothecaries' weight

CLOTHING SIZE EQUIVALENTS

Note: Size equivalents are approximate. Glove sizes are the same in every country.

CHILDREN'S CLOTHES

American	4	6	8	10	12	14
British						
Height (in)	43	48	55	58	60	62
Age	4-5	6-7	9-10	11	12	13
Continental						
Height (cm)	125	135	150	155	160	165
Age	7	9	12	13	14	15

SOCKS

American	9½	10	10½	11	11½
British	9½	10	10½	11	11½
Continental	38-39	39-40	40-41	41-42	42-43

MEN'S SHOES

American	8	8½	9½	10½	11½	12
British	7	7½	8½	9½	10½	11
Continental	41	42	43	44	45	46

WOMEN'S SHOES

American	6	6½	7	7½	8	8½
British	4½	5	5½	6	6½	7
Continental	38	38	39	39	40	41

MEN'S SUITS AND OVERCOATS

American	36	38	40	42	44	46
British	36	38	40	42	44	46
Continental	46	48	50	52	54	56

SHIRTS

American	14	14½	15	15½	16	16½	17
British	14	14½	15	15½	16	16½	17
Continental	36	37	38	39	41	42	43

WOMEN'S SUITS AND DRESSES

American	8	10	12	14	16	18
British	10	12	14	16	18	20
Continental	38	40	42	44	46	48

Clothing Size Reminders

Name	Birth Date	Chest	Waist	Hips	Inseam	Suit Dress	Shirt	Hose Sock	Shoe	Glove	Hat
•											
•											
•											
•											
•											
•											
•											
•											
•											
•											
•											
•											
•											
•											
•											
•											
•											
•											
•											
•											

YEAR-AT-A-GLANCE PLANNER

YEAR	JANUARY	FEBRUARY	MARCH	APRIL	MAY	JUNE

YEAR	JANUARY	FEBRUARY	MARCH	APRIL	MAY	JUNE

YEAR	JANUARY	FEBRUARY	MARCH	APRIL	MAY	JUNE

YEAR	JANUARY	FEBRUARY	MARCH	APRIL	MAY	JUNE

YEAR	JANUARY	FEBRUARY	MARCH	APRIL	MAY	JUNE

YEAR-AT-A-GLANCE PLANNER

JULY	AUGUST	SEPTEMBER	OCTOBER	NOVEMBER	DECEMBER

JULY	AUGUST	SEPTEMBER	OCTOBER	NOVEMBER	DECEMBER

JULY	AUGUST	SEPTEMBER	OCTOBER	NOVEMBER	DECEMBER

JULY	AUGUST	SEPTEMBER	OCTOBER	NOVEMBER	DECEMBER

JULY	AUGUST	SEPTEMBER	OCTOBER	NOVEMBER	DECEMBER

YEAR-AT-A-GLANCE PLANNER

YEAR	JANUARY	FEBRUARY	MARCH	APRIL	MAY	JUNE

YEAR	JANUARY	FEBRUARY	MARCH	APRIL	MAY	JUNE

YEAR	JANUARY	FEBRUARY	MARCH	APRIL	MAY	JUNE

YEAR	JANUARY	FEBRUARY	MARCH	APRIL	MAY	JUNE

YEAR	JANUARY	FEBRUARY	MARCH	APRIL	MAY	JUNE

YEAR-AT-A-GLANCE PLANNER

JULY	AUGUST	SEPTEMBER	OCTOBER	NOVEMBER	DECEMBER
JULY	AUGUST	SEPTEMBER	OCTOBER	NOVEMBER	DECEMBER
JULY	AUGUST	SEPTEMBER	OCTOBER	NOVEMBER	DECEMBER
JULY	AUGUST	SEPTEMBER	OCTOBER	NOVEMBER	DECEMBER
JULY	AUGUST	SEPTEMBER	OCTOBER	NOVEMBER	DECEMBER

JANUARY 1

Abies concolor
White or Silver Fir

YEAR

HIGH ______° LOW______°

YEAR

HIGH ______° LOW______°

YEAR

HIGH ______° LOW______°

YEAR

HIGH ______° LOW______°

YEAR

HIGH ______° LOW______°

YEAR

HIGH ______° LOW______°

YEAR

HIGH ______° LOW______°

YEAR

HIGH ______° LOW______°

YEAR

HIGH ______° LOW______°

YEAR

HIGH ______° LOW______°

JANUARY 2

Acer platanoides

Norway Maple

YEAR

HIGH ______° LOW______°

YEAR

HIGH ______° LOW______°

YEAR

HIGH ______° LOW______°

YEAR

HIGH ______° LOW______°

YEAR

HIGH ______° LOW______°

YEAR

HIGH ______° LOW______°

YEAR

HIGH ______° LOW______°

YEAR

HIGH ______° LOW______°

YEAR

HIGH ______° LOW______°

YEAR

HIGH ______° LOW______°

JANUARY 3

Acer rubrum

Red Maple

YEAR

HIGH ________° LOW________°

YEAR

HIGH ________° LOW________°

YEAR

HIGH ________° LOW________°

YEAR

HIGH ________° LOW________°

YEAR

HIGH ________° LOW________°

YEAR

HIGH ________° LOW________°

YEAR

HIGH ________° LOW________°

YEAR

HIGH ________° LOW________°

YEAR

HIGH ________° LOW________°

YEAR

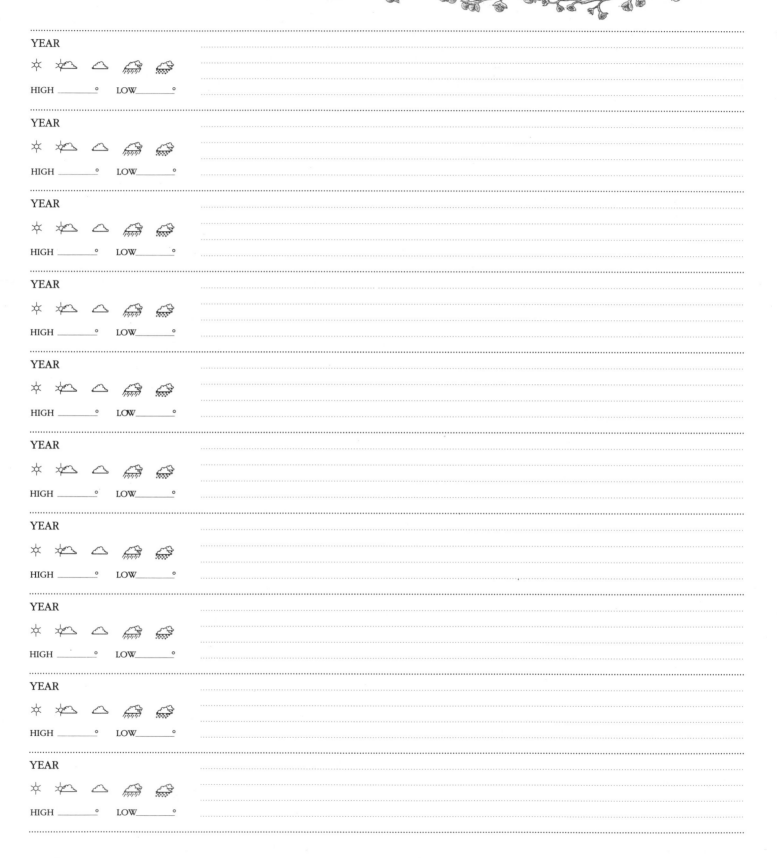

HIGH ________° LOW________°

JANUARY 4

Acer saccharinum

Silver Maple

YEAR

HIGH ______° LOW______°

YEAR

HIGH ______° LOW______°

YEAR

HIGH ______° LOW______°

YEAR

HIGH ______° LOW______°

YEAR

HIGH ______° LOW______°

YEAR

HIGH ______° LOW______°

YEAR

HIGH ______° LOW______°

YEAR

HIGH ______° LOW______°

YEAR

HIGH ______° LOW______°

YEAR

HIGH ______° LOW______°

JANUARY 5

Acer saccharum
Sugar Maple

YEAR

HIGH ______° LOW______°

YEAR

HIGH ______° LOW______°

YEAR

HIGH ______° LOW______°

YEAR

HIGH ______° LOW______°

YEAR

HIGH ______° LOW______°

YEAR

HIGH ______° LOW______°

YEAR

HIGH ______° LOW______°

YEAR

HIGH ______° LOW______°

YEAR

HIGH ______° LOW______°

YEAR

HIGH ______° LOW______°

JANUARY 6

Acer ginnala

Amur Maple

YEAR 1998

HIGH ____° LOW ____°

To Santa Barbara for Fred's procedure appt. on Wednesday
Saw Mt. lion below Rock Front Ranch on Garcia's prop.

YEAR

HIGH ____° LOW ____°

YEAR

HIGH ____° LOW ____°

YEAR

HIGH ____° LOW ____°

YEAR

HIGH ____° LOW ____°

YEAR

HIGH ____° LOW ____°

YEAR

HIGH ____° LOW ____°

YEAR

HIGH ____° LOW ____°

YEAR

HIGH ____° LOW ____°

YEAR

HIGH ____° LOW ____°

JANUARY 7

Achillea filipendulina
Fern-leaf Yarrow

YEAR 1998 Returned from Santa Barbara

HIGH ____° LOW ____°

YEAR

HIGH ____° LOW ____°

YEAR

HIGH ____° LOW ____°

YEAR

HIGH ____° LOW ____°

YEAR

HIGH ____° LOW ____°

YEAR

HIGH ____° LOW ____°

YEAR

HIGH ____° LOW ____°

YEAR

HIGH ____° LOW ____°

YEAR

HIGH ____° LOW ____°

YEAR

HIGH ____° LOW ____°

JANUARY 8

Acer palmatum "Atropurpureum"

Purple Japanese Maple

YEAR 1998 Cleaned sidewalks - Disposed of big tomato plant -

HIGH 57 ° LOW ____ °

YEAR

HIGH ____ ° LOW ____ °

YEAR

HIGH ____ ° LOW ____ °

YEAR

HIGH ____ ° LOW ____ °

YEAR

HIGH ____ ° LOW ____ °

YEAR

HIGH ____ ° LOW ____ °

YEAR

HIGH ____ ° LOW ____ °

YEAR

HIGH ____ ° LOW ____ °

YEAR

HIGH ____ ° LOW ____ °

YEAR

HIGH ____ ° LOW ____ °

JANUARY 9

Achillea millefolium
Common Yarrow

YEAR 1998

HIGH ____° LOW____°

YEAR

HIGH ____° LOW____°

YEAR

HIGH ____° LOW____°

YEAR

HIGH ____° LOW____°

YEAR

HIGH ____° LOW____°

YEAR

HIGH ____° LOW____°

YEAR

HIGH ____° LOW____°

YEAR

HIGH ____° LOW____°

YEAR

HIGH ____° LOW____°

YEAR

HIGH ____° LOW____°

JANUARY 10

Aconitum

Monkshood or Aconite

YEAR

HIGH ______° LOW______°

YEAR

HIGH ______° LOW______°

YEAR

HIGH ______° LOW______°

YEAR

HIGH ______° LOW______°

YEAR

HIGH ______° LOW______°

YEAR

HIGH ______° LOW______°

YEAR

HIGH ______° LOW______°

YEAR

HIGH ______° LOW______°

YEAR

HIGH ______° LOW______°

YEAR

HIGH ______° LOW______°

JANUARY 11

Aconitum lycoctonum
Wolfsbane Monkshood

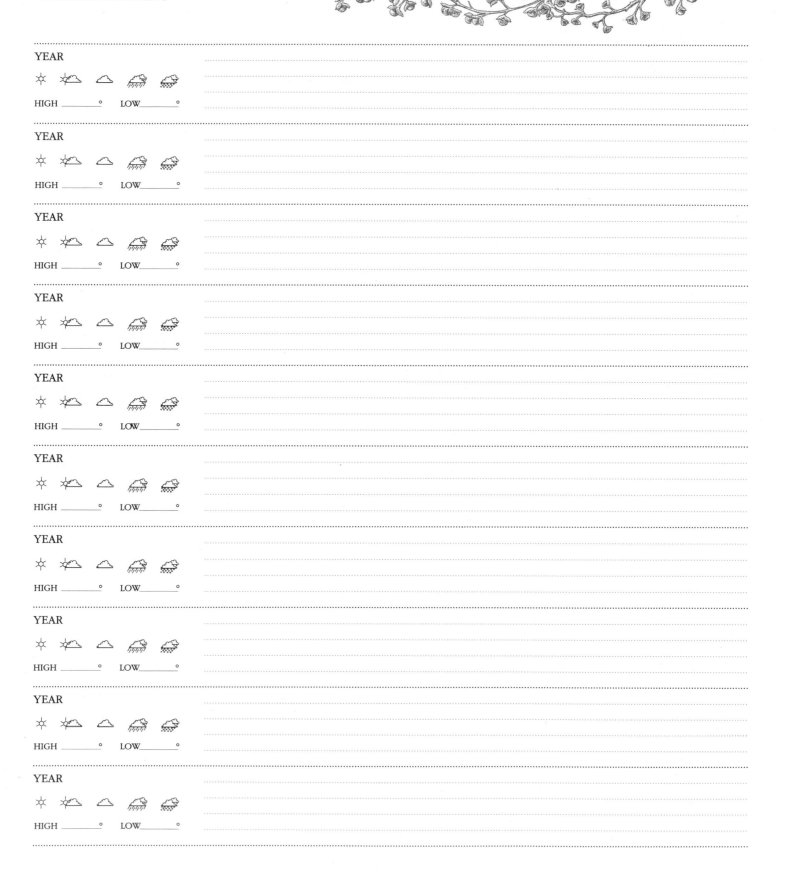

YEAR

HIGH ______° LOW ______°

YEAR

HIGH ______° LOW ______°

YEAR

HIGH ______° LOW ______°

YEAR

HIGH ______° LOW ______°

YEAR

HIGH ______° LOW ______°

YEAR

HIGH ______° LOW ______°

YEAR

HIGH ______° LOW ______°

YEAR

HIGH ______° LOW ______°

YEAR

HIGH ______° LOW ______°

YEAR

HIGH ______° LOW ______°

JANUARY 12

Acorus calamus
Sweet Flag

YEAR

HIGH ______° LOW______°

YEAR

HIGH ______° LOW______°

YEAR

HIGH ______° LOW______°

YEAR

HIGH ______° LOW______°

YEAR

HIGH ______° LOW______°

YEAR

HIGH ______° LOW______°

YEAR

HIGH ______° LOW______°

YEAR

HIGH ______° LOW______°

YEAR

HIGH ______° LOW______°

YEAR

HIGH ______° LOW______°

JANUARY 13

Aegopodium podograria
Bishop's Weed

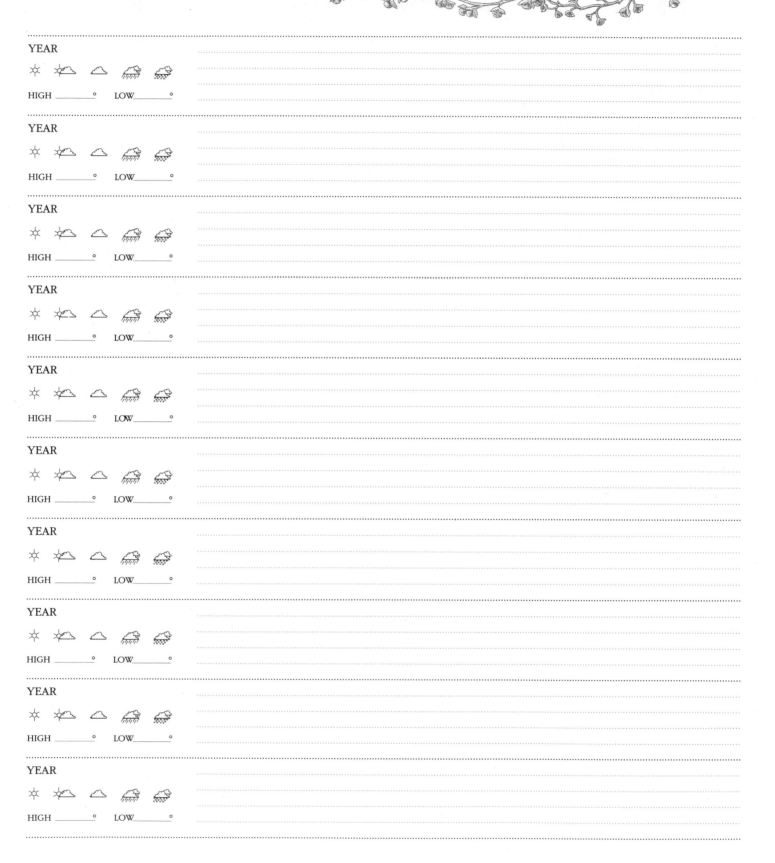

YEAR

HIGH ________° LOW________°

YEAR

HIGH ________° LOW________°

YEAR

HIGH ________° LOW________°

YEAR

HIGH ________° LOW________°

YEAR

HIGH ________° LOW________°

YEAR

HIGH ________° LOW________°

YEAR

HIGH ________° LOW________°

YEAR

HIGH ________° LOW________°

YEAR

HIGH ________° LOW________°

YEAR

HIGH ________° LOW________°

JANUARY 14

Aesculus hippocastanum

Horse Chestnut

YEAR

HIGH ______° LOW______°

YEAR

HIGH ______° LOW______°

YEAR

HIGH ______° LOW______°

YEAR

HIGH ______° LOW______°

YEAR

HIGH ______° LOW______°

YEAR

HIGH ______° LOW______°

YEAR

HIGH ______° LOW______°

YEAR

HIGH ______° LOW______°

YEAR

HIGH ______° LOW______°

YEAR

HIGH ______° LOW______°

JANUARY 15

Agrimonia eupatoria
Agrimony

YEAR

HIGH ______° LOW______°

YEAR

HIGH ______° LOW______°

YEAR

HIGH ______° LOW______°

YEAR

HIGH ______° LOW______°

YEAR

HIGH ______° LOW______°

YEAR

HIGH ______° LOW______°

YEAR

HIGH ______° LOW______°

YEAR

HIGH ______° LOW______°

YEAR

HIGH ______° LOW______°

YEAR

HIGH ______° LOW______°

JANUARY 16

Ajuga genevensis
Bugle Flowers

YEAR

HIGH ______° LOW ______°

YEAR

HIGH ______° LOW ______°

YEAR

HIGH ______° LOW ______°

YEAR

HIGH ______° LOW ______°

YEAR

HIGH ______° LOW ______°

YEAR

HIGH ______° LOW ______°

YEAR

HIGH ______° LOW ______°

YEAR

HIGH ______° LOW ______°

YEAR

HIGH ______° LOW ______°

YEAR

HIGH ______° LOW ______°

JANUARY 17

Alcea rosea

Hollyhocks

YEAR

HIGH ______° LOW______°

YEAR

HIGH ______° LOW______°

YEAR

HIGH ______° LOW______°

YEAR

HIGH ______° LOW______°

YEAR

HIGH ______° LOW______°

YEAR

HIGH ______° LOW______°

YEAR

HIGH ______° LOW______°

YEAR

HIGH ______° LOW______°

YEAR

HIGH ______° LOW______°

YEAR

HIGH ______° LOW______°

JANUARY 18

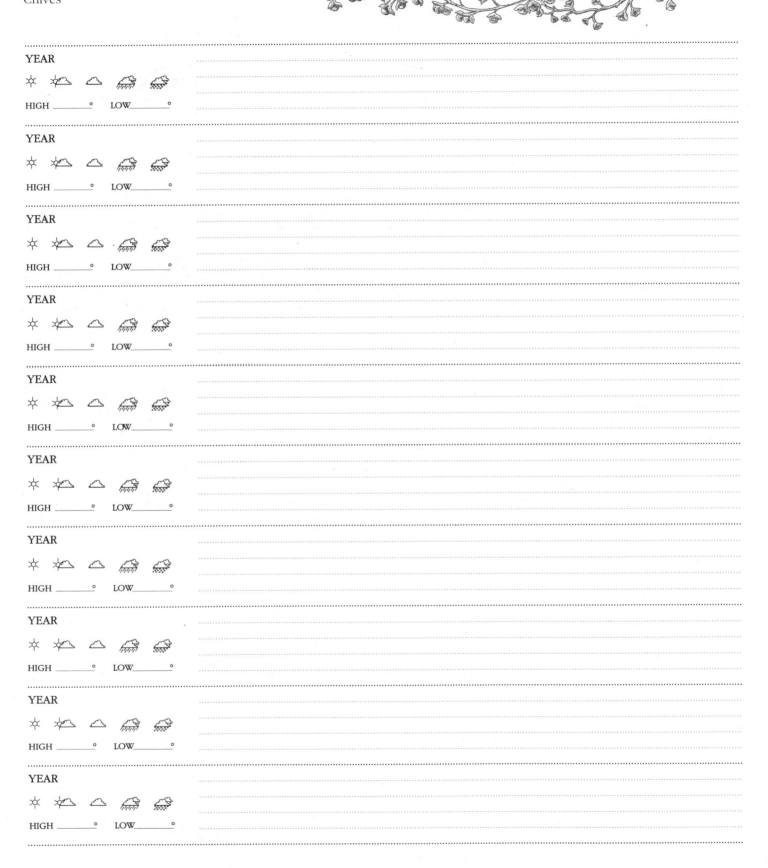

Allium schoenoprasum
Chives

YEAR

HIGH ______° LOW ______°

YEAR

HIGH ______° LOW ______°

YEAR

HIGH ______° LOW ______°

YEAR

HIGH ______° LOW ______°

YEAR

HIGH ______° LOW ______°

YEAR

HIGH ______° LOW ______°

YEAR

HIGH ______° LOW ______°

YEAR

HIGH ______° LOW ______°

YEAR

HIGH ______° LOW ______°

YEAR

HIGH ______° LOW ______°

JANUARY 19

Allium tuberosum
Garlic Chives

YEAR

HIGH ______° LOW______°

YEAR

HIGH ______° LOW______°

YEAR

HIGH ______° LOW______°

YEAR

HIGH ______° LOW______°

YEAR

HIGH ______° LOW______°

YEAR

HIGH ______° LOW______°

YEAR

HIGH ______° LOW______°

YEAR

HIGH ______° LOW______°

YEAR

HIGH ______° LOW______°

YEAR

HIGH ______° LOW______°

JANUARY 20

Allium cepa

Onion

YEAR

HIGH ______° LOW ______°

YEAR

HIGH ______° LOW ______°

YEAR

HIGH ______° LOW ______°

YEAR

HIGH ______° LOW ______°

YEAR

HIGH ______° LOW ______°

YEAR

HIGH ______° LOW ______°

YEAR

HIGH ______° LOW ______°

YEAR

HIGH ______° LOW ______°

YEAR

HIGH ______° LOW ______°

YEAR

HIGH ______° LOW ______°

JANUARY 21

Allium sativum
Garlic

YEAR

HIGH ________° LOW________°

YEAR

HIGH ________° LOW________°

YEAR

HIGH ________° LOW________°

YEAR

HIGH ________° LOW________°

YEAR

HIGH ________° LOW________°

YEAR

HIGH ________° LOW________°

YEAR

HIGH ________° LOW________°

YEAR

HIGH ________° LOW________°

YEAR

HIGH ________° LOW________°

YEAR

HIGH ________° LOW________°

JANUARY 22

Allium porrum

Leek

YEAR

HIGH ______° LOW ______°

YEAR

HIGH ______° LOW ______°

YEAR

HIGH ______° LOW ______°

YEAR

HIGH ______° LOW ______°

YEAR

HIGH ______° LOW ______°

YEAR

HIGH ______° LOW ______°

YEAR

HIGH ______° LOW ______°

YEAR

HIGH ______° LOW ______°

YEAR

HIGH ______° LOW ______°

YEAR

HIGH ______° LOW ______°

JANUARY 23

Aloysia triphylla
Lemon Verbena

YEAR

HIGH ______° LOW______°

YEAR

HIGH ______° LOW______°

YEAR

HIGH ______° LOW______°

YEAR

HIGH ______° LOW______°

YEAR

HIGH ______° LOW______°

YEAR

HIGH ______° LOW______°

YEAR

HIGH ______° LOW______°

YEAR

HIGH ______° LOW______°

YEAR

HIGH ______° LOW______°

YEAR

HIGH ______° LOW______°

JANUARY 24

Althaea officinalis
Marsh Mallow

YEAR

HIGH ______° LOW______°

YEAR

HIGH ______° LOW______°

YEAR

HIGH ______° LOW______°

YEAR

HIGH ______° LOW______°

YEAR

HIGH ______° LOW______°

YEAR

HIGH ______° LOW______°

YEAR

HIGH ______° LOW______°

YEAR

HIGH ______° LOW______°

YEAR

HIGH ______° LOW______°

YEAR

HIGH ______° LOW______°

JANUARY 25

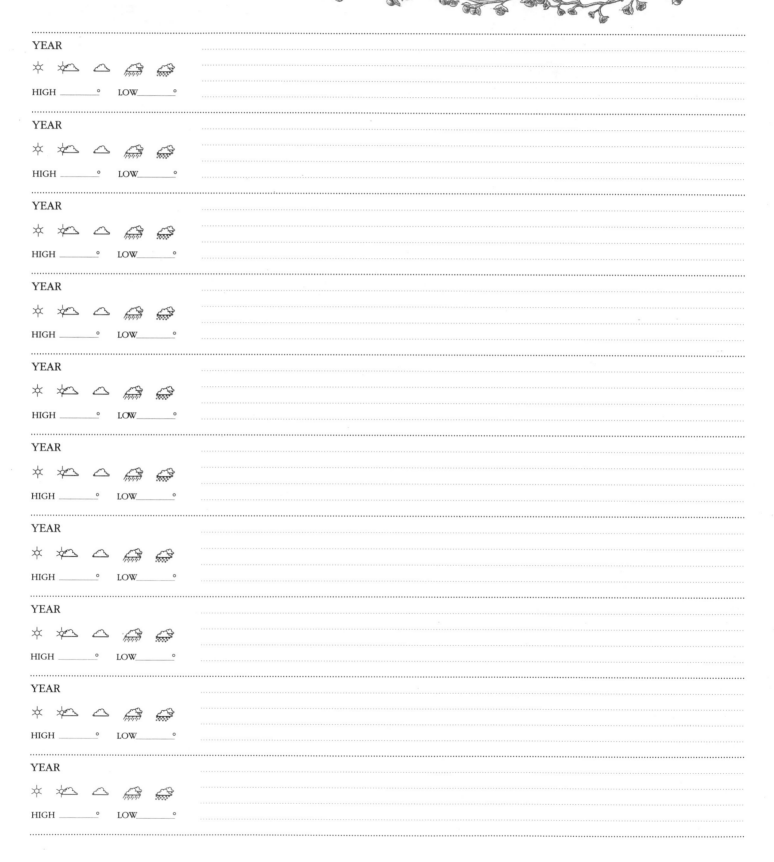

Amelanchier canadensis

Downy Serviceberry

YEAR

HIGH ______° LOW______°

YEAR

HIGH ______° LOW______°

YEAR

HIGH ______° LOW______°

YEAR

HIGH ______° LOW______°

YEAR

HIGH ______° LOW______°

YEAR

HIGH ______° LOW______°

YEAR

HIGH ______° LOW______°

YEAR

HIGH ______° LOW______°

YEAR

HIGH ______° LOW______°

YEAR

HIGH ______° LOW______°

JANUARY 26

Armoracia lapathifolia
Horseradish

YEAR

HIGH ________° LOW________°

YEAR

HIGH ________° LOW________°

YEAR

HIGH ________° LOW________°

YEAR

HIGH ________° LOW________°

YEAR

HIGH ________° LOW________°

YEAR

HIGH ________° LOW________°

YEAR

HIGH ________° LOW________°

YEAR

HIGH ________° LOW________°

YEAR

HIGH ________° LOW________°

YEAR

HIGH ________° LOW________°

JANUARY 27

Anchusa Azurea
Italian Bugloss

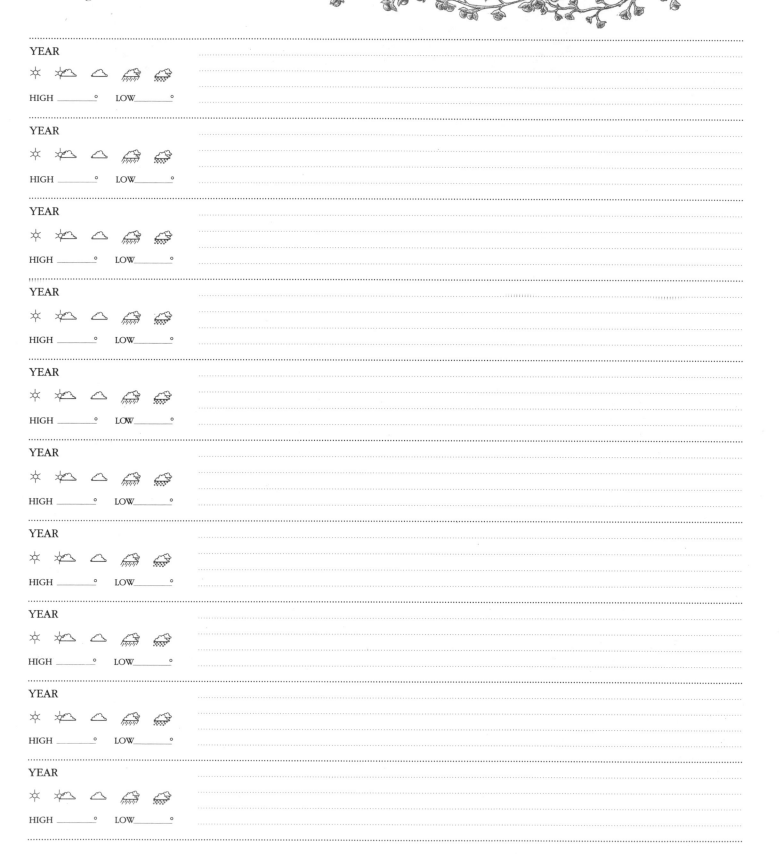

YEAR

HIGH ______° LOW ______°

YEAR

HIGH ______° LOW ______°

YEAR

HIGH ______° LOW ______°

YEAR

HIGH ______° LOW ______°

YEAR

HIGH ______° LOW ______°

YEAR

HIGH ______° LOW ______°

YEAR

HIGH ______° LOW ______°

YEAR

HIGH ______° LOW ______°

YEAR

HIGH ______° LOW ______°

YEAR

HIGH ______° LOW ______°

JANUARY 28

Anemone pulsatilla
European Pasqueflower

YEAR
HIGH ________° LOW________°

YEAR
HIGH ________° LOW________°

YEAR
HIGH ________° LOW________°

YEAR
HIGH ________° LOW________°

YEAR
HIGH ________° LOW________°

YEAR
HIGH ________° LOW________°

YEAR
HIGH ________° LOW________°

YEAR
HIGH ________° LOW________°

YEAR
HIGH ________° LOW________°

YEAR
HIGH ________° LOW________°

JANUARY 29

Anethum graveolens
Dill

YEAR

HIGH ______° LOW______°

YEAR

HIGH ______° LOW______°

YEAR

HIGH ______° LOW______°

YEAR

HIGH ______° LOW______°

YEAR

HIGH ______° LOW______°

YEAR

HIGH ______° LOW______°

YEAR

HIGH ______° LOW______°

YEAR

HIGH ______° LOW______°

YEAR

HIGH ______° LOW______°

YEAR

HIGH ______° LOW______°

JANUARY 30

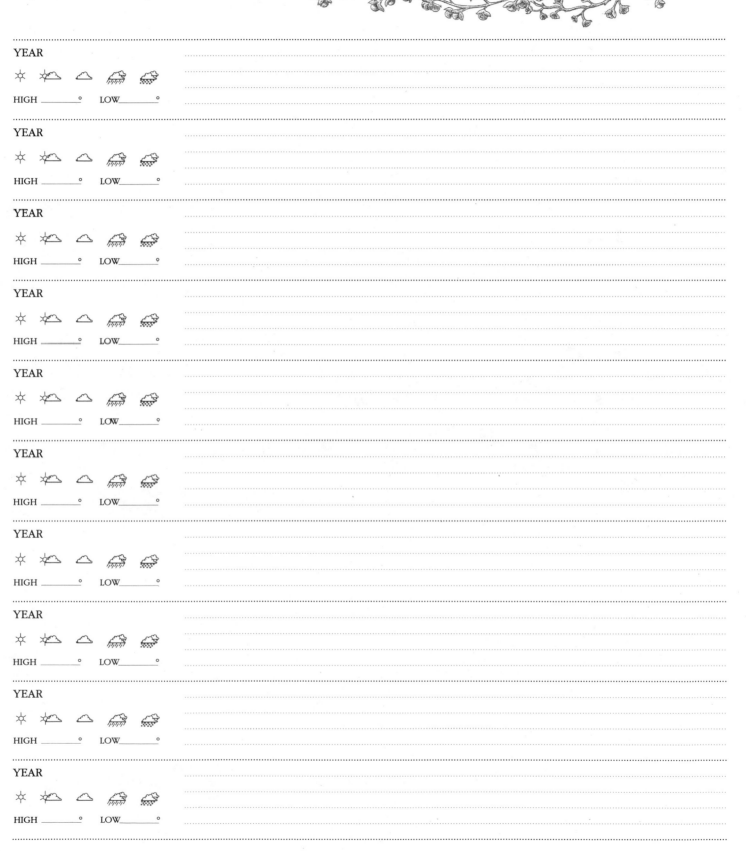

Angelica archangelica
Angelica or Wild Parsnip

YEAR

HIGH ______° LOW ______°

YEAR

HIGH ______° LOW ______°

YEAR

HIGH ______° LOW ______°

YEAR

HIGH ______° LOW ______°

YEAR

HIGH ______° LOW ______°

YEAR

HIGH ______° LOW ______°

YEAR

HIGH ______° LOW ______°

YEAR

HIGH ______° LOW ______°

YEAR

HIGH ______° LOW ______°

YEAR

HIGH ______° LOW ______°

JANUARY 31

Anthemis tinctoria
Golden Marguerite

YEAR

HIGH ________° LOW________°

YEAR

HIGH ________° LOW________°

YEAR

HIGH ________° LOW________°

YEAR

HIGH ________° LOW________°

YEAR

HIGH ________° LOW________°

YEAR

HIGH ________° LOW________°

YEAR

HIGH ________° LOW________°

YEAR

HIGH ________° LOW________°

YEAR

HIGH ________° LOW________°

YEAR

HIGH ________° LOW________°

FEBRUARY 1

Anthriscus cerefolium
Chervil

YEAR

HIGH ______° LOW ______°

YEAR

HIGH ______° LOW ______°

YEAR

HIGH ______° LOW ______°

YEAR

HIGH ______° LOW ______°

YEAR

HIGH ______° LOW ______°

YEAR

HIGH ______° LOW ______°

YEAR

HIGH ______° LOW ______°

YEAR

HIGH ______° LOW ______°

YEAR

HIGH ______° LOW ______°

YEAR

HIGH ______° LOW ______°

FEBRUARY 2

Antirrhinum majus
Snapdragons (common)

YEAR

HIGH ________° LOW________°

YEAR

HIGH ________° LOW________°

YEAR

HIGH ________° LOW________°

YEAR

HIGH ________° LOW________°

YEAR

HIGH ________° LOW________°

YEAR

HIGH ________° LOW________°

YEAR

HIGH ________° LOW________°

YEAR

HIGH ________° LOW________°

YEAR

HIGH ________° LOW________°

YEAR

HIGH ________° LOW________°

FEBRUARY 3

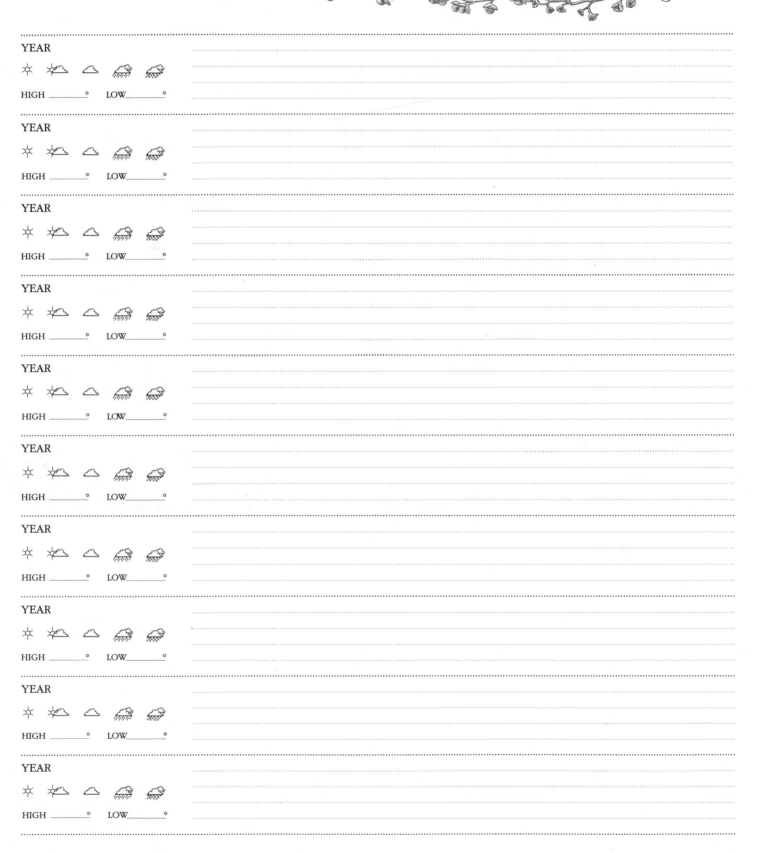

Apium graveolens dulce
Celery

YEAR

HIGH ______° LOW______°

YEAR

HIGH ______° LOW______°

YEAR

HIGH ______° LOW______°

YEAR

HIGH ______° LOW______°

YEAR

HIGH ______° LOW______°

YEAR

HIGH ______° LOW______°

YEAR

HIGH ______° LOW______°

YEAR

HIGH ______° LOW______°

YEAR

HIGH ______° LOW______°

YEAR

HIGH ______° LOW______°

FEBRUARY 4

Apium graveolens rapaceum

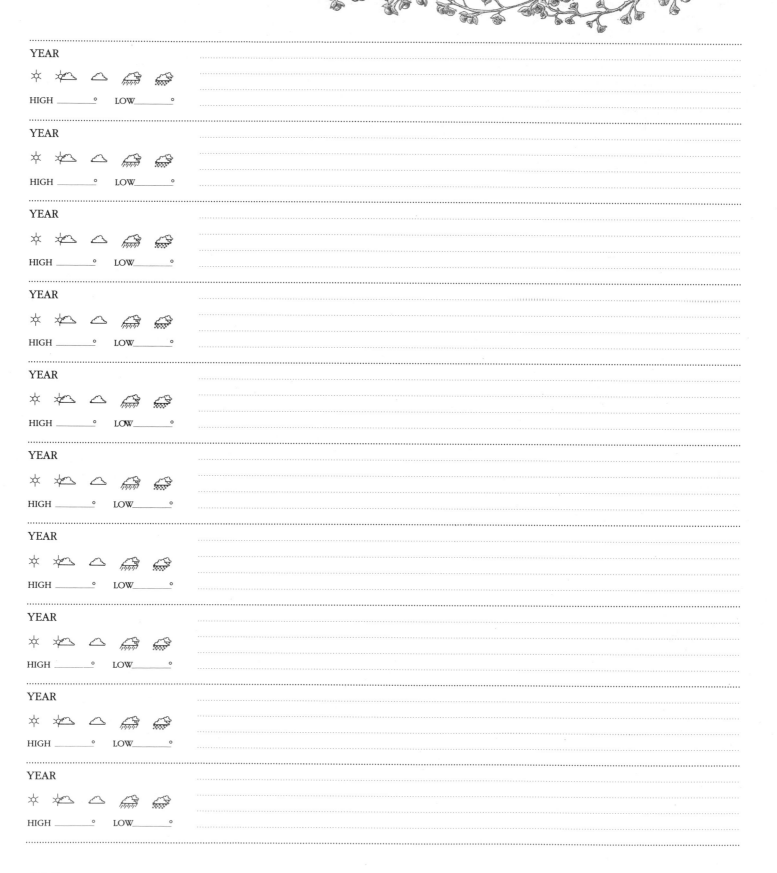

Celeriac

YEAR

HIGH ________° LOW________°

YEAR

HIGH ________° LOW________°

YEAR

HIGH ________° LOW________°

YEAR

HIGH ________° LOW________°

YEAR

HIGH ________° LOW________°

YEAR

HIGH ________° LOW________°

YEAR

HIGH ________° LOW________°

YEAR

HIGH ________° LOW________°

YEAR

HIGH ________° LOW________°

YEAR

HIGH ________° LOW________°

FEBRUARY 5

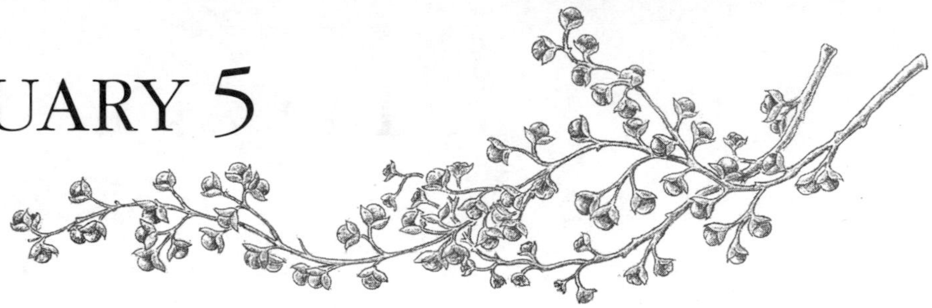

Aquilegia
Columbine

YEAR

HIGH ________° LOW________°

YEAR

HIGH ________° LOW________°

YEAR

HIGH ________° LOW________°

YEAR

HIGH ________° LOW________°

YEAR

HIGH ________° LOW________°

YEAR

HIGH ________° LOW________°

YEAR

HIGH ________° LOW________°

YEAR

HIGH ________° LOW________°

YEAR

HIGH ________° LOW________°

YEAR

HIGH ________° LOW________°

FEBRUARY 6

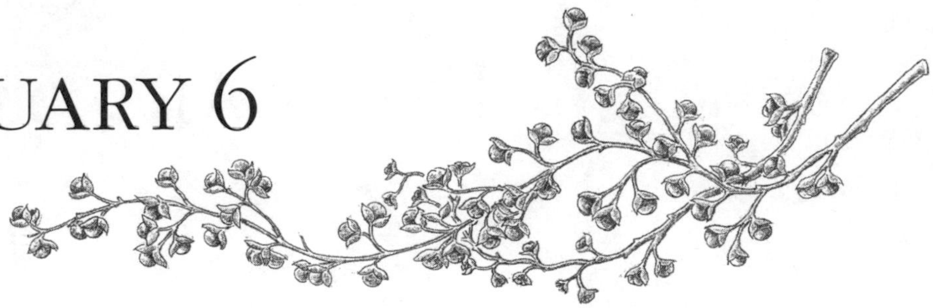

Arabis bida

Rock Cress

YEAR

HIGH ______° LOW______°

YEAR

HIGH ______° LOW______°

YEAR

HIGH ______° LOW______°

YEAR

HIGH ______° LOW______°

YEAR

HIGH ______° LOW______°

YEAR

HIGH ______° LOW______°

YEAR

HIGH ______° LOW______°

YEAR

HIGH ______° LOW______°

YEAR

HIGH ______° LOW______°

YEAR

HIGH ______° LOW______°

FEBRUARY 7

Arachis hypogaea
Peanut

YEAR
HIGH ______° LOW______°

YEAR
HIGH ______° LOW______°

YEAR
HIGH ______° LOW______°

YEAR
HIGH ______° LOW______°

YEAR
HIGH ______° LOW______°

YEAR
HIGH ______° LOW______°

YEAR
HIGH ______° LOW______°

YEAR
HIGH ______° LOW______°

YEAR
HIGH ______° LOW______°

YEAR
HIGH ______° LOW______°

FEBRUARY 8

Aralia elata
Devil's Walking Stick

YEAR

HIGH ______° LOW______°

YEAR

HIGH ______° LOW______°

YEAR

HIGH ______° LOW______°

YEAR

HIGH ______° LOW______°

YEAR

HIGH ______° LOW______°

YEAR

HIGH ______° LOW______°

YEAR

HIGH ______° LOW______°

YEAR

HIGH ______° LOW______°

YEAR

HIGH ______° LOW______°

YEAR

HIGH ______° LOW______°

FEBRUARY 9

Arctium lappa
Burdock

YEAR

HIGH ______° LOW______°

YEAR

HIGH ______° LOW______°

YEAR

HIGH ______° LOW______°

YEAR

HIGH ______° LOW______°

YEAR

HIGH ______° LOW______°

YEAR

HIGH ______° LOW______°

YEAR

HIGH ______° LOW______°

YEAR

HIGH ______° LOW______°

YEAR

HIGH ______° LOW______°

YEAR

HIGH ______° LOW______°

FEBRUARY 10

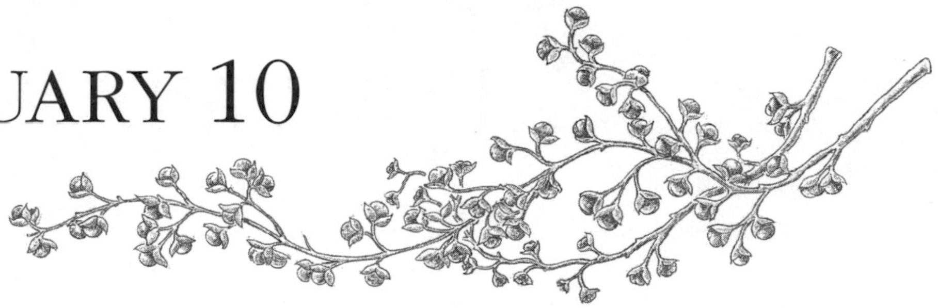

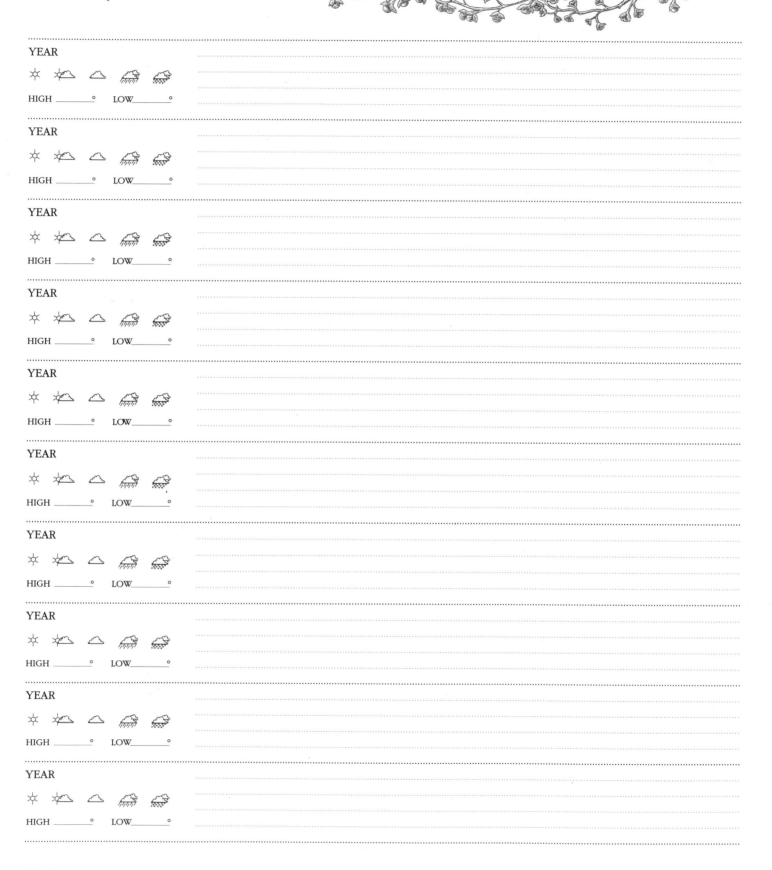

Aristolochia durior

Dutchman's Pipe

YEAR

HIGH ________° LOW________°

YEAR

HIGH ________° LOW________°

YEAR

HIGH ________° LOW________°

YEAR

HIGH ________° LOW________°

YEAR

HIGH ________° LOW________°

YEAR

HIGH ________° LOW________°

YEAR

HIGH ________° LOW________°

YEAR

HIGH ________° LOW________°

YEAR

HIGH ________° LOW________°

YEAR

HIGH ________° LOW________°

FEBRUARY 11

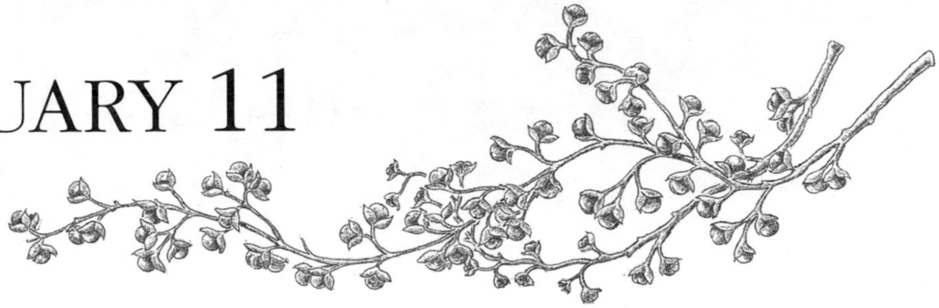

Armeria maritima

Sea Thrift

YEAR

HIGH ______° LOW______°

YEAR

HIGH ______° LOW______°

YEAR

HIGH ______° LOW______°

YEAR

HIGH ______° LOW______°

YEAR

HIGH ______° LOW______°

YEAR

HIGH ______° LOW______°

YEAR

HIGH ______° LOW______°

YEAR

HIGH ______° LOW______°

YEAR

HIGH ______° LOW______°

YEAR

HIGH ______° LOW______°

FEBRUARY 12

Arnica montana
Arnica

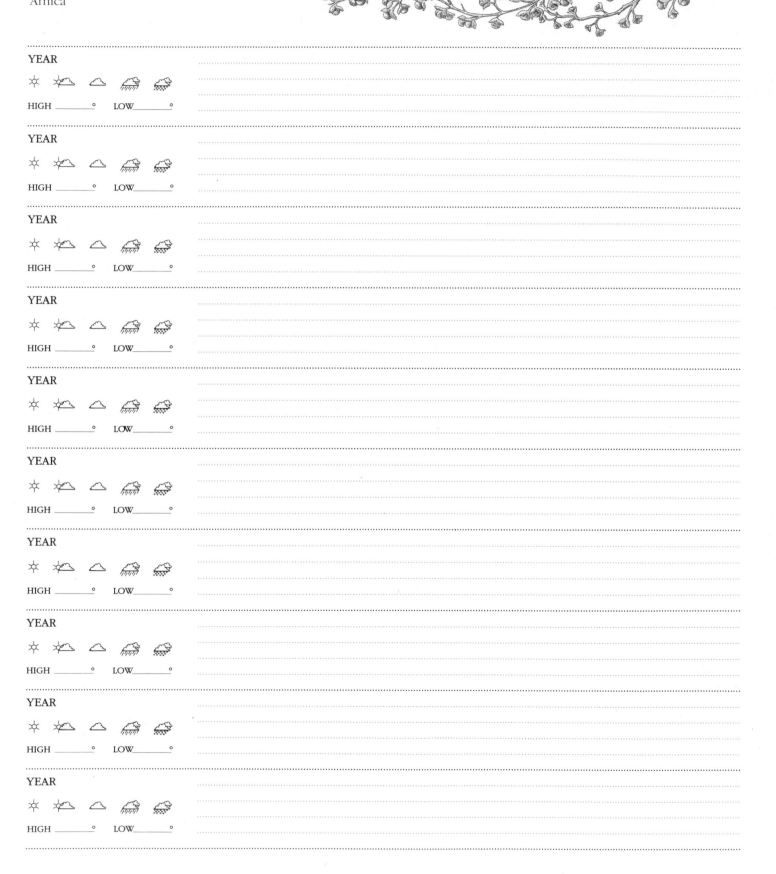

YEAR

HIGH ______° LOW______°

YEAR

HIGH ______° LOW______°

YEAR

HIGH ______° LOW______°

YEAR

HIGH ______° LOW______°

YEAR

HIGH ______° LOW______°

YEAR

HIGH ______° LOW______°

YEAR

HIGH ______° LOW______°

YEAR

HIGH ______° LOW______°

YEAR

HIGH ______° LOW______°

YEAR

HIGH ______° LOW______°

FEBRUARY 13

Artemisia absinthium

Wormwood

YEAR

HIGH ______° LOW______°

YEAR

HIGH ______° LOW______°

YEAR

HIGH ______° LOW______°

YEAR

HIGH ______° LOW______°

YEAR

HIGH ______° LOW______°

YEAR

HIGH ______° LOW______°

YEAR

HIGH ______° LOW______°

YEAR

HIGH ______° LOW______°

YEAR

HIGH ______° LOW______°

YEAR

HIGH ______° LOW______°

FEBRUARY 14

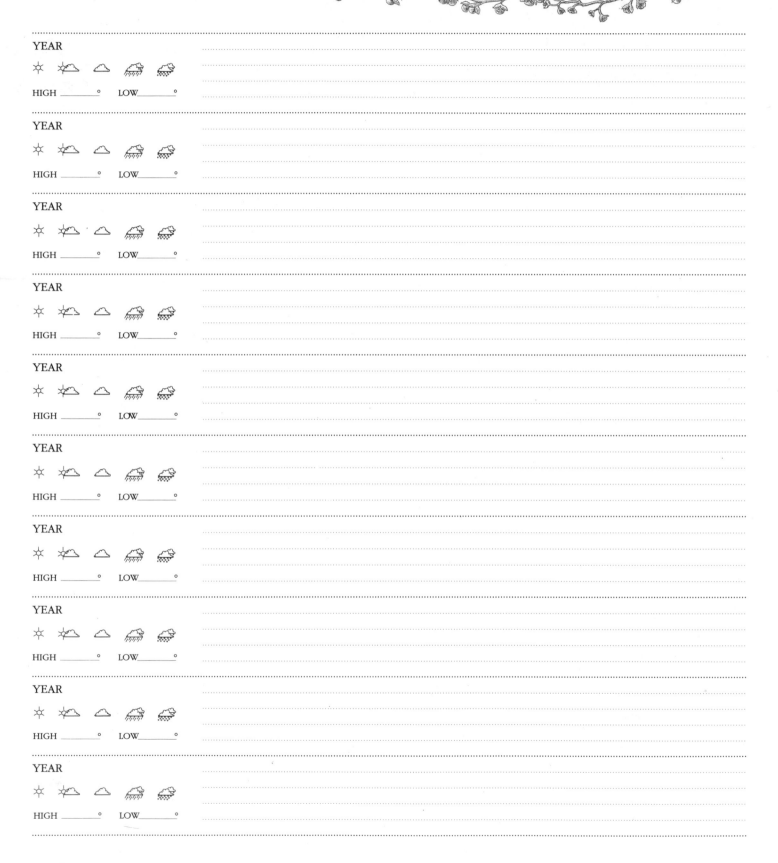

Artemisia vulgaris
Mugwort

YEAR

HIGH ______° LOW______°

YEAR

HIGH ______° LOW______°

YEAR

HIGH ______° LOW______°

YEAR

HIGH ______° LOW______°

YEAR

HIGH ______° LOW______°

YEAR

HIGH ______° LOW______°

YEAR

HIGH ______° LOW______°

YEAR

HIGH ______° LOW______°

YEAR

HIGH ______° LOW______°

YEAR

HIGH ______° LOW______°

FEBRUARY 15

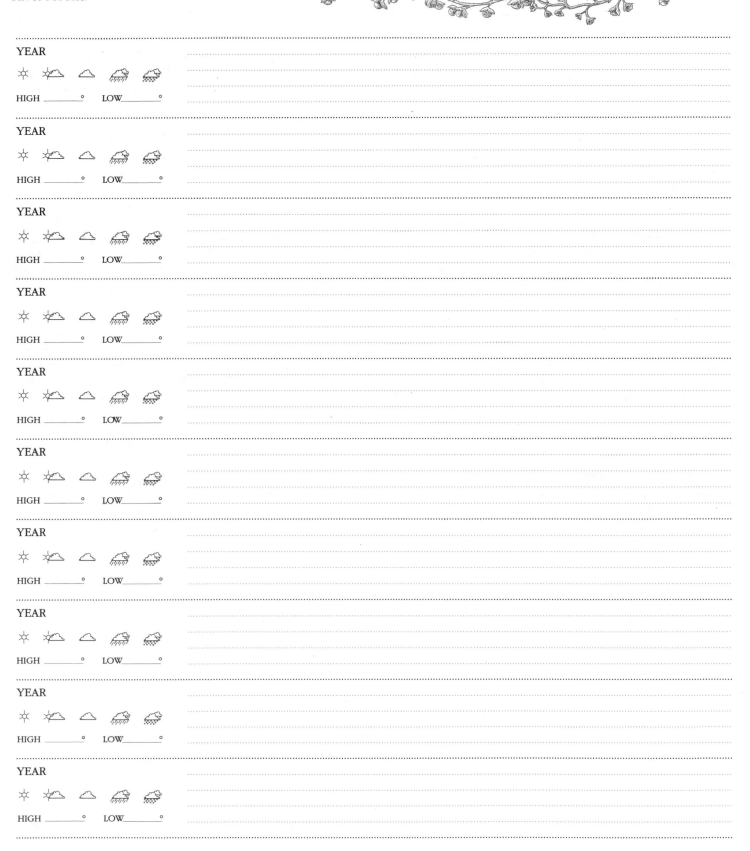

Artemisia schmidtiana "Nana"

Silver Mound

YEAR

HIGH ______° LOW______°

YEAR

HIGH ______° LOW______°

YEAR

HIGH ______° LOW______°

YEAR

HIGH ______° LOW______°

YEAR

HIGH ______° LOW______°

YEAR

HIGH ______° LOW______°

YEAR

HIGH ______° LOW______°

YEAR

HIGH ______° LOW______°

YEAR

HIGH ______° LOW______°

YEAR

HIGH ______° LOW______°

FEBRUARY 16

Artemisia dracunculus
Tarragon

YEAR

HIGH ________° LOW________°

YEAR

HIGH ________° LOW________°

YEAR

HIGH ________° LOW________°

YEAR

HIGH ________° LOW________°

YEAR

HIGH ________° LOW________°

YEAR

HIGH ________° LOW________°

YEAR

HIGH ________° LOW________°

YEAR

HIGH ________° LOW________°

YEAR

HIGH ________° LOW________°

YEAR

HIGH ________° LOW________°

FEBRUARY 17

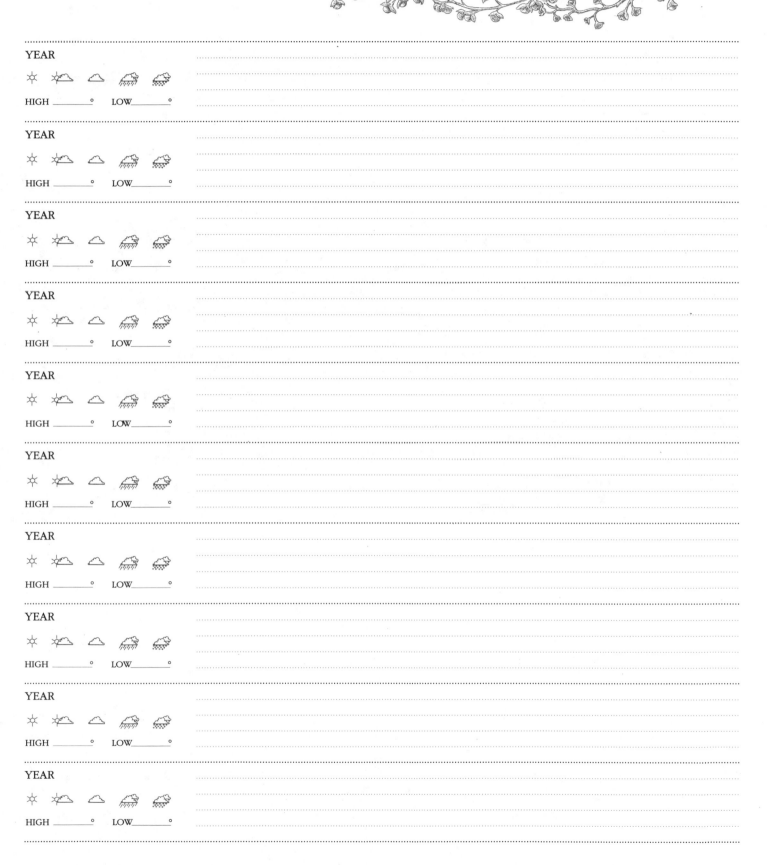

Artemisia abrotanum

Southernwood

YEAR

HIGH ______° LOW ______°

YEAR

HIGH ______° LOW ______°

YEAR

HIGH ______° LOW ______°

YEAR

HIGH ______° LOW ______°

YEAR

HIGH ______° LOW ______°

YEAR

HIGH ______° LOW ______°

YEAR

HIGH ______° LOW ______°

YEAR

HIGH ______° LOW ______°

YEAR

HIGH ______° LOW ______°

YEAR

HIGH ______° LOW ______°

FEBRUARY 18

Asclepias tuberosa

Butterfly Milkweed or Indian Paintbrush

YEAR

HIGH ______° LOW______°

YEAR

HIGH ______° LOW______°

YEAR

HIGH ______° LOW______°

YEAR

HIGH ______° LOW______°

YEAR

HIGH ______° LOW______°

YEAR

HIGH ______° LOW______°

YEAR

HIGH ______° LOW______°

YEAR

HIGH ______° LOW______°

YEAR

HIGH ______° LOW______°

YEAR

HIGH ______° LOW______°

FEBRUARY 19

Asparagus officinalis
Asparagus

YEAR

HIGH ______° LOW______°

YEAR

HIGH ______° LOW______°

YEAR

HIGH ______° LOW______°

YEAR

HIGH ______° LOW______°

YEAR

HIGH ______° LOW______°

YEAR

HIGH ______° LOW______°

YEAR

HIGH ______° LOW______°

YEAR

HIGH ______° LOW______°

YEAR

HIGH ______° LOW______°

YEAR

HIGH ______° LOW______°

FEBRUARY 20

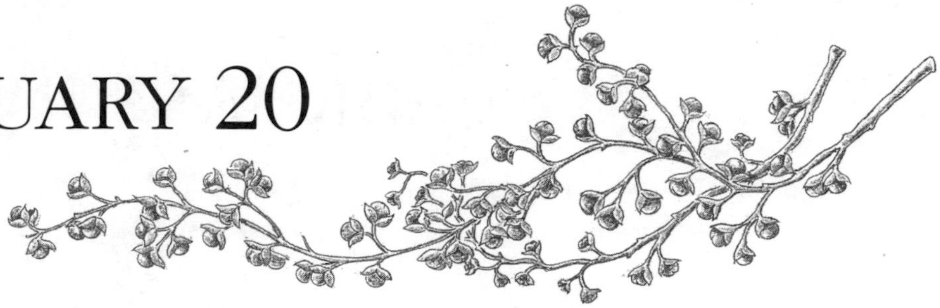

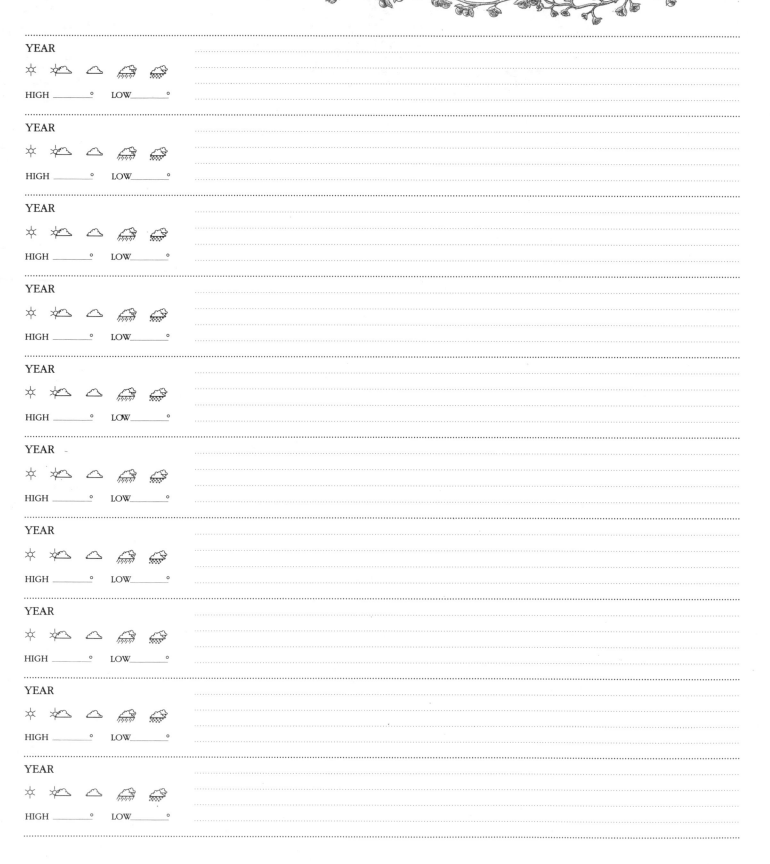

Aster alpinus
Alpine Aster

YEAR

HIGH ________° LOW________°

YEAR

HIGH ________° LOW________°

YEAR

HIGH ________° LOW________°

YEAR

HIGH ________° LOW________°

YEAR

HIGH ________° LOW________°

YEAR

HIGH ________° LOW________°

YEAR

HIGH ________° LOW________°

YEAR

HIGH ________° LOW________°

YEAR

HIGH ________° LOW________°

YEAR

HIGH ________° LOW________°

FEBRUARY 21

Atropa belladonna
Deadly Nightshade

YEAR

HIGH ______° LOW______°

YEAR

HIGH ______° LOW______°

YEAR

HIGH ______° LOW______°

YEAR

HIGH ______° LOW______°

YEAR

HIGH ______° LOW______°

YEAR

HIGH ______° LOW______°

YEAR

HIGH ______° LOW______°

YEAR

HIGH ______° LOW______°

YEAR

HIGH ______° LOW______°

YEAR

HIGH ______° LOW______°

FEBRUARY 22

Aubrieta
False Rock Cress

YEAR

HIGH ______° LOW______°

YEAR

HIGH ______° LOW______°

YEAR

HIGH ______° LOW______°

YEAR

HIGH ______° LOW______°

YEAR

HIGH ______° LOW______°

YEAR

HIGH ______° LOW______°

YEAR

HIGH ______° LOW______°

YEAR

HIGH ______° LOW______°

YEAR

HIGH ______° LOW______°

YEAR

HIGH ______° LOW______°

FEBRUARY 23

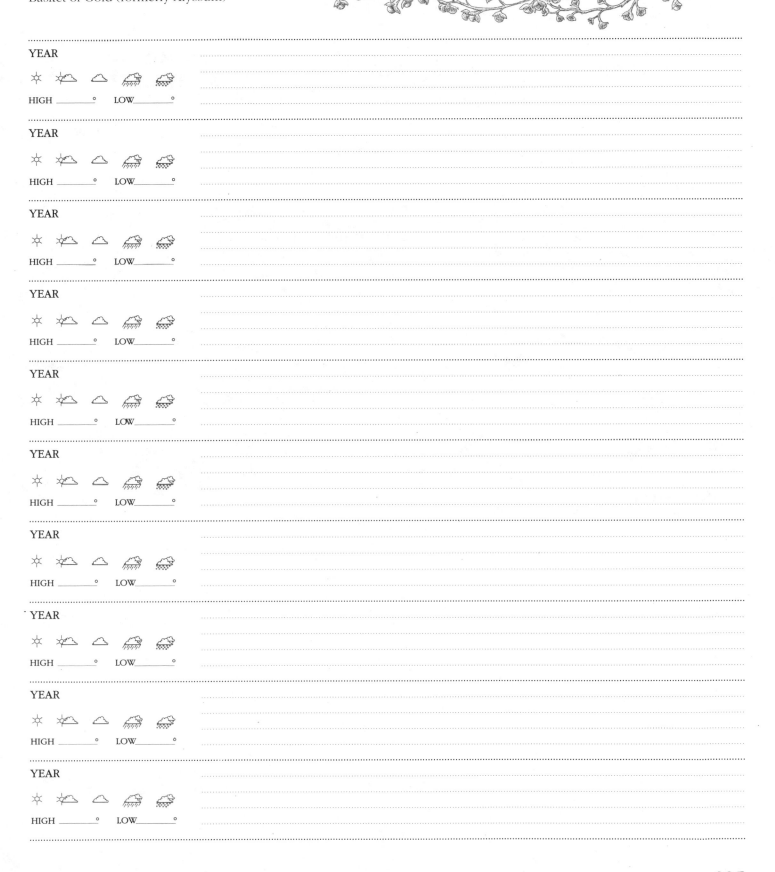

Aurinia saxatilis

Basket of Gold (formerly Alyssum)

YEAR

HIGH ______° LOW______°

YEAR

HIGH ______° LOW______°

YEAR

HIGH ______° LOW______°

YEAR

HIGH ______° LOW______°

YEAR

HIGH ______° LOW______°

YEAR

HIGH ______° LOW______°

YEAR

HIGH ______° LOW______°

YEAR

HIGH ______° LOW______°

YEAR

HIGH ______° LOW______°

YEAR

HIGH ______° LOW______°

FEBRUARY 24

Berberis vulgaris

Barberry

YEAR

HIGH ______° LOW______°

YEAR

HIGH ______° LOW______°

YEAR

HIGH ______° LOW______°

YEAR

HIGH ______° LOW______°

YEAR

HIGH ______° LOW______°

YEAR

HIGH ______° LOW______°

YEAR

HIGH ______° LOW______°

YEAR

HIGH ______° LOW______°

YEAR

HIGH ______° LOW______°

YEAR

HIGH ______° LOW______°

FEBRUARY 25

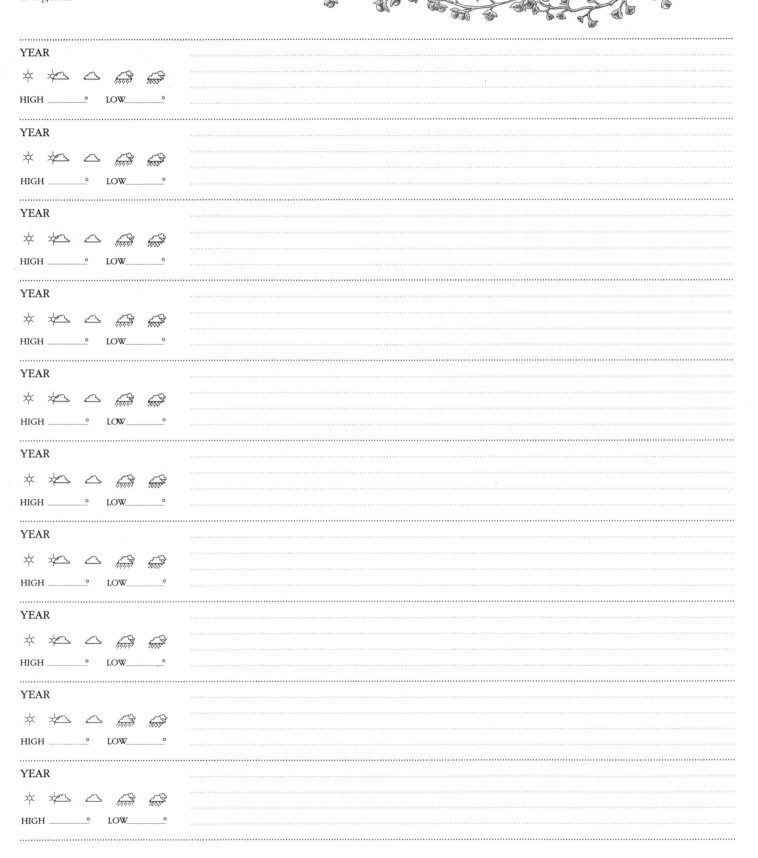

Bergenia cordifolia
Bergenia

YEAR

HIGH ______° LOW______°

YEAR

HIGH ______° LOW______°

YEAR

HIGH ______° LOW______°

YEAR

HIGH ______° LOW______°

YEAR

HIGH ______° LOW______°

YEAR

HIGH ______° LOW______°

YEAR

HIGH ______° LOW______°

YEAR

HIGH ______° LOW______°

YEAR

HIGH ______° LOW______°

YEAR

HIGH ______° LOW______°

FEBRUARY 26

Beta vulgaris cicla
Chard

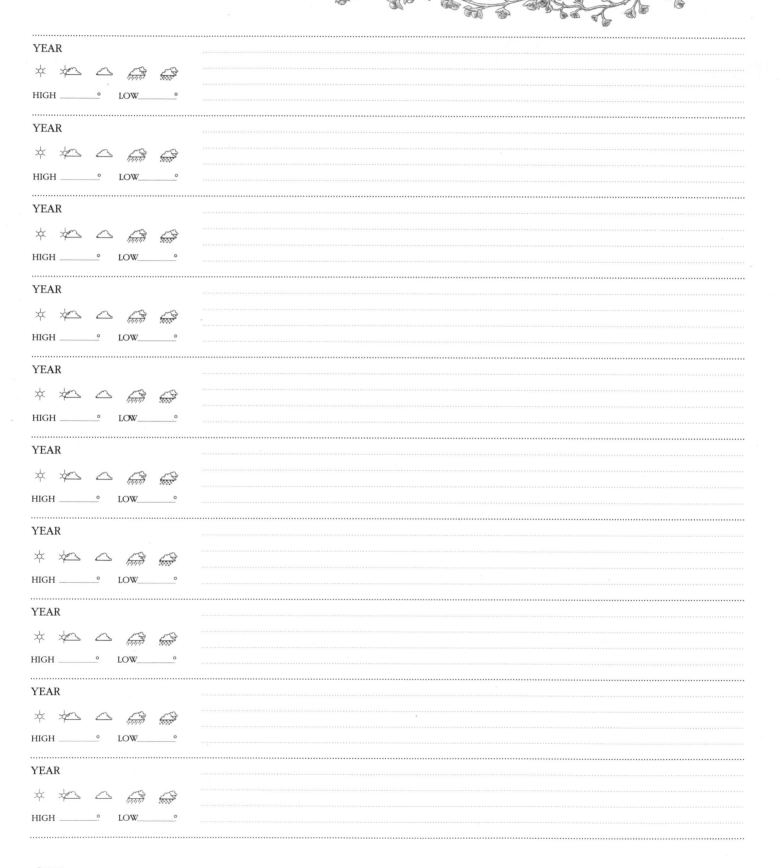

YEAR
HIGH ______° LOW______°

YEAR
HIGH ______° LOW______°

YEAR
HIGH ______° LOW______°

YEAR
HIGH ______° LOW______°

YEAR
HIGH ______° LOW______°

YEAR
HIGH ______° LOW______°

YEAR
HIGH ______° LOW______°

YEAR
HIGH ______° LOW______°

YEAR
HIGH ______° LOW______°

YEAR
HIGH ______° LOW______°

FEBRUARY 27

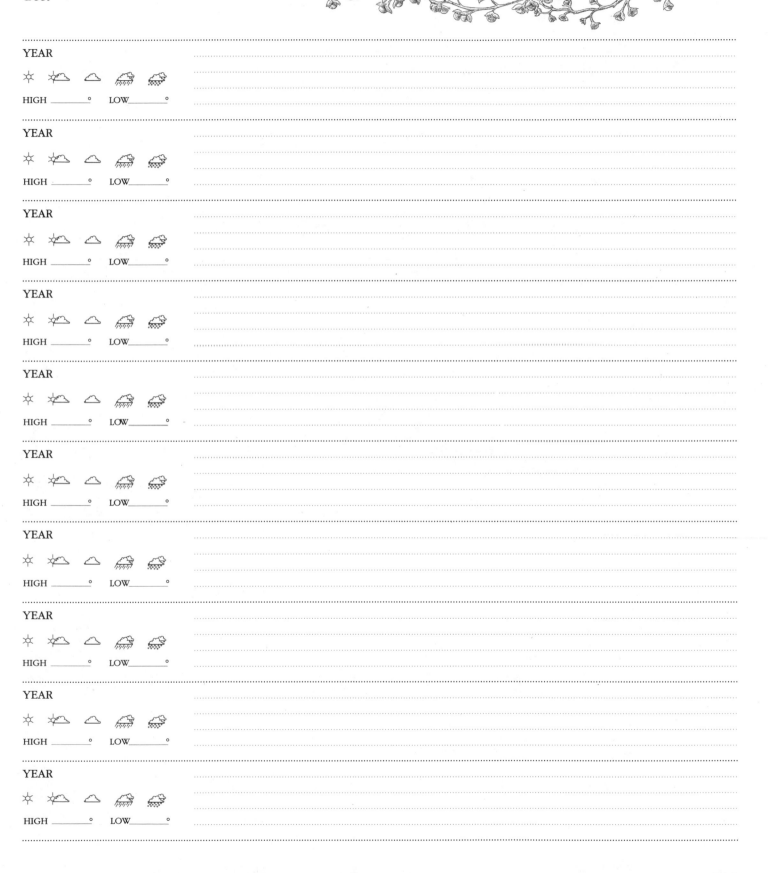

Beta vulgaris

Beet

YEAR

HIGH ________° LOW________°

YEAR

HIGH ________° LOW________°

YEAR

HIGH ________° LOW________°

YEAR

HIGH ________° LOW________°

YEAR

HIGH ________° LOW________°

YEAR

HIGH ________° LOW________°

YEAR

HIGH ________° LOW________°

YEAR

HIGH ________° LOW________°

YEAR

HIGH ________° LOW________°

YEAR

HIGH ________° LOW________°

FEBRUARY 28

Betula papyrifera
Paper Birch

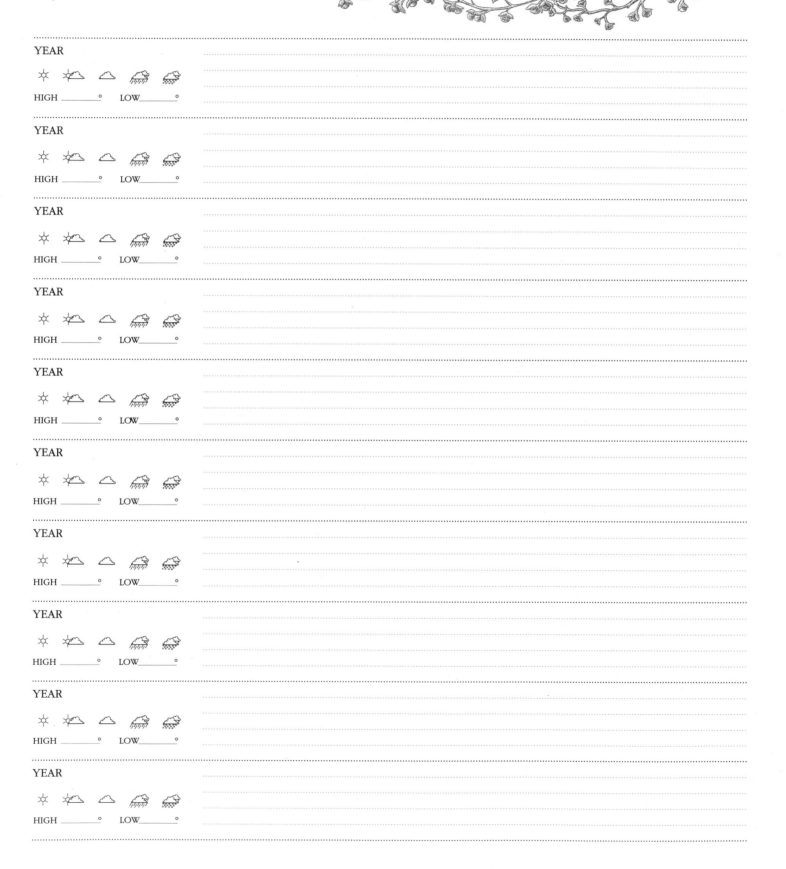

YEAR

HIGH ________° LOW________°

YEAR

HIGH ________° LOW________°

YEAR

HIGH ________° LOW________°

YEAR

HIGH ________° LOW________°

YEAR

HIGH ________° LOW________°

YEAR

HIGH ________° LOW________°

YEAR

HIGH ________° LOW________°

YEAR

HIGH ________° LOW________°

YEAR

HIGH ________° LOW________°

YEAR

HIGH ________° LOW________°

FEBRUARY 29

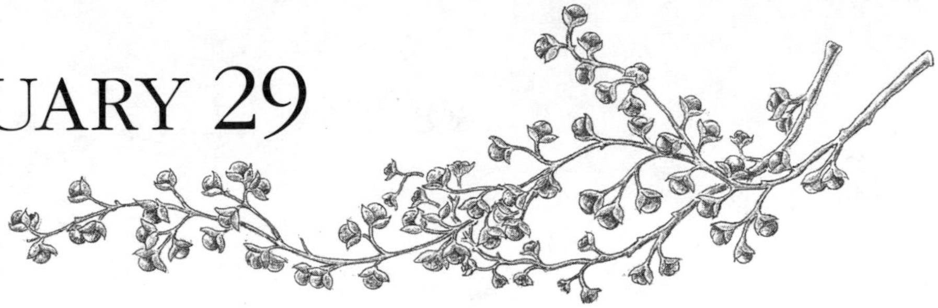

Betula pendula
European Birch

YEAR

HIGH ______° LOW______°

YEAR

HIGH ______° LOW______°

YEAR

HIGH ______° LOW______°

YEAR

HIGH ______° LOW______°

YEAR

HIGH ______° LOW______°

YEAR

HIGH ______° LOW______°

YEAR

HIGH ______° LOW______°

YEAR

HIGH ______° LOW______°

YEAR

HIGH ______° LOW______°

YEAR

HIGH ______° LOW______°

March 1

Borago officinalis

Borage

YEAR

HIGH ______° LOW ______°

YEAR

HIGH ______° LOW ______°

YEAR

HIGH ______° LOW ______°

YEAR

HIGH ______° LOW ______°

YEAR

HIGH ______° LOW ______°

YEAR

HIGH ______° LOW ______°

YEAR

HIGH ______° LOW ______°

YEAR

HIGH ______° LOW ______°

YEAR

HIGH ______° LOW ______°

YEAR

HIGH ______° LOW ______°

MARCH 2

Betula pendula "Youngii"

Young's Weeping Birch

YEAR

HIGH ______° LOW______°

YEAR

HIGH ______° LOW______°

YEAR

HIGH ______° LOW______°

YEAR

HIGH ______° LOW______°

YEAR

HIGH ______° LOW______°

YEAR

HIGH ______° LOW______°

YEAR

HIGH ______° LOW______°

YEAR

HIGH ______° LOW______°

YEAR

HIGH ______° LOW______°

YEAR

HIGH ______° LOW______°

MARCH 3

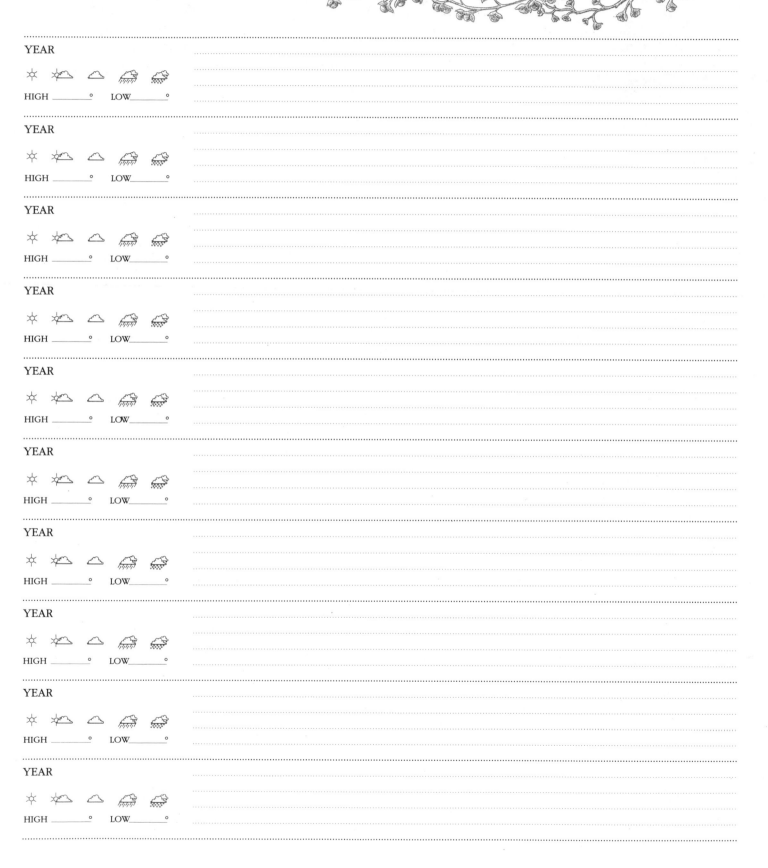

Betula pendula "Gracilis"
Cutleaf Birch

YEAR

HIGH ______° LOW______°

YEAR

HIGH ______° LOW______°

YEAR

HIGH ______° LOW______°

YEAR

HIGH ______° LOW______°

YEAR

HIGH ______° LOW______°

YEAR

HIGH ______° LOW______°

YEAR

HIGH ______° LOW______°

YEAR

HIGH ______° LOW______°

YEAR

HIGH ______° LOW______°

YEAR

HIGH ______° LOW______°

MARCH 4

Brassica oleracea gemmifera
Brussels Sprouts

YEAR

HIGH ______° LOW______°

YEAR

HIGH ______° LOW______°

YEAR

HIGH ______° LOW______°

YEAR

HIGH ______° LOW______°

YEAR

HIGH ______° LOW______°

YEAR

HIGH ______° LOW______°

YEAR

HIGH ______° LOW______°

YEAR

HIGH ______° LOW______°

YEAR

HIGH ______° LOW______°

YEAR

HIGH ______° LOW______°

MARCH 5

Brassica caulorapa
Kohlrabi

YEAR

HIGH ________° LOW________°

YEAR

HIGH ________° LOW________°

YEAR

HIGH ________° LOW________°

YEAR

HIGH ________° LOW________°

YEAR

HIGH ________° LOW________°

YEAR

HIGH ________° LOW________°

YEAR

HIGH ________° LOW________°

YEAR

HIGH ________° LOW________°

YEAR

HIGH ________° LOW________°

YEAR

HIGH ________° LOW________°

MARCH 6

Brassica rapa

Summer Turnip

YEAR

HIGH ______° LOW______°

YEAR

HIGH ______° LOW______°

YEAR

HIGH ______° LOW______°

YEAR

HIGH ______° LOW______°

YEAR

HIGH ______° LOW______°

YEAR

HIGH ______° LOW______°

YEAR

HIGH ______° LOW______°

YEAR

HIGH ______° LOW______°

YEAR

HIGH ______° LOW______°

YEAR

HIGH ______° LOW______°

MARCH 7

Brassica oleracea capitata
Cabbage

YEAR

HIGH ________° LOW________°

YEAR

HIGH ________° LOW________°

YEAR

HIGH ________° LOW________°

YEAR

HIGH ________° LOW________°

YEAR

HIGH ________° LOW________°

YEAR

HIGH ________° LOW________°

YEAR

HIGH ________° LOW________°

YEAR

HIGH ________° LOW________°

YEAR

HIGH ________° LOW________°

YEAR

HIGH ________° LOW________°

MARCH 8

Brassica napus napobrassica

Rutabaga

YEAR

HIGH ______° LOW______°

YEAR

HIGH ______° LOW______°

YEAR

HIGH ______° LOW______°

YEAR

HIGH ______° LOW______°

YEAR

HIGH ______° LOW______°

YEAR

HIGH ______° LOW______°

YEAR

HIGH ______° LOW______°

YEAR

HIGH ______° LOW______°

YEAR

HIGH ______° LOW______°

YEAR

HIGH ______° LOW______°

MARCH 9

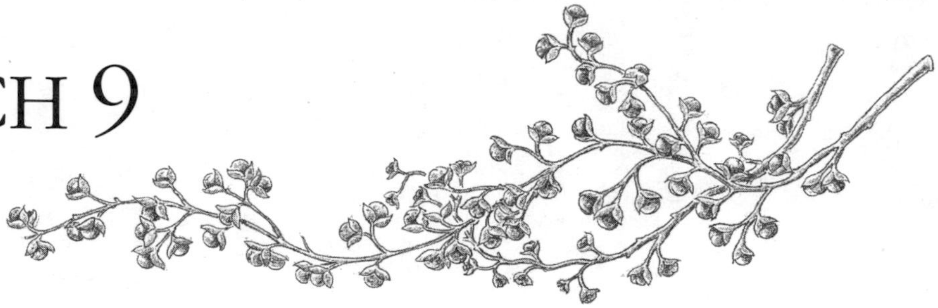

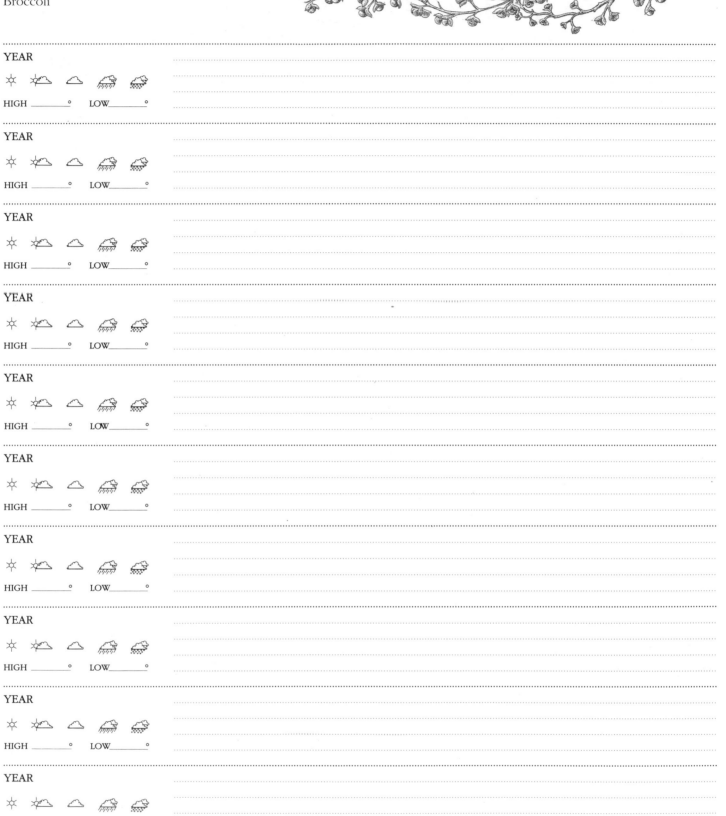

Brassica oleracea italica

Broccoli

YEAR

HIGH ________° LOW________°

YEAR

HIGH ________° LOW________°

YEAR

HIGH ________° LOW________°

YEAR

HIGH ________° LOW________°

YEAR

HIGH ________° LOW________°

YEAR

HIGH ________° LOW________°

YEAR

HIGH ________° LOW________°

YEAR

HIGH ________° LOW________°

YEAR

HIGH ________° LOW________°

YEAR

HIGH ________° LOW________°

MARCH 10

Brassica oleracea acephala
Kale

YEAR

HIGH ______° LOW______°

YEAR

HIGH ______° LOW______°

YEAR

HIGH ______° LOW______°

YEAR

HIGH ______° LOW______°

YEAR

HIGH ______° LOW______°

YEAR

HIGH ______° LOW______°

YEAR

HIGH ______° LOW______°

YEAR

HIGH ______° LOW______°

YEAR

HIGH ______° LOW______°

YEAR

HIGH ______° LOW______°

MARCH 11

Brassica oleracea botrytis
Cauliflower

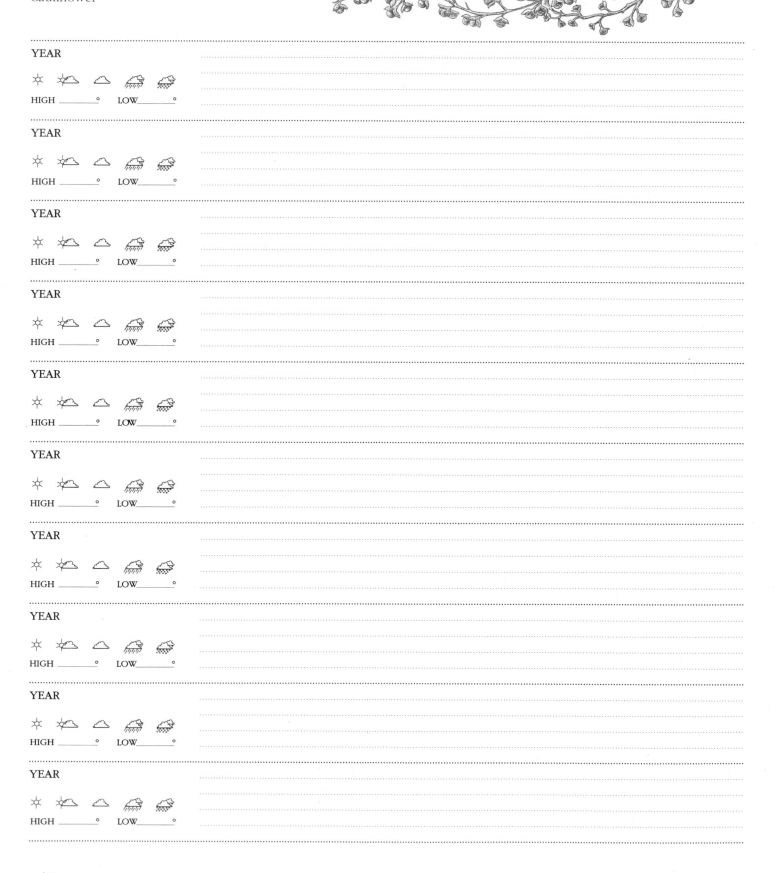

YEAR

HIGH ________° LOW________°

YEAR

HIGH ________° LOW________°

YEAR

HIGH ________° LOW________°

YEAR

HIGH ________° LOW________°

YEAR

HIGH ________° LOW________°

YEAR

HIGH ________° LOW________°

YEAR

HIGH ________° LOW________°

YEAR

HIGH ________° LOW________°

YEAR

HIGH ________° LOW________°

YEAR

HIGH ________° LOW________°

MARCH 12

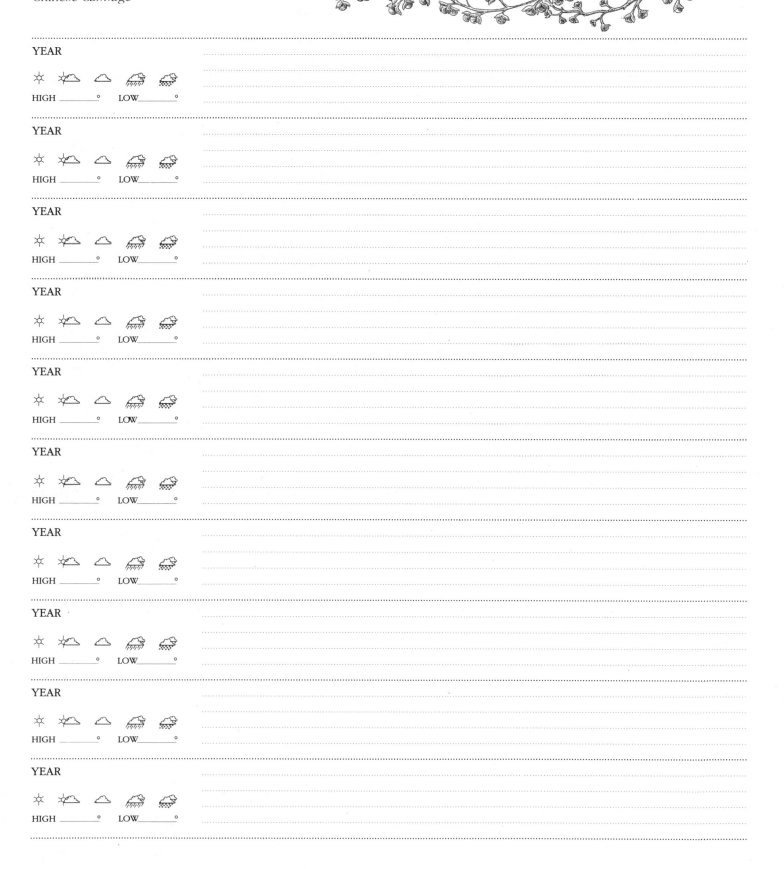

Brassica chinensis
Chinese Cabbage

YEAR

HIGH ______° LOW______°

YEAR

HIGH ______° LOW______°

YEAR

HIGH ______° LOW______°

YEAR

HIGH ______° LOW______°

YEAR

HIGH ______° LOW______°

YEAR

HIGH ______° LOW______°

YEAR

HIGH ______° LOW______°

YEAR

HIGH ______° LOW______°

YEAR

HIGH ______° LOW______°

YEAR

HIGH ______° LOW______°

MARCH 13

Buddleia davidii
Butterfly Bush

YEAR

HIGH ______° LOW ______°

YEAR

HIGH ______° LOW ______°

YEAR

HIGH ______° LOW ______°

YEAR

HIGH ______° LOW ______°

YEAR

HIGH ______° LOW ______°

YEAR

HIGH ______° LOW ______°

YEAR

HIGH ______° LOW ______°

YEAR

HIGH ______° LOW ______°

YEAR

HIGH ______° LOW ______°

YEAR

HIGH ______° LOW ______°

March 14

Buxus microphylla koreana

Korean Boxwood

YEAR

HIGH ______° LOW______°

YEAR

HIGH ______° LOW______°

YEAR

HIGH ______° LOW______°

YEAR

HIGH ______° LOW______°

YEAR

HIGH ______° LOW______°

YEAR

HIGH ______° LOW______°

YEAR

HIGH ______° LOW______°

YEAR

HIGH ______° LOW______°

YEAR

HIGH ______° LOW______°

YEAR

HIGH ______° LOW______°

MARCH 15

Calendula officinalis
Pot Marigold

YEAR

HIGH ______° LOW______°

YEAR

HIGH ______° LOW______°

YEAR

HIGH ______° LOW______°

YEAR

HIGH ______° LOW______°

YEAR

HIGH ______° LOW______°

YEAR

HIGH ______° LOW______°

YEAR

HIGH ______° LOW______°

YEAR

HIGH ______° LOW______°

YEAR

HIGH ______° LOW______°

YEAR

HIGH ______° LOW______°

MARCH 16

Calopogon tuberosus
Grass Pink Orchid

YEAR

HIGH ______° LOW______°

YEAR

HIGH ______° LOW______°

YEAR

HIGH ______° LOW______°

YEAR

HIGH ______° LOW______°

YEAR

HIGH ______° LOW______°

YEAR

HIGH ______° LOW______°

YEAR

HIGH ______° LOW______°

YEAR

HIGH ______° LOW______°

YEAR

HIGH ______° LOW______°

YEAR

HIGH ______° LOW______°

March 17

Campanula carpatica
Carpathian Bellflower

YEAR

HIGH ______° LOW ______°

YEAR

HIGH ______° LOW ______°

YEAR

HIGH ______° LOW ______°

YEAR

HIGH ______° LOW ______°

YEAR

HIGH ______° LOW ______°

YEAR

HIGH ______° LOW ______°

YEAR

HIGH ______° LOW ______°

YEAR

HIGH ______° LOW ______°

YEAR

HIGH ______° LOW ______°

YEAR

HIGH ______° LOW ______°

MARCH 18

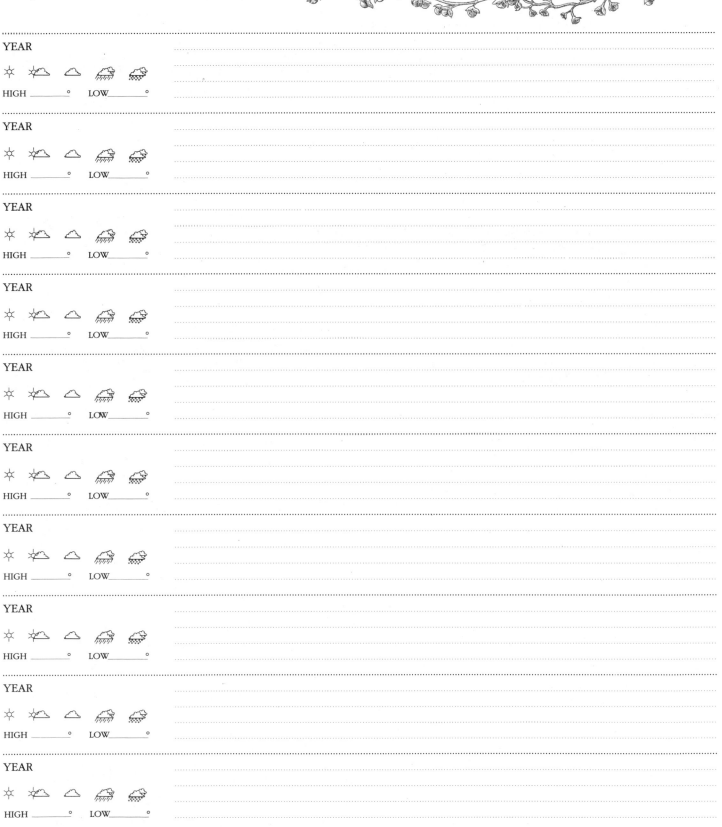

Campsis radicans

Trumpet Vine

YEAR

HIGH ______° LOW______°

YEAR

HIGH ______° LOW______°

YEAR

HIGH ______° LOW______°

YEAR

HIGH ______° LOW______°

YEAR

HIGH ______° LOW______°

YEAR

HIGH ______° LOW______°

YEAR

HIGH ______° LOW______°

YEAR

HIGH ______° LOW______°

YEAR

HIGH ______° LOW______°

YEAR

HIGH ______° LOW______°

MARCH 19

Capsicum frutescens

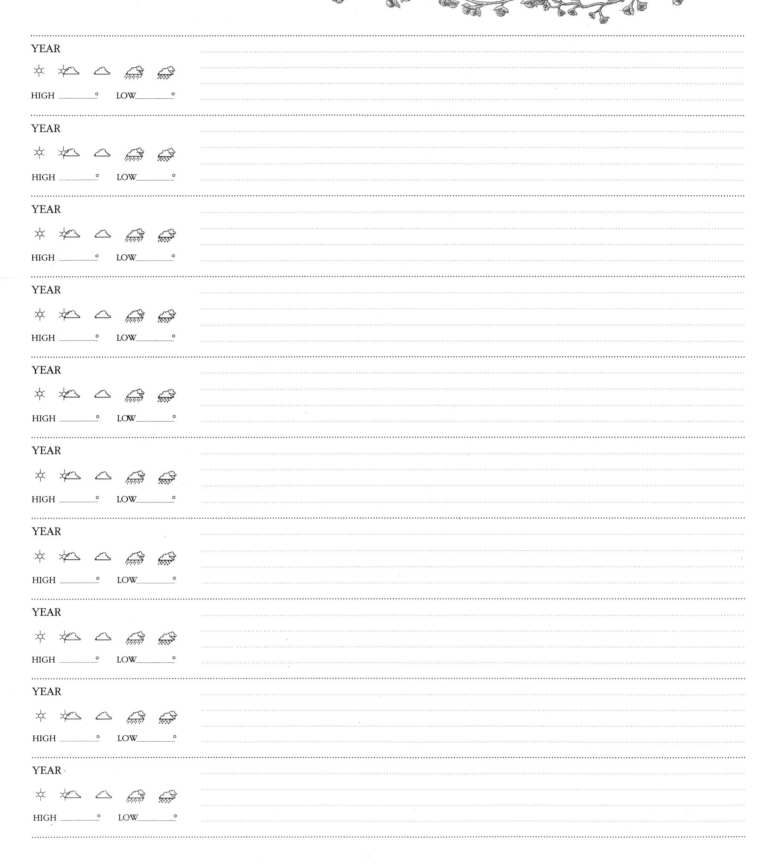

Hot Peppers

YEAR

HIGH ________° LOW________°

YEAR

HIGH ________° LOW________°

YEAR

HIGH ________° LOW________°

YEAR

HIGH ________° LOW________°

YEAR

HIGH ________° LOW________°

YEAR

HIGH ________° LOW________°

YEAR

HIGH ________° LOW________°

YEAR

HIGH ________° LOW________°

YEAR

HIGH ________° LOW________°

YEAR

HIGH ________° LOW________°

MARCH 20

Capsicum annuum
Sweet Peppers

YEAR

HIGH ______° LOW______°

YEAR

HIGH ______° LOW______°

YEAR

HIGH ______° LOW______°

YEAR

HIGH ______° LOW______°

YEAR

HIGH ______° LOW______°

YEAR

HIGH ______° LOW______°

YEAR

HIGH ______° LOW______°

YEAR

HIGH ______° LOW______°

YEAR

HIGH ______° LOW______°

YEAR

HIGH ______° LOW______°

MARCH 21

Capsella bursa-pastoris
Shepherd's-purse

YEAR

HIGH ______° LOW______°

YEAR

HIGH ______° LOW______°

YEAR

HIGH ______° LOW______°

YEAR

HIGH ______° LOW______°

YEAR

HIGH ______° LOW______°

YEAR

HIGH ______° LOW______°

YEAR

HIGH ______° LOW______°

YEAR

HIGH ______° LOW______°

YEAR

HIGH ______° LOW______°

YEAR

HIGH ______° LOW______°

MARCH 22

Caragana arborescens "Pendula"
Weeping Pea Shrub

YEAR

HIGH ________° LOW________°

YEAR

HIGH ________° LOW________°

YEAR

HIGH ________° LOW________°

YEAR

HIGH ________° LOW________°

YEAR

HIGH ________° LOW________°

YEAR

HIGH ________° LOW________°

YEAR

HIGH ________° LOW________°

YEAR

HIGH ________° LOW________°

YEAR

HIGH ________° LOW________°

YEAR

HIGH ________° LOW________°

MARCH 23

Caragana arborescens
Siberian Pea Shrub

YEAR

HIGH ______° LOW ______°

YEAR

HIGH ______° LOW ______°

YEAR

HIGH ______° LOW ______°

YEAR

HIGH ______° LOW ______°

YEAR

HIGH ______° LOW ______°

YEAR

HIGH ______° LOW ______°

YEAR

HIGH ______° LOW ______°

YEAR

HIGH ______° LOW ______°

YEAR

HIGH ______° LOW ______°

YEAR

HIGH ______° LOW ______°

MARCH 24

Carthamus tinctorius
Safflower

YEAR
HIGH ______° LOW______°

YEAR
HIGH ______° LOW______°

YEAR
HIGH ______° LOW______°

YEAR
HIGH ______° LOW______°

YEAR
HIGH ______° LOW______°

YEAR
HIGH ______° LOW______°

YEAR
HIGH ______° LOW______°

YEAR
HIGH ______° LOW______°

YEAR
HIGH ______° LOW______°

YEAR
HIGH ______° LOW______°

MARCH 25

Carum carvi
Caraway

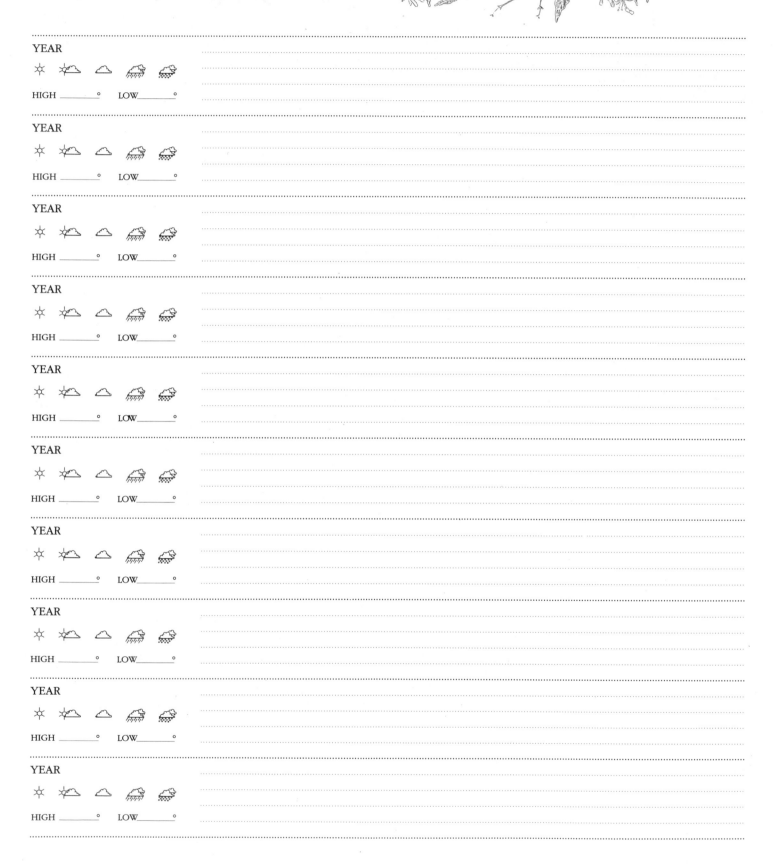

YEAR

HIGH ______° LOW ______°

YEAR

HIGH ______° LOW ______°

YEAR

HIGH ______° LOW ______°

YEAR

HIGH ______° LOW ______°

YEAR

HIGH ______° LOW ______°

YEAR

HIGH ______° LOW ______°

YEAR

HIGH ______° LOW ______°

YEAR

HIGH ______° LOW ______°

YEAR

HIGH ______° LOW ______°

YEAR

HIGH ______° LOW ______°

MARCH 26

Catalpa bignonioides "Nana"
Umbrella Catalpa

YEAR

HIGH ______° LOW ______°

YEAR

HIGH ______° LOW ______°

YEAR

HIGH ______° LOW ______°

YEAR

HIGH ______° LOW ______°

YEAR

HIGH ______° LOW ______°

YEAR

HIGH ______° LOW ______°

YEAR

HIGH ______° LOW ______°

YEAR

HIGH ______° LOW ______°

YEAR

HIGH ______° LOW ______°

YEAR

HIGH ______° LOW ______°

MARCH 27

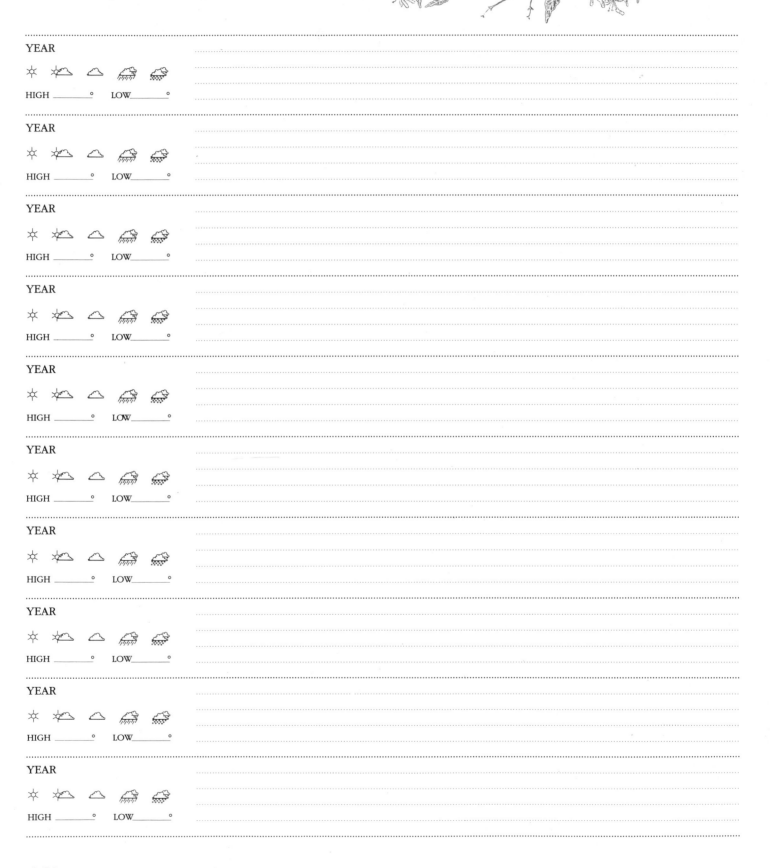

Catalpa speciosa
Northern Catalpa

YEAR

☼ ⛅ ☁ 🌧 🌨

HIGH ______° LOW______°

YEAR

☼ ⛅ ☁ 🌧 🌨

HIGH ______° LOW______°

YEAR

☼ ⛅ ☁ 🌧 🌨

HIGH ______° LOW______°

YEAR

☼ ⛅ ☁ 🌧 🌨

HIGH ______° LOW______°

YEAR

☼ ⛅ ☁ 🌧 🌨

HIGH ______° LOW______°

YEAR

☼ ⛅ ☁ 🌧 🌨

HIGH ______° LOW______°

YEAR

☼ ⛅ ☁ 🌧 🌨

HIGH ______° LOW______°

YEAR

☼ ⛅ ☁ 🌧 🌨

HIGH ______° LOW______°

YEAR

☼ ⛅ ☁ 🌧 🌨

HIGH ______° LOW______°

YEAR

☼ ⛅ ☁ 🌧 🌨

HIGH ______° LOW______°

MARCH 28

Caulophyllum thalictroides

Blue Cohosh

YEAR

HIGH ______° LOW______°

YEAR

HIGH ______° LOW______°

YEAR

HIGH ______° LOW______°

YEAR

HIGH ______° LOW______°

YEAR

HIGH ______° LOW______°

YEAR

HIGH ______° LOW______°

YEAR

HIGH ______° LOW______°

YEAR

HIGH ______° LOW______°

YEAR

HIGH ______° LOW______°

YEAR

HIGH ______° LOW______°

MARCH 29

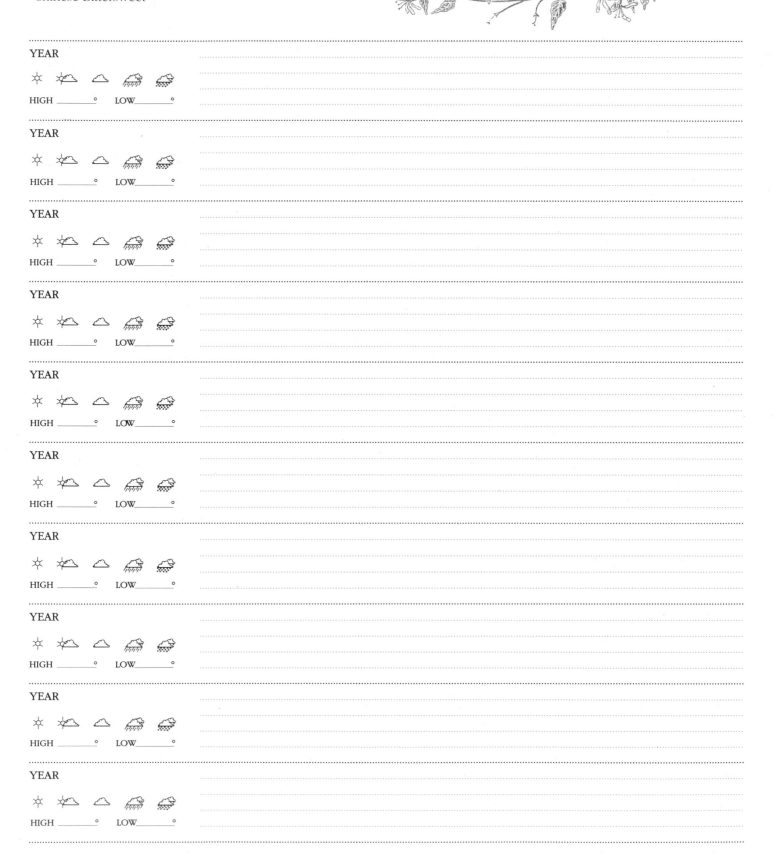

Celastrus loeseneri

Chinese Bittersweet

YEAR

HIGH _______° LOW_______°

YEAR

HIGH _______° LOW_______°

YEAR

HIGH _______° LOW_______°

YEAR

HIGH _______° LOW_______°

YEAR

HIGH _______° LOW_______°

YEAR

HIGH _______° LOW_______°

YEAR

HIGH _______° LOW_______°

YEAR

HIGH _______° LOW_______°

YEAR

HIGH _______° LOW_______°

YEAR

HIGH _______° LOW_______°

MARCH 30

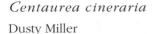

Centaurea cineraria

Dusty Miller

YEAR

HIGH ______° LOW______°

YEAR

HIGH ______° LOW______°

YEAR

HIGH ______° LOW______°

YEAR

HIGH ______° LOW______°

YEAR

HIGH ______° LOW______°

YEAR

HIGH ______° LOW______°

YEAR

HIGH ______° LOW______°

YEAR

HIGH ______° LOW______°

YEAR

HIGH ______° LOW______°

YEAR

HIGH ______° LOW______°

MARCH 31

Cerastium tomentosum

Snow-in-Summer

YEAR

HIGH ________° LOW________°

YEAR

HIGH ________° LOW________°

YEAR

HIGH ________° LOW________°

YEAR

HIGH ________° LOW________°

YEAR

HIGH ________° LOW________°

YEAR

HIGH ________° LOW________°

YEAR

HIGH ________° LOW________°

YEAR

HIGH ________° LOW________°

YEAR

HIGH ________° LOW________°

YEAR

HIGH ________° LOW________°

APRIL 1

Chaenomeles speciosa
Flowering Quince

YEAR

HIGH ______° LOW______°

YEAR

HIGH ______° LOW______°

YEAR

HIGH ______° LOW______°

YEAR

HIGH ______° LOW______°

YEAR

HIGH ______° LOW______°

YEAR

HIGH ______° LOW______°

YEAR

HIGH ______° LOW______°

YEAR

HIGH ______° LOW______°

YEAR

HIGH ______° LOW______°

YEAR

HIGH ______° LOW______°

APRIL 2

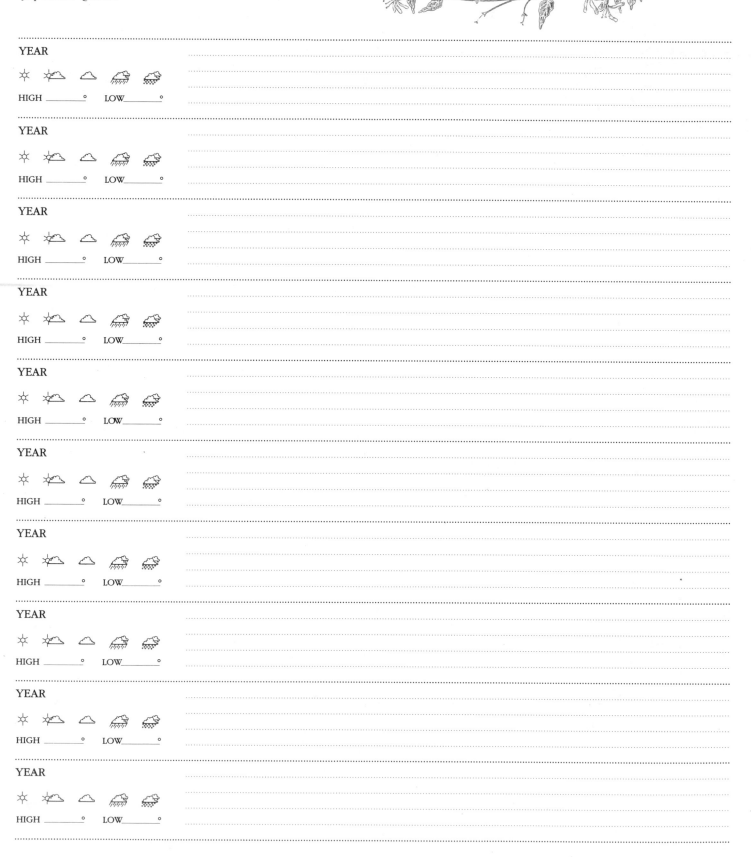

Chaenomeles japonica
Japanese Quince

YEAR
HIGH _______° LOW_______°

YEAR
HIGH _______° LOW_______°

YEAR
HIGH _______° LOW_______°

YEAR
HIGH _______° LOW_______°

YEAR
HIGH _______° LOW_______°

YEAR
HIGH _______° LOW_______°

YEAR
HIGH _______° LOW_______°

YEAR
HIGH _______° LOW_______°

YEAR
HIGH _______° LOW_______°

YEAR
HIGH _______° LOW_______°

APRIL 3

Chamaecyparis pisifera "Filifera"
Threadleaf False Cypress

YEAR

☼ ⛅ ☁ 🌧 🌨

HIGH ______° LOW______°

YEAR

☼ ⛅ ☁ 🌧 🌨

HIGH ______° LOW______°

YEAR

☼ ⛅ ☁ 🌧 🌨

HIGH ______° LOW______°

YEAR

☼ ⛅ ☁ 🌧 🌨

HIGH ______° LOW______°

YEAR

☼ ⛅ ☁ 🌧 🌨

HIGH ______° LOW______°

YEAR

☼ ⛅ ☁ 🌧 🌨

HIGH ______° LOW______°

YEAR

☼ ⛅ ☁ 🌧 🌨

HIGH ______° LOW______°

YEAR

☼ ⛅ ☁ 🌧 🌨

HIGH ______° LOW______°

YEAR

☼ ⛅ ☁ 🌧 🌨

HIGH ______° LOW______°

YEAR

☼ ⛅ ☁ 🌧 🌨

HIGH ______° LOW______°

APRIL 4

Chamaemelum nobile
Chamomile

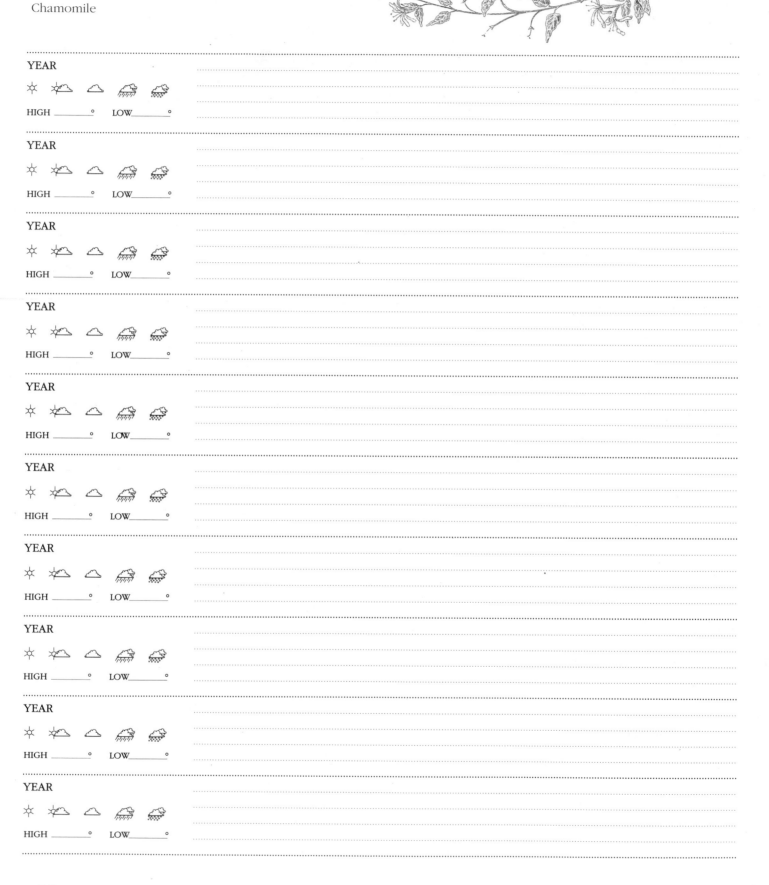

YEAR
☼ ⛅ ☁ 🌧 🌨
HIGH ____° LOW____°

YEAR
☼ ⛅ ☁ 🌧 🌨
HIGH ____° LOW____°

YEAR
☼ ⛅ ☁ 🌧 🌨
HIGH ____° LOW____°

YEAR
☼ ⛅ ☁ 🌧 🌨
HIGH ____° LOW____°

YEAR
☼ ⛅ ☁ 🌧 🌨
HIGH ____° LOW____°

YEAR
☼ ⛅ ☁ 🌧 🌨
HIGH ____° LOW____°

YEAR
☼ ⛅ ☁ 🌧 🌨
HIGH ____° LOW____°

YEAR
☼ ⛅ ☁ 🌧 🌨
HIGH ____° LOW____°

YEAR
☼ ⛅ ☁ 🌧 🌨
HIGH ____° LOW____°

YEAR
☼ ⛅ ☁ 🌧 🌨
HIGH ____° LOW____°

APRIL 5

Chimaphila umbellata
Pipsissewa

YEAR

HIGH ______° LOW ______°

YEAR

HIGH ______° LOW ______°

YEAR

HIGH ______° LOW ______°

YEAR

HIGH ______° LOW ______°

YEAR

HIGH ______° LOW ______°

YEAR

HIGH ______° LOW ______°

YEAR

HIGH ______° LOW ______°

YEAR

HIGH ______° LOW ______°

YEAR

HIGH ______° LOW ______°

YEAR

HIGH ______° LOW ______°

APRIL 6

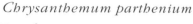

Chrysanthemum parthenium
Feverfew

YEAR

HIGH ________° LOW ________°

YEAR

HIGH ________° LOW ________°

YEAR

HIGH ________° LOW ________°

YEAR

HIGH ________° LOW ________°

YEAR

HIGH ________° LOW ________°

YEAR

HIGH ________° LOW ________°

YEAR

HIGH ________° LOW ________°

YEAR

HIGH ________° LOW ________°

YEAR

HIGH ________° LOW ________°

YEAR

HIGH ________° LOW ________°

APRIL 7

Chrysanthemum balsamita

Costmary

YEAR

HIGH ______° LOW______°

YEAR

HIGH ______° LOW______°

YEAR

HIGH ______° LOW______°

YEAR

HIGH ______° LOW______°

YEAR

HIGH ______° LOW______°

YEAR

HIGH ______° LOW______°

YEAR

HIGH ______° LOW______°

YEAR

HIGH ______° LOW______°

YEAR

HIGH ______° LOW______°

YEAR

HIGH ______° LOW______°

APRIL 8

Chrysanthemum coccineum
Pyrethrum, Painted Daisy

YEAR

HIGH ______° LOW______°

YEAR

HIGH ______° LOW______°

YEAR

HIGH ______° LOW______°

YEAR

HIGH ______° LOW______°

YEAR

HIGH ______° LOW______°

YEAR

HIGH ______° LOW______°

YEAR

HIGH ______° LOW______°

YEAR

HIGH ______° LOW______°

YEAR

HIGH ______° LOW______°

YEAR

HIGH ______° LOW______°

APRIL 9

Chrysanthemum superbum
Shasta Daisy

YEAR

HIGH ________° LOW________°

YEAR

HIGH ________° LOW________°

YEAR

HIGH ________° LOW________°

YEAR

HIGH ________° LOW________°

YEAR

HIGH ________° LOW________°

YEAR

HIGH ________° LOW________°

YEAR

HIGH ________° LOW________°

YEAR

HIGH ________° LOW________°

YEAR

HIGH ________° LOW________°

YEAR

HIGH ________° LOW________°

APRIL 10

Cichorium intybus
French Endive

YEAR

HIGH ________° LOW________°

YEAR

HIGH ________° LOW________°

YEAR

HIGH ________° LOW________°

YEAR

HIGH ________° LOW________°

YEAR

HIGH ________° LOW________°

YEAR

HIGH ________° LOW________°

YEAR

HIGH ________° LOW________°

YEAR

HIGH ________° LOW________°

YEAR

HIGH ________° LOW________°

YEAR

HIGH ________° LOW________°

APRIL 11

Cinnamomum zeylanicum
Cinnamon

YEAR

HIGH ____° LOW ____°

YEAR

HIGH ____° LOW ____°

YEAR

HIGH ____° LOW ____°

YEAR

HIGH ____° LOW ____°

YEAR

HIGH ____° LOW ____°

YEAR

HIGH ____° LOW ____°

YEAR

HIGH ____° LOW ____°

YEAR

HIGH ____° LOW ____°

YEAR

HIGH ____° LOW ____°

YEAR

HIGH ____° LOW ____°

APRIL 12

Citrullus lanatus
Watermelon

YEAR

HIGH ______° LOW ______°

YEAR

HIGH ______° LOW ______°

YEAR

HIGH ______° LOW ______°

YEAR

HIGH ______° LOW ______°

YEAR

HIGH ______° LOW ______°

YEAR

HIGH ______° LOW ______°

YEAR

HIGH ______° LOW ______°

YEAR

HIGH ______° LOW ______°

YEAR

HIGH ______° LOW ______°

YEAR

HIGH ______° LOW ______°

April 13

Cleome

Spider Flower

YEAR

HIGH ________° LOW________°

YEAR

HIGH ________° LOW________°

YEAR

HIGH ________° LOW________°

YEAR

HIGH ________° LOW________°

YEAR

HIGH ________° LOW________°

YEAR

HIGH ________° LOW________°

YEAR

HIGH ________° LOW________°

YEAR

HIGH ________° LOW________°

YEAR

HIGH ________° LOW________°

YEAR

HIGH ________° LOW________°

April 14

Coffea arabica

Coffee

YEAR

HIGH ________° LOW________°

YEAR

HIGH ________° LOW________°

YEAR

HIGH ________° LOW________°

YEAR

HIGH ________° LOW________°

YEAR

HIGH ________° LOW________°

YEAR

HIGH ________° LOW________°

YEAR

HIGH ________° LOW________°

YEAR

HIGH ________° LOW________°

YEAR

HIGH ________° LOW________°

YEAR

HIGH ________° LOW________°

APRIL 15

Colchicum autumnale
Autumn Crocus

YEAR

HIGH ________° LOW________°

YEAR

HIGH ________° LOW________°

YEAR

HIGH ________° LOW________°

YEAR

HIGH ________° LOW________°

YEAR

HIGH ________° LOW________°

YEAR

HIGH ________° LOW________°

YEAR

HIGH ________° LOW________°

YEAR

HIGH ________° LOW________°

YEAR

HIGH ________° LOW________°

YEAR

HIGH ________° LOW________°

APRIL 16

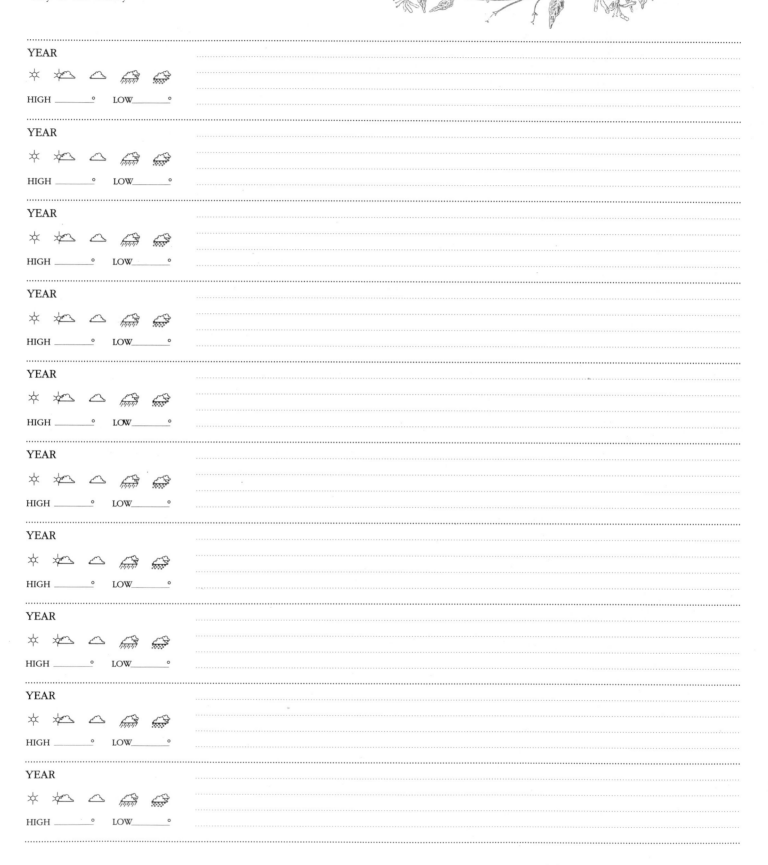

Convallaria majalis
Lily-of-the-Valley

YEAR

HIGH ______° LOW______°

YEAR

HIGH ______° LOW______°

YEAR

HIGH ______° LOW______°

YEAR

HIGH ______° LOW______°

YEAR

HIGH ______° LOW______°

YEAR

HIGH ______° LOW______°

YEAR

HIGH ______° LOW______°

YEAR

HIGH ______° LOW______°

YEAR

HIGH ______° LOW______°

YEAR

HIGH ______° LOW______°

April 17

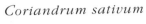

Coriandrum sativum
Coriander

YEAR

HIGH ______° LOW______°

YEAR

HIGH ______° LOW______°

YEAR

HIGH ______° LOW______°

YEAR

HIGH ______° LOW______°

YEAR

HIGH ______° LOW______°

YEAR

HIGH ______° LOW______°

YEAR

HIGH ______° LOW______°

YEAR

HIGH ______° LOW______°

YEAR

HIGH ______° LOW______°

YEAR

HIGH ______° LOW______°

APRIL 18

Cornus alba "Sibirica"
Siberian Dogwood

YEAR

HIGH ____° LOW____°

YEAR

HIGH ____° LOW____°

YEAR

HIGH ____° LOW____°

YEAR

HIGH ____° LOW____°

YEAR

HIGH ____° LOW____°

YEAR

HIGH ____° LOW____°

YEAR

HIGH ____° LOW____°

YEAR

HIGH ____° LOW____°

YEAR

HIGH ____° LOW____°

YEAR

HIGH ____° LOW____°

APRIL 19

Cornus alba "Argenteo-Marginata"

Silverleaf Dogwood

YEAR

HIGH ______° LOW______°

YEAR

HIGH ______° LOW______°

YEAR

HIGH ______° LOW______°

YEAR

HIGH ______° LOW______°

YEAR

HIGH ______° LOW______°

YEAR

HIGH ______° LOW______°

YEAR

HIGH ______° LOW______°

YEAR

HIGH ______° LOW______°

YEAR

HIGH ______° LOW______°

YEAR

HIGH ______° LOW______°

APRIL 20

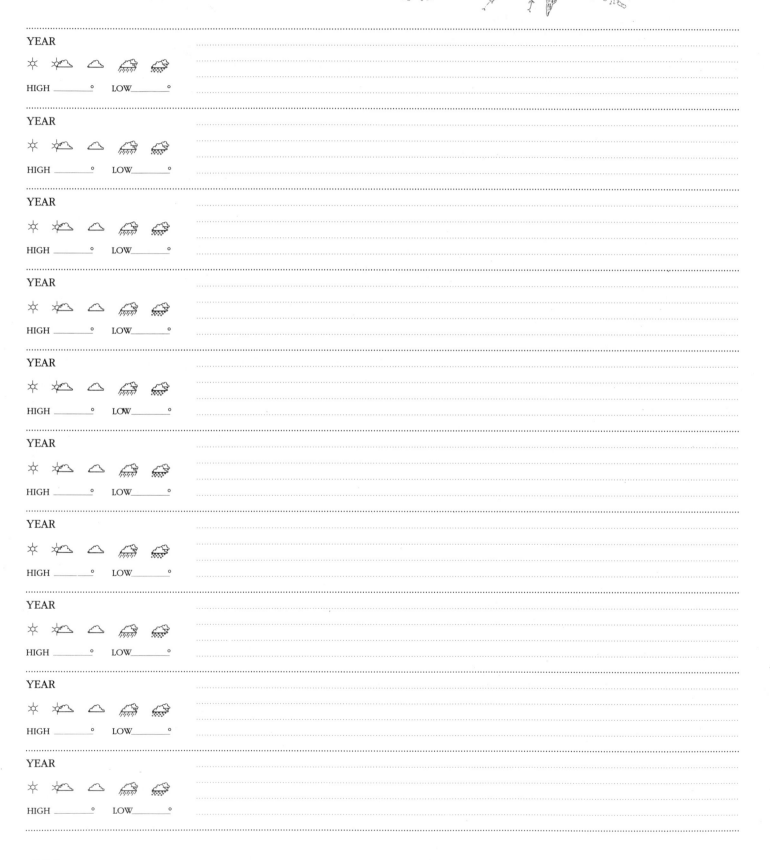

Coronilla varia
Crown vetch

YEAR

HIGH ______° LOW ______°

YEAR

HIGH ______° LOW ______°

YEAR

HIGH ______° LOW ______°

YEAR

HIGH ______° LOW ______°

YEAR

HIGH ______° LOW ______°

YEAR

HIGH ______° LOW ______°

YEAR

HIGH ______° LOW ______°

YEAR

HIGH ______° LOW ______°

YEAR

HIGH ______° LOW ______°

YEAR

HIGH ______° LOW ______°

APRIL 21

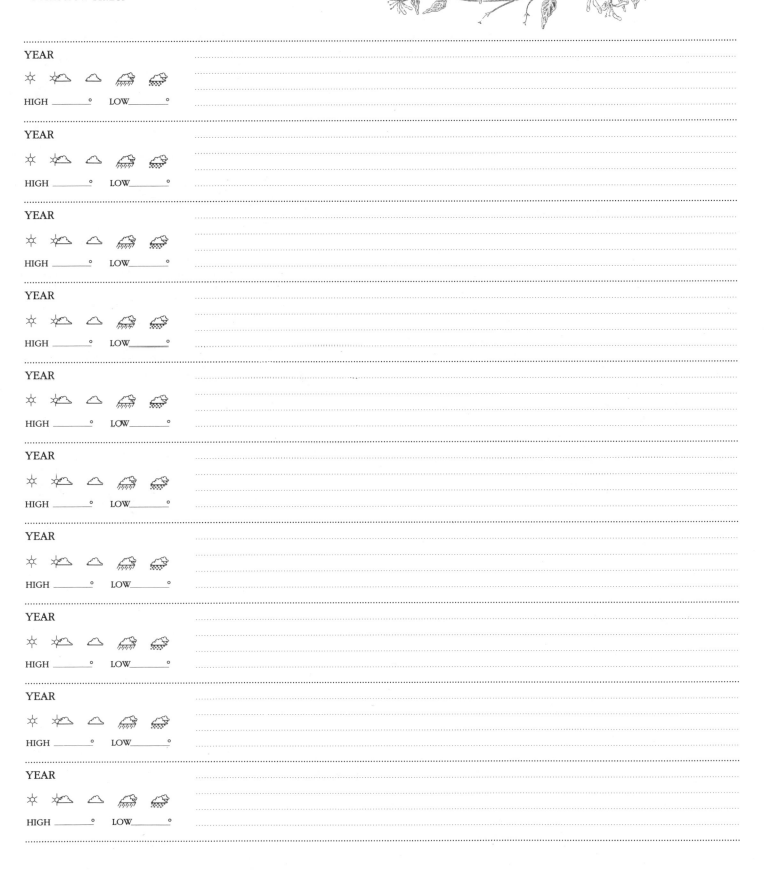

Corylus avellana "Contorta"
Corkscrew Hazel

YEAR

HIGH ______° LOW______°

YEAR

HIGH ______° LOW______°

YEAR

HIGH ______° LOW______°

YEAR

HIGH ______° LOW______°

YEAR

HIGH ______° LOW______°

YEAR

HIGH ______° LOW______°

YEAR

HIGH ______° LOW______°

YEAR

HIGH ______° LOW______°

YEAR

HIGH ______° LOW______°

YEAR

HIGH ______° LOW______°

APRIL 22

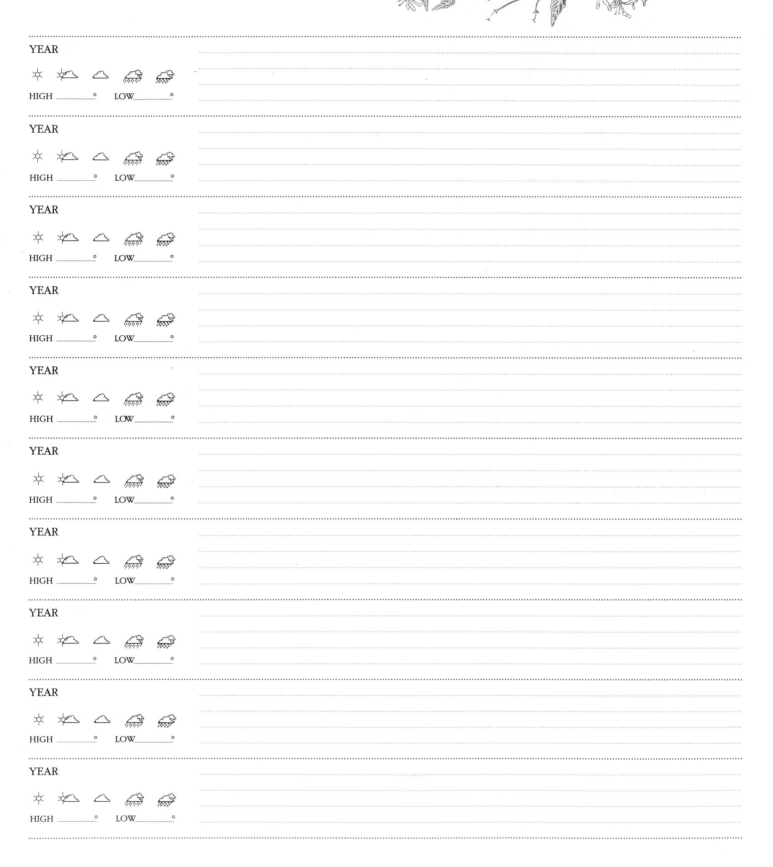

Cotinus coggygria
Smokebush

YEAR

HIGH ______° LOW______°

YEAR

HIGH ______° LOW______°

YEAR

HIGH ______° LOW______°

YEAR

HIGH ______° LOW______°

YEAR

HIGH ______° LOW______°

YEAR

HIGH ______° LOW______°

YEAR

HIGH ______° LOW______°

YEAR

HIGH ______° LOW______°

YEAR

HIGH ______° LOW______°

YEAR

HIGH ______° LOW______°

April 23

Cotoneaster apiculatus
Cranberry Cotoneaster

YEAR
HIGH ______° LOW ______°

YEAR
HIGH ______° LOW ______°

YEAR
HIGH ______° LOW ______°

YEAR
HIGH ______° LOW ______°

YEAR
HIGH ______° LOW ______°

YEAR
HIGH ______° LOW ______°

YEAR
HIGH ______° LOW ______°

YEAR
HIGH ______° LOW ______°

YEAR
HIGH ______° LOW ______°

YEAR
HIGH ______° LOW ______°

APRIL 24

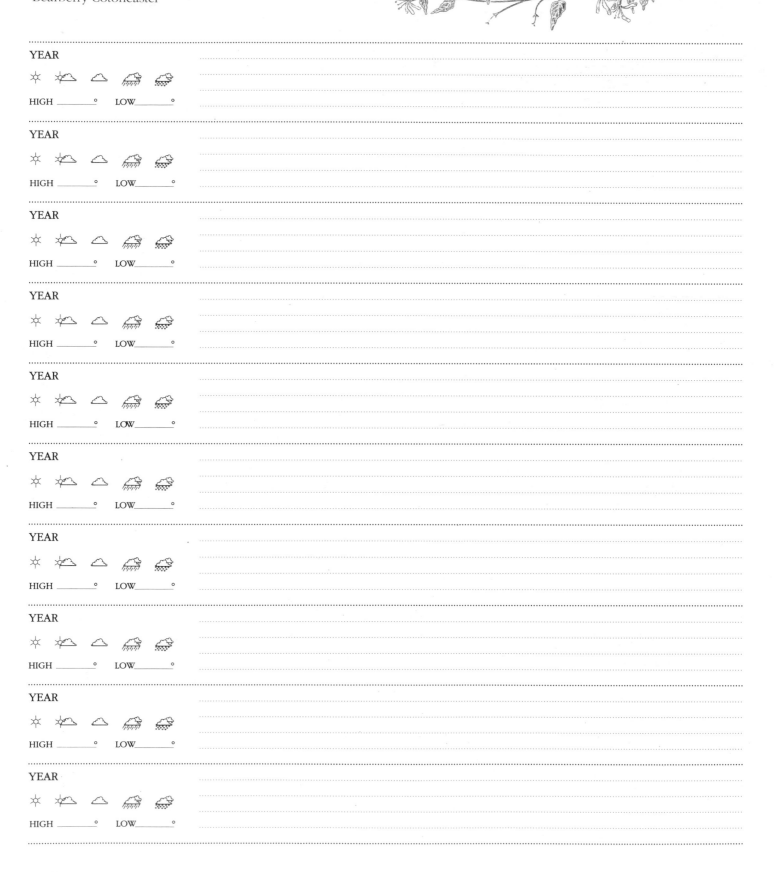

Cotoneaster dammeri

Bearberry Cotoneaster

YEAR

HIGH ______° LOW ______°

YEAR

HIGH ______° LOW ______°

YEAR

HIGH ______° LOW ______°

YEAR

HIGH ______° LOW ______°

YEAR

HIGH ______° LOW ______°

YEAR

HIGH ______° LOW ______°

YEAR

HIGH ______° LOW ______°

YEAR

HIGH ______° LOW ______°

YEAR

HIGH ______° LOW ______°

YEAR

HIGH ______° LOW ______°

APRIL 25

Cotoneaster acutifolius

Peking Cotoneaster

YEAR

HIGH ______° LOW ______°

YEAR

HIGH ______° LOW ______°

YEAR

HIGH ______° LOW ______°

YEAR

HIGH ______° LOW ______°

YEAR

HIGH ______° LOW ______°

YEAR

HIGH ______° LOW ______°

YEAR

HIGH ______° LOW ______°

YEAR

HIGH ______° LOW ______°

YEAR

HIGH ______° LOW ______°

YEAR

HIGH ______° LOW ______°

APRIL 26

Crambe maritima
Sea Kale

YEAR

HIGH ______° LOW______°

YEAR

HIGH ______° LOW______°

YEAR

HIGH ______° LOW______°

YEAR

HIGH ______° LOW______°

YEAR

HIGH ______° LOW______°

YEAR

HIGH ______° LOW______°

YEAR

HIGH ______° LOW______°

YEAR

HIGH ______° LOW______°

YEAR

HIGH ______° LOW______°

YEAR

HIGH ______° LOW______°

APRIL 27

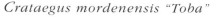

Crataegus mordenensis "Toba"

Toba Hawthorn

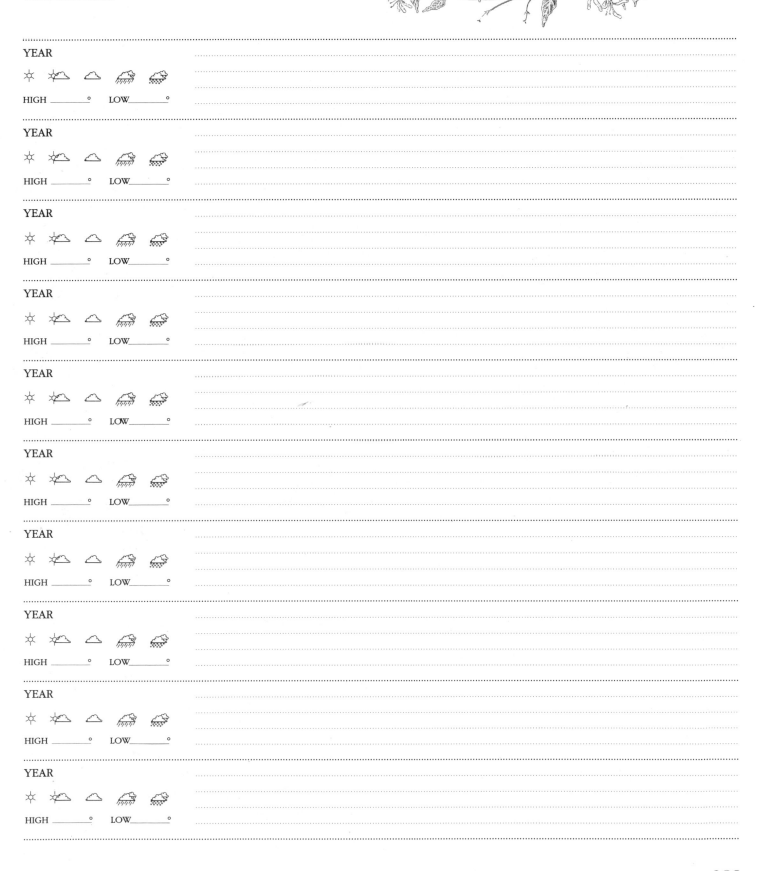

YEAR

HIGH ______° LOW______°

YEAR

HIGH ______° LOW______°

YEAR

HIGH ______° LOW______°

YEAR

HIGH ______° LOW______°

YEAR

HIGH ______° LOW______°

YEAR

HIGH ______° LOW______°

YEAR

HIGH ______° LOW______°

YEAR

HIGH ______° LOW______°

YEAR

HIGH ______° LOW______°

YEAR

HIGH ______° LOW______°

APRIL 28

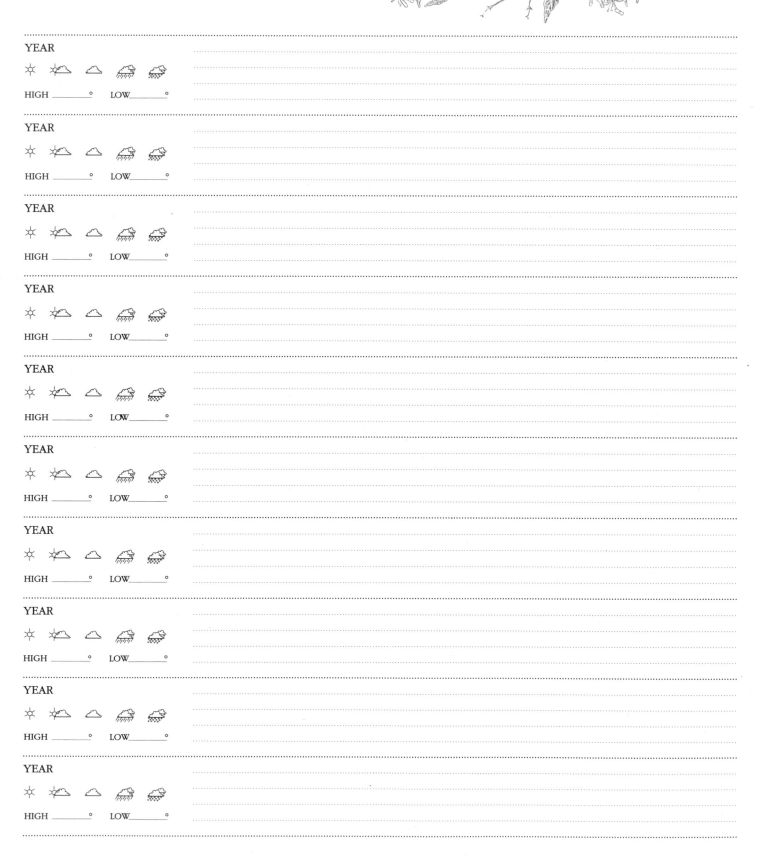

Crocus sativus

Saffron

YEAR

HIGH ________° LOW________°

YEAR

HIGH ________° LOW________°

YEAR

HIGH ________° LOW________°

YEAR

HIGH ________° LOW________°

YEAR

HIGH ________° LOW________°

YEAR

HIGH ________° LOW________°

YEAR

HIGH ________° LOW________°

YEAR

HIGH ________° LOW________°

YEAR

HIGH ________° LOW________°

YEAR

HIGH ________° LOW________°

APRIL 29

Cucumis melo

Cantaloupe

YEAR

HIGH ________° LOW________°

YEAR

HIGH ________° LOW________°

YEAR

HIGH ________° LOW________°

YEAR

HIGH ________° LOW________°

YEAR

HIGH ________° LOW________°

YEAR

HIGH ________° LOW________°

YEAR

HIGH ________° LOW________°

YEAR

HIGH ________° LOW________°

YEAR

HIGH ________° LOW________°

YEAR

HIGH ________° LOW________°

APRIL 30

Cucumis sativus
Cucumber

YEAR

HIGH ______° LOW ______°

YEAR

HIGH ______° LOW ______°

YEAR

HIGH ______° LOW ______°

YEAR

HIGH ______° LOW ______°

YEAR

HIGH ______° LOW ______°

YEAR

HIGH ______° LOW ______°

YEAR

HIGH ______° LOW ______°

YEAR

HIGH ______° LOW ______°

YEAR

HIGH ______° LOW ______°

YEAR

HIGH ______° LOW ______°

MAY 1

Cucurbita pepo "Zucchini"
Zucchini squash

YEAR

HIGH ______° LOW ______°

YEAR

HIGH ______° LOW ______°

YEAR

HIGH ______° LOW ______°

YEAR

HIGH ______° LOW ______°

YEAR

HIGH ______° LOW ______°

YEAR

HIGH ______° LOW ______°

YEAR

HIGH ______° LOW ______°

YEAR

HIGH ______° LOW ______°

YEAR

HIGH ______° LOW ______°

YEAR

HIGH ______° LOW ______°

MAY 2

Cucurbita maxima
Winter Squash

YEAR

HIGH ________° LOW________°

YEAR

HIGH ________° LOW________°

YEAR

HIGH ________° LOW________°

YEAR

HIGH ________° LOW________°

YEAR

HIGH ________° LOW________°

YEAR

HIGH ________° LOW________°

YEAR

HIGH ________° LOW________°

YEAR

HIGH ________° LOW________°

YEAR

HIGH ________° LOW________°

YEAR

HIGH ________° LOW________°

MAY 3

Cynara scolymus
Globe Artichoke

YEAR
HIGH ______° LOW______°

YEAR
HIGH ______° LOW______°

YEAR
HIGH ______° LOW______°

YEAR
HIGH ______° LOW______°

YEAR
HIGH ______° LOW______°

YEAR
HIGH ______° LOW______°

YEAR
HIGH ______° LOW______°

YEAR
HIGH ______° LOW______°

YEAR
HIGH ______° LOW______°

YEAR
HIGH ______° LOW______°

MAY 4

Cytisus albus

Broom

YEAR

HIGH ________° LOW________°

YEAR

HIGH ________° LOW________°

YEAR

HIGH ________° LOW________°

YEAR

HIGH ________° LOW________°

YEAR

HIGH ________° LOW________°

YEAR

HIGH ________° LOW________°

YEAR

HIGH ________° LOW________°

YEAR

HIGH ________° LOW________°

YEAR

HIGH ________° LOW________°

YEAR

HIGH ________° LOW________°

MAY 5

Daphne mezereum

February Daphne

YEAR

HIGH ______° LOW______°

YEAR

HIGH ______° LOW______°

YEAR

HIGH ______° LOW______°

YEAR

HIGH ______° LOW______°

YEAR

HIGH ______° LOW______°

YEAR

HIGH ______° LOW______°

YEAR

HIGH ______° LOW______°

YEAR

HIGH ______° LOW______°

YEAR

HIGH ______° LOW______°

YEAR

HIGH ______° LOW______°

May 6

Daucus carota

Carrot

YEAR

HIGH _______° LOW_______°

YEAR

HIGH _______° LOW_______°

YEAR

HIGH _______° LOW_______°

YEAR

HIGH _______° LOW_______°

YEAR

HIGH _______° LOW_______°

YEAR

HIGH _______° LOW_______°

YEAR

HIGH _______° LOW_______°

YEAR

HIGH _______° LOW_______°

YEAR

HIGH _______° LOW_______°

YEAR

HIGH _______° LOW_______°

MAY 7

Deutzia gracilis
Slender Deutzia

YEAR

HIGH ________° LOW________°

YEAR

HIGH ________° LOW________°

YEAR

HIGH ________° LOW________°

YEAR

HIGH ________° LOW________°

YEAR

HIGH ________° LOW________°

YEAR

HIGH ________° LOW________°

YEAR

HIGH ________° LOW________°

YEAR

HIGH ________° LOW________°

YEAR

HIGH ________° LOW________°

YEAR

HIGH ________° LOW________°

MAY 8

Dianthus caryophyllus
Carnation

YEAR

HIGH ______° LOW______°

YEAR

HIGH ______° LOW______°

YEAR

HIGH ______° LOW______°

YEAR

HIGH ______° LOW______°

YEAR

HIGH ______° LOW______°

YEAR

HIGH ______° LOW______°

YEAR

HIGH ______° LOW______°

YEAR

HIGH ______° LOW______°

YEAR

HIGH ______° LOW______°

YEAR

HIGH ______° LOW______°

MAY 9

Dianthus plumarius

Cottage Pink

YEAR

HIGH ______° LOW______°

YEAR

HIGH ______° LOW______°

YEAR

HIGH ______° LOW______°

YEAR

HIGH ______° LOW______°

YEAR

HIGH ______° LOW______°

YEAR

HIGH ______° LOW______°

YEAR

HIGH ______° LOW______°

YEAR

HIGH ______° LOW______°

YEAR

HIGH ______° LOW______°

YEAR

HIGH ______° LOW______°

May 10

Dicentra spectabilis
Bleeding Heart

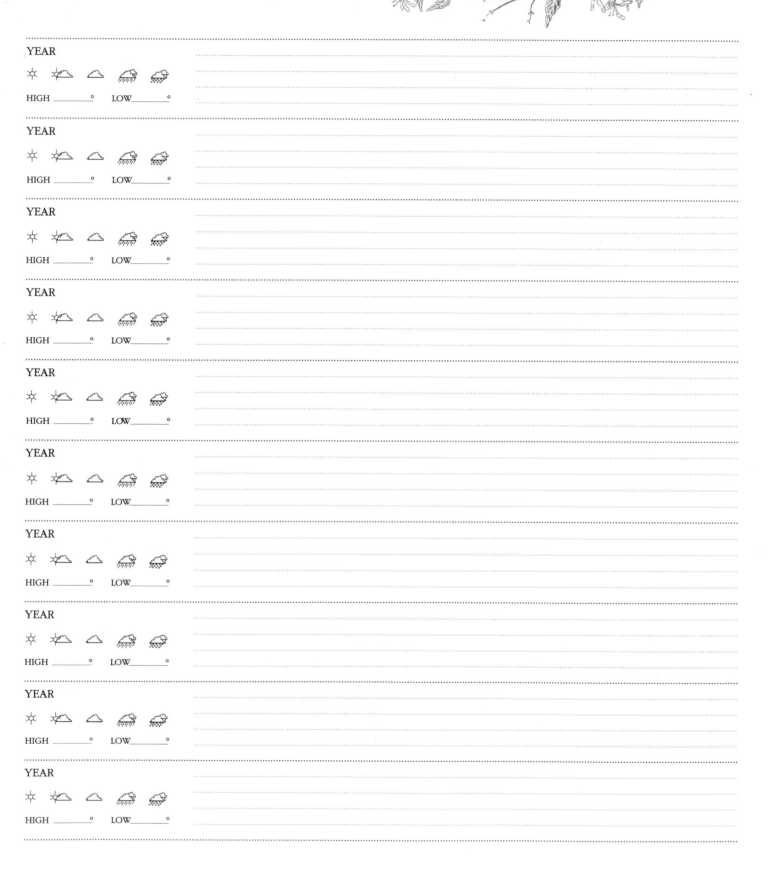

YEAR

HIGH ______° LOW______°

YEAR

HIGH ______° LOW______°

YEAR

HIGH ______° LOW______°

YEAR

HIGH ______° LOW______°

YEAR

HIGH ______° LOW______°

YEAR

HIGH ______° LOW______°

YEAR

HIGH ______° LOW______°

YEAR

HIGH ______° LOW______°

YEAR

HIGH ______° LOW______°

YEAR

HIGH ______° LOW______°

MAY 11

Dictamnus albus

Gas Plant

YEAR

HIGH ______° LOW______°

YEAR

HIGH ______° LOW______°

YEAR

HIGH ______° LOW______°

YEAR

HIGH ______° LOW______°

YEAR

HIGH ______° LOW______°

YEAR

HIGH ______° LOW______°

YEAR

HIGH ______° LOW______°

YEAR

HIGH ______° LOW______°

YEAR

HIGH ______° LOW______°

YEAR

HIGH ______° LOW______°

MAY 12

Digitalis

Foxglove

YEAR

HIGH ________° LOW________°

YEAR

HIGH ________° LOW________°

YEAR

HIGH ________° LOW________°

YEAR

HIGH ________° LOW________°

YEAR

HIGH ________° LOW________°

YEAR

HIGH ________° LOW________°

YEAR

HIGH ________° LOW________°

YEAR

HIGH ________° LOW________°

YEAR

HIGH ________° LOW________°

YEAR

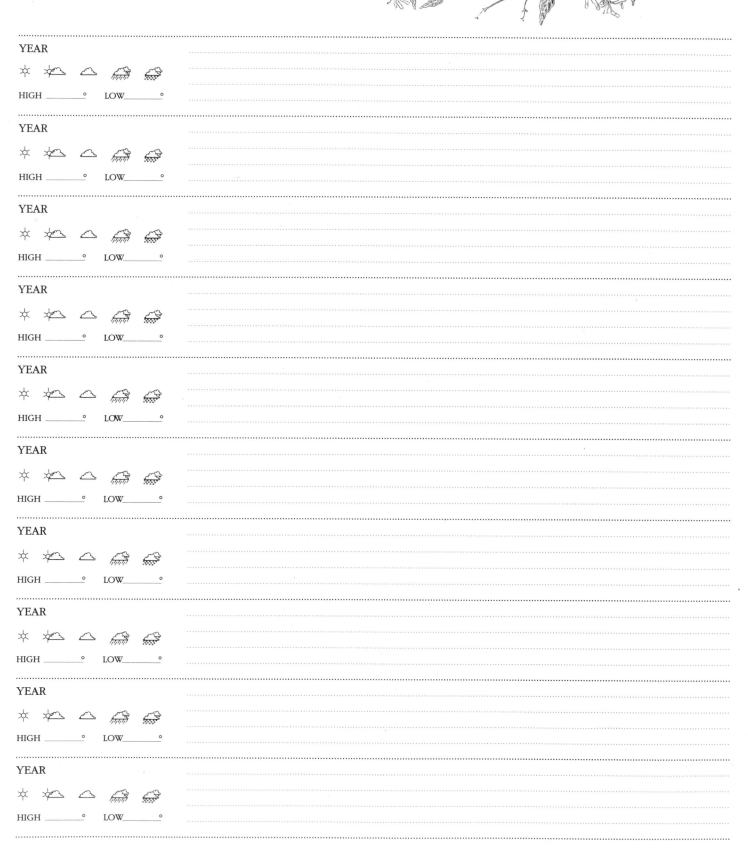

HIGH ________° LOW________°

May 13

Dombeya wallichii
Scarlet Dombeya

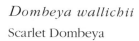

YEAR

HIGH ______° LOW______°

YEAR

HIGH ______° LOW______°

YEAR

HIGH ______° LOW______°

YEAR

HIGH ______° LOW______°

YEAR

HIGH ______° LOW______°

YEAR

HIGH ______° LOW______°

YEAR

HIGH ______° LOW______°

YEAR

HIGH ______° LOW______°

YEAR

HIGH ______° LOW______°

YEAR

HIGH ______° LOW______°

May 14

Doronicum cordatum
Leopardsbane

YEAR

HIGH ________° LOW________°

YEAR

HIGH ________° LOW________°

YEAR

HIGH ________° LOW________°

YEAR

HIGH ________° LOW________°

YEAR

HIGH ________° LOW________°

YEAR

HIGH ________° LOW________°

YEAR

HIGH ________° LOW________°

YEAR

HIGH ________° LOW________°

YEAR

HIGH ________° LOW________°

YEAR

HIGH ________° LOW________°

MAY 15

Echinacea purpurea
Coneflower

YEAR

HIGH ______° LOW______°

YEAR

HIGH ______° LOW______°

YEAR

HIGH ______° LOW______°

YEAR

HIGH ______° LOW______°

YEAR

HIGH ______° LOW______°

YEAR

HIGH ______° LOW______°

YEAR

HIGH ______° LOW______°

YEAR

HIGH ______° LOW______°

YEAR

HIGH ______° LOW______°

YEAR

HIGH ______° LOW______°

MAY 16

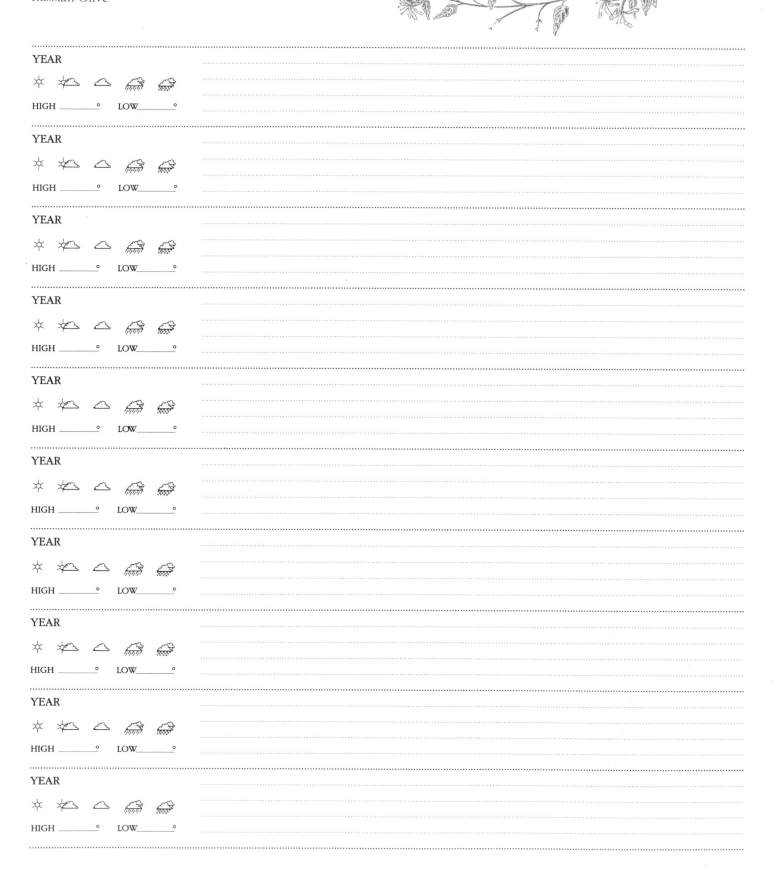

Elaeagnus angustifolia
Russian Olive

YEAR

HIGH ________° LOW________°

YEAR

HIGH ________° LOW________°

YEAR

HIGH ________° LOW________°

YEAR

HIGH ________° LOW________°

YEAR

HIGH ________° LOW________°

YEAR

HIGH ________° LOW________°

YEAR

HIGH ________° LOW________°

YEAR

HIGH ________° LOW________°

YEAR

HIGH ________° LOW________°

YEAR

HIGH ________° LOW________°

MAY 17

Elettaria cardamomum
Cardamom

YEAR

HIGH ______° LOW______°

YEAR

HIGH ______° LOW______°

YEAR

HIGH ______° LOW______°

YEAR

HIGH ______° LOW______°

YEAR

HIGH ______° LOW______°

YEAR

HIGH ______° LOW______°

YEAR

HIGH ______° LOW______°

YEAR

HIGH ______° LOW______°

YEAR

HIGH ______° LOW______°

YEAR

HIGH ______° LOW______°

May 18

Equisetum hyemale
Horsetail

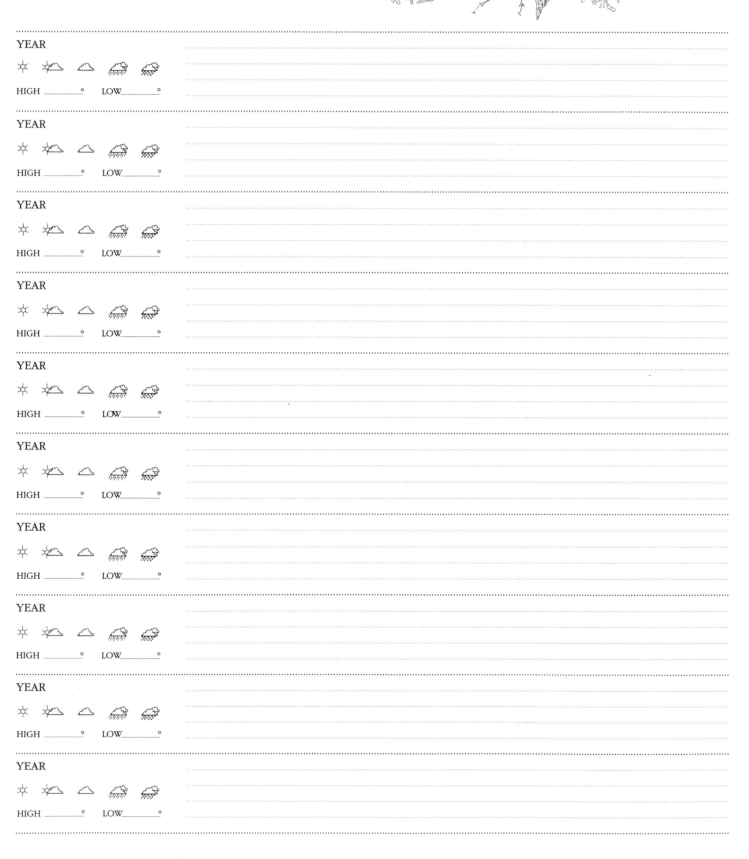

YEAR

HIGH ________° LOW________°

YEAR

HIGH ________° LOW________°

YEAR

HIGH ________° LOW________°

YEAR

HIGH ________° LOW________°

YEAR

HIGH ________° LOW________°

YEAR

HIGH ________° LOW________°

YEAR

HIGH ________° LOW________°

YEAR

HIGH ________° LOW________°

YEAR

HIGH ________° LOW________°

YEAR

HIGH ________° LOW________°

May 19

Erigeron
Fleabane

YEAR

HIGH ______° LOW______°

YEAR

HIGH ______° LOW______°

YEAR

HIGH ______° LOW______°

YEAR

HIGH ______° LOW______°

YEAR

HIGH ______° LOW______°

YEAR

HIGH ______° LOW______°

YEAR

HIGH ______° LOW______°

YEAR

HIGH ______° LOW______°

YEAR

HIGH ______° LOW______°

YEAR

HIGH ______° LOW______°

May 20

Euonymus alatus "Compactus"
Dwarf Burning Bush

YEAR

HIGH ______° LOW______°

YEAR

HIGH ______° LOW______°

YEAR

HIGH ______° LOW______°

YEAR

HIGH ______° LOW______°

YEAR

HIGH ______° LOW______°

YEAR

HIGH ______° LOW______°

YEAR

HIGH ______° LOW______°

YEAR

HIGH ______° LOW______°

YEAR

HIGH ______° LOW______°

YEAR

HIGH ______° LOW______°

MAY 21

Eupatorium perfoliatum

Boneset

YEAR

HIGH ______° LOW______°

YEAR

HIGH ______° LOW______°

YEAR

HIGH ______° LOW______°

YEAR

HIGH ______° LOW______°

YEAR

HIGH ______° LOW______°

YEAR

HIGH ______° LOW______°

YEAR

HIGH ______° LOW______°

YEAR

HIGH ______° LOW______°

YEAR

HIGH ______° LOW______°

YEAR

HIGH ______° LOW______°

MAY 22

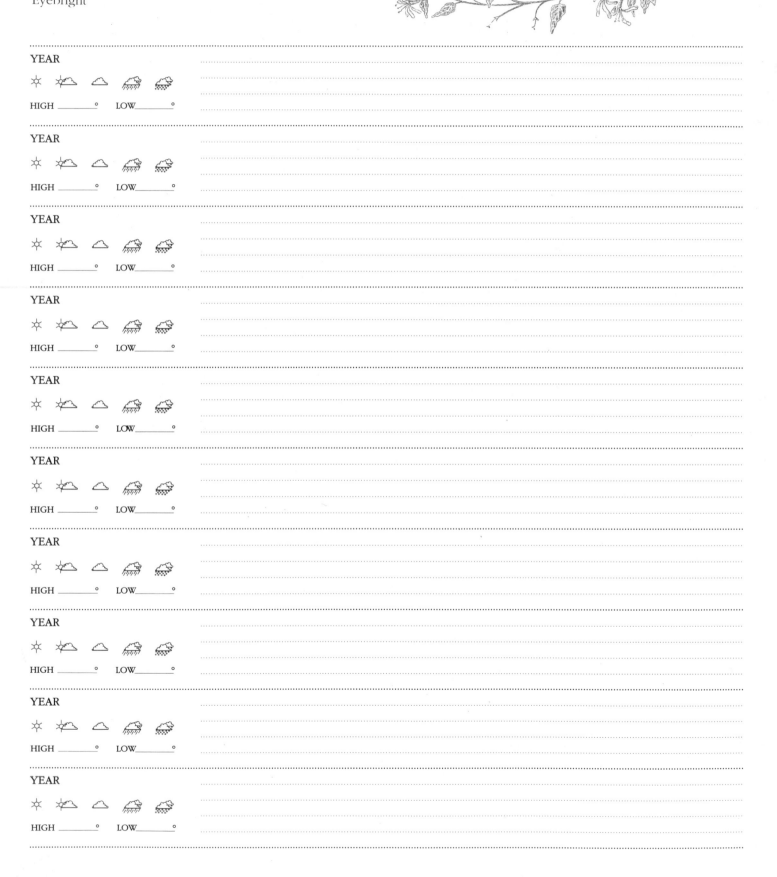

Euphrasia officinalis
Eyebright

YEAR

HIGH ______° LOW______°

YEAR

HIGH ______° LOW______°

YEAR

HIGH ______° LOW______°

YEAR

HIGH ______° LOW______°

YEAR

HIGH ______° LOW______°

YEAR

HIGH ______° LOW______°

YEAR

HIGH ______° LOW______°

YEAR

HIGH ______° LOW______°

YEAR

HIGH ______° LOW______°

YEAR

HIGH ______° LOW______°

May 23

Fagus grandifolia

American Beech

YEAR

HIGH ______° LOW______°

YEAR

HIGH ______° LOW______°

YEAR

HIGH ______° LOW______°

YEAR

HIGH ______° LOW______°

YEAR

HIGH ______° LOW______°

YEAR

HIGH ______° LOW______°

YEAR

HIGH ______° LOW______°

YEAR

HIGH ______° LOW______°

YEAR

HIGH ______° LOW______°

YEAR

HIGH ______° LOW______°

May 24

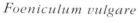

Foeniculum vulgare
Fennel

YEAR
HIGH ° LOW °

YEAR
HIGH ° LOW °

YEAR
HIGH ° LOW °

YEAR
HIGH ° LOW °

YEAR
HIGH ° LOW °

YEAR
HIGH ° LOW °

YEAR
HIGH ° LOW °

YEAR
HIGH ° LOW °

YEAR
HIGH ° LOW °

YEAR
HIGH ° LOW °

MAY 25

Forsythia suspensa

Weeping Forsythia

YEAR

HIGH _______° LOW_______°

YEAR

HIGH _______° LOW_______°

YEAR

HIGH _______° LOW_______°

YEAR

HIGH _______° LOW_______°

YEAR

HIGH _______° LOW_______°

YEAR

HIGH _______° LOW_______°

YEAR

HIGH _______° LOW_______°

YEAR

HIGH _______° LOW_______°

YEAR

HIGH _______° LOW_______°

YEAR

HIGH _______° LOW_______°

MAY 26

Fraxinus americana
White Ash

YEAR

HIGH ________° LOW________°

YEAR

HIGH ________° LOW________°

YEAR

HIGH ________° LOW________°

YEAR

HIGH ________° LOW________°

YEAR

HIGH ________° LOW________°

YEAR

HIGH ________° LOW________°

YEAR

HIGH ________° LOW________°

YEAR

HIGH ________° LOW________°

YEAR

HIGH ________° LOW________°

YEAR

HIGH ________° LOW________°

MAY 27

Fraxinus pennsylvanica
Green Ash

YEAR
HIGH ____° LOW____°

YEAR
HIGH ____° LOW____°

YEAR
HIGH ____° LOW____°

YEAR
HIGH ____° LOW____°

YEAR
HIGH ____° LOW____°

YEAR
HIGH ____° LOW____°

YEAR
HIGH ____° LOW____°

YEAR
HIGH ____° LOW____°

YEAR
HIGH ____° LOW____°

YEAR
HIGH ____° LOW____°

May 28

Gaillardia aristata

Blanket Flower

YEAR

HIGH ______° LOW______°

YEAR

HIGH ______° LOW______°

YEAR

HIGH ______° LOW______°

YEAR

HIGH ______° LOW______°

YEAR

HIGH ______° LOW______°

YEAR

HIGH ______° LOW______°

YEAR

HIGH ______° LOW______°

YEAR

HIGH ______° LOW______°

YEAR

HIGH ______° LOW______°

YEAR

HIGH ______° LOW______°

May 29

Galium odoratum
Sweet Woodruff

YEAR
HIGH _____° LOW_____°

YEAR
HIGH _____° LOW_____°

YEAR
HIGH _____° LOW_____°

YEAR
HIGH _____° LOW_____°

YEAR
HIGH _____° LOW_____°

YEAR
HIGH _____° LOW_____°

YEAR
HIGH _____° LOW_____°

YEAR
HIGH _____° LOW_____°

YEAR
HIGH _____° LOW_____°

YEAR
HIGH _____° LOW_____°

MAY 30

Galium verum

Lady's Bedstraw

YEAR

HIGH ______° LOW ______°

YEAR

HIGH ______° LOW ______°

YEAR

HIGH ______° LOW ______°

YEAR

HIGH ______° LOW ______°

YEAR

HIGH ______° LOW ______°

YEAR

HIGH ______° LOW ______°

YEAR

HIGH ______° LOW ______°

YEAR

HIGH ______° LOW ______°

YEAR

HIGH ______° LOW ______°

YEAR

HIGH ______° LOW ______°

MAY 31

Gaultheria procumbens

Wintergreen

YEAR

HIGH ______° LOW ______°

YEAR

HIGH ______° LOW ______°

YEAR

HIGH ______° LOW ______°

YEAR

HIGH ______° LOW ______°

YEAR

HIGH ______° LOW ______°

YEAR

HIGH ______° LOW ______°

YEAR

HIGH ______° LOW ______°

YEAR

HIGH ______° LOW ______°

YEAR

HIGH ______° LOW ______°

YEAR

HIGH ______° LOW ______°

June 1

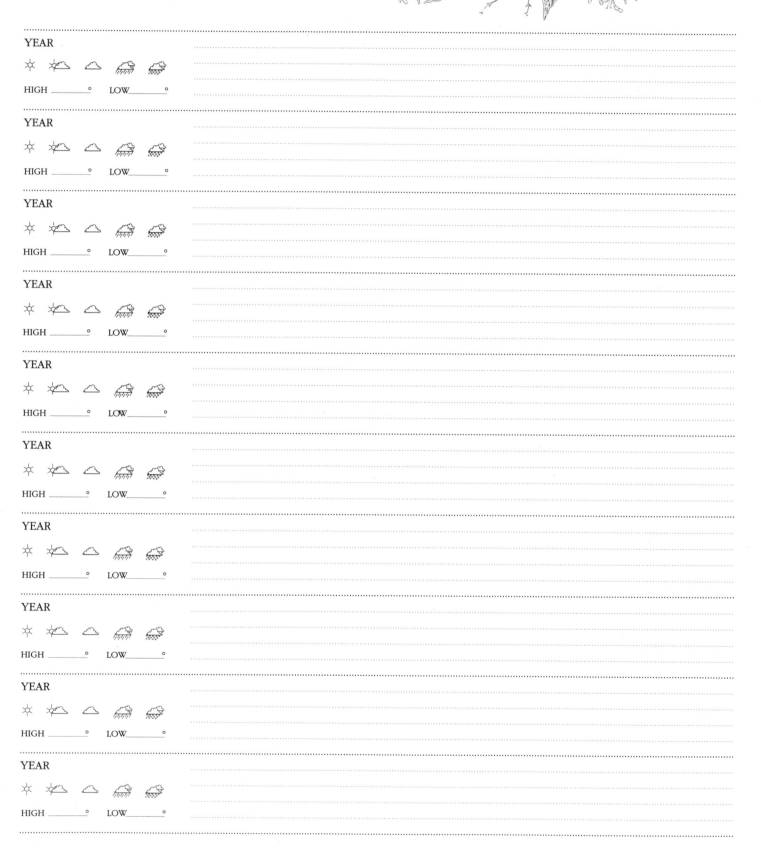

Gentiana lutea

Gentian

YEAR

HIGH ________° LOW________°

YEAR

HIGH ________° LOW________°

YEAR

HIGH ________° LOW________°

YEAR

HIGH ________° LOW________°

YEAR

HIGH ________° LOW________°

YEAR

HIGH ________° LOW________°

YEAR

HIGH ________° LOW________°

YEAR

HIGH ________° LOW________°

YEAR

HIGH ________° LOW________°

YEAR

HIGH ________° LOW________°

JUNE 2

Ginkgo biloba

Maidenhair Tree

YEAR

HIGH ______° LOW ______°

YEAR

HIGH ______° LOW ______°

YEAR

HIGH ______° LOW ______°

YEAR

HIGH ______° LOW ______°

YEAR

HIGH ______° LOW ______°

YEAR

HIGH ______° LOW ______°

YEAR

HIGH ______° LOW ______°

YEAR

HIGH ______° LOW ______°

YEAR

HIGH ______° LOW ______°

YEAR

HIGH ______° LOW ______°

JUNE 3

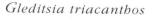

Gleditsia triacanthos
Honey locust

YEAR

HIGH ________° LOW ________°

YEAR

HIGH ________° LOW ________°

YEAR

HIGH ________° LOW ________°

YEAR

HIGH ________° LOW ________°

YEAR

HIGH ________° LOW ________°

YEAR

HIGH ________° LOW ________°

YEAR

HIGH ________° LOW ________°

YEAR

HIGH ________° LOW ________°

YEAR

HIGH ________° LOW ________°

YEAR

HIGH ________° LOW ________°

JUNE 4

Glycyrrhiza glabra

Licorice

YEAR

HIGH ________° LOW________°

YEAR

HIGH ________° LOW________°

YEAR

HIGH ________° LOW________°

YEAR

HIGH ________° LOW________°

YEAR

HIGH ________° LOW________°

YEAR

HIGH ________° LOW________°

YEAR

HIGH ________° LOW________°

YEAR

HIGH ________° LOW________°

YEAR

HIGH ________° LOW________°

YEAR

HIGH ________° LOW________°

JUNE 5

Gypsophila paniculata
Baby's Breath

YEAR

HIGH ________° LOW________°

YEAR

HIGH ________° LOW________°

YEAR

HIGH ________° LOW________°

YEAR

HIGH ________° LOW________°

YEAR

HIGH ________° LOW________°

YEAR

HIGH ________° LOW________°

YEAR

HIGH ________° LOW________°

YEAR

HIGH ________° LOW________°

YEAR

HIGH ________° LOW________°

YEAR

HIGH ________° LOW________°

June 6

Hedeoma pulegioides
American Pennyroyal

YEAR

HIGH ______° LOW ______°

YEAR

HIGH ______° LOW ______°

YEAR

HIGH ______° LOW ______°

YEAR

HIGH ______° LOW ______°

YEAR

HIGH ______° LOW ______°

YEAR

HIGH ______° LOW ______°

YEAR

HIGH ______° LOW ______°

YEAR

HIGH ______° LOW ______°

YEAR

HIGH ______° LOW ______°

YEAR

HIGH ______° LOW ______°

JUNE 7

Helenium autumnale
Common Sneezeweed

YEAR

HIGH ________° LOW________°

YEAR

HIGH ________° LOW________°

YEAR

HIGH ________° LOW________°

YEAR

HIGH ________° LOW________°

YEAR

HIGH ________° LOW________°

YEAR

HIGH ________° LOW________°

YEAR

HIGH ________° LOW________°

YEAR

HIGH ________° LOW________°

YEAR

HIGH ________° LOW________°

YEAR

HIGH ________° LOW________°

JUNE 8

Helianthus tuberosus
Jerusalem Artichoke

YEAR

HIGH ________° LOW________°

YEAR

HIGH ________° LOW________°

YEAR

HIGH ________° LOW________°

YEAR

HIGH ________° LOW________°

YEAR

HIGH ________° LOW________°

YEAR

HIGH ________° LOW________°

YEAR

HIGH ________° LOW________°

YEAR

HIGH ________° LOW________°

YEAR

HIGH ________° LOW________°

YEAR

HIGH ________° LOW________°

JUNE 9

Helleborus niger
Black Hellebore

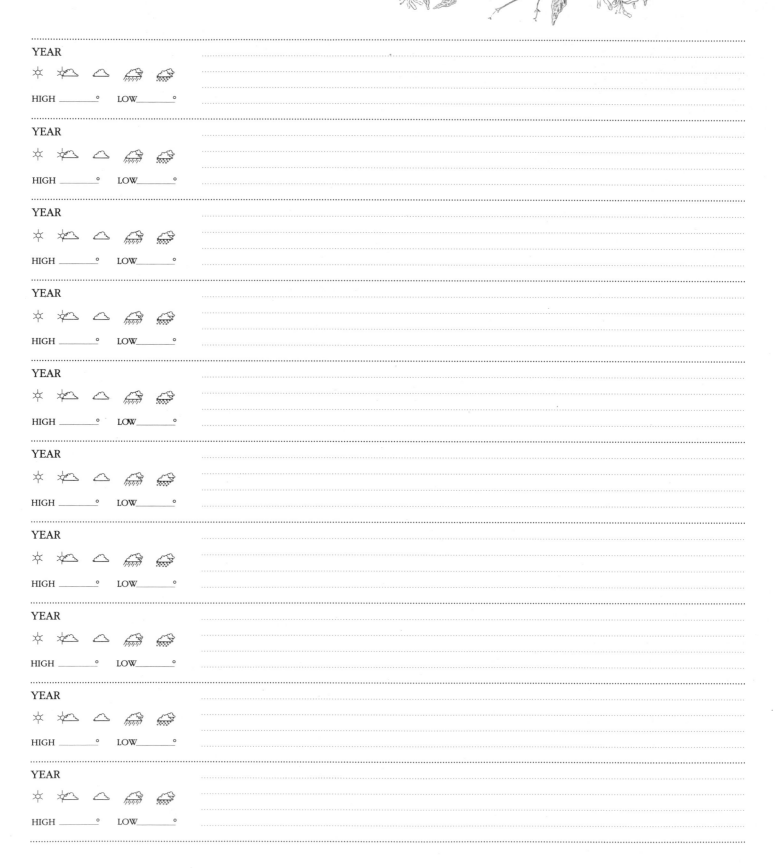

YEAR

HIGH ______° LOW ______°

YEAR

HIGH ______° LOW ______°

YEAR

HIGH ______° LOW ______°

YEAR

HIGH ______° LOW ______°

YEAR

HIGH ______° LOW ______°

YEAR

HIGH ______° LOW ______°

YEAR

HIGH ______° LOW ______°

YEAR

HIGH ______° LOW ______°

YEAR

HIGH ______° LOW ______°

YEAR

HIGH ______° LOW ______°

JUNE 10

Hemerocallis

Daylilies

YEAR

HIGH ______° LOW______°

YEAR

HIGH ______° LOW______°

YEAR

HIGH ______° LOW______°

YEAR

HIGH ______° LOW______°

YEAR

HIGH ______° LOW______°

YEAR

HIGH ______° LOW______°

YEAR

HIGH ______° LOW______°

YEAR

HIGH ______° LOW______°

YEAR

HIGH ______° LOW______°

YEAR

HIGH ______° LOW______°

JUNE 11

Heuchera sanguinea

Coral Bell

YEAR

HIGH ________° LOW________°

YEAR

HIGH ________° LOW________°

YEAR

HIGH ________° LOW________°

YEAR

HIGH ________° LOW________°

YEAR

HIGH ________° LOW________°

YEAR

HIGH ________° LOW________°

YEAR

HIGH ________° LOW________°

YEAR

HIGH ________° LOW________°

YEAR

HIGH ________° LOW________°

YEAR

HIGH ________° LOW________°

JUNE 12

Hibiscus syriacus

Rose of Sharon

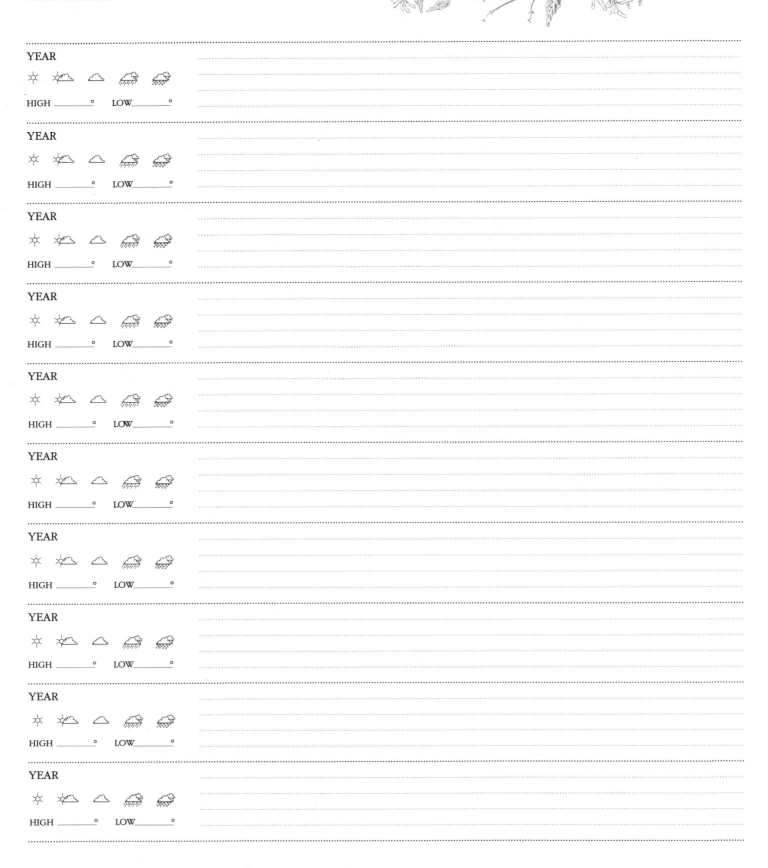

YEAR

HIGH ________° LOW________°

YEAR

HIGH ________° LOW________°

YEAR

HIGH ________° LOW________°

YEAR

HIGH ________° LOW________°

YEAR

HIGH ________° LOW________°

YEAR

HIGH ________° LOW________°

YEAR

HIGH ________° LOW________°

YEAR

HIGH ________° LOW________°

YEAR

HIGH ________° LOW________°

YEAR

HIGH ________° LOW________°

June 13

Hibiscus esculentus
Okra

YEAR

HIGH ______° LOW ______°

YEAR

HIGH ______° LOW ______°

YEAR

HIGH ______° LOW ______°

YEAR

HIGH ______° LOW ______°

YEAR

HIGH ______° LOW ______°

YEAR

HIGH ______° LOW ______°

YEAR

HIGH ______° LOW ______°

YEAR

HIGH ______° LOW ______°

YEAR

HIGH ______° LOW ______°

YEAR

HIGH ______° LOW ______°

JUNE 14

Hosta

Plantain Lily

YEAR

HIGH ______° LOW______°

YEAR

HIGH ______° LOW______°

YEAR

HIGH ______° LOW______°

YEAR

HIGH ______° LOW______°

YEAR

HIGH ______° LOW______°

YEAR

HIGH ______° LOW______°

YEAR

HIGH ______° LOW______°

YEAR

HIGH ______° LOW______°

YEAR

HIGH ______° LOW______°

YEAR

HIGH ______° LOW______°

JUNE 15

Hydrangea anomala petiolaris

Climbing Hydrangea

YEAR

HIGH ________° LOW________°

YEAR

HIGH ________° LOW________°

YEAR

HIGH ________° LOW________°

YEAR

HIGH ________° LOW________°

YEAR

HIGH ________° LOW________°

YEAR

HIGH ________° LOW________°

YEAR

HIGH ________° LOW________°

YEAR

HIGH ________° LOW________°

YEAR

HIGH ________° LOW________°

YEAR

HIGH ________° LOW________°

JUNE 16

Hydrangea paniculata "Grandiflora"

Peegee Hydrangea

YEAR

HIGH ______° LOW ______°

YEAR

HIGH ______° LOW ______°

YEAR

HIGH ______° LOW ______°

YEAR

HIGH ______° LOW ______°

YEAR

HIGH ______° LOW ______°

YEAR

HIGH ______° LOW ______°

YEAR

HIGH ______° LOW ______°

YEAR

HIGH ______° LOW ______°

YEAR

HIGH ______° LOW ______°

YEAR

HIGH ______° LOW ______°

JUNE 17

Hydrangea arborescens "Grandiflora"
Snowhill Hydrangea

YEAR

HIGH ______° LOW ______°

YEAR

HIGH ______° LOW ______°

YEAR

HIGH ______° LOW ______°

YEAR

HIGH ______° LOW ______°

YEAR

HIGH ______° LOW ______°

YEAR

HIGH ______° LOW ______°

YEAR

HIGH ______° LOW ______°

YEAR

HIGH ______° LOW ______°

YEAR

HIGH ______° LOW ______°

YEAR

HIGH ______° LOW ______°

JUNE 18

Hydrastis canadensis
Goldenseal

YEAR

HIGH ______° LOW______°

YEAR

HIGH ______° LOW______°

YEAR

HIGH ______° LOW______°

YEAR

HIGH ______° LOW______°

YEAR

HIGH ______° LOW______°

YEAR

HIGH ______° LOW______°

YEAR

HIGH ______° LOW______°

YEAR

HIGH ______° LOW______°

YEAR

HIGH ______° LOW______°

YEAR

HIGH ______° LOW______°

June 19

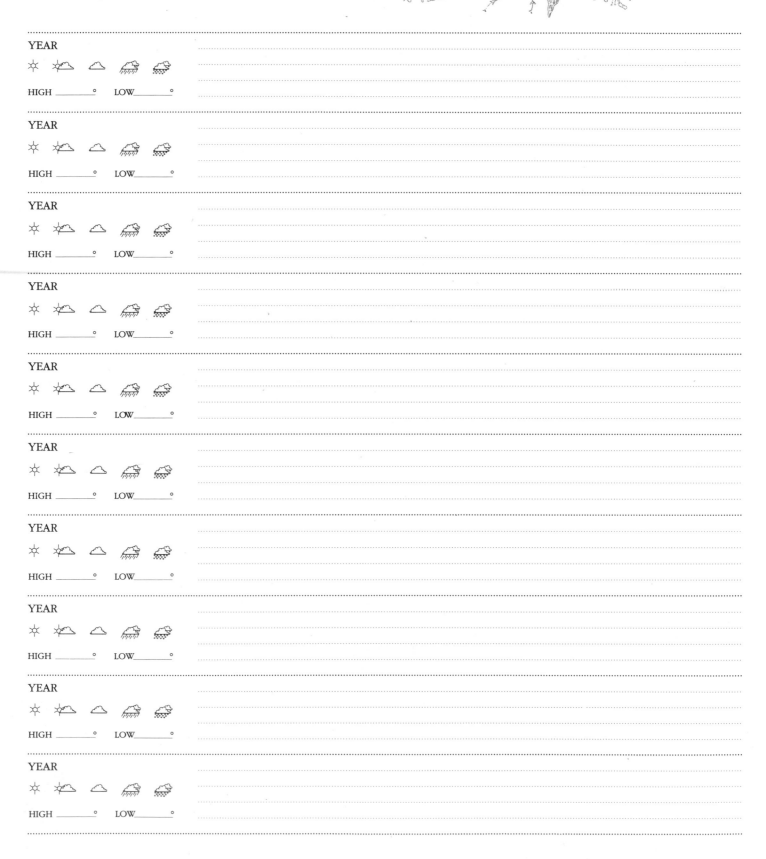

Hypericum perforatum
St.-John's-Wort

YEAR

HIGH ________° LOW________°

YEAR

HIGH ________° LOW________°

YEAR

HIGH ________° LOW________°

YEAR

HIGH ________° LOW________°

YEAR

HIGH ________° LOW________°

YEAR

HIGH ________° LOW________°

YEAR

HIGH ________° LOW________°

YEAR

HIGH ________° LOW________°

YEAR

HIGH ________° LOW________°

YEAR

HIGH ________° LOW________°

JUNE 20

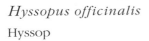

Hyssopus officinalis
Hyssop

YEAR
HIGH ________° LOW________°

YEAR
HIGH ________° LOW________°

YEAR
HIGH ________° LOW________°

YEAR
HIGH ________° LOW________°

YEAR
HIGH ________° LOW________°

YEAR
HIGH ________° LOW________°

YEAR
HIGH ________° LOW________°

YEAR
HIGH ________° LOW________°

YEAR
HIGH ________° LOW________°

YEAR
HIGH ________° LOW________°

JUNE 21

Iberis sempervirens
Candytuft

YEAR

HIGH ______° LOW______°

YEAR

HIGH ______° LOW______°

YEAR

HIGH ______° LOW______°

YEAR

HIGH ______° LOW______°

YEAR

HIGH ______° LOW______°

YEAR

HIGH ______° LOW______°

YEAR

HIGH ______° LOW______°

YEAR

HIGH ______° LOW______°

YEAR

HIGH ______° LOW______°

YEAR

HIGH ______° LOW______°

JUNE 22

Indigofera tinctoria
Indigo

YEAR
HIGH ______° LOW______°

YEAR
HIGH ______° LOW______°

YEAR
HIGH ______° LOW______°

YEAR
HIGH ______° LOW______°

YEAR
HIGH ______° LOW______°

YEAR
HIGH ______° LOW______°

YEAR
HIGH ______° LOW______°

YEAR
HIGH ______° LOW______°

YEAR
HIGH ______° LOW______°

YEAR
HIGH ______° LOW______°

JUNE 23

Inula helenium
Elecampane

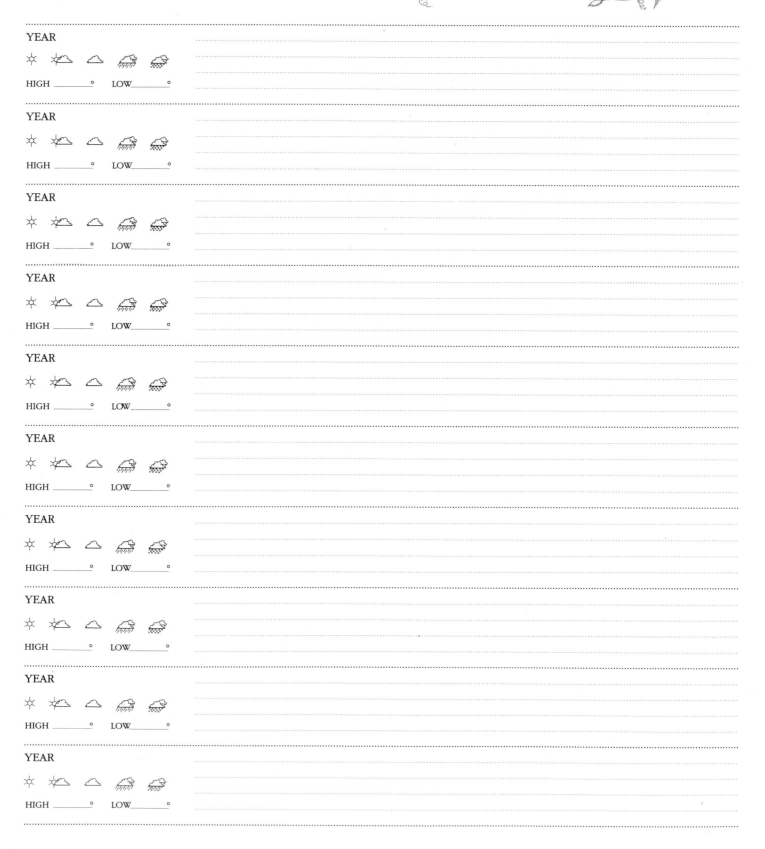

YEAR

HIGH ________° LOW________°

YEAR

HIGH ________° LOW________°

YEAR

HIGH ________° LOW________°

YEAR

HIGH ________° LOW________°

YEAR

HIGH ________° LOW________°

YEAR

HIGH ________° LOW________°

YEAR

HIGH ________° LOW________°

YEAR

HIGH ________° LOW________°

YEAR

HIGH ________° LOW________°

YEAR

HIGH ________° LOW________°

JUNE 24

Ipomoea batatas
Sweet Potato

YEAR
HIGH ____° LOW ____°

YEAR
HIGH ____° LOW ____°

YEAR
HIGH ____° LOW ____°

YEAR
HIGH ____° LOW ____°

YEAR
HIGH ____° LOW ____°

YEAR
HIGH ____° LOW ____°

YEAR
HIGH ____° LOW ____°

YEAR
HIGH ____° LOW ____°

YEAR
HIGH ____° LOW ____°

YEAR
HIGH ____° LOW ____°

JUNE 25

Iris sibirica
Siberian Iris

YEAR

HIGH ________° LOW________°

YEAR

HIGH ________° LOW________°

YEAR

HIGH ________° LOW________°

YEAR

HIGH ________° LOW________°

YEAR

HIGH ________° LOW________°

YEAR

HIGH ________° LOW________°

YEAR

HIGH ________° LOW________°

YEAR

HIGH ________° LOW________°

YEAR

HIGH ________° LOW________°

YEAR

HIGH ________° LOW________°

JUNE 26

Iris pumila
Dwarf Iris

YEAR

HIGH ______° LOW______°

YEAR

HIGH ______° LOW______°

YEAR

HIGH ______° LOW______°

YEAR

HIGH ______° LOW______°

YEAR

HIGH ______° LOW______°

YEAR

HIGH ______° LOW______°

YEAR

HIGH ______° LOW______°

YEAR

HIGH ______° LOW______°

YEAR

HIGH ______° LOW______°

YEAR

HIGH ______° LOW______°

JUNE 27

Iris persica

Persian Iris

YEAR

HIGH ______° LOW ______°

YEAR

HIGH ______° LOW ______°

YEAR

HIGH ______° LOW ______°

YEAR

HIGH ______° LOW ______°

YEAR

HIGH ______° LOW ______°

YEAR

HIGH ______° LOW ______°

YEAR

HIGH ______° LOW ______°

YEAR

HIGH ______° LOW ______°

YEAR

HIGH ______° LOW ______°

YEAR

HIGH ______° LOW ______°

JUNE 28

Isatis tinctoria

Woad

YEAR

HIGH ______° LOW ______°

YEAR

HIGH ______° LOW ______°

YEAR

HIGH ______° LOW ______°

YEAR

HIGH ______° LOW ______°

YEAR

HIGH ______° LOW ______°

YEAR

HIGH ______° LOW ______°

YEAR

HIGH ______° LOW ______°

YEAR

HIGH ______° LOW ______°

YEAR

HIGH ______° LOW ______°

YEAR

HIGH ______° LOW ______°

JUNE 29

Juniperus chinensis "Mintjulep"

Mint Julep Juniper

YEAR

HIGH ______° LOW ______°

YEAR

HIGH ______° LOW ______°

YEAR

HIGH ______° LOW ______°

YEAR

HIGH ______° LOW ______°

YEAR

HIGH ______° LOW ______°

YEAR

HIGH ______° LOW ______°

YEAR

HIGH ______° LOW ______°

YEAR

HIGH ______° LOW ______°

YEAR

HIGH ______° LOW ______°

YEAR

HIGH ______° LOW ______°

JUNE 30

Juniperus chinensis "Pfitzerana"
Pfitzer Juniper

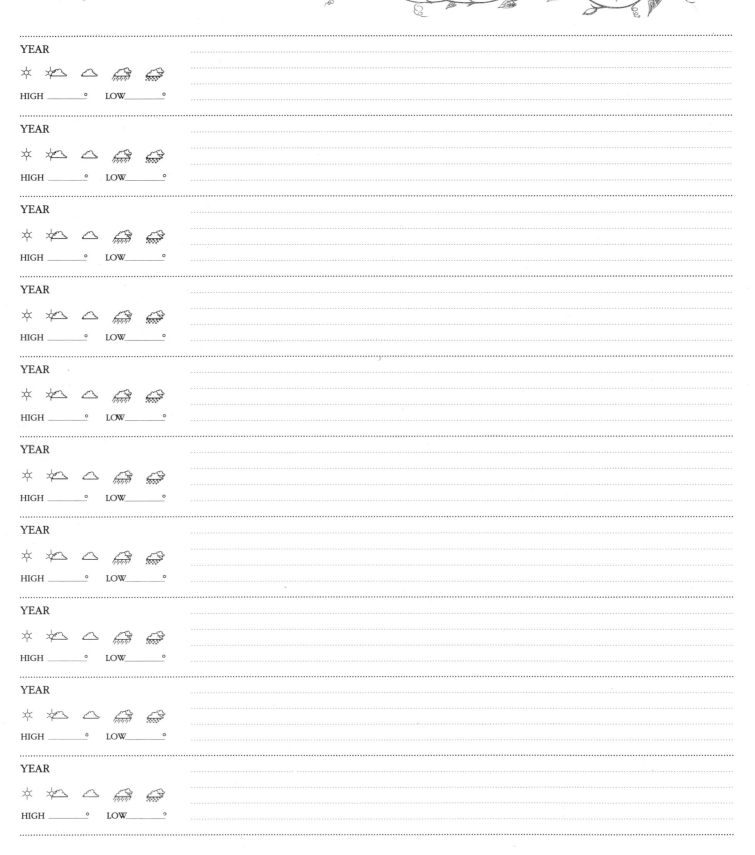

YEAR

HIGH ______° LOW ______°

YEAR

HIGH ______° LOW ______°

YEAR

HIGH ______° LOW ______°

YEAR

HIGH ______° LOW ______°

YEAR

HIGH ______° LOW ______°

YEAR

HIGH ______° LOW ______°

YEAR

HIGH ______° LOW ______°

YEAR

HIGH ______° LOW ______°

YEAR

HIGH ______° LOW ______°

YEAR

HIGH ______° LOW ______°

JULY 1

Juniperus chinensis "Fairview"

Fairview Juniper

YEAR

HIGH ______° LOW______°

YEAR

HIGH ______° LOW______°

YEAR

HIGH ______° LOW______°

YEAR

HIGH ______° LOW______°

YEAR

HIGH ______° LOW______°

YEAR

HIGH ______° LOW______°

YEAR

HIGH ______° LOW______°

YEAR

HIGH ______° LOW______°

YEAR

HIGH ______° LOW______°

YEAR

HIGH ______° LOW______°

JULY 2

Juniperus chinensis "Old Gold"

Old Gold Juniper

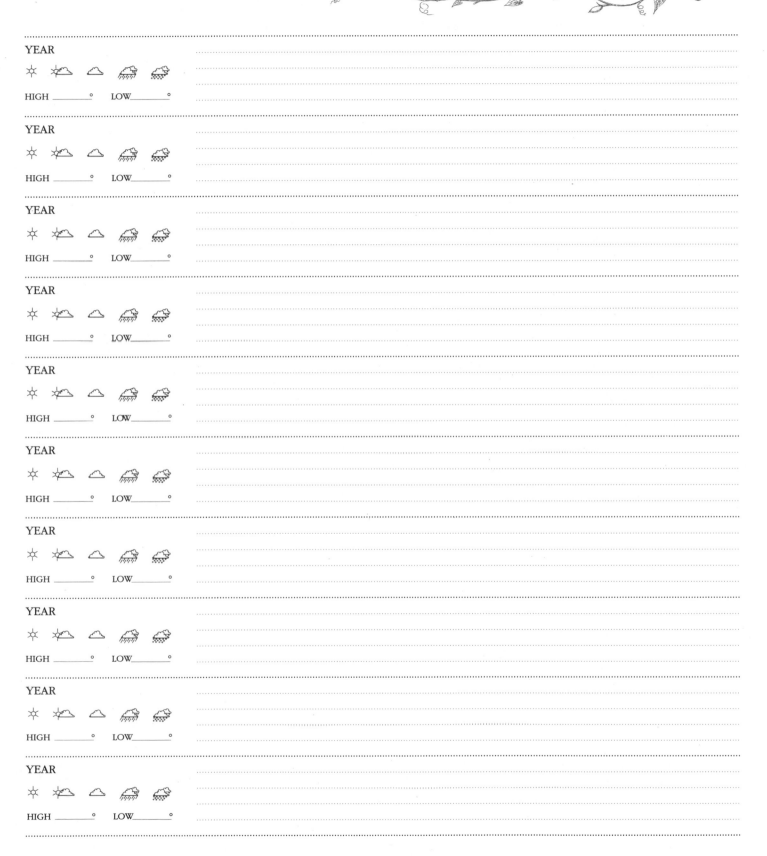

YEAR

HIGH ______° LOW______°

YEAR

HIGH ______° LOW______°

YEAR

HIGH ______° LOW______°

YEAR

HIGH ______° LOW______°

YEAR

HIGH ______° LOW______°

YEAR

HIGH ______° LOW______°

YEAR

HIGH ______° LOW______°

YEAR

HIGH ______° LOW______°

YEAR

HIGH ______° LOW______°

YEAR

HIGH ______° LOW______°

JULY 3

Juniperus chinensis "Blaauw"
Blaauw Juniper

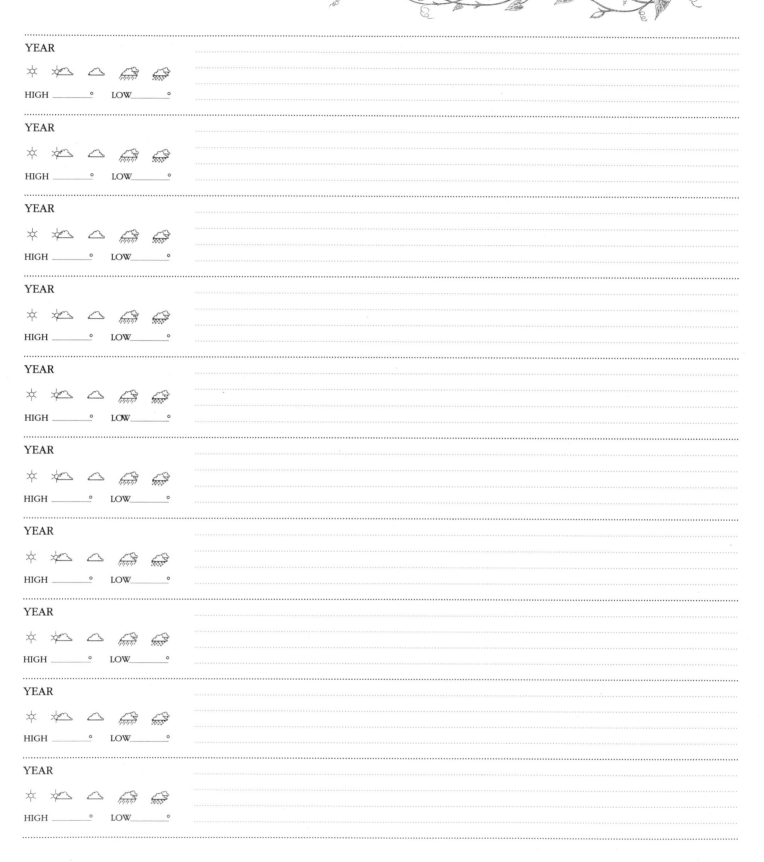

YEAR

HIGH ______° LOW______°

YEAR

HIGH ______° LOW______°

YEAR

HIGH ______° LOW______°

YEAR

HIGH ______° LOW______°

YEAR

HIGH ______° LOW______°

YEAR

HIGH ______° LOW______°

YEAR

HIGH ______° LOW______°

YEAR

HIGH ______° LOW______°

YEAR

HIGH ______° LOW______°

YEAR

HIGH ______° LOW______°

JULY 4

Juniperus chinensis "Mountbatten"

Mountbatten Juniper

YEAR

HIGH ________° LOW________°

YEAR

HIGH ________° LOW________°

YEAR

HIGH ________° LOW________°

YEAR

HIGH ________° LOW________°

YEAR

HIGH ________° LOW________°

YEAR

HIGH ________° LOW________°

YEAR

HIGH ________° LOW________°

YEAR

HIGH ________° LOW________°

YEAR

HIGH ________° LOW________°

YEAR

HIGH ________° LOW________°

JULY 5

Juniperus horizontalis "Plumosa"
Andorra Juniper

YEAR

HIGH ______° LOW______°

YEAR

HIGH ______° LOW______°

YEAR

HIGH ______° LOW______°

YEAR

HIGH ______° LOW______°

YEAR

HIGH ______° LOW______°

YEAR

HIGH ______° LOW______°

YEAR

HIGH ______° LOW______°

YEAR

HIGH ______° LOW______°

YEAR

HIGH ______° LOW______°

YEAR

HIGH ______° LOW______°

JULY 6

Juniperus sabina
Savin Juniper

YEAR

HIGH ________° LOW________°

YEAR

HIGH ________° LOW________°

YEAR

HIGH ________° LOW________°

YEAR

HIGH ________° LOW________°

YEAR

HIGH ________° LOW________°

YEAR

HIGH ________° LOW________°

YEAR

HIGH ________° LOW________°

YEAR

HIGH ________° LOW________°

YEAR

HIGH ________° LOW________°

YEAR

HIGH ________° LOW________°

JULY 7

Juniperus virginiana
Eastern Red Cedar

YEAR

HIGH ________° LOW________°

YEAR

HIGH ________° LOW________°

YEAR

HIGH ________° LOW________°

YEAR

HIGH ________° LOW________°

YEAR

HIGH ________° LOW________°

YEAR

HIGH ________° LOW________°

YEAR

HIGH ________° LOW________°

YEAR

HIGH ________° LOW________°

YEAR

HIGH ________° LOW________°

YEAR

HIGH ________° LOW________°

JULY 8

Juniperus scopulorum "Skyrocket"
Skyrocket Juniper

YEAR

HIGH ______° LOW ______°

YEAR

HIGH ______° LOW ______°

YEAR

HIGH ______° LOW ______°

YEAR

HIGH ______° LOW ______°

YEAR

HIGH ______° LOW ______°

YEAR

HIGH ______° LOW ______°

YEAR

HIGH ______° LOW ______°

YEAR

HIGH ______° LOW ______°

YEAR

HIGH ______° LOW ______°

YEAR

HIGH ______° LOW ______°

JULY 9

Juniperus chinensis "Hetzii"
Hetz Juniper

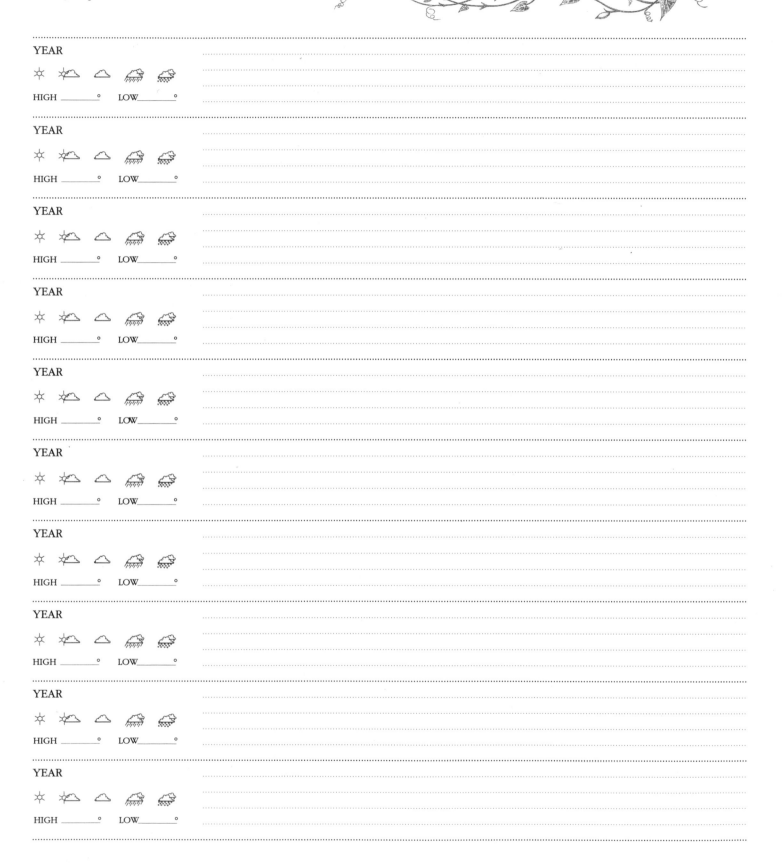

YEAR

HIGH ______° LOW ______°

YEAR

HIGH ______° LOW ______°

YEAR

HIGH ______° LOW ______°

YEAR

HIGH ______° LOW ______°

YEAR

HIGH ______° LOW ______°

YEAR

HIGH ______° LOW ______°

YEAR

HIGH ______° LOW ______°

YEAR

HIGH ______° LOW ______°

YEAR

HIGH ______° LOW ______°

YEAR

HIGH ______° LOW ______°

JULY 10

Kerria japonica
Japanese kerria

YEAR

HIGH ______° LOW ______°

YEAR

HIGH ______° LOW ______°

YEAR

HIGH ______° LOW ______°

YEAR

HIGH ______° LOW ______°

YEAR

HIGH ______° LOW ______°

YEAR

HIGH ______° LOW ______°

YEAR

HIGH ______° LOW ______°

YEAR

HIGH ______° LOW ______°

YEAR

HIGH ______° LOW ______°

YEAR

HIGH ______° LOW ______°

JULY 11

Kochia

Burning Bush (annual)

YEAR

HIGH ________° LOW________°

YEAR

HIGH ________° LOW________°

YEAR

HIGH ________° LOW________°

YEAR

HIGH ________° LOW________°

YEAR

HIGH ________° LOW________°

YEAR

HIGH ________° LOW________°

YEAR

HIGH ________° LOW________°

YEAR

HIGH ________° LOW________°

YEAR

HIGH ________° LOW________°

YEAR

HIGH ________° LOW________°

JULY 12

Kolkwitzia amabilis
Beautybush

YEAR

HIGH ______° LOW______°

YEAR

HIGH ______° LOW______°

YEAR

HIGH ______° LOW______°

YEAR

HIGH ______° LOW______°

YEAR

HIGH ______° LOW______°

YEAR

HIGH ______° LOW______°

YEAR

HIGH ______° LOW______°

YEAR

HIGH ______° LOW______°

YEAR

HIGH ______° LOW______°

YEAR

HIGH ______° LOW______°

JULY 13

Lactuca sativa

Lettuce

YEAR

HIGH ________° LOW________°

YEAR

HIGH ________° LOW________°

YEAR

HIGH ________° LOW________°

YEAR

HIGH ________° LOW________°

YEAR

HIGH ________° LOW________°

YEAR

HIGH ________° LOW________°

YEAR

HIGH ________° LOW________°

YEAR

HIGH ________° LOW________°

YEAR

HIGH ________° LOW________°

YEAR

HIGH ________° LOW________°

JULY 14

Larix laricina

American Larch or Tamarack

YEAR

HIGH ______° LOW ______°

YEAR

HIGH ______° LOW ______°

YEAR

HIGH ______° LOW ______°

YEAR

HIGH ______° LOW ______°

YEAR

HIGH ______° LOW ______°

YEAR

HIGH ______° LOW ______°

YEAR

HIGH ______° LOW ______°

YEAR

HIGH ______° LOW ______°

YEAR

HIGH ______° LOW ______°

YEAR

HIGH ______° LOW ______°

JULY 15

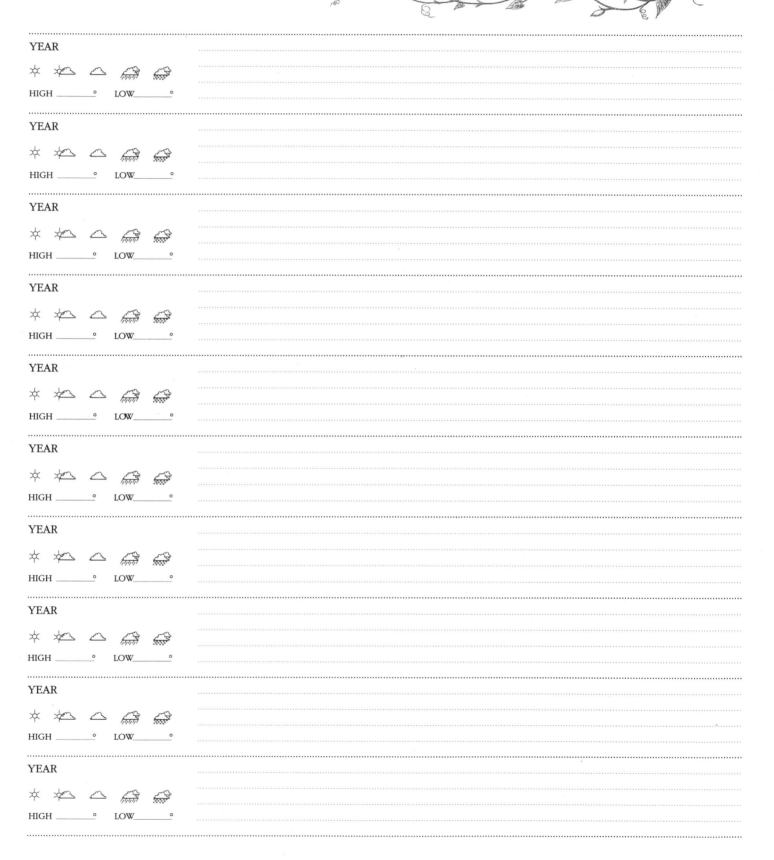

Lathyrus latifolius
Perennial Pea Vine

YEAR

HIGH ________° LOW________°

YEAR

HIGH ________° LOW________°

YEAR

HIGH ________° LOW________°

YEAR

HIGH ________° LOW________°

YEAR

HIGH ________° LOW________°

YEAR

HIGH ________° LOW________°

YEAR

HIGH ________° LOW________°

YEAR

HIGH ________° LOW________°

YEAR

HIGH ________° LOW________°

YEAR

HIGH ________° LOW________°

JULY 16

Laurus nobilis

Bay

YEAR

HIGH ________° LOW________°

YEAR

HIGH ________° LOW________°

YEAR

HIGH ________° LOW________°

YEAR

HIGH ________° LOW________°

YEAR

HIGH ________° LOW________°

YEAR

HIGH ________° LOW________°

YEAR

HIGH ________° LOW________°

YEAR

HIGH ________° LOW________°

YEAR

HIGH ________° LOW________°

YEAR

HIGH ________° LOW________°

JULY 17

Lavandula angustifolia
Lavender

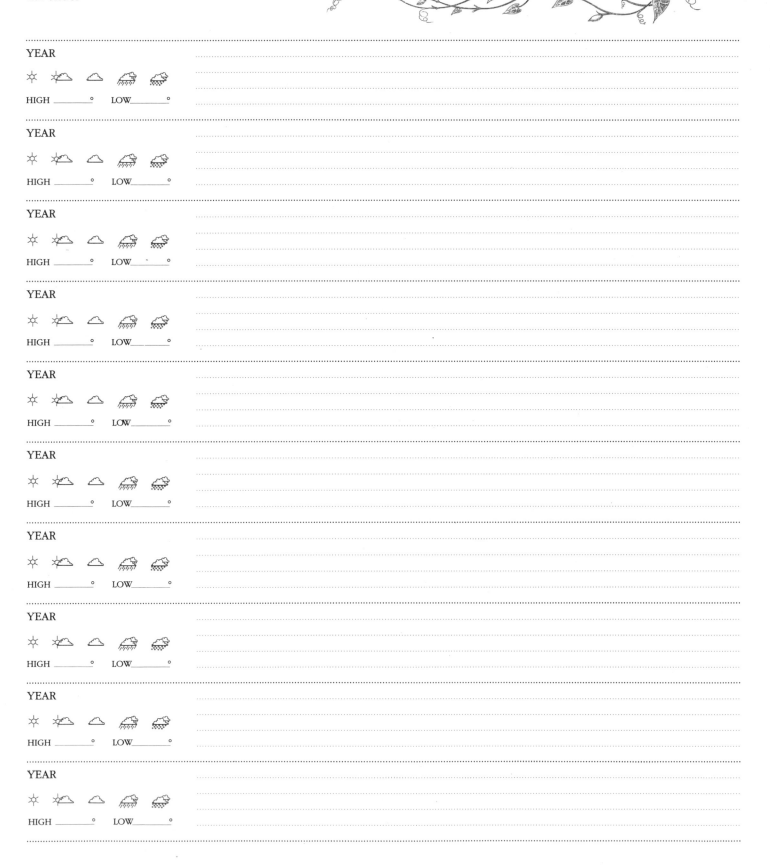

YEAR

HIGH ______° LOW______°

YEAR

HIGH ______° LOW______°

YEAR

HIGH ______° LOW______°

YEAR

HIGH ______° LOW______°

YEAR

HIGH ______° LOW______°

YEAR

HIGH ______° LOW______°

YEAR

HIGH ______° LOW______°

YEAR

HIGH ______° LOW______°

YEAR

HIGH ______° LOW______°

YEAR

HIGH ______° LOW______°

July 18

Lens culinaris

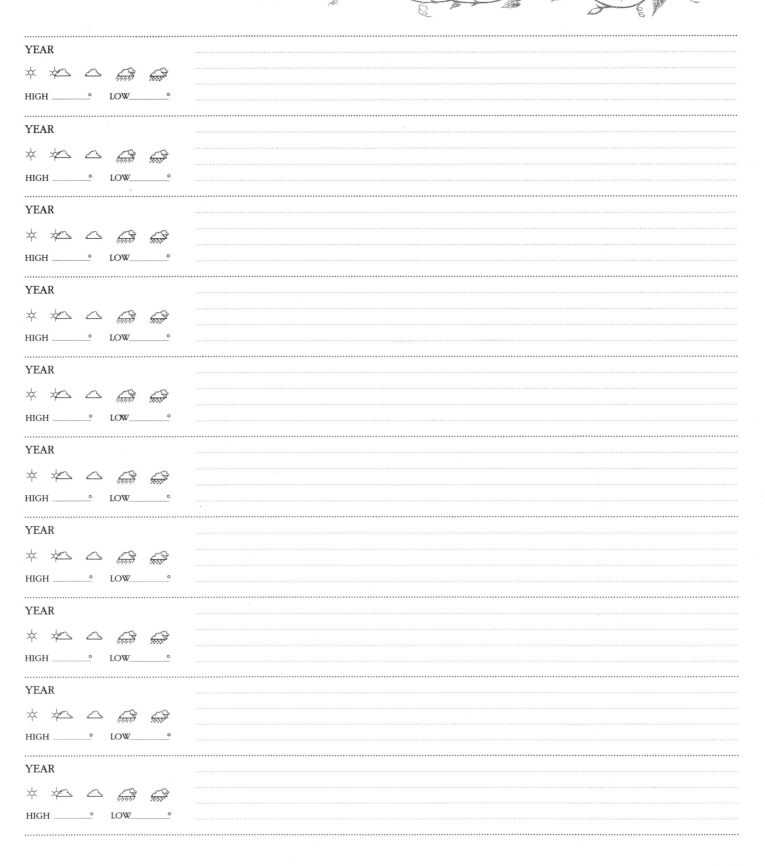

Lentil

YEAR

HIGH ______° LOW______°

YEAR

HIGH ______° LOW______°

YEAR

HIGH ______° LOW______°

YEAR

HIGH ______° LOW______°

YEAR

HIGH ______° LOW______°

YEAR

HIGH ______° LOW______°

YEAR

HIGH ______° LOW______°

YEAR

HIGH ______° LOW______°

YEAR

HIGH ______° LOW______°

YEAR

HIGH ______° LOW______°

July 19

Leontopodium alpinum
Edelweiss

YEAR

HIGH ________° LOW ________°

YEAR

HIGH ________° LOW ________°

YEAR

HIGH ________° LOW ________°

YEAR

HIGH ________° LOW ________°

YEAR

HIGH ________° LOW ________°

YEAR

HIGH ________° LOW ________°

YEAR

HIGH ________° LOW ________°

YEAR

HIGH ________° LOW ________°

YEAR

HIGH ________° LOW ________°

YEAR

HIGH ________° LOW ________°

JULY 20

Lepidium sativum

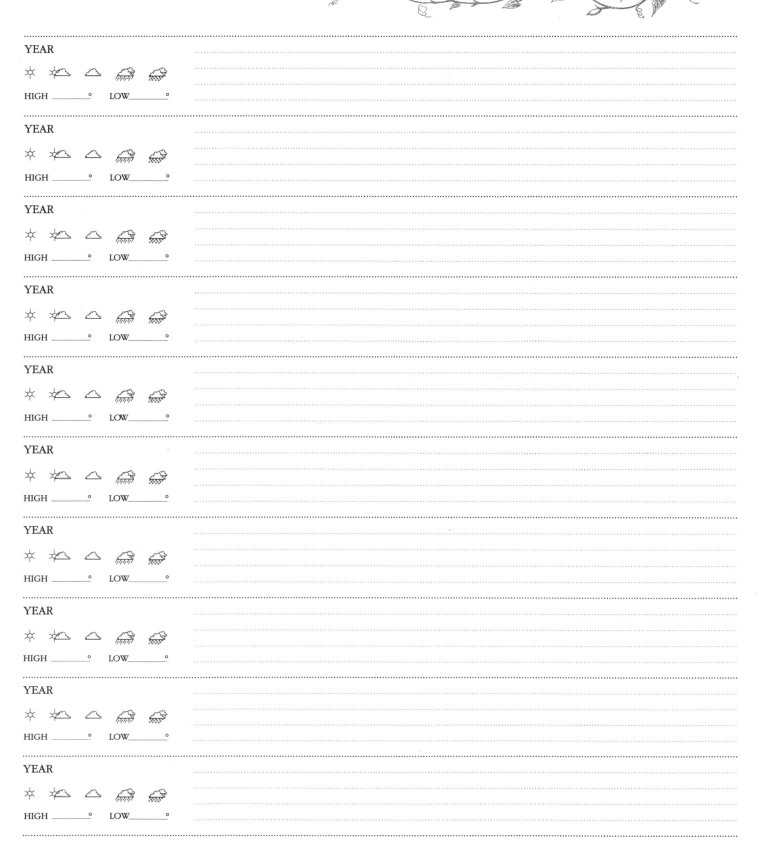

Cress

YEAR

HIGH ______° LOW______°

YEAR

HIGH ______° LOW______°

YEAR

HIGH ______° LOW______°

YEAR

HIGH ______° LOW______°

YEAR

HIGH ______° LOW______°

YEAR

HIGH ______° LOW______°

YEAR

HIGH ______° LOW______°

YEAR

HIGH ______° LOW______°

YEAR

HIGH ______° LOW______°

YEAR

HIGH ______° LOW______°

July 21

Levisticum officinale

Lovage

YEAR

HIGH ______° LOW ______°

YEAR

HIGH ______° LOW ______°

YEAR

HIGH ______° LOW ______°

YEAR

HIGH ______° LOW ______°

YEAR

HIGH ______° LOW ______°

YEAR

HIGH ______° LOW ______°

YEAR

HIGH ______° LOW ______°

YEAR

HIGH ______° LOW ______°

YEAR

HIGH ______° LOW ______°

YEAR

HIGH ______° LOW ______°

JULY 22

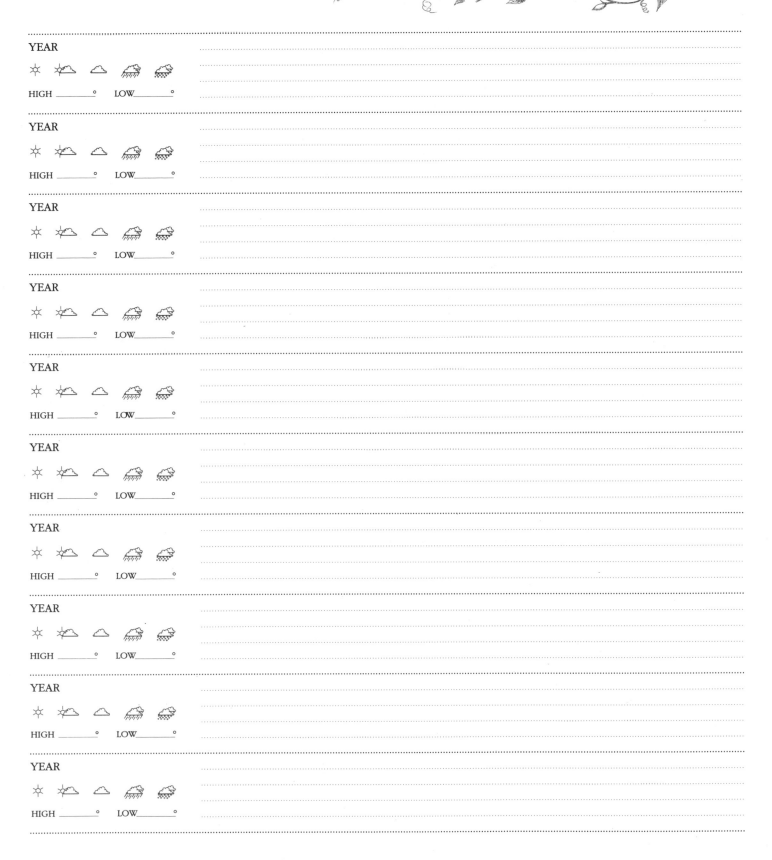

Liatris pycnostachya
Gayfeather

YEAR

HIGH ________° LOW________°

YEAR

HIGH ________° LOW________°

YEAR

HIGH ________° LOW________°

YEAR

HIGH ________° LOW________°

YEAR

HIGH ________° LOW________°

YEAR

HIGH ________° LOW________°

YEAR

HIGH ________° LOW________°

YEAR

HIGH ________° LOW________°

YEAR

HIGH ________° LOW________°

YEAR

HIGH ________° LOW________°

JULY 23

Ligustrum amurense
Amur privet

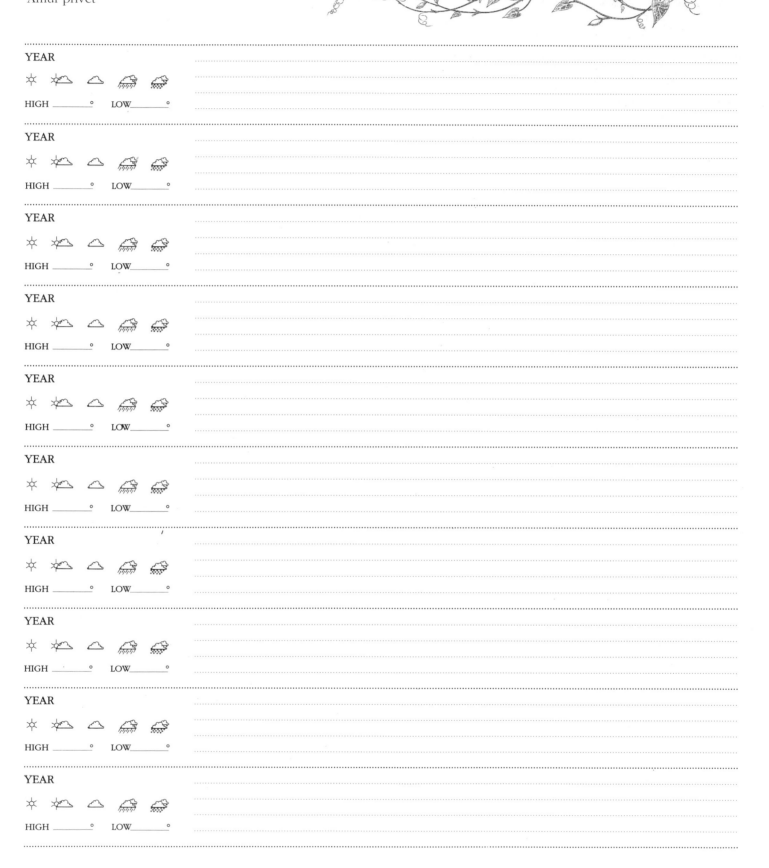

YEAR

HIGH ______° LOW______°

YEAR

HIGH ______° LOW______°

YEAR

HIGH ______° LOW______°

YEAR

HIGH ______° LOW______°

YEAR

HIGH ______° LOW______°

YEAR

HIGH ______° LOW______°

YEAR

HIGH ______° LOW______°

YEAR

HIGH ______° LOW______°

YEAR

HIGH ______° LOW______°

YEAR

HIGH ______° LOW______°

JULY 24

Lilium

Lily

YEAR

HIGH ____° LOW ____°

YEAR

HIGH ____° LOW ____°

YEAR

HIGH ____° LOW ____°

YEAR

HIGH ____° LOW ____°

YEAR

HIGH ____° LOW ____°

YEAR

HIGH ____° LOW ____°

YEAR

HIGH ____° LOW ____°

YEAR

HIGH ____° LOW ____°

YEAR

HIGH ____° LOW ____°

YEAR

HIGH ____° LOW ____°

JULY 25

Linum usitatissimum
Flax

YEAR

HIGH ________° LOW________°

YEAR

HIGH ________° LOW________°

YEAR

HIGH ________° LOW________°

YEAR

HIGH ________° LOW________°

YEAR

HIGH ________° LOW________°

YEAR

HIGH ________° LOW________°

YEAR

HIGH ________° LOW________°

YEAR

HIGH ________° LOW________°

YEAR

HIGH ________° LOW________°

YEAR

HIGH ________° LOW________°

JULY 26

Liriodendron tulipifera

Tulip Tree

YEAR

HIGH ________° LOW________°

YEAR

HIGH ________° LOW________°

YEAR

HIGH ________° LOW________°

YEAR

HIGH ________° LOW________°

YEAR

HIGH ________° LOW________°

YEAR

HIGH ________° LOW________°

YEAR

HIGH ________° LOW________°

YEAR

HIGH ________° LOW________°

YEAR

HIGH ________° LOW________°

YEAR

HIGH ________° LOW________°

JULY 27

Lobelia inflata
Lobelia

YEAR

HIGH ______° LOW______°

YEAR

HIGH ______° LOW______°

YEAR

HIGH ______° LOW______°

YEAR

HIGH ______° LOW______°

YEAR

HIGH ______° LOW______°

YEAR

HIGH ______° LOW______°

YEAR

HIGH ______° LOW______°

YEAR

HIGH ______° LOW______°

YEAR

HIGH ______° LOW______°

YEAR

HIGH ______° LOW______°

JULY 28

Lonicera x heckrottii
Goldflame Honeysuckle

YEAR

HIGH ______° LOW ______°

YEAR

HIGH ______° LOW ______°

YEAR

HIGH ______° LOW ______°

YEAR

HIGH ______° LOW ______°

YEAR

HIGH ______° LOW ______°

YEAR

HIGH ______° LOW ______°

YEAR

HIGH ______° LOW ______°

YEAR

HIGH ______° LOW ______°

YEAR

HIGH ______° LOW ______°

YEAR

HIGH ______° LOW ______°

JULY 29

Lonicera korolkowii zabelii
Zabel's Honeysuckle

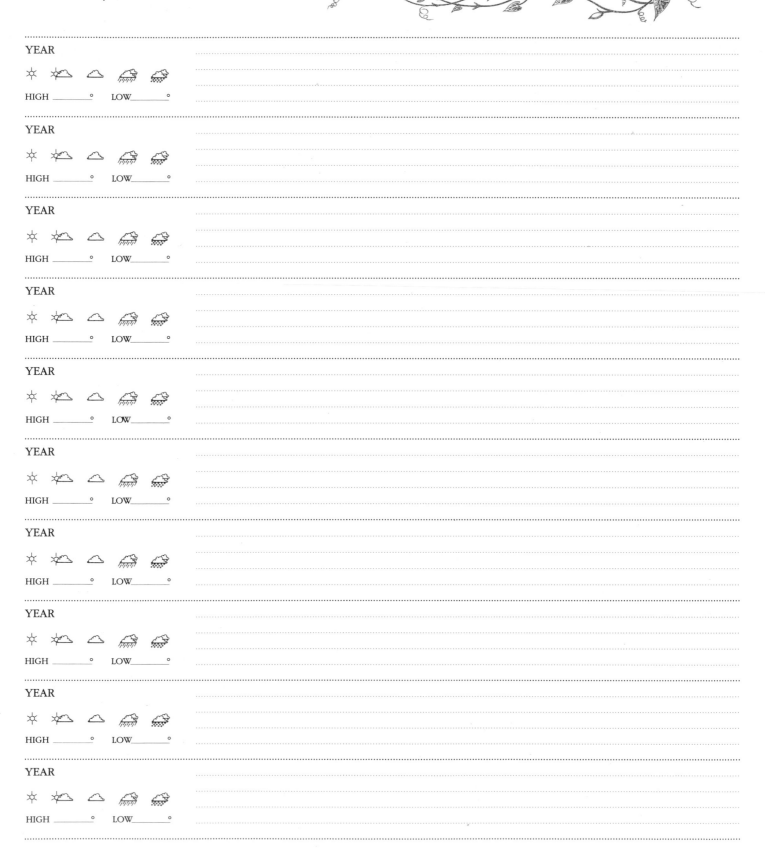

YEAR

HIGH ________° LOW ________°

YEAR

HIGH ________° LOW ________°

YEAR

HIGH ________° LOW ________°

YEAR

HIGH ________° LOW ________°

YEAR

HIGH ________° LOW ________°

YEAR

HIGH ________° LOW ________°

YEAR

HIGH ________° LOW ________°

YEAR

HIGH ________° LOW ________°

YEAR

HIGH ________° LOW ________°

YEAR

HIGH ________° LOW ________°

July 30

Lupinus
Lupine

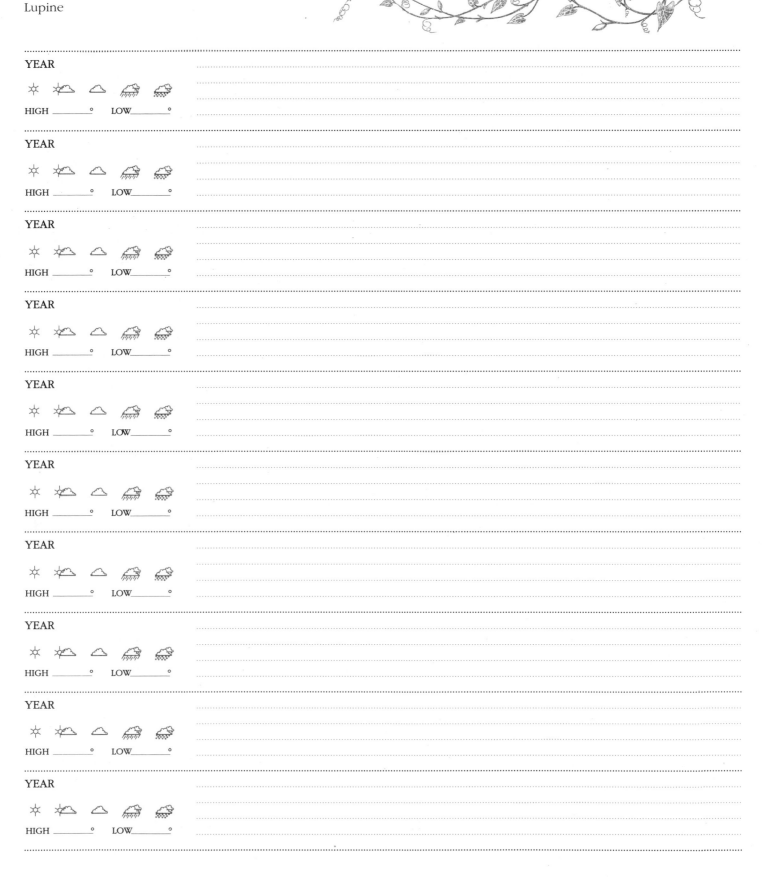

YEAR

HIGH ____° LOW____°

YEAR

HIGH ____° LOW____°

YEAR

HIGH ____° LOW____°

YEAR

HIGH ____° LOW____°

YEAR

HIGH ____° LOW____°

YEAR

HIGH ____° LOW____°

YEAR

HIGH ____° LOW____°

YEAR

HIGH ____° LOW____°

YEAR

HIGH ____° LOW____°

YEAR

HIGH ____° LOW____°

JULY 31

Lychnis chalcedonica
Maltese Cross

YEAR

HIGH ________° LOW________°

YEAR

HIGH ________° LOW________°

YEAR

HIGH ________° LOW________°

YEAR

HIGH ________° LOW________°

YEAR

HIGH ________° LOW________°

YEAR

HIGH ________° LOW________°

YEAR

HIGH ________° LOW________°

YEAR

HIGH ________° LOW________°

YEAR

HIGH ________° LOW________°

YEAR

HIGH ________° LOW________°

AUGUST 1

Lychnis viscaria
German Catchfly

YEAR

HIGH ______° LOW______°

YEAR

HIGH ______° LOW______°

YEAR

HIGH ______° LOW______°

YEAR

HIGH ______° LOW______°

YEAR

HIGH ______° LOW______°

YEAR

HIGH ______° LOW______°

YEAR

HIGH ______° LOW______°

YEAR

HIGH ______° LOW______°

YEAR

HIGH ______° LOW______°

YEAR

HIGH ______° LOW______°

AUGUST 2

Lycopersicon esculentum
Tomato

YEAR

HIGH ______° LOW ______°

YEAR

HIGH ______° LOW ______°

YEAR

HIGH ______° LOW ______°

YEAR

HIGH ______° LOW ______°

YEAR

HIGH ______° LOW ______°

YEAR

HIGH ______° LOW ______°

YEAR

HIGH ______° LOW ______°

YEAR

HIGH ______° LOW ______°

YEAR

HIGH ______° LOW ______°

YEAR

HIGH ______° LOW ______°

AUGUST 3

Lythrum salicaria
Purple Loosestrife

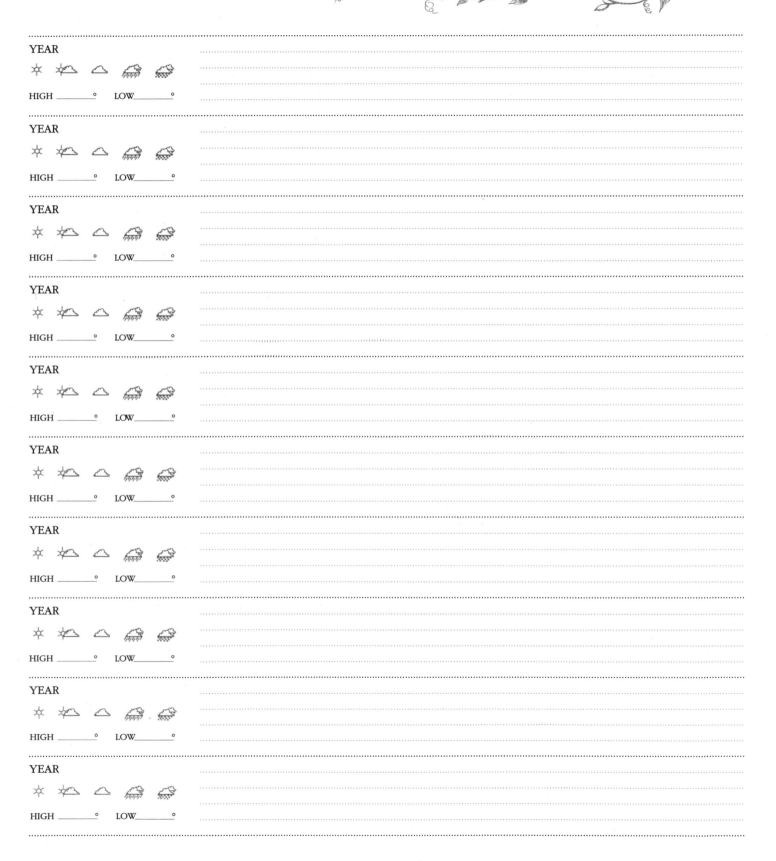

YEAR

HIGH ________° LOW________°

YEAR

HIGH ________° LOW________°

YEAR

HIGH ________° LOW________°

YEAR

HIGH ________° LOW________°

YEAR

HIGH ________° LOW________°

YEAR

HIGH ________° LOW________°

YEAR

HIGH ________° LOW________°

YEAR

HIGH ________° LOW________°

YEAR

HIGH ________° LOW________°

YEAR

HIGH ________° LOW________°

AUGUST 4

Magnolia soulangiana
Saucer Magnolia

YEAR

HIGH ________° LOW________°

YEAR

HIGH ________° LOW________°

YEAR

HIGH ________° LOW________°

YEAR

HIGH ________° LOW________°

YEAR

HIGH ________° LOW________°

YEAR

HIGH ________° LOW________°

YEAR

HIGH ________° LOW________°

YEAR

HIGH ________° LOW________°

YEAR

HIGH ________° LOW________°

YEAR

HIGH ________° LOW________°

AUGUST 5

Mahonia aquifolium
Oregon Grape

YEAR

HIGH ______° LOW______°

YEAR

HIGH ______° LOW______°

YEAR

HIGH ______° LOW______°

YEAR

HIGH ______° LOW______°

YEAR

HIGH ______° LOW______°

YEAR

HIGH ______° LOW______°

YEAR

HIGH ______° LOW______°

YEAR

HIGH ______° LOW______°

YEAR

HIGH ______° LOW______°

YEAR

HIGH ______° LOW______°

AUGUST 6

Malus
Apples

YEAR

HIGH ______° LOW______°

YEAR

HIGH ______° LOW______°

YEAR

HIGH ______° LOW______°

YEAR

HIGH ______° LOW______°

YEAR

HIGH ______° LOW______°

YEAR

HIGH ______° LOW______°

YEAR

HIGH ______° LOW______°

YEAR

HIGH ______° LOW______°

YEAR

HIGH ______° LOW______°

YEAR

HIGH ______° LOW______°

AUGUST 7

Magnolia kobus
Star Magnolia

YEAR

HIGH ______° LOW ______°

YEAR

HIGH ______° LOW ______°

YEAR

HIGH ______° LOW ______°

YEAR

HIGH ______° LOW ______°

YEAR

HIGH ______° LOW ______°

YEAR

HIGH ______° LOW ______°

YEAR

HIGH ______° LOW ______°

YEAR

HIGH ______° LOW ______°

YEAR

HIGH ______° LOW ______°

YEAR

HIGH ______° LOW ______°

AUGUST 8

Marrubium vulgare
Horehound

YEAR

HIGH ______° LOW ______°

YEAR

HIGH ______° LOW ______°

YEAR

HIGH ______° LOW ______°

YEAR

HIGH ______° LOW ______°

YEAR

HIGH ______° LOW ______°

YEAR

HIGH ______° LOW ______°

YEAR

HIGH ______° LOW ______°

YEAR

HIGH ______° LOW ______°

YEAR

HIGH ______° LOW ______°

YEAR

HIGH ______° LOW ______°

August 9

Melissa officinalis

Lemon Balm

YEAR

HIGH ______° LOW ______°

YEAR

HIGH ______° LOW ______°

YEAR

HIGH ______° LOW ______°

YEAR

HIGH ______° LOW ______°

YEAR

HIGH ______° LOW ______°

YEAR

HIGH ______° LOW ______°

YEAR

HIGH ______° LOW ______°

YEAR

HIGH ______° LOW ______°

YEAR

HIGH ______° LOW ______°

YEAR

HIGH ______° LOW ______°

AUGUST 10

Mentha spicata
Spearmint

YEAR

HIGH ______° LOW______°

YEAR

HIGH ______° LOW______°

YEAR

HIGH ______° LOW______°

YEAR

HIGH ______° LOW______°

YEAR

HIGH ______° LOW______°

YEAR

HIGH ______° LOW______°

YEAR

HIGH ______° LOW______°

YEAR

HIGH ______° LOW______°

YEAR

HIGH ______° LOW______°

YEAR

HIGH ______° LOW______°

August 11

Mentha pulegium

European Pennyroyal

YEAR

HIGH ______° LOW______°

YEAR

HIGH ______° LOW______°

YEAR

HIGH ______° LOW______°

YEAR

HIGH ______° LOW______°

YEAR

HIGH ______° LOW______°

YEAR

HIGH ______° LOW______°

YEAR

HIGH ______° LOW______°

YEAR

HIGH ______° LOW______°

YEAR

HIGH ______° LOW______°

YEAR

HIGH ______° LOW______°

AUGUST 12

Monarda didyma
Bee Balm

YEAR

HIGH ________° LOW________°

YEAR

HIGH ________° LOW________°

YEAR

HIGH ________° LOW________°

YEAR

HIGH ________° LOW________°

YEAR

HIGH ________° LOW________°

YEAR

HIGH ________° LOW________°

YEAR

HIGH ________° LOW________°

YEAR

HIGH ________° LOW________°

YEAR

HIGH ________° LOW________°

YEAR

HIGH ________° LOW________°

AUGUST 13

Morus alba "Pendula"

Weeping Mulberry

YEAR

HIGH ______° LOW ______°

YEAR

HIGH ______° LOW ______°

YEAR

HIGH ______° LOW ______°

YEAR

HIGH ______° LOW ______°

YEAR

HIGH ______° LOW ______°

YEAR

HIGH ______° LOW ______°

YEAR

HIGH ______° LOW ______°

YEAR

HIGH ______° LOW ______°

YEAR

HIGH ______° LOW ______°

YEAR

HIGH ______° LOW ______°

AUGUST 14

Myosotis sylvatica
Forget-me-not

YEAR

HIGH ______° LOW______°

YEAR

HIGH ______° LOW______°

YEAR

HIGH ______° LOW______°

YEAR

HIGH ______° LOW______°

YEAR

HIGH ______° LOW______°

YEAR

HIGH ______° LOW______°

YEAR

HIGH ______° LOW______°

YEAR

HIGH ______° LOW______°

YEAR

HIGH ______° LOW______°

YEAR

HIGH ______° LOW______°

AUGUST 15

Myrica cerifera

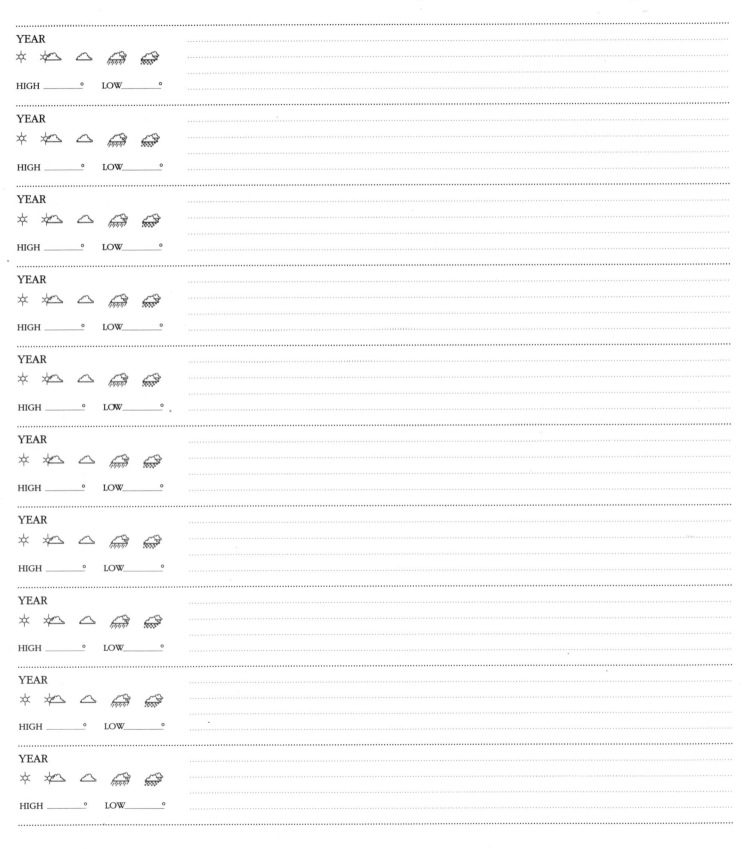

Bayberry

YEAR

HIGH ______° LOW______°

YEAR

HIGH ______° LOW______°

YEAR

HIGH ______° LOW______°

YEAR

HIGH ______° LOW______°

YEAR

HIGH ______° LOW______°

YEAR

HIGH ______° LOW______°

YEAR

HIGH ______° LOW______°

YEAR

HIGH ______° LOW______°

YEAR

HIGH ______° LOW______°

YEAR

HIGH ______° LOW______°

AUGUST 16

Myrrhis odorata
Sweet Cicely

YEAR

HIGH ________° LOW________°

YEAR

HIGH ________° LOW________°

YEAR

HIGH ________° LOW________°

YEAR

HIGH ________° LOW________°

YEAR

HIGH ________° LOW________°

YEAR

HIGH ________° LOW________°

YEAR

HIGH ________° LOW________°

YEAR

HIGH ________° LOW________°

YEAR

HIGH ________° LOW________°

YEAR

HIGH ________° LOW________°

AUGUST 17

Myrtus communis
Myrtle

YEAR

HIGH ______° LOW______°

YEAR

HIGH ______° LOW______°

YEAR

HIGH ______° LOW______°

YEAR

HIGH ______° LOW______°

YEAR

HIGH ______° LOW______°

YEAR

HIGH ______° LOW______°

YEAR

HIGH ______° LOW______°

YEAR

HIGH ______° LOW______°

YEAR

HIGH ______° LOW______°

YEAR

HIGH ______° LOW______°

AUGUST 18

Nasturtium officinale

Water Cress

YEAR

HIGH ______° LOW ______°

YEAR

HIGH ______° LOW ______°

YEAR

HIGH ______° LOW ______°

YEAR

HIGH ______° LOW ______°

YEAR

HIGH ______° LOW ______°

YEAR

HIGH ______° LOW ______°

YEAR

HIGH ______° LOW ______°

YEAR

HIGH ______° LOW ______°

YEAR

HIGH ______° LOW ______°

YEAR

HIGH ______° LOW ______°

AUGUST 19

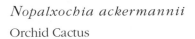

Nopalxochia ackermannii
Orchid Cactus

YEAR

HIGH _______° LOW_______°

YEAR

HIGH _______° LOW_______°

YEAR

HIGH _______° LOW_______°

YEAR

HIGH _______° LOW_______°

YEAR

HIGH _______° LOW_______°

YEAR

HIGH _______° LOW_______°

YEAR

HIGH _______° LOW_______°

YEAR

HIGH _______° LOW_______°

YEAR

HIGH _______° LOW_______°

YEAR

HIGH _______° LOW_______°

AUGUST 20

Nepeta cataria
Catnip

YEAR

HIGH ______° LOW______°

YEAR

HIGH ______° LOW______°

YEAR

HIGH ______° LOW______°

YEAR

HIGH ______° LOW______°

YEAR

HIGH ______° LOW______°

YEAR

HIGH ______° LOW______°

YEAR

HIGH ______° LOW______°

YEAR

HIGH ______° LOW______°

YEAR

HIGH ______° LOW______°

YEAR

HIGH ______° LOW______°

AUGUST 21

Ocimum basilicum

Sweet Basil

YEAR

HIGH ______° LOW ______°

YEAR

HIGH ______° LOW ______°

YEAR

HIGH ______° LOW ______°

YEAR

HIGH ______° LOW ______°

YEAR

HIGH ______° LOW ______°

YEAR

HIGH ______° LOW ______°

YEAR

HIGH ______° LOW ______°

YEAR

HIGH ______° LOW ______°

YEAR

HIGH ______° LOW ______°

YEAR

HIGH ______° LOW ______°

AUGUST 22

Oenothera biennis
Evening Primrose

YEAR

HIGH ________° LOW________°

YEAR

HIGH ________° LOW________°

YEAR

HIGH ________° LOW________°

YEAR

HIGH ________° LOW________°

YEAR

HIGH ________° LOW________°

YEAR

HIGH ________° LOW________°

YEAR

HIGH ________° LOW________°

YEAR

HIGH ________° LOW________°

YEAR

HIGH ________° LOW________°

YEAR

HIGH ________° LOW________°

AUGUST 23

Origanum majorana

Marjoram

YEAR

HIGH ________° LOW________°

YEAR

HIGH ________° LOW________°

YEAR

HIGH ________° LOW________°

YEAR

HIGH ________° LOW________°

YEAR

HIGH ________° LOW________°

YEAR

HIGH ________° LOW________°

YEAR

HIGH ________° LOW________°

YEAR

HIGH ________° LOW________°

YEAR

HIGH ________° LOW________°

YEAR

HIGH ________° LOW________°

AUGUST 24

Origanum vulgare
Oregano

YEAR

HIGH ________° LOW________°

YEAR

HIGH ________° LOW________°

YEAR

HIGH ________° LOW________°

YEAR

HIGH ________° LOW________°

YEAR

HIGH ________° LOW________°

YEAR

HIGH ________° LOW________°

YEAR

HIGH ________° LOW________°

YEAR

HIGH ________° LOW________°

YEAR

HIGH ________° LOW________°

YEAR

HIGH ________° LOW________°

AUGUST 25

Paxistima canbyi
Canby Pachistima

YEAR

HIGH ________° LOW________°

YEAR

HIGH ________° LOW________°

YEAR

HIGH ________° LOW________°

YEAR

HIGH ________° LOW________°

YEAR

HIGH ________° LOW________°

YEAR

HIGH ________° LOW________°

YEAR

HIGH ________° LOW________°

YEAR

HIGH ________° LOW________°

YEAR

HIGH ________° LOW________°

YEAR

HIGH ________° LOW________°

AUGUST 26

Pachysandra terminalis

Japanese Spurge

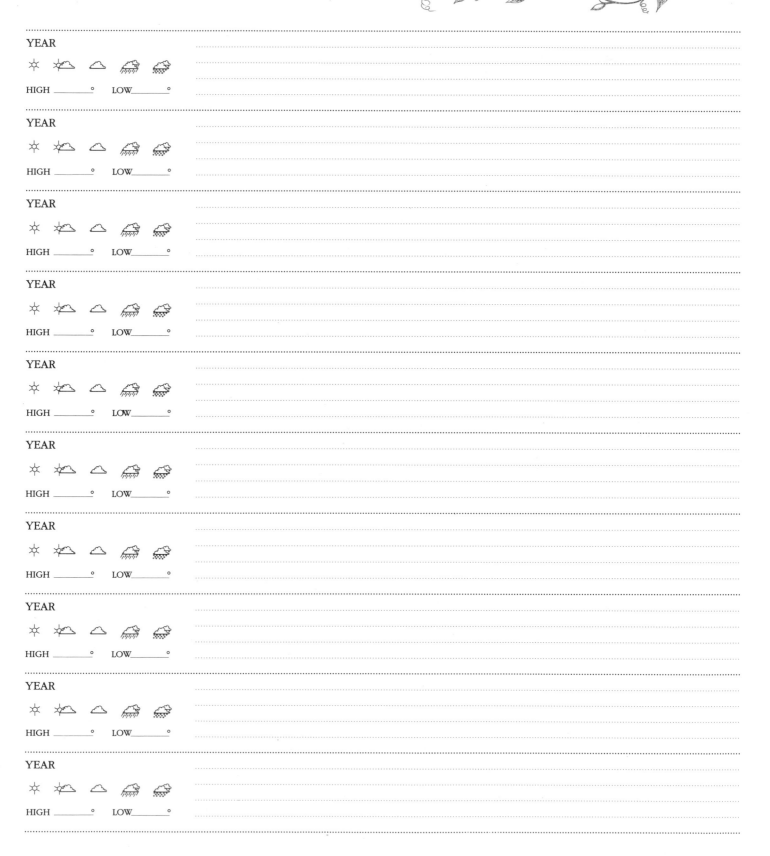

YEAR

HIGH ______° LOW______°

YEAR

HIGH ______° LOW______°

YEAR

HIGH ______° LOW______°

YEAR

HIGH ______° LOW______°

YEAR

HIGH ______° LOW______°

YEAR

HIGH ______° LOW______°

YEAR

HIGH ______° LOW______°

YEAR

HIGH ______° LOW______°

YEAR

HIGH ______° LOW______°

YEAR

HIGH ______° LOW______°

AUGUST 27

Paeonia lactiflora
Chinese Peony

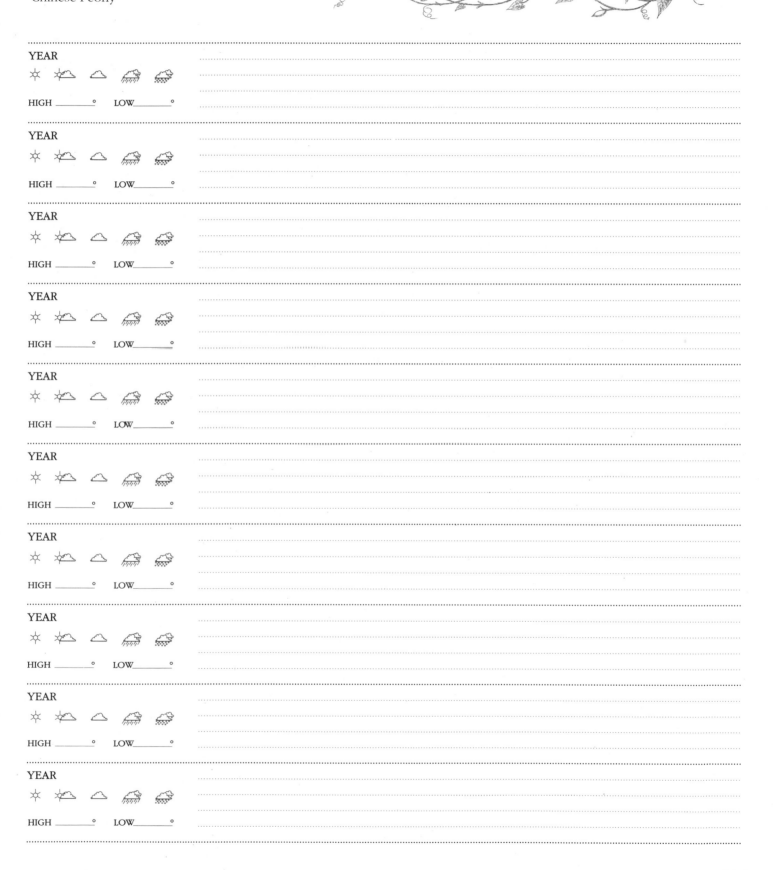

YEAR

HIGH ________° LOW ________°

YEAR

HIGH ________° LOW ________°

YEAR

HIGH ________° LOW ________°

YEAR

HIGH ________° LOW ________°

YEAR

HIGH ________° LOW ________°

YEAR

HIGH ________° LOW ________°

YEAR

HIGH ________° LOW ________°

YEAR

HIGH ________° LOW ________°

YEAR

HIGH ________° LOW ________°

YEAR

HIGH ________° LOW ________°

AUGUST 28

Panax quinquefolius
Ginseng

YEAR

HIGH ______° LOW______°

YEAR

HIGH ______° LOW______°

YEAR

HIGH ______° LOW______°

YEAR

HIGH ______° LOW______°

YEAR

HIGH ______° LOW______°

YEAR

HIGH ______° LOW______°

YEAR

HIGH ______° LOW______°

YEAR

HIGH ______° LOW______°

YEAR

HIGH ______° LOW______°

YEAR

HIGH ______° LOW______°

AUGUST 29

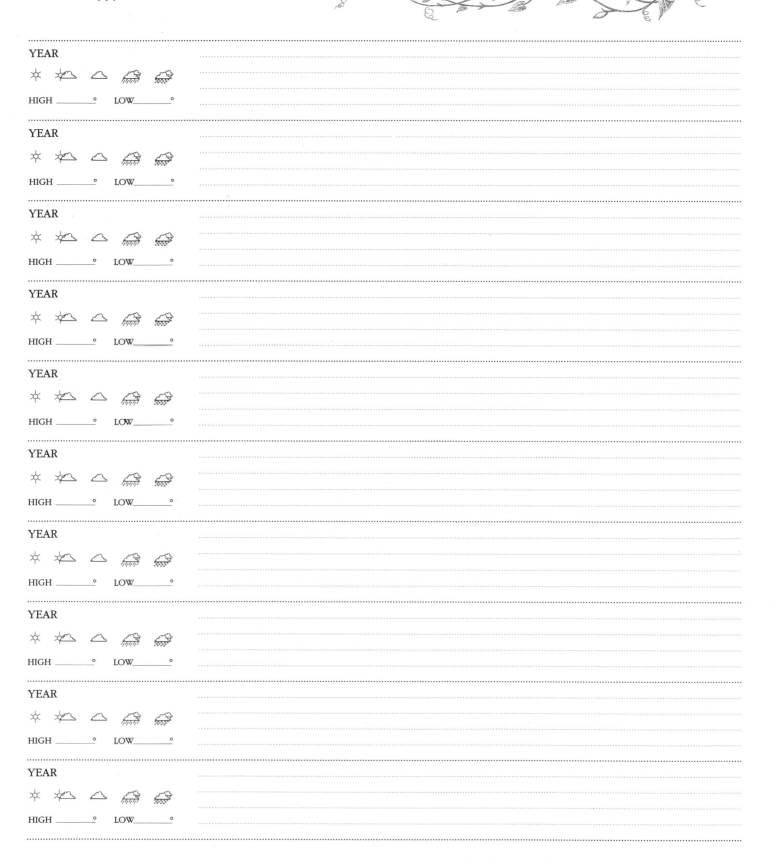

Papaver orientale
Oriental Poppy

YEAR
HIGH ____° LOW____°

YEAR
HIGH ____° LOW____°

YEAR
HIGH ____° LOW____°

YEAR
HIGH ____° LOW____°

YEAR
HIGH ____° LOW____°

YEAR
HIGH ____° LOW____°

YEAR
HIGH ____° LOW____°

YEAR
HIGH ____° LOW____°

YEAR
HIGH ____° LOW____°

YEAR
HIGH ____° LOW____°

AUGUST 30

Parthenocissus quinquefolia
Virginia Creeper

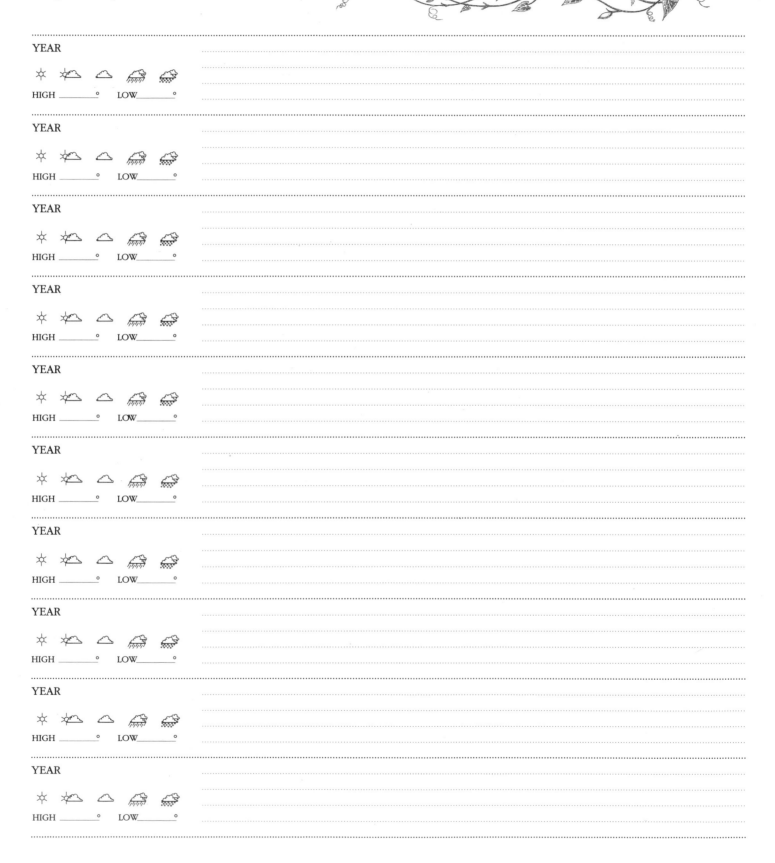

YEAR

HIGH ______° LOW ______°

YEAR

HIGH ______° LOW ______°

YEAR

HIGH ______° LOW ______°

YEAR

HIGH ______° LOW ______°

YEAR

HIGH ______° LOW ______°

YEAR

HIGH ______° LOW ______°

YEAR

HIGH ______° LOW ______°

YEAR

HIGH ______° LOW ______°

YEAR

HIGH ______° LOW ______°

YEAR

HIGH ______° LOW ______°

AUGUST 31

Parthenocissus tricuspidata "Veitchii"
Boston Ivy

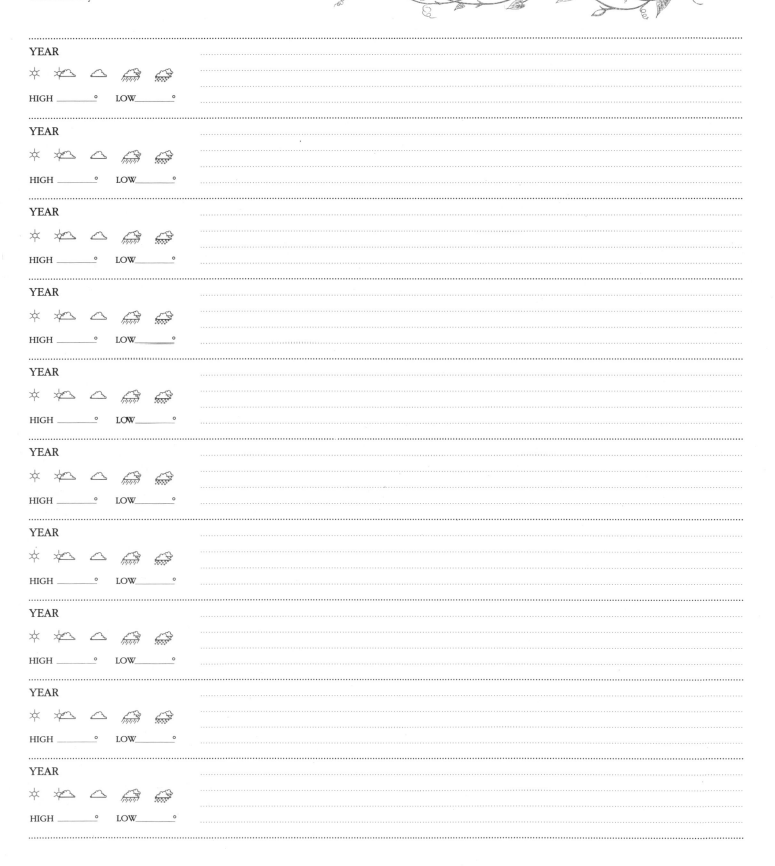

YEAR
HIGH ______° LOW ______°

YEAR
HIGH ______° LOW ______°

YEAR
HIGH ______° LOW ______°

YEAR
HIGH ______° LOW ______°

YEAR
HIGH ______° LOW ______°

YEAR
HIGH ______° LOW ______°

YEAR
HIGH ______° LOW ______°

YEAR
HIGH ______° LOW ______°

YEAR
HIGH ______° LOW ______°

YEAR
HIGH ______° LOW ______°

SEPTEMBER 1

Pastinaca sativa
Parsnip

YEAR

HIGH ________° LOW________°

YEAR

HIGH ________° LOW________°

YEAR

HIGH ________° LOW________°

YEAR

HIGH ________° LOW________°

YEAR

HIGH ________° LOW________°

YEAR

HIGH ________° LOW________°

YEAR

HIGH ________° LOW________°

YEAR

HIGH ________° LOW________°

YEAR

HIGH ________° LOW________°

YEAR

HIGH ________° LOW________°

SEPTEMBER 2

Petroselinum crispum
Parsley

YEAR

HIGH _______° LOW_______°

YEAR

HIGH _______° LOW_______°

YEAR

HIGH _______° LOW_______°

YEAR

HIGH _______° LOW_______°

YEAR

HIGH _______° LOW_______°

YEAR

HIGH _______° LOW_______°

YEAR

HIGH _______° LOW_______°

YEAR

HIGH _______° LOW_______°

YEAR

HIGH _______° LOW_______°

YEAR

HIGH _______° LOW_______°

SEPTEMBER 3

Phaseolus vulgaris
Bush Snap Bean

YEAR

HIGH ________° LOW ________°

YEAR

HIGH ________° LOW ________°

YEAR

HIGH ________° LOW ________°

YEAR

HIGH ________° LOW ________°

YEAR

HIGH ________° LOW ________°

YEAR

HIGH ________° LOW ________°

YEAR

HIGH ________° LOW ________°

YEAR

HIGH ________° LOW ________°

YEAR

HIGH ________° LOW ________°

YEAR

HIGH ________° LOW ________°

SEPTEMBER 4

Phaseolus coccineus
Scarlet Runner Bean

YEAR

HIGH ______° LOW______°

YEAR

HIGH ______° LOW______°

YEAR

HIGH ______° LOW______°

YEAR

HIGH ______° LOW______°

YEAR

HIGH ______° LOW______°

YEAR

HIGH ______° LOW______°

YEAR

HIGH ______° LOW______°

YEAR

HIGH ______° LOW______°

YEAR

HIGH ______° LOW______°

YEAR

HIGH ______° LOW______°

SEPTEMBER 5

Phaseolus lunatus
Lima Bean

YEAR

HIGH ______° LOW______°

YEAR

HIGH ______° LOW______°

YEAR

HIGH ______° LOW______°

YEAR

HIGH ______° LOW______°

YEAR

HIGH ______° LOW______°

YEAR

HIGH ______° LOW______°

YEAR

HIGH ______° LOW______°

YEAR

HIGH ______° LOW______°

YEAR

HIGH ______° LOW______°

YEAR

HIGH ______° LOW______°

SEPTEMBER 6

Philadelphus coronarius "Aureus"
Golden Mock Orange

YEAR

HIGH ______° LOW______°

YEAR

HIGH ______° LOW______°

YEAR

HIGH ______° LOW______°

YEAR

HIGH ______° LOW______°

YEAR

HIGH ______° LOW______°

YEAR

HIGH ______° LOW______°

YEAR

HIGH ______° LOW______°

YEAR

HIGH ______° LOW______°

YEAR

HIGH ______° LOW______°

YEAR

HIGH ______° LOW______°

SEPTEMBER 7

Philadelphus virginalis
Double Mock Orange

YEAR

HIGH ______° LOW______°

YEAR

HIGH ______° LOW______°

YEAR

HIGH ______° LOW______°

YEAR

HIGH ______° LOW______°

YEAR

HIGH ______° LOW______°

YEAR

HIGH ______° LOW______°

YEAR

HIGH ______° LOW______°

YEAR

HIGH ______° LOW______°

YEAR

HIGH ______° LOW______°

YEAR

HIGH ______° LOW______°

SEPTEMBER 8

Phlox subulata
Moss Pink

YEAR

HIGH ______° LOW______°

YEAR

HIGH ______° LOW______°

YEAR

HIGH ______° LOW______°

YEAR

HIGH ______° LOW______°

YEAR

HIGH ______° LOW______°

YEAR

HIGH ______° LOW______°

YEAR

HIGH ______° LOW______°

YEAR

HIGH ______° LOW______°

YEAR

HIGH ______° LOW______°

YEAR

HIGH ______° LOW______°

SEPTEMBER 9

Physalis pruinosa
Ground Cherry

YEAR

HIGH ______° LOW______°

YEAR

HIGH ______° LOW______°

YEAR

HIGH ______° LOW______°

YEAR

HIGH ______° LOW______°

YEAR

HIGH ______° LOW______°

YEAR

HIGH ______° LOW______°

YEAR

HIGH ______° LOW______°

YEAR

HIGH ______° LOW______°

YEAR

HIGH ______° LOW______°

YEAR

HIGH ______° LOW______°

SEPTEMBER 10

Physostegia virginiana
False Dragonhead

YEAR

HIGH ____° LOW____°

YEAR

HIGH ____° LOW____°

YEAR

HIGH ____° LOW____°

YEAR

HIGH ____° LOW____°

YEAR

HIGH ____° LOW____°

YEAR

HIGH ____° LOW____°

YEAR

HIGH ____° LOW____°

YEAR

HIGH ____° LOW____°

YEAR

HIGH ____° LOW____°

YEAR

HIGH ____° LOW____°

SEPTEMBER 11

Phytolacca americana
Pokeweed

YEAR

HIGH ________° LOW________°

YEAR

HIGH ________° LOW________°

YEAR

HIGH ________° LOW________°

YEAR

HIGH ________° LOW________°

YEAR

HIGH ________° LOW________°

YEAR

HIGH ________° LOW________°

YEAR

HIGH ________° LOW________°

YEAR

HIGH ________° LOW________°

YEAR

HIGH ________° LOW________°

YEAR

HIGH ________° LOW________°

SEPTEMBER 12

Picea pungens glauca
Blue Spruce

YEAR

HIGH ______° LOW ______°

YEAR

HIGH ______° LOW ______°

YEAR

HIGH ______° LOW ______°

YEAR

HIGH ______° LOW ______°

YEAR

HIGH ______° LOW ______°

YEAR

HIGH ______° LOW ______°

YEAR

HIGH ______° LOW ______°

YEAR

HIGH ______° LOW ______°

YEAR

HIGH ______° LOW ______°

YEAR

HIGH ______° LOW ______°

SEPTEMBER 13

Picea abies

Norway Spruce

YEAR

HIGH ________° LOW________°

YEAR

HIGH ________° LOW________°

YEAR

HIGH ________° LOW________°

YEAR

HIGH ________° LOW________°

YEAR

HIGH ________° LOW________°

YEAR

HIGH ________° LOW________°

YEAR

HIGH ________° LOW________°

YEAR

HIGH ________° LOW________°

YEAR

HIGH ________° LOW________°

YEAR

HIGH ________° LOW________°

SEPTEMBER 14

Picea glauca
White Spruce

YEAR

HIGH ______° LOW______°

YEAR

HIGH ______° LOW______°

YEAR

HIGH ______° LOW______°

YEAR

HIGH ______° LOW______°

YEAR

HIGH ______° LOW______°

YEAR

HIGH ______° LOW______°

YEAR

HIGH ______° LOW______°

YEAR

HIGH ______° LOW______°

YEAR

HIGH ______° LOW______°

YEAR

HIGH ______° LOW______°

SEPTEMBER 15

Picea pungens
Colorado Spruce

YEAR

HIGH ________° LOW________°

YEAR

HIGH ________° LOW________°

YEAR

HIGH ________° LOW________°

YEAR

HIGH ________° LOW________°

YEAR

HIGH ________° LOW________°

YEAR

HIGH ________° LOW________°

YEAR

HIGH ________° LOW________°

YEAR

HIGH ________° LOW________°

YEAR

HIGH ________° LOW________°

YEAR

HIGH ________° LOW________°

SEPTEMBER 16

Picea abies "Nidiformis"
Nest Spruce

YEAR

HIGH ______° LOW ______°

YEAR

HIGH ______° LOW ______°

YEAR

HIGH ______° LOW ______°

YEAR

HIGH ______° LOW ______°

YEAR

HIGH ______° LOW ______°

YEAR

HIGH ______° LOW ______°

YEAR

HIGH ______° LOW ______°

YEAR

HIGH ______° LOW ______°

YEAR

HIGH ______° LOW ______°

YEAR

HIGH ______° LOW ______°

SEPTEMBER 17

Picea glauca "Conica"
Dwarf Alberta Spruce

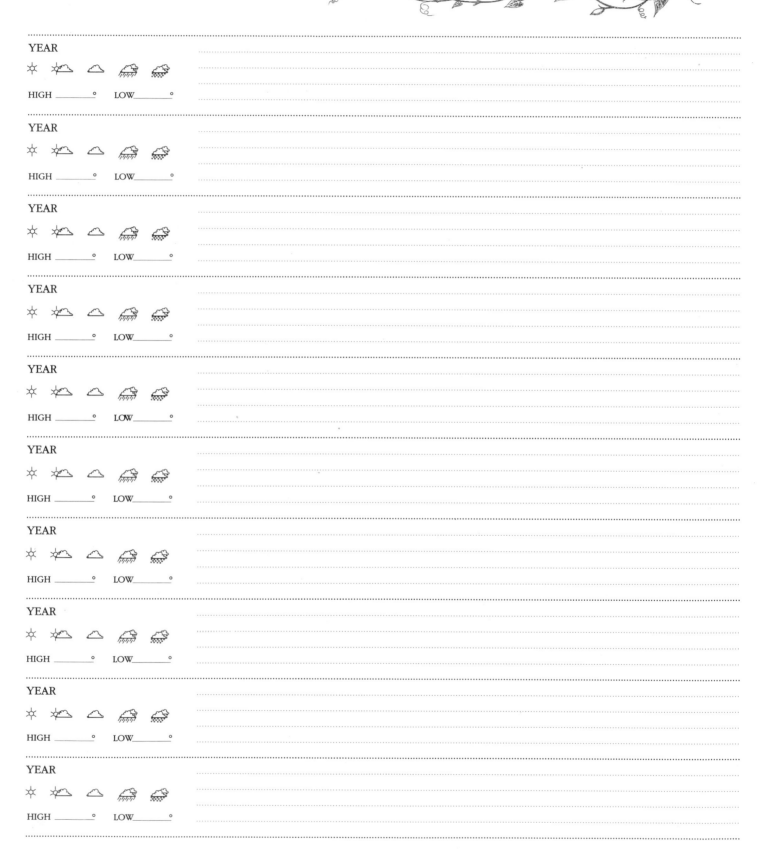

YEAR

HIGH ________° LOW________°

YEAR

HIGH ________° LOW________°

YEAR

HIGH ________° LOW________°

YEAR

HIGH ________° LOW________°

YEAR

HIGH ________° LOW________°

YEAR

HIGH ________° LOW________°

YEAR

HIGH ________° LOW________°

YEAR

HIGH ________° LOW________°

YEAR

HIGH ________° LOW________°

YEAR

HIGH ________° LOW________°

SEPTEMBER 18

Pimpinella anisum

Anise

YEAR

HIGH ______° LOW______°

YEAR

HIGH ______° LOW______°

YEAR

HIGH ______° LOW______°

YEAR

HIGH ______° LOW______°

YEAR

HIGH ______° LOW______°

YEAR

HIGH ______° LOW______°

YEAR

HIGH ______° LOW______°

YEAR

HIGH ______° LOW______°

YEAR

HIGH ______° LOW______°

YEAR

HIGH ______° LOW______°

SEPTEMBER 19

Pinus nigra

Austrian Pine

YEAR

HIGH ______° LOW______°

YEAR

HIGH ______° LOW______°

YEAR

HIGH ______° LOW______°

YEAR

HIGH ______° LOW______°

YEAR

HIGH ______° LOW______°

YEAR

HIGH ______° LOW______°

YEAR

HIGH ______° LOW______°

YEAR

HIGH ______° LOW______°

YEAR

HIGH ______° LOW______°

YEAR

HIGH ______° LOW______°

SEPTEMBER 20

Pinus strobus

Eastern White Pine

YEAR

HIGH ______° LOW ______°

YEAR

HIGH ______° LOW ______°

YEAR

HIGH ______° LOW ______°

YEAR

HIGH ______° LOW ______°

YEAR

HIGH ______° LOW ______°

YEAR

HIGH ______° LOW ______°

YEAR

HIGH ______° LOW ______°

YEAR

HIGH ______° LOW ______°

YEAR

HIGH ______° LOW ______°

YEAR

HIGH ______° LOW ______°

SEPTEMBER 21

Pinus sylvestris
Scots Pine

YEAR

HIGH ______° LOW______°

YEAR

HIGH ______° LOW______°

YEAR

HIGH ______° LOW______°

YEAR

HIGH ______° LOW______°

YEAR

HIGH ______° LOW______°

YEAR

HIGH ______° LOW______°

YEAR

HIGH ______° LOW______°

YEAR

HIGH ______° LOW______°

YEAR

HIGH ______° LOW______°

YEAR

HIGH ______° LOW______°

SEPTEMBER 22

Pinus mugo mugo

Mugo Pine

YEAR

HIGH ______° LOW______°

YEAR

HIGH ______° LOW______°

YEAR

HIGH ______° LOW______°

YEAR

HIGH ______° LOW______°

YEAR

HIGH ______° LOW______°

YEAR

HIGH ______° LOW______°

YEAR

HIGH ______° LOW______°

YEAR

HIGH ______° LOW______°

YEAR

HIGH ______° LOW______°

YEAR

HIGH ______° LOW______°

SEPTEMBER 23

Pisum sativum macrocarpon

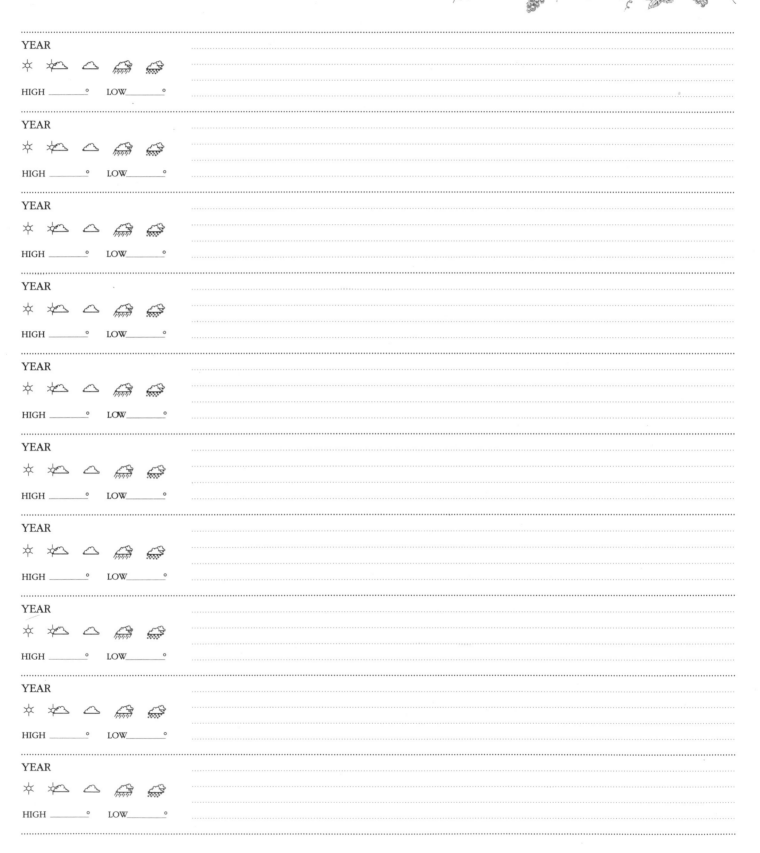

Snow Pea

YEAR

HIGH ______° LOW______°

YEAR

HIGH ______° LOW______°

YEAR

HIGH ______° LOW______°

YEAR

HIGH ______° LOW______°

YEAR

HIGH ______° LOW______°

YEAR

HIGH ______° LOW______°

YEAR

HIGH ______° LOW______°

YEAR

HIGH ______° LOW______°

YEAR

HIGH ______° LOW______°

YEAR

HIGH ______° LOW______°

SEPTEMBER 24

Pisum sativum

Pea

YEAR

HIGH ________° LOW________°

YEAR

HIGH ________° LOW________°

YEAR

HIGH ________° LOW________°

YEAR

HIGH ________° LOW________°

YEAR

HIGH ________° LOW________°

YEAR

HIGH ________° LOW________°

YEAR

HIGH ________° LOW________°

YEAR

HIGH ________° LOW________°

YEAR

HIGH ________° LOW________°

YEAR

HIGH ________° LOW________°

SEPTEMBER 25

Plantago major
Plantain

YEAR

HIGH ______° LOW______°

YEAR

HIGH ______° LOW______°

YEAR

HIGH ______° LOW______°

YEAR

HIGH ______° LOW______°

YEAR

HIGH ______° LOW______°

YEAR

HIGH ______° LOW______°

YEAR

HIGH ______° LOW______°

YEAR

HIGH ______° LOW______°

YEAR

HIGH ______° LOW______°

YEAR

HIGH ______° LOW______°

SEPTEMBER 26

Platycodon grandiflorus

Balloon Flower

YEAR

HIGH ________° LOW________°

YEAR

HIGH ________° LOW________°

YEAR

HIGH ________° LOW________°

YEAR

HIGH ________° LOW________°

YEAR

HIGH ________° LOW________°

YEAR

HIGH ________° LOW________°

YEAR

HIGH ________° LOW________°

YEAR

HIGH ________° LOW________°

YEAR

HIGH ________° LOW________°

YEAR

HIGH ________° LOW________°

SEPTEMBER 27

Podophyllum peltatum
Mayapple

YEAR

HIGH ______° LOW______°

YEAR

HIGH ______° LOW______°

YEAR

HIGH ______° LOW______°

YEAR

HIGH ______° LOW______°

YEAR

HIGH ______° LOW______°

YEAR

HIGH ______° LOW______°

YEAR

HIGH ______° LOW______°

YEAR

HIGH ______° LOW______°

YEAR

HIGH ______° LOW______°

YEAR

HIGH ______° LOW______°

SEPTEMBER 28

Polemonium caeruleum
Jacob's Ladder

YEAR

HIGH ______° LOW______°

YEAR

HIGH ______° LOW______°

YEAR

HIGH ______° LOW______°

YEAR

HIGH ______° LOW______°

YEAR

HIGH ______° LOW______°

YEAR

HIGH ______° LOW______°

YEAR

HIGH ______° LOW______°

YEAR

HIGH ______° LOW______°

YEAR

HIGH ______° LOW______°

YEAR

HIGH ______° LOW______°

SEPTEMBER 29

Polygonum aubertii
Silver Lace Vine

YEAR

HIGH ________° LOW________°

YEAR

HIGH ________° LOW________°

YEAR

HIGH ________° LOW________°

YEAR

HIGH ________° LOW________°

YEAR

HIGH ________° LOW________°

YEAR

HIGH ________° LOW________°

YEAR

HIGH ________° LOW________°

YEAR

HIGH ________° LOW________°

YEAR

HIGH ________° LOW________°

YEAR

HIGH ________° LOW________°

SEPTEMBER 30

Populus nigra italica
Lombardy Poplar

YEAR

HIGH ____° LOW ____°

YEAR

HIGH ____° LOW ____°

YEAR

HIGH ____° LOW ____°

YEAR

HIGH ____° LOW ____°

YEAR

HIGH ____° LOW ____°

YEAR

HIGH ____° LOW ____°

YEAR

HIGH ____° LOW ____°

YEAR

HIGH ____° LOW ____°

YEAR

HIGH ____° LOW ____°

YEAR

HIGH ____° LOW ____°

OCTOBER 1

Populus alba "Pyramidalis"
Boleana Poplar

YEAR

HIGH ______° LOW______°

YEAR

HIGH ______° LOW______°

YEAR

HIGH ______° LOW______°

YEAR

HIGH ______° LOW______°

YEAR

HIGH ______° LOW______°

YEAR

HIGH ______° LOW______°

YEAR

HIGH ______° LOW______°

YEAR

HIGH ______° LOW______°

YEAR

HIGH ______° LOW______°

YEAR

HIGH ______° LOW______°

OCTOBER 2

Populus canadensis "Eugenei"
Carolina Poplar

YEAR

HIGH ______° LOW ______°

YEAR

HIGH ______° LOW ______°

YEAR

HIGH ______° LOW ______°

YEAR

HIGH ______° LOW ______°

YEAR

HIGH ______° LOW ______°

YEAR

HIGH ______° LOW ______°

YEAR

HIGH ______° LOW ______°

YEAR

HIGH ______° LOW ______°

YEAR

HIGH ______° LOW ______°

YEAR

HIGH ______° LOW ______°

OCTOBER 3

Potentilla fruticosa
Cinquefoils (Buttercup Bush)

YEAR

HIGH ______° LOW ______°

YEAR

HIGH ______° LOW ______°

YEAR

HIGH ______° LOW ______°

YEAR

HIGH ______° LOW ______°

YEAR

HIGH ______° LOW ______°

YEAR

HIGH ______° LOW ______°

YEAR

HIGH ______° LOW ______°

YEAR

HIGH ______° LOW ______°

YEAR

HIGH ______° LOW ______°

YEAR

HIGH ______° LOW ______°

OCTOBER 4

Poterium sanguisorba

Salad Burnet

YEAR

HIGH ____° LOW ____°

YEAR

HIGH ____° LOW ____°

YEAR

HIGH ____° LOW ____°

YEAR

HIGH ____° LOW ____°

YEAR

HIGH ____° LOW ____°

YEAR

HIGH ____° LOW ____°

YEAR

HIGH ____° LOW ____°

YEAR

HIGH ____° LOW ____°

YEAR

HIGH ____° LOW ____°

YEAR

HIGH ____° LOW ____°

OCTOBER 5

Primula polyantha
Primrose

YEAR

HIGH ______° LOW______°

YEAR

HIGH ______° LOW______°

YEAR

HIGH ______° LOW______°

YEAR

HIGH ______° LOW______°

YEAR

HIGH ______° LOW______°

YEAR

HIGH ______° LOW______°

YEAR

HIGH ______° LOW______°

YEAR

HIGH ______° LOW______°

YEAR

HIGH ______° LOW______°

YEAR

HIGH ______° LOW______°

OCTOBER 6

Prunus triloba "Multiplex"
Flowering Almond

YEAR

HIGH ________° LOW ________°

YEAR

HIGH ________° LOW ________°

YEAR

HIGH ________° LOW ________°

YEAR

HIGH ________° LOW ________°

YEAR

HIGH ________° LOW ________°

YEAR

HIGH ________° LOW ________°

YEAR

HIGH ________° LOW ________°

YEAR

HIGH ________° LOW ________°

YEAR

HIGH ________° LOW ________°

YEAR

HIGH ________° LOW ________°

October 7

Prunus glandulosa
Dwarf Flowering Almond

YEAR

HIGH ______° LOW ______°

YEAR

HIGH ______° LOW ______°

YEAR

HIGH ______° LOW ______°

YEAR

HIGH ______° LOW ______°

YEAR

HIGH ______° LOW ______°

YEAR

HIGH ______° LOW ______°

YEAR

HIGH ______° LOW ______°

YEAR

HIGH ______° LOW ______°

YEAR

HIGH ______° LOW ______°

YEAR

HIGH ______° LOW ______°

OCTOBER 8

Prunus virginiana "Schubert"

Schubert Cherry

YEAR

HIGH ______° LOW______°

YEAR

HIGH ______° LOW______°

YEAR

HIGH ______° LOW______°

YEAR

HIGH ______° LOW______°

YEAR

HIGH ______° LOW______°

YEAR

HIGH ______° LOW______°

YEAR

HIGH ______° LOW______°

YEAR

HIGH ______° LOW______°

YEAR

HIGH ______° LOW______°

YEAR

HIGH ______° LOW______°

OCTOBER 9

Prunus cistena

Purpleleaf Sand Cherry

YEAR

HIGH ______° LOW______°

YEAR

HIGH ______° LOW______°

YEAR

HIGH ______° LOW______°

YEAR

HIGH ______° LOW______°

YEAR

HIGH ______° LOW______°

YEAR

HIGH ______° LOW______°

YEAR

HIGH ______° LOW______°

YEAR

HIGH ______° LOW______°

YEAR

HIGH ______° LOW______°

YEAR

HIGH ______° LOW______°

OCTOBER 10

Pseudotsuga menziesii glauca

Douglas Fir

YEAR

HIGH ______° LOW ______°

YEAR

HIGH ______° LOW ______°

YEAR

HIGH ______° LOW ______°

YEAR

HIGH ______° LOW ______°

YEAR

HIGH ______° LOW ______°

YEAR

HIGH ______° LOW ______°

YEAR

HIGH ______° LOW ______°

YEAR

HIGH ______° LOW ______°

YEAR

HIGH ______° LOW ______°

YEAR

HIGH ______° LOW ______°

OCTOBER 11

Pulmonaria saccharata

Bethlehem Sage

YEAR

HIGH ________° LOW________°

YEAR

HIGH ________° LOW________°

YEAR

HIGH ________° LOW________°

YEAR

HIGH ________° LOW________°

YEAR

HIGH ________° LOW________°

YEAR

HIGH ________° LOW________°

YEAR

HIGH ________° LOW________°

YEAR

HIGH ________° LOW________°

YEAR

HIGH ________° LOW________°

YEAR

HIGH ________° LOW________°

OCTOBER 12

Pyracantha coccinea

Fire Thorn

YEAR

HIGH ______° LOW______°

YEAR

HIGH ______° LOW______°

YEAR

HIGH ______° LOW______°

YEAR

HIGH ______° LOW______°

YEAR

HIGH ______° LOW______°

YEAR

HIGH ______° LOW______°

YEAR

HIGH ______° LOW______°

YEAR

HIGH ______° LOW______°

YEAR

HIGH ______° LOW______°

YEAR

HIGH ______° LOW______°

OCTOBER 13

Quercus alba

White Oak

YEAR

HIGH ________° LOW________°

YEAR

HIGH ________° LOW________°

YEAR

HIGH ________° LOW________°

YEAR

HIGH ________° LOW________°

YEAR

HIGH ________° LOW________°

YEAR

HIGH ________° LOW________°

YEAR

HIGH ________° LOW________°

YEAR

HIGH ________° LOW________°

YEAR

HIGH ________° LOW________°

YEAR

HIGH ________° LOW________°

OCTOBER 14

Quercus rubra

Red Oak

YEAR

HIGH ________ ° LOW________ °

YEAR

HIGH ________ ° LOW________ °

YEAR

HIGH ________ ° LOW________ °

YEAR

HIGH ________ ° LOW________ °

YEAR

HIGH ________ ° LOW________ °

YEAR

HIGH ________ ° LOW________ °

YEAR

HIGH ________ ° LOW________ °

YEAR

HIGH ________ ° LOW________ °

YEAR

HIGH ________ ° LOW________ °

YEAR

HIGH ________ ° LOW________ °

OCTOBER 15

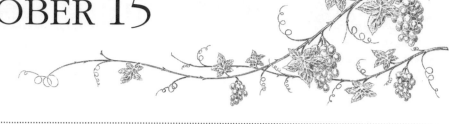

Quercus robur "Fastigiata"
Pyramidal English Oak

YEAR

HIGH ______° LOW______°

YEAR

HIGH ______° LOW______°

YEAR

HIGH ______° LOW______°

YEAR

HIGH ______° LOW______°

YEAR

HIGH ______° LOW______°

YEAR

HIGH ______° LOW______°

YEAR

HIGH ______° LOW______°

YEAR

HIGH ______° LOW______°

YEAR

HIGH ______° LOW______°

YEAR

HIGH ______° LOW______°

OCTOBER 16

Quercus palustris

Pin Oak

YEAR

HIGH ________° LOW ________°

YEAR

HIGH ________° LOW ________°

YEAR

HIGH ________° LOW ________°

YEAR

HIGH ________° LOW ________°

YEAR

HIGH ________° LOW ________°

YEAR

HIGH ________° LOW ________°

YEAR

HIGH ________° LOW ________°

YEAR

HIGH ________° LOW ________°

YEAR

HIGH ________° LOW ________°

YEAR

HIGH ________° LOW ________°

OCTOBER 17

Raphanus sativus
Radish

YEAR

HIGH ______° LOW______°

YEAR

HIGH ______° LOW______°

YEAR

HIGH ______° LOW______°

YEAR

HIGH ______° LOW______°

YEAR

HIGH ______° LOW______°

YEAR

HIGH ______° LOW______°

YEAR

HIGH ______° LOW______°

YEAR

HIGH ______° LOW______°

YEAR

HIGH ______° LOW______°

YEAR

HIGH ______° LOW______°

OCTOBER 18

Rhamnus purshiana
Cascara Buckthorn

YEAR

HIGH ______° LOW ______°

YEAR

HIGH ______° LOW ______°

YEAR

HIGH ______° LOW ______°

YEAR

HIGH ______° LOW ______°

YEAR

HIGH ______° LOW ______°

YEAR

HIGH ______° LOW ______°

YEAR

HIGH ______° LOW ______°

YEAR

HIGH ______° LOW ______°

YEAR

HIGH ______° LOW ______°

YEAR

HIGH ______° LOW ______°

OCTOBER 19

Rheum rhabarbarum

Rhubarb

YEAR

HIGH ______° LOW______°

YEAR

HIGH ______° LOW______°

YEAR

HIGH ______° LOW______°

YEAR

HIGH ______° LOW______°

YEAR

HIGH ______° LOW______°

YEAR

HIGH ______° LOW______°

YEAR

HIGH ______° LOW______°

YEAR

HIGH ______° LOW______°

YEAR

HIGH ______° LOW______°

YEAR

HIGH ______° LOW______°

OCTOBER 20

Rhus typhina
Staghorn Sumac

YEAR

HIGH ____° LOW ____°

YEAR

HIGH ____° LOW ____°

YEAR

HIGH ____° LOW ____°

YEAR

HIGH ____° LOW ____°

YEAR

HIGH ____° LOW ____°

YEAR

HIGH ____° LOW ____°

YEAR

HIGH ____° LOW ____°

YEAR

HIGH ____° LOW ____°

YEAR

HIGH ____° LOW ____°

YEAR

HIGH ____° LOW ____°

OCTOBER 21

Ribes alpinum

Alpine Currant

YEAR

HIGH ______° LOW______°

YEAR

HIGH ______° LOW______°

YEAR

HIGH ______° LOW______°

YEAR

HIGH ______° LOW______°

YEAR

HIGH ______° LOW______°

YEAR

HIGH ______° LOW______°

YEAR

HIGH ______° LOW______°

YEAR

HIGH ______° LOW______°

YEAR

HIGH ______° LOW______°

YEAR

HIGH ______° LOW______°

OCTOBER 22

Ricinus communis

Castor Bean

YEAR

HIGH ________° LOW________°

YEAR

HIGH ________° LOW________°

YEAR

HIGH ________° LOW________°

YEAR

HIGH ________° LOW________°

YEAR

HIGH ________° LOW________°

YEAR

HIGH ________° LOW________°

YEAR

HIGH ________° LOW________°

YEAR

HIGH ________° LOW________°

YEAR

HIGH ________° LOW________°

YEAR

HIGH ________° LOW________°

OCTOBER 23

Rosmarinus officinalis
Rosemary

YEAR

HIGH ______° LOW______°

YEAR

HIGH ______° LOW______°

YEAR

HIGH ______° LOW______°

YEAR

HIGH ______° LOW______°

YEAR

HIGH ______° LOW______°

YEAR

HIGH ______° LOW______°

YEAR

HIGH ______° LOW______°

YEAR

HIGH ______° LOW______°

YEAR

HIGH ______° LOW______°

YEAR

HIGH ______° LOW______°

OCTOBER 24

Rosa

Roses

YEAR

HIGH ____° LOW ____°

YEAR

HIGH ____° LOW ____°

YEAR

HIGH ____° LOW ____°

YEAR

HIGH ____° LOW ____°

YEAR

HIGH ____° LOW ____°

YEAR

HIGH ____° LOW ____°

YEAR

HIGH ____° LOW ____°

YEAR

HIGH ____° LOW ____°

YEAR

HIGH ____° LOW ____°

YEAR

HIGH ____° LOW ____°

OCTOBER 25

Rosa rugosa

Rugosa Rose

YEAR

HIGH ________° LOW________°

YEAR

HIGH ________° LOW________°

YEAR

HIGH ________° LOW________°

YEAR

HIGH ________° LOW________°

YEAR

HIGH ________° LOW________°

YEAR

HIGH ________° LOW________°

YEAR

HIGH ________° LOW________°

YEAR

HIGH ________° LOW________°

YEAR

HIGH ________° LOW________°

YEAR

HIGH ________° LOW________°

October 26

Rubia tinctorum
Common Madder

YEAR

HIGH ____° LOW ____°

YEAR

HIGH ____° LOW ____°

YEAR

HIGH ____° LOW ____°

YEAR

HIGH ____° LOW ____°

YEAR

HIGH ____° LOW ____°

YEAR

HIGH ____° LOW ____°

YEAR

HIGH ____° LOW ____°

YEAR

HIGH ____° LOW ____°

YEAR

HIGH ____° LOW ____°

YEAR

HIGH ____° LOW ____°

OCTOBER 27

Rudbeckia hirta
Black-eyed Susan

YEAR

HIGH ______° LOW______°

YEAR

HIGH ______° LOW______°

YEAR

HIGH ______° LOW______°

YEAR

HIGH ______° LOW______°

YEAR

HIGH ______° LOW______°

YEAR

HIGH ______° LOW______°

YEAR

HIGH ______° LOW______°

YEAR

HIGH ______° LOW______°

YEAR

HIGH ______° LOW______°

YEAR

HIGH ______° LOW______°

OCTOBER 28

Rumex acetosa

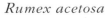

Sorrel

YEAR

HIGH ______° LOW______°

YEAR

HIGH ______° LOW______°

YEAR

HIGH ______° LOW______°

YEAR

HIGH ______° LOW______°

YEAR

HIGH ______° LOW______°

YEAR

HIGH ______° LOW______°

YEAR

HIGH ______° LOW______°

YEAR

HIGH ______° LOW______°

YEAR

HIGH ______° LOW______°

YEAR

HIGH ______° LOW______°

OCTOBER 29

Ruta graveolens

Rue

YEAR

HIGH ______° LOW ______°

YEAR

HIGH ______° LOW ______°

YEAR

HIGH ______° LOW ______°

YEAR

HIGH ______° LOW ______°

YEAR

HIGH ______° LOW ______°

YEAR

HIGH ______° LOW ______°

YEAR

HIGH ______° LOW ______°

YEAR

HIGH ______° LOW ______°

YEAR

HIGH ______° LOW ______°

YEAR

HIGH ______° LOW ______°

OCTOBER 30

Salix matsudana "Tortuosa"

Corkscrew Willow

YEAR

HIGH ______° LOW ______°

YEAR

HIGH ______° LOW ______°

YEAR

HIGH ______° LOW ______°

YEAR

HIGH ______° LOW ______°

YEAR

HIGH ______° LOW ______°

YEAR

HIGH ______° LOW ______°

YEAR

HIGH ______° LOW ______°

YEAR

HIGH ______° LOW ______°

YEAR

HIGH ______° LOW ______°

YEAR

HIGH ______° LOW ______°

OCTOBER 31

Salix alba tristis

Golden Weeping Willow

YEAR

HIGH ________° LOW________°

YEAR

HIGH ________° LOW________°

YEAR

HIGH ________° LOW________°

YEAR

HIGH ________° LOW________°

YEAR

HIGH ________° LOW________°

YEAR

HIGH ________° LOW________°

YEAR

HIGH ________° LOW________°

YEAR

HIGH ________° LOW________°

YEAR

HIGH ________° LOW________°

YEAR

HIGH ________° LOW________°

NOVEMBER 1

Salix purpurea "Gracilis"

Arctic Willow

YEAR

HIGH ______° LOW ______°

YEAR

HIGH ______° LOW ______°

YEAR

HIGH ______° LOW ______°

YEAR

HIGH ______° LOW ______°

YEAR

HIGH ______° LOW ______°

YEAR

HIGH ______° LOW ______°

YEAR

HIGH ______° LOW ______°

YEAR

HIGH ______° LOW ______°

YEAR

HIGH ______° LOW ______°

YEAR

HIGH ______° LOW ______°

NOVEMBER 2

Salix caprea

Pussy Willow

YEAR

HIGH ______° LOW ______°

YEAR

HIGH ______° LOW ______°

YEAR

HIGH ______° LOW ______°

YEAR

HIGH ______° LOW ______°

YEAR

HIGH ______° LOW ______°

YEAR

HIGH ______° LOW ______°

YEAR

HIGH ______° LOW ______°

YEAR

HIGH ______° LOW ______°

YEAR

HIGH ______° LOW ______°

YEAR

HIGH ______° LOW ______°

NOVEMBER 3

Salvia officinalis

Sage

YEAR

HIGH ______° LOW______°

YEAR

HIGH ______° LOW______°

YEAR

HIGH ______° LOW______°

YEAR

HIGH ______° LOW______°

YEAR

HIGH ______° LOW______°

YEAR

HIGH ______° LOW______°

YEAR

HIGH ______° LOW______°

YEAR

HIGH ______° LOW______°

YEAR

HIGH ______° LOW______°

YEAR

HIGH ______° LOW______°

NOVEMBER 4

Salvia Sclarea

Clary

YEAR

HIGH ______° LOW______°

YEAR

HIGH ______° LOW______°

YEAR

HIGH ______° LOW______°

YEAR

HIGH ______° LOW______°

YEAR

HIGH ______° LOW______°

YEAR

HIGH ______° LOW______°

YEAR

HIGH ______° LOW______°

YEAR

HIGH ______° LOW______°

YEAR

HIGH ______° LOW______°

YEAR

HIGH ______° LOW______°

NOVEMBER 5

Sanguinaria canadensis
Bloodroot

YEAR
HIGH ____° LOW ____°

YEAR
HIGH ____° LOW ____°

YEAR
HIGH ____° LOW ____°

YEAR
HIGH ____° LOW ____°

YEAR
HIGH ____° LOW ____°

YEAR
HIGH ____° LOW ____°

YEAR
HIGH ____° LOW ____°

YEAR
HIGH ____° LOW ____°

YEAR
HIGH ____° LOW ____°

YEAR
HIGH ____° LOW ____°

NOVEMBER 6

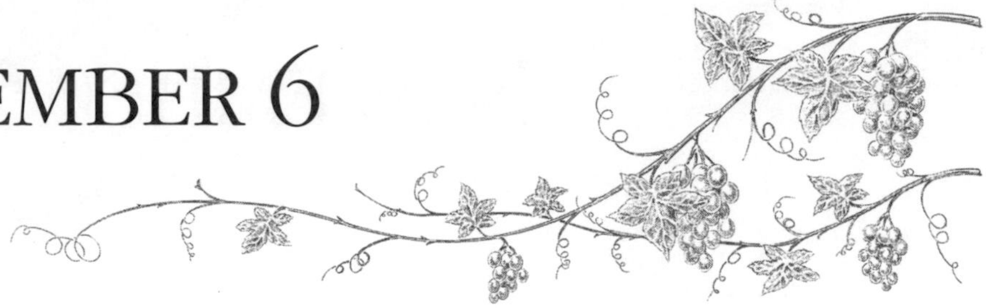

Saponaria officinalis
Soapwort

YEAR

HIGH ______° LOW______°

YEAR

HIGH ______° LOW______°

YEAR

HIGH ______° LOW______°

YEAR

HIGH ______° LOW______°

YEAR

HIGH ______° LOW______°

YEAR

HIGH ______° LOW______°

YEAR

HIGH ______° LOW______°

YEAR

HIGH ______° LOW______°

YEAR

HIGH ______° LOW______°

YEAR

HIGH ______° LOW______°

NOVEMBER 7

Satureja hortensis
Summer Savory

YEAR
HIGH ______° LOW ______°

YEAR
HIGH ______° LOW ______°

YEAR
HIGH ______° LOW ______°

YEAR
HIGH ______° LOW ______°

YEAR
HIGH ______° LOW ______°

YEAR
HIGH ______° LOW ______°

YEAR
HIGH ______° LOW ______°

YEAR
HIGH ______° LOW ______°

YEAR
HIGH ______° LOW ______°

YEAR
HIGH ______° LOW ______°

NOVEMBER 8

Satureja montana
Winter Savory

YEAR

HIGH ______° LOW______°

YEAR

HIGH ______° LOW______°

YEAR

HIGH ______° LOW______°

YEAR

HIGH ______° LOW______°

YEAR

HIGH ______° LOW______°

YEAR

HIGH ______° LOW______°

YEAR

HIGH ______° LOW______°

YEAR

HIGH ______° LOW______°

YEAR

HIGH ______° LOW______°

YEAR

HIGH ______° LOW______°

November 9

Solanum nigrum

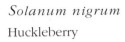

Huckleberry

YEAR

HIGH ____° LOW ____°

YEAR

HIGH ____° LOW ____°

YEAR

HIGH ____° LOW ____°

YEAR

HIGH ____° LOW ____°

YEAR

HIGH ____° LOW ____°

YEAR

HIGH ____° LOW ____°

YEAR

HIGH ____° LOW ____°

YEAR

HIGH ____° LOW ____°

YEAR

HIGH ____° LOW ____°

YEAR

HIGH ____° LOW ____°

NOVEMBER 10

Solanum tuberosum
Potato

YEAR

HIGH ________° LOW________°

YEAR

HIGH ________° LOW________°

YEAR

HIGH ________° LOW________°

YEAR

HIGH ________° LOW________°

YEAR

HIGH ________° LOW________°

YEAR

HIGH ________° LOW________°

YEAR

HIGH ________° LOW________°

YEAR

HIGH ________° LOW________°

YEAR

HIGH ________° LOW________°

YEAR

HIGH ________° LOW________°

NOVEMBER 11

Solanum melongena

Eggplant

YEAR

HIGH ______° LOW______°

YEAR

HIGH ______° LOW______°

YEAR

HIGH ______° LOW______°

YEAR

HIGH ______° LOW______°

YEAR

HIGH ______° LOW______°

YEAR

HIGH ______° LOW______°

YEAR

HIGH ______° LOW______°

YEAR

HIGH ______° LOW______°

YEAR

HIGH ______° LOW______°

YEAR

HIGH ______° LOW______°

NOVEMBER 12

Solidago canadensis
Canada Goldenrod

YEAR

HIGH ______° LOW______°

YEAR

HIGH ______° LOW______°

YEAR

HIGH ______° LOW______°

YEAR

HIGH ______° LOW______°

YEAR

HIGH ______° LOW______°

YEAR

HIGH ______° LOW______°

YEAR

HIGH ______° LOW______°

YEAR

HIGH ______° LOW______°

YEAR

HIGH ______° LOW______°

YEAR

HIGH ______° LOW______°

NOVEMBER 13

Sorbus aucuparia "Rossica"
European Mountain Ash

YEAR

HIGH ______° LOW______°

YEAR

HIGH ______° LOW______°

YEAR

HIGH ______° LOW______°

YEAR

HIGH ______° LOW______°

YEAR

HIGH ______° LOW______°

YEAR

HIGH ______° LOW______°

YEAR

HIGH ______° LOW______°

YEAR

HIGH ______° LOW______°

YEAR

HIGH ______° LOW______°

YEAR

HIGH ______° LOW______°

NOVEMBER 14

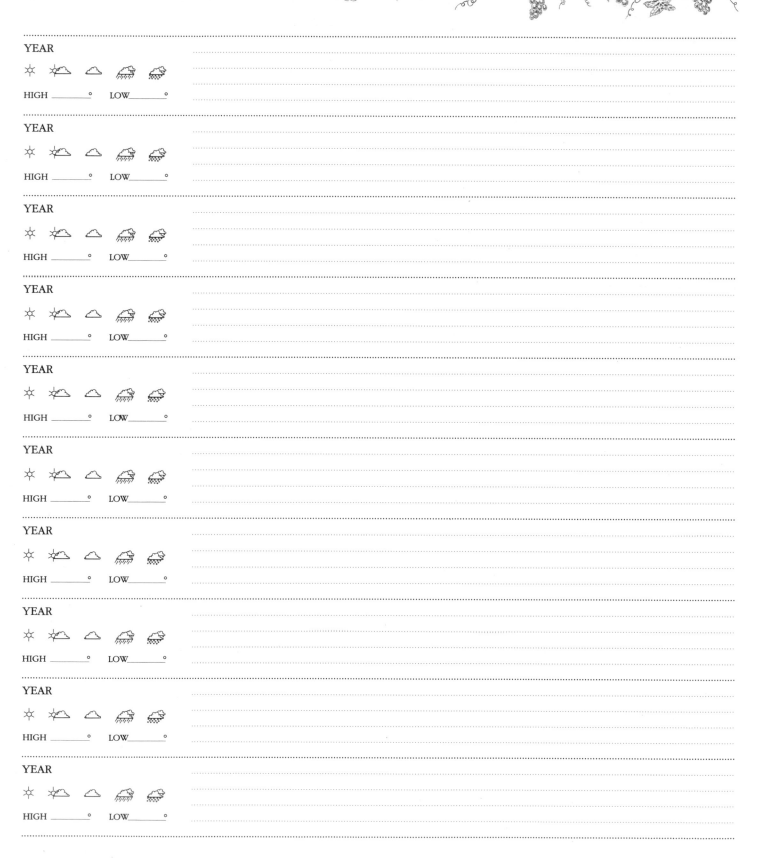

Spinacia oleracea
Spinach

YEAR

HIGH ____° LOW____°

YEAR

HIGH ____° LOW____°

YEAR

HIGH ____° LOW____°

YEAR

HIGH ____° LOW____°

YEAR

HIGH ____° LOW____°

YEAR

HIGH ____° LOW____°

YEAR

HIGH ____° LOW____°

YEAR

HIGH ____° LOW____°

YEAR

HIGH ____° LOW____°

YEAR

HIGH ____° LOW____°

NOVEMBER 15

Spiraea arguta "Graciosa"
Garland Spirea

YEAR

HIGH ______° LOW ______°

YEAR

HIGH ______° LOW ______°

YEAR

HIGH ______° LOW ______°

YEAR

HIGH ______° LOW ______°

YEAR

HIGH ______° LOW ______°

YEAR

HIGH ______° LOW ______°

YEAR

HIGH ______° LOW ______°

YEAR

HIGH ______° LOW ______°

YEAR

HIGH ______° LOW ______°

YEAR

HIGH ______° LOW ______°

NOVEMBER 16

Spiraea vanhouttei
Bridalwreath Spirea

YEAR

HIGH ____° LOW____°

YEAR

HIGH ____° LOW____°

YEAR

HIGH ____° LOW____°

YEAR

HIGH ____° LOW____°

YEAR

HIGH ____° LOW____°

YEAR

HIGH ____° LOW____°

YEAR

HIGH ____° LOW____°

YEAR

HIGH ____° LOW____°

YEAR

HIGH ____° LOW____°

YEAR

HIGH ____° LOW____°

NOVEMBER 17

Spiraea bumalda

Red Spirea

YEAR

HIGH ______° LOW______°

YEAR

HIGH ______° LOW______°

YEAR

HIGH ______° LOW______°

YEAR

HIGH ______° LOW______°

YEAR

HIGH ______° LOW______°

YEAR

HIGH ______° LOW______°

YEAR

HIGH ______° LOW______°

YEAR

HIGH ______° LOW______°

YEAR

HIGH ______° LOW______°

YEAR

HIGH ______° LOW______°

NOVEMBER 18

Stachys officinalis

Betony

YEAR

HIGH ________° LOW________°

YEAR

HIGH ________° LOW________°

YEAR

HIGH ________° LOW________°

YEAR

HIGH ________° LOW________°

YEAR

HIGH ________° LOW________°

YEAR

HIGH ________° LOW________°

YEAR

HIGH ________° LOW________°

YEAR

HIGH ________° LOW________°

YEAR

HIGH ________° LOW________°

YEAR

HIGH ________° LOW________°

NOVEMBER 19

Symphoricarpos albus
Snowberry

YEAR

HIGH ________° LOW________°

YEAR

HIGH ________° LOW________°

YEAR

HIGH ________° LOW________°

YEAR

HIGH ________° LOW________°

YEAR

HIGH ________° LOW________°

YEAR

HIGH ________° LOW________°

YEAR

HIGH ________° LOW________°

YEAR

HIGH ________° LOW________°

YEAR

HIGH ________° LOW________°

YEAR

HIGH ________° LOW________°

NOVEMBER 20

Symphytum officinale
Comfrey

YEAR

HIGH ______° LOW ______°

YEAR

HIGH ______° LOW ______°

YEAR

HIGH ______° LOW ______°

YEAR

HIGH ______° LOW ______°

YEAR

HIGH ______° LOW ______°

YEAR

HIGH ______° LOW ______°

YEAR

HIGH ______° LOW ______°

YEAR

HIGH ______° LOW ______°

YEAR

HIGH ______° LOW ______°

YEAR

HIGH ______° LOW ______°

NOVEMBER 21

Syringa vulgaris
Common Lilac

YEAR

HIGH ______° LOW______°

YEAR

HIGH ______° LOW______°

YEAR

HIGH ______° LOW______°

YEAR

HIGH ______° LOW______°

YEAR

HIGH ______° LOW______°

YEAR

HIGH ______° LOW______°

YEAR

HIGH ______° LOW______°

YEAR

HIGH ______° LOW______°

YEAR

HIGH ______° LOW______°

YEAR

HIGH ______° LOW______°

NOVEMBER 22

Syringa velutina
Lilac (Dwarf)

YEAR

HIGH _______° LOW_______°

YEAR

HIGH _______° LOW_______°

YEAR

HIGH _______° LOW_______°

YEAR

HIGH _______° LOW_______°

YEAR

HIGH _______° LOW_______°

YEAR

HIGH _______° LOW_______°

YEAR

HIGH _______° LOW_______°

YEAR

HIGH _______° LOW_______°

YEAR

HIGH _______° LOW_______°

YEAR

HIGH _______° LOW_______°

NOVEMBER 23

Syringa reticulata "Ivory Silk"
Ivory Silk Tree

YEAR

HIGH ________° LOW________°

YEAR

HIGH ________° LOW________°

YEAR

HIGH ________° LOW________°

YEAR

HIGH ________° LOW________°

YEAR

HIGH ________° LOW________°

YEAR

HIGH ________° LOW________°

YEAR

HIGH ________° LOW________°

YEAR

HIGH ________° LOW________°

YEAR

HIGH ________° LOW________°

YEAR

HIGH ________° LOW________°

NOVEMBER 24

Syzygium aromaticum

Cloves

YEAR

HIGH ______° LOW______°

YEAR

HIGH ______° LOW______°

YEAR

HIGH ______° LOW______°

YEAR

HIGH ______° LOW______°

YEAR

HIGH ______° LOW______°

YEAR

HIGH ______° LOW______°

YEAR

HIGH ______° LOW______°

YEAR

HIGH ______° LOW______°

YEAR

HIGH ______° LOW______°

YEAR

HIGH ______° LOW______°

NOVEMBER 25

Tagetes patula
French Marigold

YEAR

HIGH ______° LOW______°

YEAR

HIGH ______° LOW______°

YEAR

HIGH ______° LOW______°

YEAR

HIGH ______° LOW______°

YEAR

HIGH ______° LOW______°

YEAR

HIGH ______° LOW______°

YEAR

HIGH ______° LOW______°

YEAR

HIGH ______° LOW______°

YEAR

HIGH ______° LOW______°

YEAR

HIGH ______° LOW______°

NOVEMBER 26

Tamarix pentandra
Amur Tamarisk

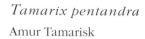

YEAR

HIGH ________° LOW________°

YEAR

HIGH ________° LOW________°

YEAR

HIGH ________° LOW________°

YEAR

HIGH ________° LOW________°

YEAR

HIGH ________° LOW________°

YEAR

HIGH ________° LOW________°

YEAR

HIGH ________° LOW________°

YEAR

HIGH ________° LOW________°

YEAR

HIGH ________° LOW________°

YEAR

HIGH ________° LOW________°

NOVEMBER 27

Tanacetum vulgare

Tansy

YEAR

HIGH ________° LOW________°

YEAR

HIGH ________° LOW________°

YEAR

HIGH ________° LOW________°

YEAR

HIGH ________° LOW________°

YEAR

HIGH ________° LOW________°

YEAR

HIGH ________° LOW________°

YEAR

HIGH ________° LOW________°

YEAR

HIGH ________° LOW________°

YEAR

HIGH ________° LOW________°

YEAR

HIGH ________° LOW________°

NOVEMBER 28

Taraxacum officinale
Dandelion

YEAR

HIGH ______° LOW ______°

YEAR

HIGH ______° LOW ______°

YEAR

HIGH ______° LOW ______°

YEAR

HIGH ______° LOW ______°

YEAR

HIGH ______° LOW ______°

YEAR

HIGH ______° LOW ______°

YEAR

HIGH ______° LOW ______°

YEAR

HIGH ______° LOW ______°

YEAR

HIGH ______° LOW ______°

YEAR

HIGH ______° LOW ______°

NOVEMBER 29

Taxus media "Hicksii"
Hicks Yew

YEAR

HIGH ______° LOW______°

YEAR

HIGH ______° LOW______°

YEAR

HIGH ______° LOW______°

YEAR

HIGH ______° LOW______°

YEAR

HIGH ______° LOW______°

YEAR

HIGH ______° LOW______°

YEAR

HIGH ______° LOW______°

YEAR

HIGH ______° LOW______°

YEAR

HIGH ______° LOW______°

YEAR

HIGH ______° LOW______°

NOVEMBER 30

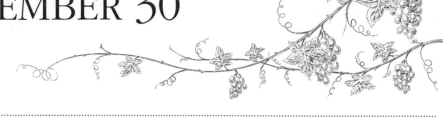

Taxus media "Densiformis"

Dense Yew

YEAR

HIGH ________° LOW________°

YEAR

HIGH ________° LOW________°

YEAR

HIGH ________° LOW________°

YEAR

HIGH ________° LOW________°

YEAR

HIGH ________° LOW________°

YEAR

HIGH ________° LOW________°

YEAR

HIGH ________° LOW________°

YEAR

HIGH ________° LOW________°

YEAR

HIGH ________° LOW________°

YEAR

HIGH ________° LOW________°

DECEMBER 1

Taxus cuspidata
Japanese Yew

YEAR

HIGH ________° LOW________°

YEAR

HIGH ________° LOW________°

YEAR

HIGH ________° LOW________°

YEAR

HIGH ________° LOW________°

YEAR

HIGH ________° LOW________°

YEAR

HIGH ________° LOW________°

YEAR

HIGH ________° LOW________°

YEAR

HIGH ________° LOW________°

YEAR

HIGH ________° LOW________°

YEAR

HIGH ________° LOW________°

DECEMBER 2

Tetragonia expansa
New Zealand Spinach

YEAR

HIGH ____° LOW ____°

YEAR

HIGH ____° LOW ____°

YEAR

HIGH ____° LOW ____°

YEAR

HIGH ____° LOW ____°

YEAR

HIGH ____° LOW ____°

YEAR

HIGH ____° LOW ____°

YEAR

HIGH ____° LOW ____°

YEAR

HIGH ____° LOW ____°

YEAR

HIGH ____° LOW ____°

YEAR

HIGH ____° LOW ____°

DECEMBER 3

Teucrium Chamaedrys
Germander

YEAR

HIGH ________° LOW________°

YEAR

HIGH ________° LOW________°

YEAR

HIGH ________° LOW________°

YEAR

HIGH ________° LOW________°

YEAR

HIGH ________° LOW________°

YEAR

HIGH ________° LOW________°

YEAR

HIGH ________° LOW________°

YEAR

HIGH ________° LOW________°

YEAR

HIGH ________° LOW________°

YEAR

HIGH ________° LOW________°

DECEMBER 4

Thuja occidentalis
White Cedar

YEAR

HIGH ______° LOW______°

YEAR

HIGH ______° LOW______°

YEAR

HIGH ______° LOW______°

YEAR

HIGH ______° LOW______°

YEAR

HIGH ______° LOW______°

YEAR

HIGH ______° LOW______°

YEAR

HIGH ______° LOW______°

YEAR

HIGH ______° LOW______°

YEAR

HIGH ______° LOW______°

YEAR

HIGH ______° LOW______°

DECEMBER 5

Thuja occidentalis "Woodwardii"
Globe Cedar

YEAR
HIGH ° LOW °

YEAR
HIGH ° LOW °

YEAR
HIGH ° LOW °

YEAR
HIGH ° LOW °

YEAR
HIGH ° LOW °

YEAR
HIGH ° LOW °

YEAR
HIGH ° LOW °

YEAR
HIGH ° LOW °

YEAR
HIGH ° LOW °

YEAR
HIGH ° LOW °

DECEMBER 6

Thymus vulgaris
Thyme

YEAR

HIGH ________° LOW________°

YEAR

HIGH ________° LOW________°

YEAR

HIGH ________° LOW________°

YEAR

HIGH ________° LOW________°

YEAR

HIGH ________° LOW________°

YEAR

HIGH ________° LOW________°

YEAR

HIGH ________° LOW________°

YEAR

HIGH ________° LOW________°

YEAR

HIGH ________° LOW________°

YEAR

HIGH ________° LOW________°

DECEMBER 7

Tilia cordata

Littleleaf Linden

YEAR

HIGH ______° LOW______°

YEAR

HIGH ______° LOW______°

YEAR

HIGH ______° LOW______°

YEAR

HIGH ______° LOW______°

YEAR

HIGH ______° LOW______°

YEAR

HIGH ______° LOW______°

YEAR

HIGH ______° LOW______°

YEAR

HIGH ______° LOW______°

YEAR

HIGH ______° LOW______°

YEAR

HIGH ______° LOW______°

DECEMBER 8

Trigonella foenum-graecum
Fenugreek

YEAR

HIGH ________° LOW ________°

YEAR

HIGH ________° LOW ________°

YEAR

HIGH ________° LOW ________°

YEAR

HIGH ________° LOW ________°

YEAR

HIGH ________° LOW ________°

YEAR

HIGH ________° LOW ________°

YEAR

HIGH ________° LOW ________°

YEAR

HIGH ________° LOW ________°

YEAR

HIGH ________° LOW ________°

YEAR

HIGH ________° LOW ________°

DECEMBER 9

Tropaeolum majus

Nasturtium

YEAR

HIGH ______° LOW______°

YEAR

HIGH ______° LOW______°

YEAR

HIGH ______° LOW______°

YEAR

HIGH ______° LOW______°

YEAR

HIGH ______° LOW______°

YEAR

HIGH ______° LOW______°

YEAR

HIGH ______° LOW______°

YEAR

HIGH ______° LOW______°

YEAR

HIGH ______° LOW______°

YEAR

HIGH ______° LOW______°

DECEMBER 10

Tsuga canadensis
Canadian Hemlock

YEAR

HIGH ________° LOW________°

YEAR

HIGH ________° LOW________°

YEAR

HIGH ________° LOW________°

YEAR

HIGH ________° LOW________°

YEAR

HIGH ________° LOW________°

YEAR

HIGH ________° LOW________°

YEAR

HIGH ________° LOW________°

YEAR

HIGH ________° LOW________°

YEAR

HIGH ________° LOW________°

YEAR

HIGH ________° LOW________°

DECEMBER 11

Tussilago farfara

Coltsfoot

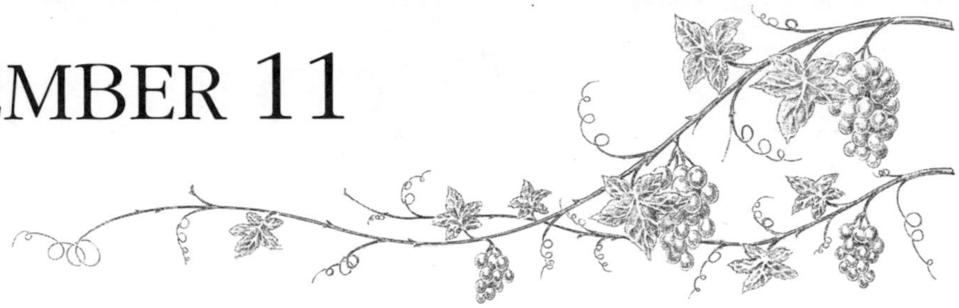

YEAR

HIGH ______° LOW______°

YEAR

HIGH ______° LOW______°

YEAR

HIGH ______° LOW______°

YEAR

HIGH ______° LOW______°

YEAR

HIGH ______° LOW______°

YEAR

HIGH ______° LOW______°

YEAR

HIGH ______° LOW______°

YEAR

HIGH ______° LOW______°

YEAR

HIGH ______° LOW______°

YEAR

HIGH ______° LOW______°

DECEMBER 12

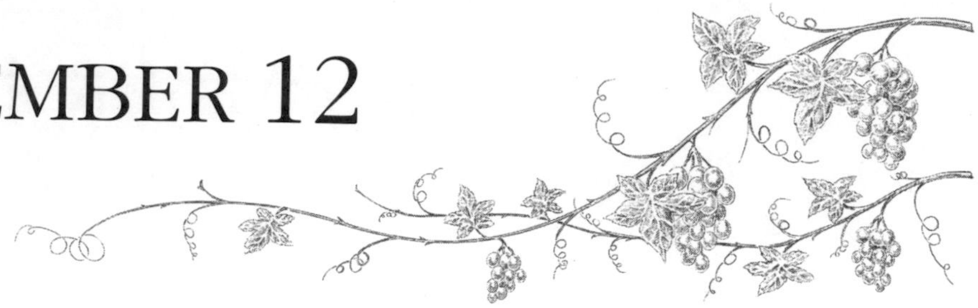

Ulmus glabra "Pendula"

Camperdown Elm

YEAR

HIGH ______° LOW______°

YEAR

HIGH ______° LOW______°

YEAR

HIGH ______° LOW______°

YEAR

HIGH ______° LOW______°

YEAR

HIGH ______° LOW______°

YEAR

HIGH ______° LOW______°

YEAR

HIGH ______° LOW______°

YEAR

HIGH ______° LOW______°

YEAR

HIGH ______° LOW______°

YEAR

HIGH ______° LOW______°

DECEMBER 13

Valeriana officinalis
Valerian

YEAR

HIGH ______° LOW ______°

YEAR

HIGH ______° LOW ______°

YEAR

HIGH ______° LOW ______°

YEAR

HIGH ______° LOW ______°

YEAR

HIGH ______° LOW ______°

YEAR

HIGH ______° LOW ______°

YEAR

HIGH ______° LOW ______°

YEAR

HIGH ______° LOW ______°

YEAR

HIGH ______° LOW ______°

YEAR

HIGH ______° LOW ______°

DECEMBER 14

Veratrum viride
American Hellebore

YEAR

HIGH ________° LOW________°

YEAR

HIGH ________° LOW________°

YEAR

HIGH ________° LOW________°

YEAR

HIGH ________° LOW________°

YEAR

HIGH ________° LOW________°

YEAR

HIGH ________° LOW________°

YEAR

HIGH ________° LOW________°

YEAR

HIGH ________° LOW________°

YEAR

HIGH ________° LOW________°

YEAR

HIGH ________° LOW________°

DECEMBER 15

Verbascum thapsus

Mullein

YEAR

HIGH ______° LOW______°

YEAR

HIGH ______° LOW______°

YEAR

HIGH ______° LOW______°

YEAR

HIGH ______° LOW______°

YEAR

HIGH ______° LOW______°

YEAR

HIGH ______° LOW______°

YEAR

HIGH ______° LOW______°

YEAR

HIGH ______° LOW______°

YEAR

HIGH ______° LOW______°

YEAR

HIGH ______° LOW______°

DECEMBER 16

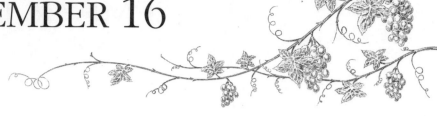

Viburnum opulus "Roseum"
European Snowball

YEAR
HIGH ____° LOW ____°

YEAR
HIGH ____° LOW ____°

YEAR
HIGH ____° LOW ____°

YEAR
HIGH ____° LOW ____°

YEAR
HIGH ____° LOW ____°

YEAR
HIGH ____° LOW ____°

YEAR
HIGH ____° LOW ____°

YEAR
HIGH ____° LOW ____°

YEAR
HIGH ____° LOW ____°

YEAR
HIGH ____° LOW ____°

DECEMBER 17

Viburnum trilobum
Highbush Cranberry

YEAR

HIGH ______° LOW ______°

YEAR

HIGH ______° LOW ______°

YEAR

HIGH ______° LOW ______°

YEAR

HIGH ______° LOW ______°

YEAR

HIGH ______° LOW ______°

YEAR

HIGH ______° LOW ______°

YEAR

HIGH ______° LOW ______°

YEAR

HIGH ______° LOW ______°

YEAR

HIGH ______° LOW ______°

YEAR

HIGH ______° LOW ______°

DECEMBER 18

Viburnum lantana
Wayfaring Tree

YEAR

HIGH _______° LOW_______°

YEAR

HIGH _______° LOW_______°

YEAR

HIGH _______° LOW_______°

YEAR

HIGH _______° LOW_______°

YEAR

HIGH _______° LOW_______°

YEAR

HIGH _______° LOW_______°

YEAR

HIGH _______° LOW_______°

YEAR

HIGH _______° LOW_______°

YEAR

HIGH _______° LOW_______°

YEAR

HIGH _______° LOW_______°

DECEMBER 19

Viburnum carlcephalum

Fragrant Viburnum

YEAR

HIGH ______° LOW______°

YEAR

HIGH ______° LOW______°

YEAR

HIGH ______° LOW______°

YEAR

HIGH ______° LOW______°

YEAR

HIGH ______° LOW______°

YEAR

HIGH ______° LOW______°

YEAR

HIGH ______° LOW______°

YEAR

HIGH ______° LOW______°

YEAR

HIGH ______° LOW______°

YEAR

HIGH ______° LOW______°

DECEMBER 20

Vicia faba
Fava Bean

YEAR

HIGH ______° LOW ______°

YEAR

HIGH ______° LOW ______°

YEAR

HIGH ______° LOW ______°

YEAR

HIGH ______° LOW ______°

YEAR

HIGH ______° LOW ______°

YEAR

HIGH ______° LOW ______°

YEAR

HIGH ______° LOW ______°

YEAR

HIGH ______° LOW ______°

YEAR

HIGH ______° LOW ______°

YEAR

HIGH ______° LOW ______°

DECEMBER 21

Vinca minor
Periwinkle

YEAR

HIGH ______° LOW ______°

YEAR

HIGH ______° LOW ______°

YEAR

HIGH ______° LOW ______°

YEAR

HIGH ______° LOW ______°

YEAR

HIGH ______° LOW ______°

YEAR

HIGH ______° LOW ______°

YEAR

HIGH ______° LOW ______°

YEAR

HIGH ______° LOW ______°

YEAR

HIGH ______° LOW ______°

YEAR

HIGH ______° LOW ______°

December 22

Viola odorata

Violet

YEAR

HIGH ______° LOW ______°

YEAR

HIGH ______° LOW ______°

YEAR

HIGH ______° LOW ______°

YEAR

HIGH ______° LOW ______°

YEAR

HIGH ______° LOW ______°

YEAR

HIGH ______° LOW ______°

YEAR

HIGH ______° LOW ______°

YEAR

HIGH ______° LOW ______°

YEAR

HIGH ______° LOW ______°

YEAR

HIGH ______° LOW ______°

DECEMBER 23

Viola x wittrockiana
Pansy

YEAR

HIGH ______° LOW______°

YEAR

HIGH ______° LOW______°

YEAR

HIGH ______° LOW______°

YEAR

HIGH ______° LOW______°

YEAR

HIGH ______° LOW______°

YEAR

HIGH ______° LOW______°

YEAR

HIGH ______° LOW______°

YEAR

HIGH ______° LOW______°

YEAR

HIGH ______° LOW______°

YEAR

HIGH ______° LOW______°

DECEMBER 24

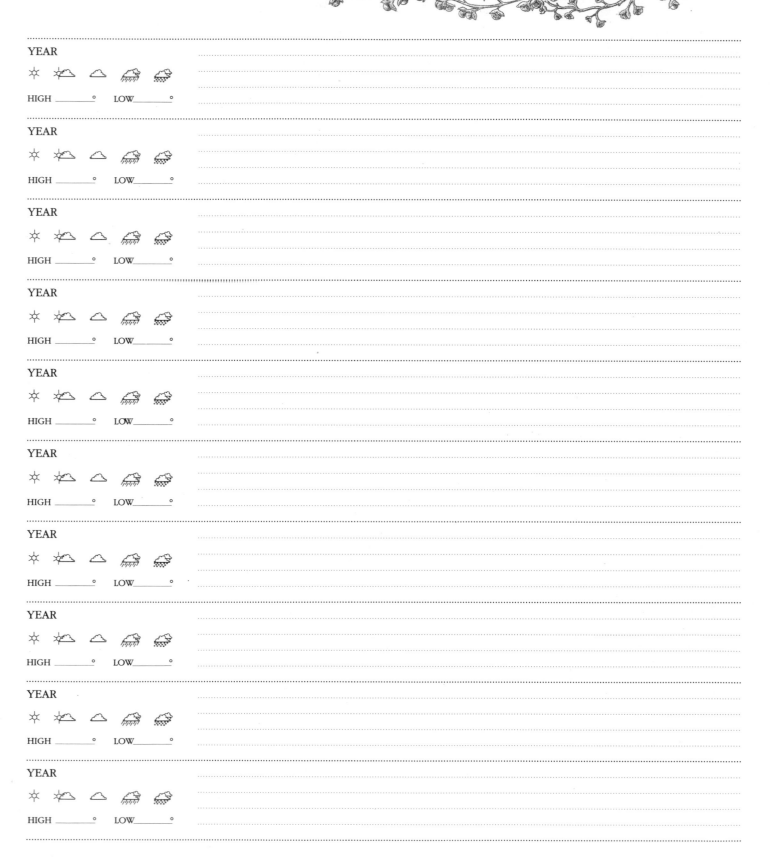

Euphorbia pulcherrima
Poinsettia

YEAR

HIGH ________° LOW________°

YEAR

HIGH ________° LOW________°

YEAR

HIGH ________° LOW________°

YEAR

HIGH ________° LOW________°

YEAR

HIGH ________° LOW________°

YEAR

HIGH ________° LOW________°

YEAR

HIGH ________° LOW________°

YEAR

HIGH ________° LOW________°

YEAR

HIGH ________° LOW________°

YEAR

HIGH ________° LOW________°

DECEMBER 25

Ilex aquifolium

English Holly

YEAR

HIGH ______° LOW ______°

YEAR

HIGH ______° LOW ______°

YEAR

HIGH ______° LOW ______°

YEAR

HIGH ______° LOW ______°

YEAR

HIGH ______° LOW ______°

YEAR

HIGH ______° LOW ______°

YEAR

HIGH ______° LOW ______°

YEAR

HIGH ______° LOW ______°

YEAR

HIGH ______° LOW ______°

YEAR

HIGH ______° LOW ______°

DECEMBER 26

Yucca filamentosa
Adam's Needle

YEAR

HIGH ______° LOW ______°

YEAR

HIGH ______° LOW ______°

YEAR

HIGH ______° LOW ______°

YEAR

HIGH ______° LOW ______°

YEAR

HIGH ______° LOW ______°

YEAR

HIGH ______° LOW ______°

YEAR

HIGH ______° LOW ______°

YEAR

HIGH ______° LOW ______°

YEAR

HIGH ______° LOW ______°

YEAR

HIGH ______° LOW ______°

DECEMBER 27

Zea mays

Corn

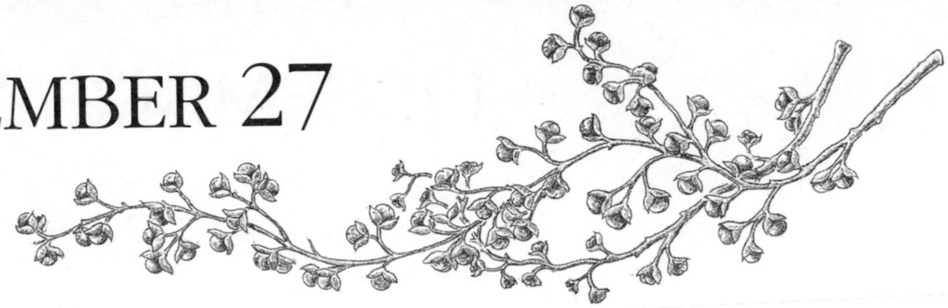

YEAR

HIGH ______° LOW______°

YEAR

HIGH ______° LOW______°

YEAR

HIGH ______° LOW______°

YEAR

HIGH ______° LOW______°

YEAR

HIGH ______° LOW______°

YEAR

HIGH ______° LOW______°

YEAR

HIGH ______° LOW______°

YEAR

HIGH ______° LOW______°

YEAR

HIGH ______° LOW______°

YEAR

HIGH ______° LOW______°

DECEMBER 28

Zingiber officinale
Ginger

YEAR

HIGH ______° LOW______°

YEAR

HIGH ______° LOW______°

YEAR

HIGH ______° LOW______°

YEAR

HIGH ______° LOW______°

YEAR

HIGH ______° LOW______°

YEAR

HIGH ______° LOW______°

YEAR

HIGH ______° LOW______°

YEAR

HIGH ______° LOW______°

YEAR

HIGH ______° LOW______°

YEAR

HIGH ______° LOW______°

DECEMBER 29

Zinnia elegans
Common Zinnia

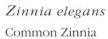

YEAR

HIGH ______° LOW ______°

YEAR

HIGH ______° LOW ______°

YEAR

HIGH ______° LOW ______°

YEAR

HIGH ______° LOW ______°

YEAR

HIGH ______° LOW ______°

YEAR

HIGH ______° LOW ______°

YEAR

HIGH ______° LOW ______°

YEAR

HIGH ______° LOW ______°

YEAR

HIGH ______° LOW ______°

YEAR

HIGH ______° LOW ______°

DECEMBER 30

Zephyranthes atamasco
Zephyr Lily

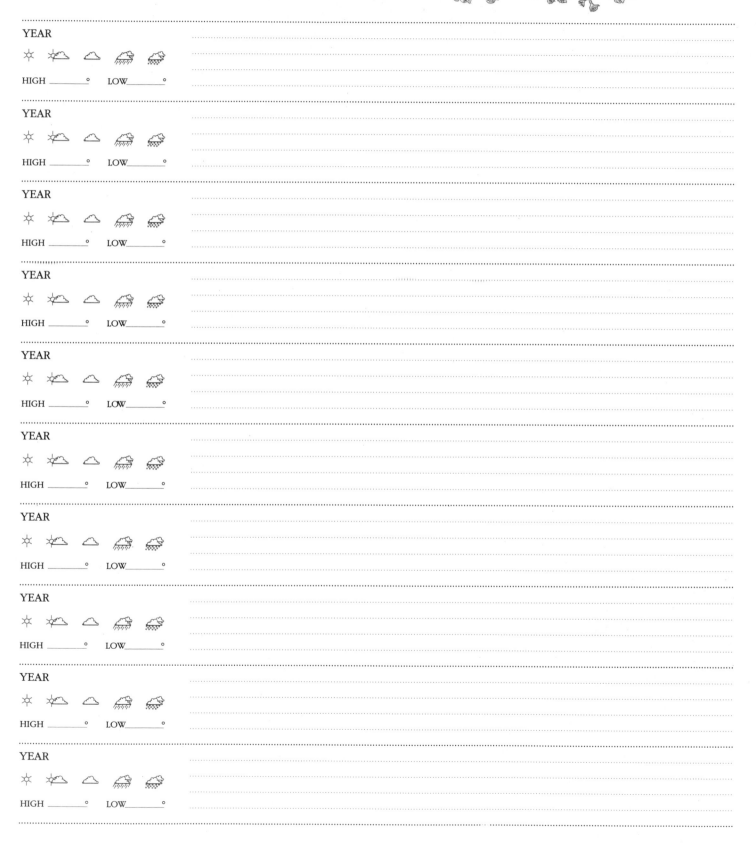

YEAR

HIGH ________° LOW ________°

YEAR

HIGH ________° LOW ________°

YEAR

HIGH ________° LOW ________°

YEAR

HIGH ________° LOW ________°

YEAR

HIGH ________° LOW ________°

YEAR

HIGH ________° LOW ________°

YEAR

HIGH ________° LOW ________°

YEAR

HIGH ________° LOW ________°

YEAR

HIGH ________° LOW ________°

YEAR

HIGH ________° LOW ________°

DECEMBER 31

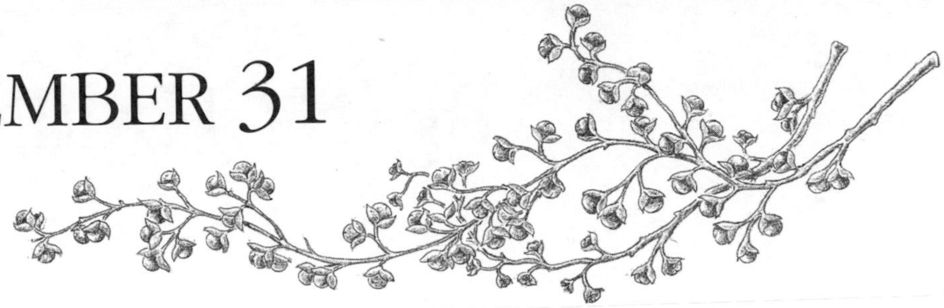

Zizania aquatica
Annual Wild Rice

YEAR

HIGH ________° LOW________°

YEAR

HIGH ________° LOW________°

YEAR

HIGH ________° LOW________°

YEAR

HIGH ________° LOW________°

YEAR

HIGH ________° LOW________°

YEAR

HIGH ________° LOW________°

YEAR

HIGH ________° LOW________°

YEAR

HIGH ________° LOW________°

YEAR

HIGH ________° LOW________°

YEAR

HIGH ________° LOW________°

Plant Hardiness

Last and First Frost Dates

The first well-known meteorologist in America was Commodore Matthew Fontaine Maury, who experimented on meteorology's value to agriculture around 1840. He noted the differences in temperatures between high and low areas, and made recommendations to fruit farmers on how to avoid the dangers of frost.

Average Frost Dates Canada

	Last Spring Frost	*First Fall Frost*
Vancouver, BC	Mar 31	Nov 3
Yellowknife, NT	May 27	Sept 16
Whitehorse, YT	June 8	Aug 30
Calgary, AB	May 25	Sept 15
Edmonton, AB	May 6	Sept 24
Regina, SK	May 24	Sept 11
Winnipeg, MB	May 23	Sept 22
Kingston, ON	May 7	Oct 10
Niagara Falls, ON	May 3	Oct 23
Ottawa, ON	May 8	Sept 30
Sault Ste. Marie, ON	May 24	Sept 29
Sudbury, ON	May 12	Oct 2
Timmins, ON	May 28	Sept 13
Toronto, ON	Apr 20	Oct 29
Thunder Bay, ON	May 30	Sept 12
Windsor, ON	Apr 26	Oct 21
Montreal, PQ	Apr 19	Oct 14
Quebec City, PQ	May 10	Oct 15
Saint John, NB	May 2	Oct 21
Halifax, NS	Apr 30	Oct 19
Charlottetown, PE	May 16	Oct 14
St. John's, NF	June 1	Oct 11

Average Frost Dates United States

	Last Spring Frost	*First Fall Frost*
Albuquerque, NM	Apr 13	Oct 28
Asheville, NC	Apr 12	Oct 24
Atlanta, GA	Mar 21	Nov 18
Baltimore, MD	Mar 28	Nov 19
Bangor, ME	May 1	Oct 4
Birmingham, AL	Mar 19	Nov 14
Bismarck, ND	May 11	Sep 24
Boise, ID	Apr 23	Oct 17
Boston, MA	Apr 5	Nov 8
Buffalo, NY	Apr 30	Oct 25
Burlington, VT	May 8	Oct 3
Caribou, ME	May 19	Sep 21
Charleston, SC	Feb 19	Dec 10
Charleston, WV	Apr 18	Oct 28
Cheyenne, WY	May 14	Oct 2
Chicago, IL	Apr 19	Oct 28
Cleveland, OH	Apr 21	Nov 2
Concord, NH	May 11	Sep 30
Dallas, TX	Mar 18	Nov 17
Denver, CO	Apr 26	Oct 14
Des Moines, IA	Apr 24	Oct 16
Detroit, MI	Apr 21	Oct 20
Duluth, MN	May 22	Sep 24
Eugene, OR	Apr 13	Nov 4
Grand Rapids, MI	Apr 23	Oct 30
Gt. Falls, MT	May 9	Sep 25
Harrisburg, PA	Apr 9	Oct 30
Hartford, CT	Apr 22	Oct 19
Houston, TX	Mar 14	Nov 21
Indianapolis, IN	Apr 17	Oct 27
Jacksonville, FL	Feb 16	Dec 16
Kansas City, MO	Apr 6	Oct 30
Las Vegas, NV	Mar 16	Nov 10
Lexington, KY	Apr 13	Oct 28
Little Rock, AR	Mar 17	Nov 13
Los Angeles, CA	Jan 3	Dec 28
Lubbock, TX	Apr 1	Nov 9
Memphis, TN	Mar 20	Nov 12
Milwaukee, WI	Apr 20	Oct 25
Minneapolis, MN	Apr 30	Oct 13
Montgomery, AL	Feb 27	Dec 3
Nashville, TN	Mar 28	Nov 7
New Orleans, LA	Feb 20	Dec 9
New York City, NY	Apr 7	Nov 12
Norfolk, VA	Mar 19	Nov 16
Okla. City, OK	Mar 28	Nov 7
Omaha, NE	Apr 14	Oct 20
Philadelphia, PA	Mar 30	Nov 17
Phoenix, AZ	Feb 5	Dec 6
Pittsburgh, PA	Apr 20	Oct 23
Pocatello, ID	Apr 28	Oct 6
Portland, ME	Apr 29	Oct 15
Portland, OR	Mar 6	Nov 24
Providence, RI	Apr 13	Oct 27
Pueblo, CO	Apr 23	Oct 14
Raleigh, NC	Mar 24	Nov 16
Rapid City, SD	May 7	Oct 4
Reno, NV	May 8	Oct 10
Richmond, VA	Mar 29	Nov 2
Salt Lake City, UT	Apr 13	Oct 22
San Francisco, CA	Jan 7	Dec 29
Santa Fe, NM	Apr 24	Oct 19
Savannah, GA	Feb 27	Nov 29
Seattle, WA	Mar 14	Nov 24
Shreveport, LA	Mar 8	Nov 15
Sioux City, IA	Apr 27	Oct 13
Sioux Falls, SD	May 5	Oct 3
Springfield, IL	Apr 20	Oct 23
Springfield, MO	Apr 12	Oct 30
Syracuse, NY	Apr 30	Oct 15
Tampa, FL	Jan 10	Dec 26
Texarkana, AR	Mar 21	Nov 9
Trenton, NJ	Apr 4	Nov 8
Tucson, AZ	Mar 19	Nov 19
Washington, DC	Mar 29	Nov 9
Wichita, KS	Apr 5	Nov 1
Wilmington, DE	Apr 18	Oct 26

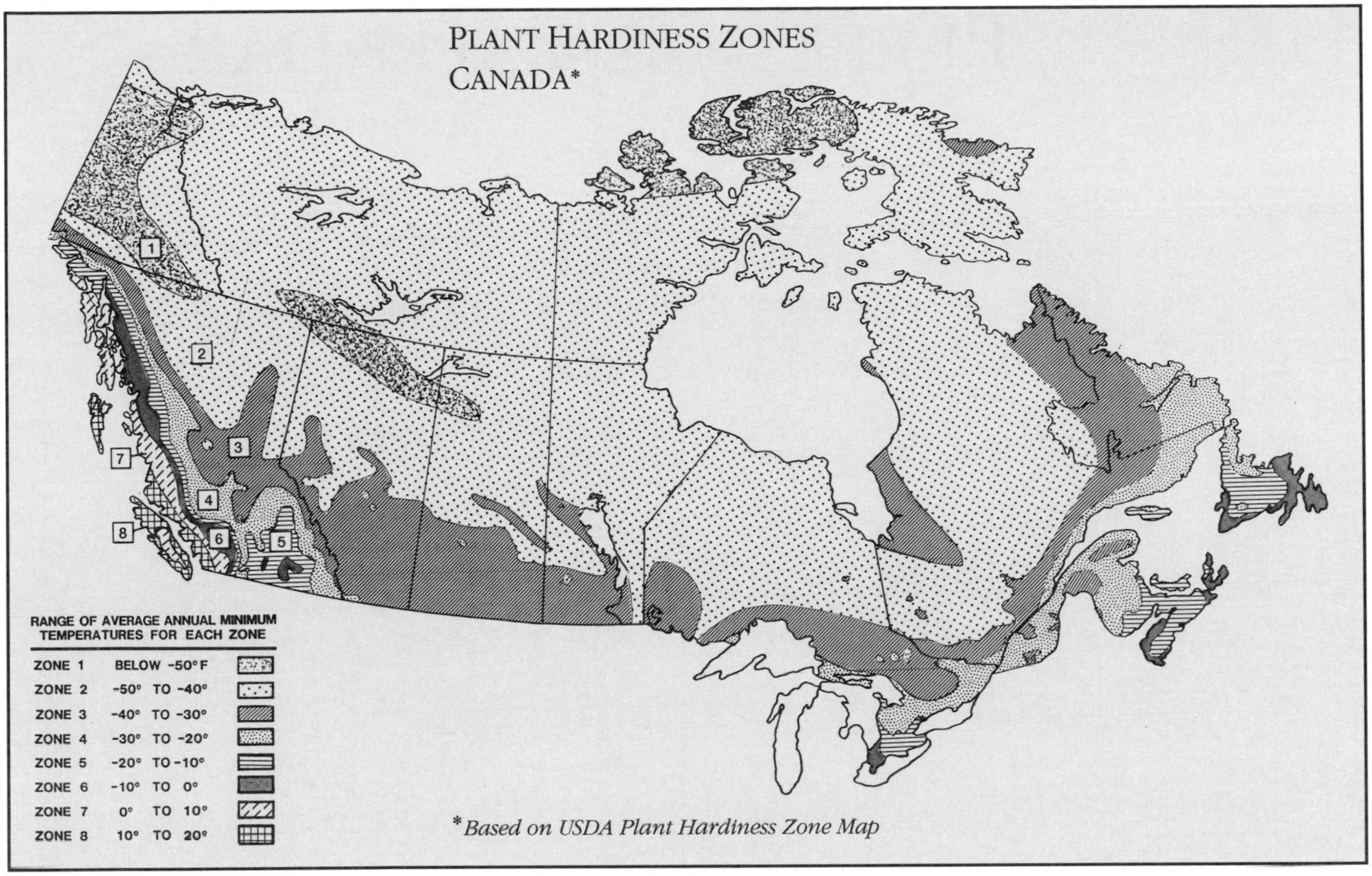
PLANT HARDINESS ZONES
CANADA*
RANGE OF AVERAGE ANNUAL MINIMUM TEMPERATURES FOR EACH ZONE
ZONE 1 BELOW -50°F
ZONE 2 -50° TO -40°
ZONE 3 -40° TO -30°
ZONE 4 -30° TO -20°
ZONE 5 -20° TO -10°
ZONE 6 -10° TO 0°
ZONE 7 0° TO 10°
ZONE 8 10° TO 20°
*Based on USDA Plant Hardiness Zone Map

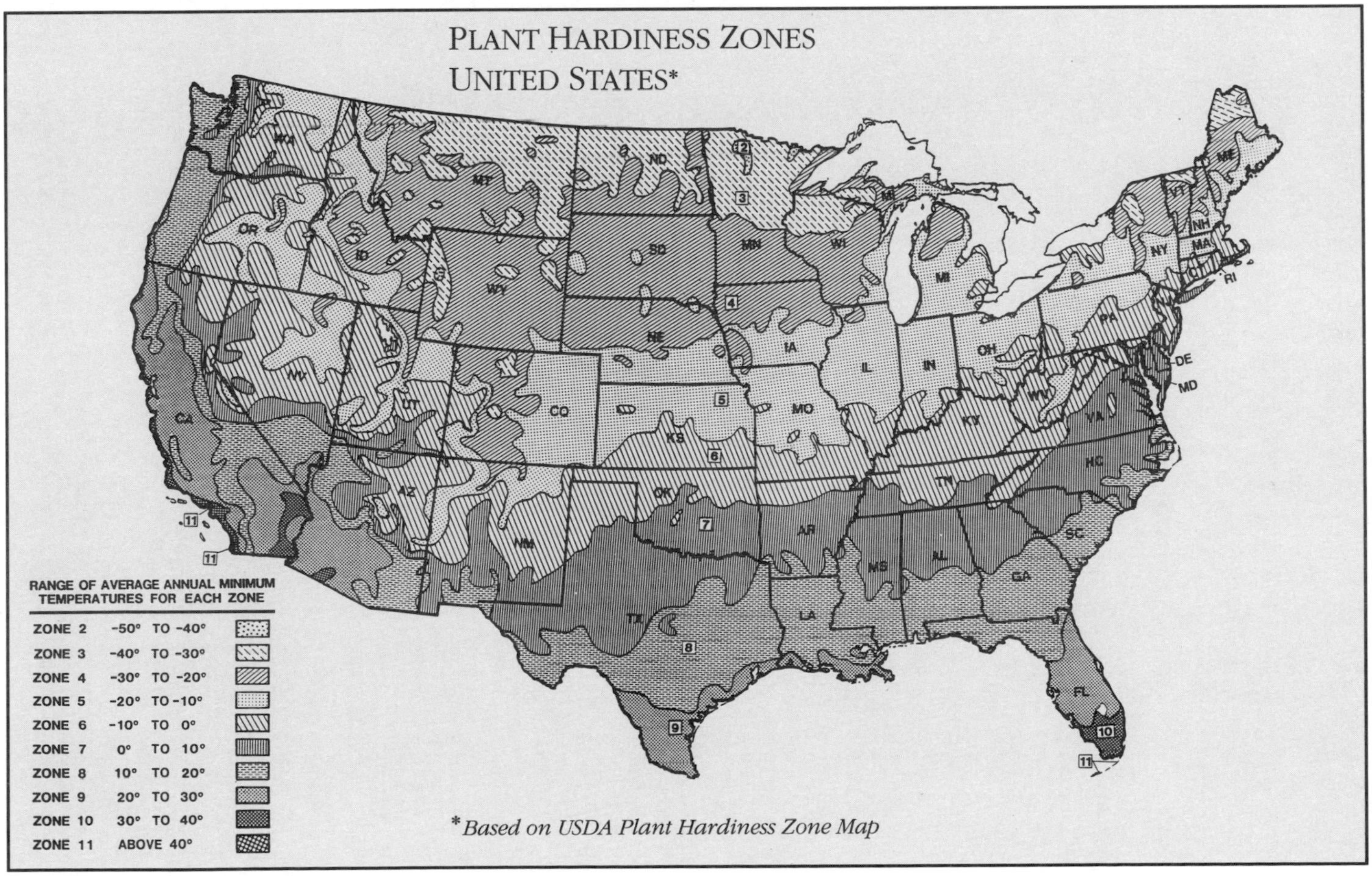
PLANT HARDINESS ZONES
UNITED STATES*
RANGE OF AVERAGE ANNUAL MINIMUM TEMPERATURES FOR EACH ZONE
ZONE 2 -50° TO -40°
ZONE 3 -40° TO -30°
ZONE 4 -30° TO -20°
ZONE 5 -20° TO -10°
ZONE 6 -10° TO 0°
ZONE 7 0° TO 10°
ZONE 8 10° TO 20°
ZONE 9 20° TO 30°
ZONE 10 30° TO 40°
ZONE 11 ABOVE 40°
*Based on USDA Plant Hardiness Zone Map

Perpetual Calendar

INDEX

1901...3	1952.10
1902...4	1953..5
1903...5	1954..6
1904.13	1955..7
1905..1	1956..8
1906..2	1957..3
1907..3	1958..4
1908.11	1959..5
1909..6	1960.13
1910..7	1961..1
1911..1	1962..2
1912..9	1963..3
1913..4	1964.11
1914..5	1965..6
1915..6	1966..7
1916.14	1967..1
1917..2	1968..9
1918..3	1969..4
1919..4	1970..5
1920.12	1971..6
1921..7	1972.14
1922..1	1973..2
1923..2	1974..3
1924.10	1975..4
1925..5	1976.12
1926..6	1977..7
1927..7	1978..1
1928..8	1979..2
1929..3	1980.10
1930..4	1981..5
1931..5	1982..6
1932.13	1983..7
1933..1	1984..8
1934..2	1985..3
1935..3	1986..4
1936.11	1987..5
1937..6	1988.13
1938..7	1989..1
1939..1	1990..2
1940..9	1991..3
1941..4	1992.11
1942..5	1993..6
1943..6	1994..7
1944.14	1995..1
1945..2	1996..9
1946..3	1997..4
1947..4	1998..5
1948.12	1999..6
1949..7	2000.14
1950..1	2001..2
1951..2	2002..3

1

January

S	M	T	W	T	F	S
1	2	3	4	5	6	7
8	9	10	11	12	13	14
15	16	17	18	19	20	21
22	23	24	25	26	27	28
29	30	31				

February

S	M	T	W	T	F	S
			1	2	3	4
5	6	7	8	9	10	11
12	13	14	15	16	17	18
19	20	21	22	23	24	25
26	27	28				

March

S	M	T	W	T	F	S
			1	2	3	4
5	6	7	8	9	10	11
12	13	14	15	16	17	18
19	20	21	22	23	24	25
26	27	28	29	30	31	

April

S	M	T	W	T	F	S
						1
2	3	4	5	6	7	8
9	10	11	12	13	14	15
16	17	18	19	20	21	22
23	24	25	26	27	28	29
30						

May

S	M	T	W	T	F	S
	1	2	3	4	5	6
7	8	9	10	11	12	13
14	15	16	17	18	19	20
21	22	23	24	25	26	27
28	29	30	31			

June

S	M	T	W	T	F	S
				1	2	3
4	5	6	7	8	9	10
11	12	13	14	15	16	17
18	19	20	21	22	23	24
25	26	27	28	29	30	

July

S	M	T	W	T	F	S
						1
2	3	4	5	6	7	8
9	10	11	12	13	14	15
16	17	18	19	20	21	22
23	24	25	26	27	28	29
30	31					

August

S	M	T	W	T	F	S
		1	2	3	4	5
6	7	8	9	10	11	12
13	14	15	16	17	18	19
20	21	22	23	24	25	26
27	28	29	30	31		

September

S	M	T	W	T	F	S
					1	2
3	4	5	6	7	8	9
10	11	12	13	14	15	16
17	18	19	20	21	22	23
24	25	26	27	28	29	30

October

S	M	T	W	T	F	S
1	2	3	4	5	6	7
8	9	10	11	12	13	14
15	16	17	18	19	20	21
22	23	24	25	26	27	28
29	30	31				

November

S	M	T	W	T	F	S
			1	2	3	4
5	6	7	8	9	10	11
12	13	14	15	16	17	18
19	20	21	22	23	24	25
26	27	28	29	30		

December

S	M	T	W	T	F	S
					1	2
3	4	5	6	7	8	9
10	11	12	13	14	15	16
17	18	19	20	21	22	23
24	25	26	27	28	29	30
31						

2

January

S	M	T	W	T	F	S
	1	2	3	4	5	6
7	8	9	10	11	12	13
14	15	16	17	18	19	20
21	22	23	24	25	26	27
28	29	30	31			

February

S	M	T	W	T	F	S
				1	2	3
4	5	6	7	8	9	10
11	12	13	14	15	16	17
18	19	20	21	22	23	24
25	26	27	28			

March

S	M	T	W	T	F	S
				1	2	3
4	5	6	7	8	9	10
11	12	13	14	15	16	17
18	19	20	21	22	23	24
25	26	27	28	29	30	31

April

S	M	T	W	T	F	S
1	2	3	4	5	6	7
8	9	10	11	12	13	14
15	16	17	18	19	20	21
22	23	24	25	26	27	28
29	30					

May

S	M	T	W	T	F	S
		1	2	3	4	5
6	7	8	9	10	11	12
13	14	15	16	17	18	19
20	21	22	23	24	25	26
27	28	29	30	31		

June

S	M	T	W	T	F	S
					1	2
3	4	5	6	7	8	9
10	11	12	13	14	15	16
17	18	19	20	21	22	23
24	25	26	27	28	29	30

July

S	M	T	W	T	F	S
1	2	3	4	5	6	7
8	9	10	11	12	13	14
15	16	17	18	19	20	21
22	23	24	25	26	27	28
29	30	31				

August

S	M	T	W	T	F	S
			1	2	3	4
5	6	7	8	9	10	11
12	13	14	15	16	17	18
19	20	21	22	23	24	25
26	27	28	29	30	31	

September

S	M	T	W	T	F	S
						1
2	3	4	5	6	7	8
9	10	11	12	13	14	15
16	17	18	19	20	21	22
23	24	25	26	27	28	29
30						

October

S	M	T	W	T	F	S
	1	2	3	4	5	6
7	8	9	10	11	12	13
14	15	16	17	18	19	20
21	22	23	24	25	26	27
28	29	30	31			

November

S	M	T	W	T	F	S
				1	2	3
4	5	6	7	8	9	10
11	12	13	14	15	16	17
18	19	20	21	22	23	24
25	26	27	28	29	30	

December

S	M	T	W	T	F	S
						1
2	3	4	5	6	7	8
9	10	11	12	13	14	15
16	17	18	19	20	21	22
23	24	25	26	27	28	29
30	31					

3

January

S	M	T	W	T	F	S
		1	2	3	4	5
6	7	8	9	10	11	12
13	14	15	16	17	18	19
20	21	22	23	24	25	26
27	28	29	30	31		

February

S	M	T	W	T	F	S
					1	2
3	4	5	6	7	8	9
10	11	12	13	14	15	16
17	18	19	20	21	22	23
24	25	26	27	28		

March

S	M	T	W	T	F	S
					1	2
3	4	5	6	7	8	9
10	11	12	13	14	15	16
17	18	19	20	21	22	23
24	25	26	27	28	29	30
31						

April

S	M	T	W	T	F	S
	1	2	3	4	5	6
7	8	9	10	11	12	13
14	15	16	17	18	19	20
21	22	23	24	25	26	27
28	29	30				

May

S	M	T	W	T	F	S
			1	2	3	4
5	6	7	8	9	10	11
12	13	14	15	16	17	18
19	20	21	22	23	24	25
26	27	28	29	30	31	

June

S	M	T	W	T	F	S
						1
2	3	4	5	6	7	8
9	10	11	12	13	14	15
16	17	18	19	20	21	22
23	24	25	26	27	28	29
30						

July

S	M	T	W	T	F	S
	1	2	3	4	5	6
7	8	9	10	11	12	13
14	15	16	17	18	19	20
21	22	23	24	25	26	27
28	29	30	31			

August

S	M	T	W	T	F	S
				1	2	3
4	5	6	7	8	9	10
11	12	13	14	15	16	17
18	19	20	21	22	23	24
25	26	27	28	29	30	31

September

S	M	T	W	T	F	S
1	2	3	4	5	6	7
8	9	10	11	12	13	14
15	16	17	18	19	20	21
22	23	24	25	26	27	28
29	30					

October

S	M	T	W	T	F	S
		1	2	3	4	5
6	7	8	9	10	11	12
13	14	15	16	17	18	19
20	21	22	23	24	25	26
27	28	29	30	31		

November

S	M	T	W	T	F	S
					1	2
3	4	5	6	7	8	9
10	11	12	13	14	15	16
17	18	19	20	21	22	23
24	25	26	27	28	29	30

December

S	M	T	W	T	F	S
1	2	3	4	5	6	7
8	9	10	11	12	13	14
15	16	17	18	19	20	21
22	23	24	25	26	27	28
29	30	31				

4

January

S	M	T	W	T	F	S
			1	2	3	4
5	6	7	8	9	10	11
12	13	14	15	16	17	18
19	20	21	22	23	24	25
26	27	28	29	30	31	

February

S	M	T	W	T	F	S
						1
2	3	4	5	6	7	8
9	10	11	12	13	14	15
16	17	18	19	20	21	22
23	24	25	26	27	28	

March

S	M	T	W	T	F	S
						1
2	3	4	5	6	7	8
9	10	11	12	13	14	15
16	17	18	19	20	21	22
23	24	25	26	27	28	29
30	31					

April

S	M	T	W	T	F	S
		1	2	3	4	5
6	7	8	9	10	11	12
13	14	15	16	17	18	19
20	21	22	23	24	25	26
27	28	29	30			

May

S	M	T	W	T	F	S
				1	2	3
4	5	6	7	8	9	10
11	12	13	14	15	16	17
18	19	20	21	22	23	24
25	26	27	28	29	30	31

June

S	M	T	W	T	F	S
1	2	3	4	5	6	7
8	9	10	11	12	13	14
15	16	17	18	19	20	21
22	23	24	25	26	27	28
29	30					

July

S	M	T	W	T	F	S
		1	2	3	4	5
6	7	8	9	10	11	12
13	14	15	16	17	18	19
20	21	22	23	24	25	26
27	28	29	30	31		

August

S	M	T	W	T	F	S
					1	2
3	4	5	6	7	8	9
10	11	12	13	14	15	16
17	18	19	20	21	22	23
24	25	26	27	28	29	30
31						

September

S	M	T	W	T	F	S
	1	2	3	4	5	6
7	8	9	10	11	12	13
14	15	16	17	18	19	20
21	22	23	24	25	26	27
28	29	30				

October

S	M	T	W	T	F	S
			1	2	3	4
5	6	7	8	9	10	11
12	13	14	15	16	17	18
19	20	21	22	23	24	25
26	27	28	29	30	31	

November

S	M	T	W	T	F	S
						1
2	3	4	5	6	7	8
9	10	11	12	13	14	15
16	17	18	19	20	21	22
23	24	25	26	27	28	29
30						

December

S	M	T	W	T	F	S
	1	2	3	4	5	6
7	8	9	10	11	12	13
14	15	16	17	18	19	20
21	22	23	24	25	26	27
28	29	30	31			

5

January

S	M	T	W	T	F	S
				1	2	3
4	5	6	7	8	9	10
11	12	13	14	15	16	17
18	19	20	21	22	23	24
25	26	27	28	29	30	31

February

S	M	T	W	T	F	S
1	2	3	4	5	6	7
8	9	10	11	12	13	14
15	16	17	18	19	20	21
22	23	24	25	26	27	28

March

S	M	T	W	T	F	S
1	2	3	4	5	6	7
8	9	10	11	12	13	14
15	16	17	18	19	20	21
22	23	24	25	26	27	28
29	30	31				

April

S	M	T	W	T	F	S
			1	2	3	4
5	6	7	8	9	10	11
12	13	14	15	16	17	18
19	20	21	22	23	24	25
26	27	28	29	30		

May

S	M	T	W	T	F	S
					1	2
3	4	5	6	7	8	9
10	11	12	13	14	15	16
17	18	19	20	21	22	23
24	25	26	27	28	29	30
31						

June

S	M	T	W	T	F	S
	1	2	3	4	5	6
7	8	9	10	11	12	13
14	15	16	17	18	19	20
21	22	23	24	25	26	27
28	29	30				

July

S	M	T	W	T	F	S
			1	2	3	4
5	6	7	8	9	10	11
12	13	14	15	16	17	18
19	20	21	22	23	24	25
26	27	28	29	30	31	

August

S	M	T	W	T	F	S
						1
2	3	4	5	6	7	8
9	10	11	12	13	14	15
16	17	18	19	20	21	22
23	24	25	26	27	28	29
30	31					

September

S	M	T	W	T	F	S
		1	2	3	4	5
6	7	8	9	10	11	12
13	14	15	16	17	18	19
20	21	22	23	24	25	26
27	28	29	30			

October

S	M	T	W	T	F	S
				1	2	3
4	5	6	7	8	9	10
11	12	13	14	15	16	17
18	19	20	21	22	23	24
25	26	27	28	29	30	31

November

S	M	T	W	T	F	S
1	2	3	4	5	6	7
8	9	10	11	12	13	14
15	16	17	18	19	20	21
22	23	24	25	26	27	28
29	30					

December

S	M	T	W	T	F	S
		1	2	3	4	5
6	7	8	9	10	11	12
13	14	15	16	17	18	19
20	21	22	23	24	25	26
27	28	29	30	31		

6

January

S	M	T	W	T	F	S
					1	2
3	4	5	6	7	8	9
10	11	12	13	14	15	16
17	18	19	20	21	22	23
24	25	26	27	28	29	30
31						

February

S	M	T	W	T	F	S
	1	2	3	4	5	6
7	8	9	10	11	12	13
14	15	16	17	18	19	20
21	22	23	24	25	26	27
28						

March

S	M	T	W	T	F	S
	1	2	3	4	5	6
7	8	9	10	11	12	13
14	15	16	17	18	19	20
21	22	23	24	25	26	27
28	29	30	31			

April

S	M	T	W	T	F	S
				1	2	3
4	5	6	7	8	9	10
11	12	13	14	15	16	17
18	19	20	21	22	23	24
25	26	27	28	29	30	

May

S	M	T	W	T	F	S
						1
2	3	4	5	6	7	8
9	10	11	12	13	14	15
16	17	18	19	20	21	22
23	24	25	26	27	28	29
30	31					

June

S	M	T	W	T	F	S
		1	2	3	4	5
6	7	8	9	10	11	12
13	14	15	16	17	18	19
20	21	22	23	24	25	26
27	28	29	30			

July

S	M	T	W	T	F	S
				1	2	3
4	5	6	7	8	9	10
11	12	13	14	15	16	17
18	19	20	21	22	23	24
25	26	27	28	29	30	31

August

S	M	T	W	T	F	S
1	2	3	4	5	6	7
8	9	10	11	12	13	14
15	16	17	18	19	20	21
22	23	24	25	26	27	28
29	30	31				

September

S	M	T	W	T	F	S
			1	2	3	4
5	6	7	8	9	10	11
12	13	14	15	16	17	18
19	20	21	22	23	24	25
26	27	28	29	30		

October

S	M	T	W	T	F	S
					1	2
3	4	5	6	7	8	9
10	11	12	13	14	15	16
17	18	19	20	21	22	23
24	25	26	27	28	29	30
31						

November

S	M	T	W	T	F	S
	1	2	3	4	5	6
7	8	9	10	11	12	13
14	15	16	17	18	19	20
21	22	23	24	25	26	27
28	29	30				

December

S	M	T	W	T	F	S
			1	2	3	4
5	6	7	8	9	10	11
12	13	14	15	16	17	18
19	20	21	22	23	24	25
26	27	28	29	30	31	

7

January

S	M	T	W	T	F	S
						1
2	3	4	5	6	7	8
9	10	11	12	13	14	15
16	17	18	19	20	21	22
23	24	25	26	27	28	29
30	31					

February

S	M	T	W	T	F	S
		1	2	3	4	5
6	7	8	9	10	11	12
13	14	15	16	17	18	19
20	21	22	23	24	25	26
27	28					

March

S	M	T	W	T	F	S
		1	2	3	4	5
6	7	8	9	10	11	12
13	14	15	16	17	18	19
20	21	22	23	24	25	26
27	28	29	30	31		

April

S	M	T	W	T	F	S
					1	2
3	4	5	6	7	8	9
10	11	12	13	14	15	16
17	18	19	20	21	22	23
24	25	26	27	28	29	30

May

S	M	T	W	T	F	S
1	2	3	4	5	6	7
8	9	10	11	12	13	14
15	16	17	18	19	20	21
22	23	24	25	26	27	28
29	30	31				

June

S	M	T	W	T	F	S
			1	2	3	4
5	6	7	8	9	10	11
12	13	14	15	16	17	18
19	20	21	22	23	24	25
26	27	28	29	30		

July

S	M	T	W	T	F	S
					1	2
3	4	5	6	7	8	9
10	11	12	13	14	15	16
17	18	19	20	21	22	23
24	25	26	27	28	29	30
31						

August

S	M	T	W	T	F	S
	1	2	3	4	5	6
7	8	9	10	11	12	13
14	15	16	17	18	19	20
21	22	23	24	25	26	27
28	29	30	31			

September

S	M	T	W	T	F	S
				1	2	3
4	5	6	7	8	9	10
11	12	13	14	15	16	17
18	19	20	21	22	23	24
25	26	27	28	29	30	

October

S	M	T	W	T	F	S
						1
2	3	4	5	6	7	8
9	10	11	12	13	14	15
16	17	18	19	20	21	22
23	24	25	26	27	28	29
30	31					

November

S	M	T	W	T	F	S
		1	2	3	4	5
6	7	8	9	10	11	12
13	14	15	16	17	18	19
20	21	22	23	24	25	26
27	28	29	30			

December

S	M	T	W	T	F	S
				1	2	3
4	5	6	7	8	9	10
11	12	13	14	15	16	17
18	19	20	21	22	23	24
25	26	27	28	29	30	31

There are only 14 different calendars possible. They are given here with an index at the sides covering the years from 1901 to 2099. The calendar to use for a given year is indicated by the number beside it.

8

January

S	M	T	W	T	F	S
1	2	3	4	5	6	7
8	9	10	11	12	13	14
15	16	17	18	19	20	21
22	23	24	25	26	27	28
29	30	31				

February

S	M	T	W	T	F	S
			1	2	3	4
5	6	7	8	9	10	11
12	13	14	15	16	17	18
19	20	21	22	23	24	25
26	27	28	29			

March

S	M	T	W	T	F	S
				1	2	3
4	5	6	7	8	9	10
11	12	13	14	15	16	17
18	19	20	21	22	23	24
25	26	27	28	29	30	31

April

S	M	T	W	T	F	S
1	2	3	4	5	6	7
8	9	10	11	12	13	14
15	16	17	18	19	20	21
22	23	24	25	26	27	28
29	30					

May

S	M	T	W	T	F	S
		1	2	3	4	5
6	7	8	9	10	11	12
13	14	15	16	17	18	19
20	21	22	23	24	25	26
27	28	29	30	31		

June

S	M	T	W	T	F	S
					1	2
3	4	5	6	7	8	9
10	11	12	13	14	15	16
17	18	19	20	21	22	23
24	25	26	27	28	29	30

July

S	M	T	W	T	F	S
1	2	3	4	5	6	7
8	9	10	11	12	13	14
15	16	17	18	19	20	21
22	23	24	25	26	27	28
29	30	31				

August

S	M	T	W	T	F	S
			1	2	3	4
5	6	7	8	9	10	11
12	13	14	15	16	17	18
19	20	21	22	23	24	25
26	27	28	29	30	31	

September

S	M	T	W	T	F	S
						1
2	3	4	5	6	7	8
9	10	11	12	13	14	15
16	17	18	19	20	21	22
23	24	25	26	27	28	29
30						

October

S	M	T	W	T	F	S
	1	2	3	4	5	6
7	8	9	10	11	12	13
14	15	16	17	18	19	20
21	22	23	24	25	26	27
28	29	30	31			

November

S	M	T	W	T	F	S
				1	2	3
4	5	6	7	8	9	10
11	12	13	14	15	16	17
18	19	20	21	22	23	24
25	26	27	28	29	30	

December

S	M	T	W	T	F	S
						1
2	3	4	5	6	7	8
9	10	11	12	13	14	15
16	17	18	19	20	21	22
23	24	25	26	27	28	29
30	31					

9

January

S	M	T	W	T	F	S
	1	2	3	4	5	6
7	8	9	10	11	12	13
14	15	16	17	18	19	20
21	22	23	24	25	26	27
28	29	30	31			

February

S	M	T	W	T	F	S
				1	2	3
4	5	6	7	8	9	10
11	12	13	14	15	16	17
18	19	20	21	22	23	24
25	26	27	28	29		

March

S	M	T	W	T	F	S
					1	2
3	4	5	6	7	8	9
10	11	12	13	14	15	16
17	18	19	20	21	22	23
24	25	26	27	28	29	30
31						

April

S	M	T	W	T	F	S
	1	2	3	4	5	6
7	8	9	10	11	12	13
14	15	16	17	18	19	20
21	22	23	24	25	26	27
28	29	30				

May

S	M	T	W	T	F	S
			1	2	3	4
5	6	7	8	9	10	11
12	13	14	15	16	17	18
19	20	21	22	23	24	25
26	27	28	29	30	31	

June

S	M	T	W	T	F	S
						1
2	3	4	5	6	7	8
9	10	11	12	13	14	15
16	17	18	19	20	21	22
23	24	25	26	27	28	29
30						

July

S	M	T	W	T	F	S
	1	2	3	4	5	6
7	8	9	10	11	12	13
14	15	16	17	18	19	20
21	22	23	24	25	26	27
28	29	30	31			

August

S	M	T	W	T	F	S
				1	2	3
4	5	6	7	8	9	10
11	12	13	14	15	16	17
18	19	20	21	22	23	24
25	26	27	28	29	30	31

September

S	M	T	W	T	F	S
1	2	3	4	5	6	7
8	9	10	11	12	13	14
15	16	17	18	19	20	21
22	23	24	25	26	27	28
29	30					

October

S	M	T	W	T	F	S
		1	2	3	4	5
6	7	8	9	10	11	12
13	14	15	16	17	18	19
20	21	22	23	24	25	26
27	28	29	30	31		

November

S	M	T	W	T	F	S
					1	2
3	4	5	6	7	8	9
10	11	12	13	14	15	16
17	18	19	20	21	22	23
24	25	26	27	28	29	30

December

S	M	T	W	T	F	S
1	2	3	4	5	6	7
8	9	10	11	12	13	14
15	16	17	18	19	20	21
22	23	24	25	26	27	28
29	30	31				

10

January

S	M	T	W	T	F	S
		1	2	3	4	5
6	7	8	9	10	11	12
13	14	15	16	17	18	19
20	21	22	23	24	25	26
27	28	29	30	31		

February

S	M	T	W	T	F	S
					1	2
3	4	5	6	7	8	9
10	11	12	13	14	15	16
17	18	19	20	21	22	23
24	25	26	27	28	29	

March

S	M	T	W	T	F	S
						1
2	3	4	5	6	7	8
9	10	11	12	13	14	15
16	17	18	19	20	21	22
23	24	25	26	27	28	29
30	31					

April

S	M	T	W	T	F	S
		1	2	3	4	5
6	7	8	9	10	11	12
13	14	15	16	17	18	19
20	21	22	23	24	25	26
27	28	29	30			

May

S	M	T	W	T	F	S
				1	2	3
4	5	6	7	8	9	10
11	12	13	14	15	16	17
18	19	20	21	22	23	24
25	26	27	28	29	30	31

June

S	M	T	W	T	F	S
1	2	3	4	5	6	7
8	9	10	11	12	13	14
15	16	17	18	19	20	21
22	23	24	25	26	27	28
29	30					

July

S	M	T	W	T	F	S
		1	2	3	4	5
6	7	8	9	10	11	12
13	14	15	16	17	18	19
20	21	22	23	24	25	26
27	28	29	30	31		

August

S	M	T	W	T	F	S
					1	2
3	4	5	6	7	8	9
10	11	12	13	14	15	16
17	18	19	20	21	22	23
24	25	26	27	28	29	30
31						

September

S	M	T	W	T	F	S
	1	2	3	4	5	6
7	8	9	10	11	12	13
14	15	16	17	18	19	20
21	22	23	24	25	26	27
28	29	30				

October

S	M	T	W	T	F	S
			1	2	3	4
5	6	7	8	9	10	11
12	13	14	15	16	17	18
19	20	21	22	23	24	25
26	27	28	29	30	31	

November

S	M	T	W	T	F	S
						1
2	3	4	5	6	7	8
9	10	11	12	13	14	15
16	17	18	19	20	21	22
23	24	25	26	27	28	29
30						

December

S	M	T	W	T	F	S
	1	2	3	4	5	6
7	8	9	10	11	12	13
14	15	16	17	18	19	20
21	22	23	24	25	26	27
28	29	30	31			

11

January

S	M	T	W	T	F	S
			1	2	3	4
5	6	7	8	9	10	11
12	13	14	15	16	17	18
19	20	21	22	23	24	25
26	27	28	29	30	31	

February

S	M	T	W	T	F	S
						1
2	3	4	5	6	7	8
9	10	11	12	13	14	15
16	17	18	19	20	21	22
23	24	25	26	27	28	29

March

S	M	T	W	T	F	S
1	2	3	4	5	6	7
8	9	10	11	12	13	14
15	16	17	18	19	20	21
22	23	24	25	26	27	28
29	30	31				

April

S	M	T	W	T	F	S
			1	2	3	4
5	6	7	8	9	10	11
12	13	14	15	16	17	18
19	20	21	22	23	24	25
26	27	28	29	30		

May

S	M	T	W	T	F	S
					1	2
3	4	5	6	7	8	9
10	11	12	13	14	15	16
17	18	19	20	21	22	23
24	25	26	27	28	29	30
31						

June

S	M	T	W	T	F	S
	1	2	3	4	5	6
7	8	9	10	11	12	13
14	15	16	17	18	19	20
21	22	23	24	25	26	27
28	29	30				

July

S	M	T	W	T	F	S
			1	2	3	4
5	6	7	8	9	10	11
12	13	14	15	16	17	18
19	20	21	22	23	24	25
26	27	28	29	30	31	

August

S	M	T	W	T	F	S
						1
2	3	4	5	6	7	8
9	10	11	12	13	14	15
16	17	18	19	20	21	22
23	24	25	26	27	28	29
30	31					

September

S	M	T	W	T	F	S
		1	2	3	4	5
6	7	8	9	10	11	12
13	14	15	16	17	18	19
20	21	22	23	24	25	26
27	28	29	30			

October

S	M	T	W	T	F	S
				1	2	3
4	5	6	7	8	9	10
11	12	13	14	15	16	17
18	19	20	21	22	23	24
25	26	27	28	29	30	31

November

S	M	T	W	T	F	S
1	2	3	4	5	6	7
8	9	10	11	12	13	14
15	16	17	18	19	20	21
22	23	24	25	26	27	28
29	30					

December

S	M	T	W	T	F	S
		1	2	3	4	5
6	7	8	9	10	11	12
13	14	15	16	17	18	19
20	21	22	23	24	25	26
27	28	29	30	31		

12

January

S	M	T	W	T	F	S
				1	2	3
4	5	6	7	8	9	10
11	12	13	14	15	16	17
18	19	20	21	22	23	24
25	26	27	28	29	30	31

February

S	M	T	W	T	F	S
1	2	3	4	5	6	7
8	9	10	11	12	13	14
15	16	17	18	19	20	21
22	23	24	25	26	27	28
29						

March

S	M	T	W	T	F	S
	1	2	3	4	5	6
7	8	9	10	11	12	13
14	15	16	17	18	19	20
21	22	23	24	25	26	27
28	29	30	31			

April

S	M	T	W	T	F	S
				1	2	3
4	5	6	7	8	9	10
11	12	13	14	15	16	17
18	19	20	21	22	23	24
25	26	27	28	29	30	

May

S	M	T	W	T	F	S
						1
2	3	4	5	6	7	8
9	10	11	12	13	14	15
16	17	18	19	20	21	22
23	24	25	26	27	28	29
30	31					

June

S	M	T	W	T	F	S
		1	2	3	4	5
6	7	8	9	10	11	12
13	14	15	16	17	18	19
20	21	22	23	24	25	26
27	28	29	30			

July

S	M	T	W	T	F	S
				1	2	3
4	5	6	7	8	9	10
11	12	13	14	15	16	17
18	19	20	21	22	23	24
25	26	27	28	29	30	31

August

S	M	T	W	T	F	S
1	2	3	4	5	6	7
8	9	10	11	12	13	14
15	16	17	18	19	20	21
22	23	24	25	26	27	28
29	30	31				

September

S	M	T	W	T	F	S
			1	2	3	4
5	6	7	8	9	10	11
12	13	14	15	16	17	18
19	20	21	22	23	24	25
26	27	28	29	30		

October

S	M	T	W	T	F	S
					1	2
3	4	5	6	7	8	9
10	11	12	13	14	15	16
17	18	19	20	21	22	23
24	25	26	27	28	29	30
31						

November

S	M	T	W	T	F	S
	1	2	3	4	5	6
7	8	9	10	11	12	13
14	15	16	17	18	19	20
21	22	23	24	25	26	27
28	29	30				

December

S	M	T	W	T	F	S
			1	2	3	4
5	6	7	8	9	10	11
12	13	14	15	16	17	18
19	20	21	22	23	24	25
26	27	28	29	30	31	

13

January

S	M	T	W	T	F	S
					1	2
3	4	5	6	7	8	9
10	11	12	13	14	15	16
17	18	19	20	21	22	23
24	25	26	27	28	29	30
31						

February

S	M	T	W	T	F	S
	1	2	3	4	5	6
7	8	9	10	11	12	13
14	15	16	17	18	19	20
21	22	23	24	25	26	27
28	29					

March

S	M	T	W	T	F	S
		1	2	3	4	5
6	7	8	9	10	11	12
13	14	15	16	17	18	19
20	21	22	23	24	25	26
27	28	29	30	31		

April

S	M	T	W	T	F	S
					1	2
3	4	5	6	7	8	9
10	11	12	13	14	15	16
17	18	19	20	21	22	23
24	25	26	27	28	29	30

May

S	M	T	W	T	F	S
1	2	3	4	5	6	7
8	9	10	11	12	13	14
15	16	17	18	19	20	21
22	23	24	25	26	27	28
29	30	31				

June

S	M	T	W	T	F	S
			1	2	3	4
5	6	7	8	9	10	11
12	13	14	15	16	17	18
19	20	21	22	23	24	25
26	27	28	29	30		

July

S	M	T	W	T	F	S
					1	2
3	4	5	6	7	8	9
10	11	12	13	14	15	16
17	18	19	20	21	22	23
24	25	26	27	28	29	30
31						

August

S	M	T	W	T	F	S
	1	2	3	4	5	6
7	8	9	10	11	12	13
14	15	16	17	18	19	20
21	22	23	24	25	26	27
28	29	30	31			

September

S	M	T	W	T	F	S
				1	2	3
4	5	6	7	8	9	10
11	12	13	14	15	16	17
18	19	20	21	22	23	24
25	26	27	28	29	30	

October

S	M	T	W	T	F	S
						1
2	3	4	5	6	7	8
9	10	11	12	13	14	15
16	17	18	19	20	21	22
23	24	25	26	27	28	29
30	31					

November

S	M	T	W	T	F	S
		1	2	3	4	5
6	7	8	9	10	11	12
13	14	15	16	17	18	19
20	21	22	23	24	25	26
27	28	29	30			

December

S	M	T	W	T	F	S
				1	2	3
4	5	6	7	8	9	10
11	12	13	14	15	16	17
18	19	20	21	22	23	24
25	26	27	28	29	30	31

14

January

S	M	T	W	T	F	S
						1
2	3	4	5	6	7	8
9	10	11	12	13	14	15
16	17	18	19	20	21	22
23	24	25	26	27	28	29
30	31					

February

S	M	T	W	T	F	S
		1	2	3	4	5
6	7	8	9	10	11	12
13	14	15	16	17	18	19
20	21	22	23	24	25	26
27	28	29				

March

S	M	T	W	T	F	S
			1	2	3	4
5	6	7	8	9	10	11
12	13	14	15	16	17	18
19	20	21	22	23	24	25
26	27	28	29	30	31	

April

S	M	T	W	T	F	S
						1
2	3	4	5	6	7	8
9	10	11	12	13	14	15
16	17	18	19	20	21	22
23	24	25	26	27	28	29
30						

May

S	M	T	W	T	F	S
	1	2	3	4	5	6
7	8	9	10	11	12	13
14	15	16	17	18	19	20
21	22	23	24	25	26	27
28	29	30	31			

June

S	M	T	W	T	F	S
				1	2	3
4	5	6	7	8	9	10
11	12	13	14	15	16	17
18	19	20	21	22	23	24
25	26	27	28	29	30	

July

S	M	T	W	T	F	S
						1
2	3	4	5	6	7	8
9	10	11	12	13	14	15
16	17	18	19	20	21	22
23	24	25	26	27	28	29
30	31					

August

S	M	T	W	T	F	S
		1	2	3	4	5
6	7	8	9	10	11	12
13	14	15	16	17	18	19
20	21	22	23	24	25	26
27	28	29	30	31		

September

S	M	T	W	T	F	S
					1	2
3	4	5	6	7	8	9
10	11	12	13	14	15	16
17	18	19	20	21	22	23
24	25	26	27	28	29	30

October

S	M	T	W	T	F	S
1	2	3	4	5	6	7
8	9	10	11	12	13	14
15	16	17	18	19	20	21
22	23	24	25	26	27	28
29	30	31				

November

S	M	T	W	T	F	S
			1	2	3	4
5	6	7	8	9	10	11
12	13	14	15	16	17	18
19	20	21	22	23	24	25
26	27	28	29	30		

December

S	M	T	W	T	F	S
					1	2
3	4	5	6	7	8	9
10	11	12	13	14	15	16
17	18	19	20	21	22	23
24	25	26	27	28	29	30
31						

INDEX

2003..4	2053..4
2004.12	2054..5
2005..7	2055..6
2006..1	2056..14
2007..2	2057..2
2008.10	2058..3
2009..5	2059..4
2010..6	2060.12
2011..7	2061..7
2012..8	2062..1
2013..3	2063..2
2014..4	2064.10
2015..5	2065..5
2016.13	2066..6
2017..1	2067..7
2018..2	2068..8
2019..3	2069..3
2020.11	2070..4
2021..6	2071..5
2022..7	2072.13
2023..1	2073..1
2024..9	2074..2
2025..4	2075..3
2026..5	2076.11
2027..6	2077..6
2028..14	2078..7
2029..2	2079..1
2030..3	2080..9
2031..4	2081..4
2032.12	2082..5
2033..7	2083..6
2034..1	2084.14
2035..2	2085..2
2036.10	2086..3
2037..5	2087..4
2038..6	2088..12
2039..7	2089..7
2040..8	2090..1
2041..3	2091..2
2042..4	2092.10
2043..5	2093..5
2044.13	2094..6
2045..1	2095..7
2046..2	2096..8
2047..3	2097..3
2048..11	2098..4
2049..6	2099..5
2050..7	
2051..1	
2052..9	

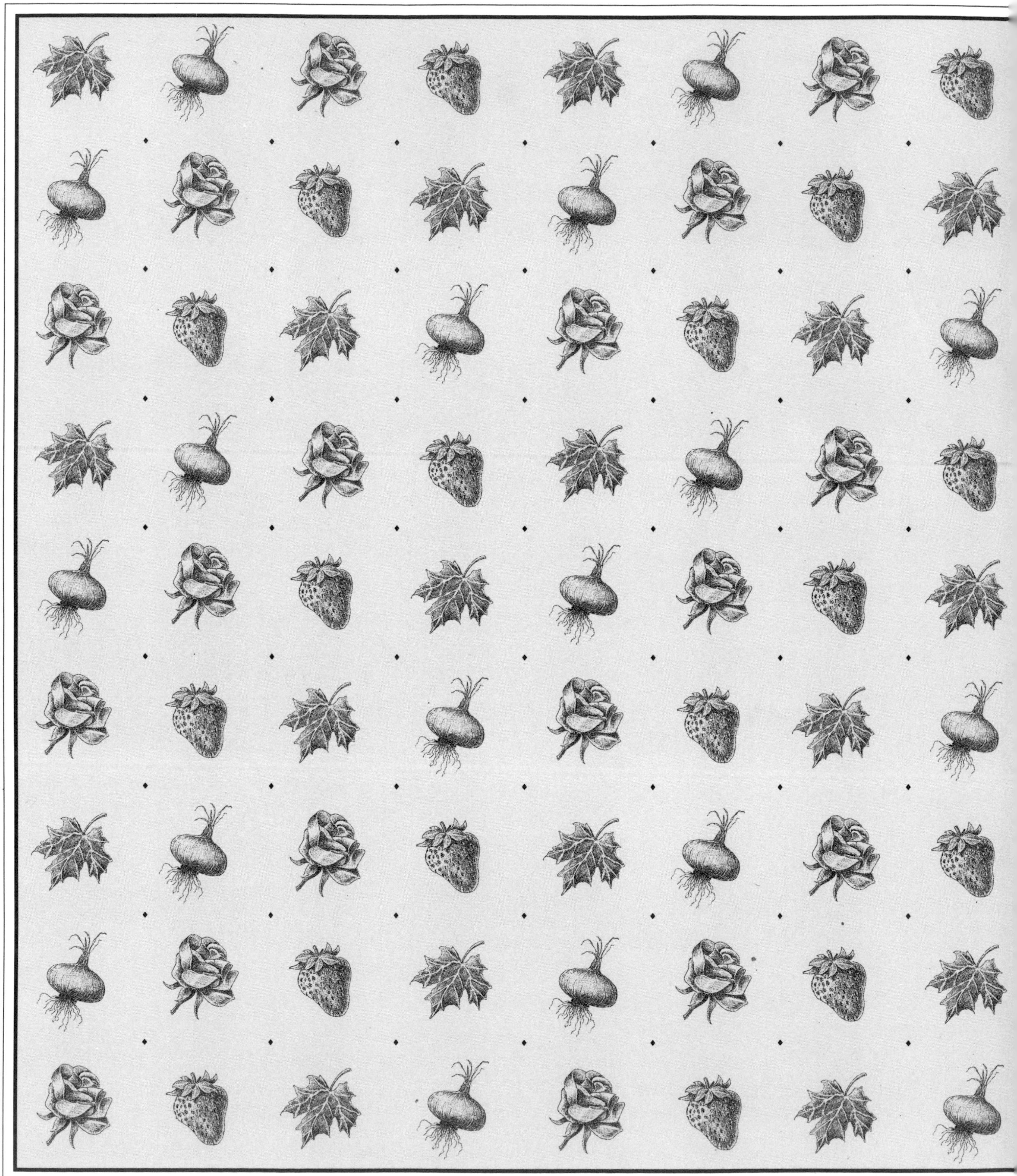